EXCEPTIONAL State

New Americanists

A Series Edited by Donald E. Pease

EXCEPTIONAL State

Contemporary U.S. Culture and the New Imperialism

Edited by
Ashley Dawson
and
Malini Johar Schueller

DUKE UNIVERSITY PRESS DURHAM AND LONDON 2007

Printed in the United States of America on acid-free paper ∞
Designed by Heather Hensley
Typeset in Linotype Janson by Keystone Typesetting, Inc.
Library of Congress Cataloging-in-Publication Data appear on the last printed page of this book.

In memory of Edward Said

and for all those resisting imperialism

Contents

Acknowledgments

The editors would like to thank the two anonymous readers for Duke University Press for their careful reading of the book and their helpful suggestions for revision. The book has also been improved by the comments given to us by the readers for Routledge Press. At Routledge, we wish to thank Matthew Byrnie for his interest in the book, as well as his professionalism. Permission for reprinting "Updating the Gendered Empire: Where Are the Women of Occupied Afghanistan and Iraq?" from *The Curious Feminist: Searching for Women in a New Age of Empire* (2005) by Cynthia Enloe has been granted by the University of California Press. Most important, we thank Reynolds Smith of Duke University Press for his help from submission to production.

ASHLEY DAWSON AND
MALINI JOHAR SCHUELLER

☆ ☆ ☆ **Introduction:** Rethinking Imperialism Today

> As I shall be using the term, "imperialism" means the practice, the theory and the attitudes of a dominating metropolitan center ruling a distant territory; "colonialism," which is almost always a consequence of imperialism, is the implanting of settlements on distant territory. . . . In our time, direct colonialism has largely ended; imperialism, as we shall see, lingers where it has always been, in a kind of general cultural sphere as well as in specific political, ideological, economic, and social practices.—**Edward Said,** ***Culture and Imperialism***

Any doubts that imperialism was central to the United States's understand-ing of itself were put to rest in the aftermath of September 11, when the operative question was not whether the United States was an imperial power, but rather what kind. Repeated invocations of differences between "our" civilization and "their" barbarity, entreaties for a "new imperialism," and calls for reinstating a nineteenth-century-type colonialism, now with the United States replacing Britain and France, as well as cheers for colonialism, circulated almost immediately after 9/11.[1] The passage of the USA PATRIOT Act, the creation of the Department of Homeland Security, the prolonged detention of prisoners at Guantánamo Bay and, most important, the unilateral invasion of Iraq in 2003 suggest that a new kind of imperialism—though of a particularly insidious kind, requiring disciplining at home and abroad through the inculcation of an imperial culture—might be at hand.

And yet, treating September 11 as a watershed moment problematically endorses the justifications of the Bush regime both for the curtailing of liberties at home and for installing repressive measures abroad. Instead, we need to see the tragedy of September 11 as a moment that helped popularize in the public sphere the coveted aims of the neocons. What marks current US imperialism is the punitive, unilateral, militaristic ideology of the neocons solidified in the 1990s in the aftermath of the Cold War and in opposition to the perceived weakness of the Clinton administration.[2] This ideology, which we argue is a compensatory response to the decline of US economic and political hegemony, found its allies in the Christian Right and among certain segments of the business elite and gained popular currency through conservative talk shows, Christian TV news channels, and giant media networks such as FOX.[3] Key liberal commentators also became apologists for US policy in the name of so-called humanitarian interventions.[4] In keeping with long-standing discourses of US exceptionalism, such apologists argue that the United States, as a kind of light to the nations of the world, has a unique obligation to export its exemplary blend of market-based representative democracy to the rest of the world. Ironically, such representations of US benevolence have been accompanied by the displacement of a democratic political realm by multiple instances of what Giorgio Agamben, following Carl Schmitt, calls sovereign exception.[5] From the extrajudicial zone at Camp X-Ray to the National Security Agency's illegal wiretapping program, the rule of law has been suspended in the name of sovereign power in more and more sites both at home and abroad. This new imperialism has permeated the US cultural imaginary, but it has also generated unprecedented levels of resistance. It is this highly contested contemporary imperial culture that we plan to examine in *Exceptional State*.

US IMPERIAL CULTURE AND POLITICS: A HISTORICAL PERSPECTIVE

Obviously, imperialism is not new to US politics or culture. The racial coordinates of imperialism were in place from the beginnings of white settlement, so that even an anticolonial rebellion against the British Empire coexisted with a belief in the destiny of settler colonists to expropriate Native Americans and enslave African Americans. White hegemony remained a crucial factor in determining the creation of the nation. At the same time, these settlers, going back to John Winthrop, also saw their settlement as the "city on the hill," as a model of idealized decolonization. The paradoxical combination of ferociously anticolonial and acutely imperial attitudes that Edward Said saw as characteristic of nineteenth- and early twentieth-century US culture thus has earlier precedents.[6] Imaginings of the nation as empire formed part of the cultural imaginary from the early days of the republic. The new empire as the fulfillment of world historical progress was articulated by political statesmen such as John Adams and historians such as John Fiske in visions of the westerly movement of empire, running its course through Europe and culminating in the United States.[7]

Such conceptions of empire received material impetus from the great imperial expansions of the nineteenth century. These included the incorporation of much of the South and West through war with Mexico, finalized in the Treaty of Guadalupe-Hidalgo, and the annexation of the Philippines, Guam, and Puerto Rico by the United States at the end of the Spanish-American War. Rudyard Kipling's "The White Man's Burden," written in response to the takeover of the Philippines, established for many a confirmation of the role of the United States as the newest empire with its obligation to liberate its "new-caught, sullen peoples / Half-devil and half-child."[8] Although bitter differences broke out between supporters of imperialist expansion and the Anti-imperialist League at the turn of the century, both sides (with the exception of a few idealists) believed in the degeneracy of the natives in the conquered territories. While imperialists felt a moral obligation to take up Kipling's burden, anti-imperialists, particularly white Southerners who were prominent in the movement, feared cultural and physical miscegenation. That the war of 1898 took place in the wake of considerable internal dissent that was violently suppressed, as in the Haymarket Riot of 1886, or juridically controlled, as with the Dawes Act of 1887, the Chinese Exclusion Act of 1881, and Supreme Court ruling in *Plessy v. Ferguson* in 1896, suggests an imbrication of internal and external colonialism that continues today.

The year 1898 marks an important moment for most historians because it exemplifies a shift from continental westward expansion to the control of far-flung territories. It is also seen as an aberration in the history of an otherwise nonimperial United States. An official rhetoric of anti-imperialism dominated the public sphere during and after World War I. Both progressives and Wilsonian liberals rightly viewed imperialism as the cause of the war and excoriated it. Thus the reluctant entry of the United States into World War II and the subsequent rise of US power have been seen by many historians as an "empire by invitation" by Western European countries willing to let the United States shoulder the burden of fending off the Soviet threat.[9] US support for and help with installing dictatorial, anticommunist regimes in, among others, Chile, Nicaragua, and Brazil; its training of South Americans in assassination methods at the School of the Americas; and the Vietnam War can all be explained through this call to empire, which is sharply differentiated from the imperial greed of former European powers. This narrative, aptly summed up in Reagan's credo of combating the "evil empire," has been summoned to explain the country's international role until the end of the Cold War.

However, political analyses alone do not account for the way in which imperial culture works. Foreign policy, for instance, forms an integral part of nationhood and becomes part of the way a citizenry imagines itself culturally. In the United States, colonial narratives of racial uplift and beliefs in Anglo-Saxon supremacy continued, in different ways, to affect policy arguments for both imperialism and anti-imperialism. Thus despite Franklin D. Roosevelt's strident opposition to European colonialism and his own role in ending the US annexation of the Philippines, he had no hesitation in recommending United Nations trusteeships for several nations as yet not ready in the schema of historical evolution for nationhood: "For a time at least there are many children among the peoples of the world that need trustees."[10] Indeed, as Michael Hunt has argued, US foreign policy has been guided by three major principles: a belief in the exceptional greatness of the nation and its promotion of liberty; racial hierarchy; and a distrust of revolution based on the assumption that the American Revolution was unique and unrepeatable. These three principles, Hunt argues, assumed the status of a potent ideology that not only directed foreign policy but also significantly defined the substance of American life.[11] Arguably, these principles continue, in the cultural imaginary, to construct the nation as chosen to make history.

AMERICAN STUDIES AND IMPERIAL CULTURE

Foreign policy, the culture industry, and American studies — conceived of as a study of national culture — are inextricably linked. The Cold War period saw not only the massive buildup of defense against the communist threat but also a concerted attempt to advertise US culture abroad—Hollywood, popular music, even political movements—in order to "foster the desire to emulate the American way."[12] The Voice of America, established just before the US entry in World War II, and which experienced dwindling support immediately after the war, saw its funds dramatically raised with the beginning of the Cold War. Simultaneously, the Smith-Mundt Act established international US information and cultural programs. As J. W. Fulbright made clear, "educational exchange is not merely a laudable experiment, but a positive instrument of foreign policy, designed to mobilize human resources just as military and economic policies seek to mobilize physical resources."[13] American studies was soon internationalized, its export functioning as an instrument of postwar US hegemony.[14]

Thus it is not surprising that when American studies was consolidated as a discipline after World War II, the major imperative for literary and cultural historians was to offer different paradigms of exceptionalism as maps for reading US culture. The two most dominant models for US culture were Perry Miller's mappings of Puritan origins exemplified in works such as *Errand into the Wilderness* (1956), continued in later works such as Sacvan Bercovitch's *The Puritan Origins of the American Self* (1975), and Frederick Jackson Turner's thesis about the "vacant" frontier as the enabling condition of American democracy, which animated studies like R. W. B. Lewis's *The American Adam* (1955). Ironically, at the very moment that radical anticolonial treatises questioning the universality of modernity were being written by Franz Fanon, George Lamming, and Aimé Césaire, major texts of American studies were consolidating American exceptionalism. We mention these well-known facts about American studies and post–World War II politics in order to make an obvious point: that imperial politics and culture are inextricably linked. Indeed, the question of whether culture follows politics or vice versa is based on the premise that the two can be separated.[15] What we can say is that imperial policies are both the consequence and cause of a certain kind of culture, a conjuncture explored by John Carlos Rowe in his essay in this collection.

Starting in the 1960s, during the period of worldwide decolonization, when Cold War paranoia had paradoxically caused the United States to engage in bolstering French colonization in Vietnam, histories of the nation as empire began to be written. Thus R. W. Van Alstyne in *The Rising American Empire*

(1960) demonstrated the centrality of the idea of empire to US history from the revolutionary period; Carl Eblen in *The First and Second American Empires* (1967) postulated a link between the imperial subjugation of various Others who threatened a singular American identity before 1898 and the pacification of overseas populations thereafter.[16] By 1980, Richard Drinnon had published his landmark literary and cultural study *Facing West: The Metaphysics of Indian-Hating and Empire-Building*, in which he traced a continuity between the rhetoric of the dehumanization of Native Americans, which was then used as a justification to "subdue" them, and the rhetoric mobilized in the Philippines and later in Vietnam.

Yet despite these revisionist analyses, which were centrally dependent on a continuity between racism at home and imperial racism abroad, much of American studies scholarship marginalized questions of imperialism, even though radical questionings of the singularity of a consensual American identity (by examining the role of raced Others in the construction of the nation) were being initiated. In this omission, American studies scholarship replicated the official rhetoric of neoliberalism, which presented its strategy of forcing free-market reforms on other nations without recourse to the word *imperialism*. It was only after the Gulf War that the next major work addressing culture and imperialism, *Cultures of United States Imperialism*, appeared.

Although imperialism has now been accepted as central to an understanding of US culture through works such as John Carlos Rowe's *Literary Culture and U.S. Imperialism: From the Revolution to World War II* (2000) and Melani McAlister's *Epic Encounters: Culture, Media, and U.S. Interests in the Middle East since 1945* (2005), the role of contemporary culture in legitimating US imperialism continues to be marginalized. Following the implosion of the Soviet Union, for example, numerous political and economic works theorized globalization and imperialism—usually to the exclusion of any consideration of cultural factors.[17] Foremost among those postulating the end of imperialism were Michael Hardt and Antonio Negri's philosophical treatise *Empire* (2000) and Thomas Friedman's more journalistic and economic endorsement of globalization, *The Lexus and the Olive Tree* (1999). Despite its many provocative moves, we reject Hardt and Negri's argument that a decentered empire has replaced imperialism, particularly because their contention about the American basis of this empire, one that is called into being and functions in the name of global right, reiterates American studies exceptionalism.[18] In addition, its Eurocentric focus on information technology, the emphasis on migration from South to North, and the rejection of the unevenness of cultural flows belies the imperialism all too evident since the preemptive invasion of Iraq.

September 11 has also produced a myriad of specifically focused studies analyzing the significance of the event.[19] In many instances, such interventions either ignore imperialism or give short shrift to the mobilization of US culture to legitimate imperial policies. *Exceptional State* builds on the momentum generated by previous work on the nexus of US culture and imperial power while refusing to privilege 9/11 as the single originary moment for understanding contemporary imperialism. Instead, we stress both the continuities and discontinuities embodied in present-day US imperialism, constituted as it is through the articulation of millennialism, exceptionalism, technological might, and visions of world dominance.

PERIODIZING CONTEMPORARY CAPITALIST IMPERIALISM

Can contemporary imperialism be explained as a continuation of the political, economic, military, and cultural aspects of past imperial culture? The answer is both yes and no. Obviously, contemporary imperialism draws on a legacy of the nation's past. Yet to posit an unchanging imperialism would be to deny the relevance of world historical events that have direct relevance to imperialism, for instance, the worldwide decolonization movements of the 1950s and 1960s. What, then, are the continuities and changes that describe contemporary imperialism? How do we mark the contemporary imperial moment?

Classic works such as William Appleman Williams's *The Tragedy of American Diplomacy* (1962) can be invoked to demonstrate continuities of imperialism. Williams argued persuasively how US foreign policy since the nineteenth century was driven by an ideology of open-door expansionism, or an imperialism of free trade that created an informal empire through economic expansion. Tested in China at the turn of the century, it was soon applied globally. The foreign policy of the United States thus relied on a long-standing assumption about the world being available to it.[20] As a result, many imperial ventures, from David Porter's attempts to annex the Marquesas to the takeover of the Philippines to the 2003 invasion of Iraq, can be seen as open-door imperialism, attempts to control trade routes and markets.[21] The frequent failure of such policies to further US imperial ambitions, as, for instance, in the military debacle in Iraq—an ironic outcome of the free market fundamentalism that animated neoconservative plans for the rebuilding of Iraq following the defeat of Saddam Hussein's military—does not seem to impede their zealous reapplication.[22]

Contemporary political and cultural critics also find it important to stress the continuities between contemporary imperialism and that of the past. The political critic Noam Chomsky argues that the unilateralism of the George W. Bush administration, particularly the philosophy of preemptive war, simply constitutes a continuation of the past fifty years of US foreign policy as evidenced by the military's actions in Cuba, Nicaragua, Turkey, and so on.[23] Gabriel Kolko takes an analogous view, arguing that the military industrial complex built by the United States during the Cold War has become an unstoppable and dangerously autonomous juggernaut.[24] The permeation of this complex into all facets of life in the United States remorselessly pushes the country to substitute militarist adventurism for diplomatic solutions to political crises. For Kolko, the wreckage and bitterness left in the wake of exertions of asymmetrical military power around the world inevitably come back to haunt the United States.

Similarly, some cultural critics argue for the importance of seeing continuities before and after September 11. Elaine Tyler May, for instance, sees post–9/11 policies and rhetoric as a continuation of Cold War ideologies. Bush's term, *axis of evil*, for example, combines the language of World War II (*axis*) and that of Ronald Reagan (*evil empire*). She also notes a resurgence of the 1950s-style emphasis on marriage and family.[25] Others analyze the specificity of new power configurations (such as the racialization of Middle Eastern people, Arab or Muslim) within a continuity of old discourses such as Orientalism.[26]

Yet despite such connections, US unilateralist policies today are clearly being deployed in a significantly different historical context from that of the Cold War or even the 1990s. In order to periodize contemporary imperialism adequately, we need to take a step back to examine the changing economic and political conditions out of which it emerged. The crucial shift in this regard centers on the emergence of neoliberal doctrines during the 1970s. By the late 1960s, the integrated political and economic system created by the United States after World War II began foundering on its own internal contradictions. With Germany and Japan back at full strength and competing economically with the United States, a classic crisis of overaccumulation developed in the world economy.[27] When the OPEC oil embargo of 1973 threw the world into recession, these contradictions became insurmountable and a fresh strategy for accumulation and political regulation had to be developed. This new approach involved the rupture of the tripartite compact between capital, labor, and government that had characterized the postwar period.[28] Corporations in the United States began moving production abroad in order to realize greater surplus value by exploiting cheap labor. In the process, they were able largely to liquidate the power of the organized working class in the United States. The financial sector also became increasingly powerful within the country and globally as the OPEC surplus was recycled by US banks in the form of loans to developing countries.[29]

Neoliberalism, based on a revival of nineteenth-century market fundamentalism, emerged during the Reagan and Thatcher administrations as measures to make the global South "consent" (and therefore accept and work with the hegemony of the United States and, to some extent, Britain) to the imperatives of the so-called free market through institutions controlled by the United States. Presented as common sense and the ultimate good for all, neoliberalism worked through the imperial formula of opening up all markets and combined deregulating all industries, privatizing government concerns, and minimizing social services for citizens. Associated most closely with the so-called Washington consensus of the 1980s and 1990s, neoliberalism sought a "centralized multilateralism" through the operation of institutions such as the International Monetary Fund (IMF), the World Bank, and the World Trade Organization (WTO).[30] Although the debt crises of developing countries and the draconian structural adjustment policies administered by such international institutions to deal with debt created significant turmoil during the 1980s, there were no significant challenges to neoliberal hegemony during this period. Instead, popular unrest and the democratization movements that often developed from such unrest in Latin America, Eastern Europe, Africa, and East Asia ironically led to the proliferation of neoliberal programs.[31] When the Soviet Union collapsed in 1989, the last barrier to the global dissemination of the neoliberal model was removed and the US formula of liberal representative democracy twinned with increasingly unrestrained corporate power appeared to many commentators to have triumphed for good.[32]

Yet neoliberalism would not have achieved the level of public popularity it has at home had it not been for the Right's harnessing of the culture wars to economic ends. Increasingly since the 1970s, the rhetoric of cultural authenticity—real Americanness, driven by market fundamentalism versus elite welfarism—has been marshaled to support neoliberalism. For instance, the former Vermont governor Howard Dean was excoriated in an ad by the conservative Club for Growth and advised to take his "tax-hiking, government-expanding, latte-drinking, sushi-eating, Volvo-driving, *New York Times*-reading, Hollywood-loving, left-wing freak show back to Vermont where it belongs."[33] Thus, as Thomas Frank has aptly demonstrated, the working class, appropriating the persecution rhetoric of the labor movement of the 1930s to cultural ends, has contradictorily voted against its own economic interests and in favor of privatization, deregulation, and deunionization.[34]

However, simultaneous with this consensus, the struggle against globalization that had been unfolding in developing countries since the early 1980s reached the United States in the so-called battle of Seattle.[35] Protestors from the traditional labor union movements joined radical environmentalists, feminists, indigenous people, and anarchists in 1999 to blockade the streets of Seattle, where the WTO was meeting to pursue its agenda of concentrating power on a supranational level. In the two preceding years, Asia's central banks had blown apart their own financial system trying to prop up the dollar in order to finance the United States' unsustainable trade deficit and ensure exports. As a result of these policies, which allowed Americans to keep living beyond their means, there was a run on Asian currencies, leading to the imposition of devastating structural adjustment policies that revealed the fundamental inequalities of the neoliberal dispensation. The Washington consensus was thrown into turmoil, with insiders such as Joseph Stiglitz publishing searing critiques of the policies administered around the globe in the name of trade liberalization.[36] An international movement began to coalesce whose slogan, "Another World Is Possible," was a direct riposte to the dominant "There Is No Alternative" ideology of the preceding twenty years. This movement targeted its protests on the privatization of the global commons, or what David Harvey calls "accumulation by dispossession," a perspective Harvey derives from antiglobalization activists such as Arundhati Roy and Naomi Klein.[37]

In tandem with this progressive movement, significant populist reactionary movements began to develop in response to the privations caused by the Washington consensus around the globe. Many of these movements were spawned by reactions against the disruptive impact created by neoliberalism, which tended to unsettle political and cultural, as well as economic, borders. Christian, Hindu, and Muslim fundamentalism, in particular, are now significant forces both within particular states and on an international level.[38] It is, of course, the latter that has received the most attention in the United States in response to the devastating attacks of 9/11, although it should properly be seen as part of a broader antisystemic reaction. Like so many other aspects of the present crisis, al-Qaeda is a form of blowback from the United States' own superpower politics, in this case the unflinching support lent by successive administrations since 1945 to the corrupt and authoritarian but nonetheless pro-Western Saudi regime.[39]

It is out of this crisis of the doctrines of neoliberalism and the US hegemony that implemented it that contemporary imperialism has developed. While the country's aggressive militarism appears to be a sign of its unrivaled power on the world stage, in fact, we believe it should be seen as a symptom of its weakness. Commentators such as David Harvey, Emmanuel Todd, Michael Mann, and Immanuel Wallerstein have all argued that having lost both its economic and its financial supremacy, the United States is left with only one component of its former hegemony: military power.[40] Chalmers Johnson, for example, identifies a post–September 11 imperialism based on militarism and a massive transfer of power from the representatives of the people to the Pentagon. This militarism, going back to the late nineteenth century and continuing with the 1990s interventions in Panama, the Gulf, Somalia, Haiti, and Bosnia, witnessed a change after September 11 in that leaders began openly seeing the country as an empire, a new Rome: "Since 9/11, our country has undergone a transformation from republic to empire that may well prove irreversible."[41] What constitutes this new empire are the 725 US military bases that are all exempt from the laws of home states and that instill youths with the ingredients of racial superiority.[42] Johnson, who, like Harvey, views neoliberal market fundamentalism/globalization as economic imperialism, sees a shift after 9/11 that marked the end of globalization.[43]

Although it is impossible to predict precisely how the endgame of US hegemony will play out, it is clear that current policies have only succeeded in intensifying the contradictions bequeathed by twenty years of neoliberalism. For while attempting to retain the neoliberal formula of free markets and free elections, the United States has jettisoned the element of international co-operation and consent on which the free circulation of capital depends. In addition, having allowed its industrial base to atrophy, the United States is currently in the process of frittering away what remains of its financial power through an extremely costly military occupation in Iraq, which is yoked to the implementation of ideologically driven, regressive domestic tax cuts.[44] Like many empires before it, the United States seems to have been pushed by its reliance on military might into a critical economic and political overextension.[45] Since the United States remains the global consumer of last resort, export-oriented countries such as Japan and China have been forced to foot the bill for the country's unsustainable militarism. Yet US unilateralism and adventurism are likely to produce a defensive response from such lenders, encouraging them to pull the financial plug sooner rather than later. The recent decision by the East Asian nations to begin denominating cross-border debt in the region in Asian currency rather than the dollar is a sign that the United States cannot count on other nations to continue financing its mammoth foreign debt (now over $3 trillion) indefinitely.

Certainly, Operation Iraqi Freedom may be seen as the first of the twenty-first century's resource wars.[46] In such a reading, the United States is exerting its sole remaining asset—immense military power—in order to gain control of the planet's major petroleum reserves. If it can maintain control of Iraq and Saudi Arabia—the odds do not look good at present—the United States will be in a position to exercise economic, political, and cultural hegemony over industrialized powers such as the European Union, Japan, and China for the next half century. The United States will, in other words, use its military muscle to extract surplus value from the rest of the world in order to continue its own unsustainable levels of consumption. Whether or not such a far-reaching geopolitical objective was in the minds of the Bush administration's ideologues, their bellicose actions have ratcheted up the pressure on US hegemony rather than helping consolidate it. The US invasion of Iraq sparked the largest demonstrations of popular discontent in the history of the planet and has managed to alienate even stalwart allies among the elite sectors of the industrialized nations. Thus, in addition to running the danger of overextension, this unilateralist aggression also threatens to revive the kind of interimperialist competition discussed by V. I. Lenin, with regional trading blocs such as the EU-Russia and Japan-China-Korea allying to challenge US attempts to exert unilateral control over the world's resources and economic development.[47] How will the United States react to and cope with the increasing turbulence and resistance that the neocons' unilateralist policies are likely to spark?

IDEOLOGIES OF CONTEMPORARY IMPERIAL CULTURE

In the summer of 2004, Michael Moore's antiwar documentary *Fahrenheit 9/11* opened in theaters around the United States after having won great international acclaim and enduring an attention-getting scuffle over censorship with the Disney Corporation. Moore's relatively restrained attack on belligerent US foreign policy immediately shot to number one at the box office.[48] Yet after only one week of such success, *Spider-Man 2* replaced Moore's film as the top box-office draw. Despite their apparent disconnection from the political realm, films like *Spider-Man 2* deliver a powerful counternarrative to *Fahrenheit 9/11*. Peter Parker, the hero of *Spider-Man 2*, has deep misgivings about his superhuman powers. He basically wants nothing more than to lead the life of a normal US college student. Unfortunately for him, the world is populated by vicious people who prey on the weak and innocent. When the monstrous Doctor Octopus threatens his girlfriend, Parker is forced to reassume his guise as Spider-Man and do battle with his enemy. *Spider-Man 2*, in other words, is a saga of what Richard Slotkin calls "regeneration through violence."[49] Such narratives typically feature a naive hero whose calm world is turned upside down by a desperado who usually kidnaps innocent women and menaces helpless average citizens. The violence of the bad guys destroys social order. To restore calm, the hero of these narratives rejects the torturously slow workings of the legal system and resorts to extralegal justice. In this way, American popular culture recycles the ethos of the lynch mob.

Although regeneration through violence is a staple of US cinema, in recent years Hollywood has churned out scores of films based on vigilantism, most of them far more steeped in patriotic gore than the relatively nuanced tale of Peter Parker. From Quentin Tarantino's *Kill Bill* to Steven Spielberg's *Saving Private Ryan*, from *Gladiator* to *The Gangs of New York*, the American appetite for fantasies of revenge has been indulged in virtually every genre and historical period.[50] Such fantasies are likely to receive increasing plaudits given the ideology of victimization through which US imperialism has been justified since 9/11. It should be no surprise that the other hit movie of 2004 was Mel Gibson's *The Passion of the Christ*, essentially an extended allegory of wronged innocence. Gibson's torturous movie implicitly calls not for the universalistic humanitarianism of the Sermon on the Mount but for the apocalyptic ethnic cleansing of the best-selling fundamentalist Christian Left Behind novel series examined in Melani McAlister's essay in this collection. Not surprisingly, the most popular video rental after 9/11 was *Independence Day*, a retributive call to arms.

The tragic events of 9/11 are all too easy to read according to this retributive narrative. In fact, the suicide attacks on the World Trade Center towers and the Pentagon were almost immediately seen by the news media and by politicians as warranting some form of purgative retaliation. Less than two hours after the first plane hit the first tower in New York, Peter Jennings of ABC News said that the United States would have to strike back with massive force.[51] The attacks thus intensified the now habitual tendency of many Americans to see themselves as the dispensers of morally legitimate violence, albeit now as victims. In addition, the carnage of the suicide attacks on 9/11 seemed to demolish all standards of civilization and thereby solicit acts of extralegal retribution. As in Hollywood revenge fantasies, the brutality of the attacks suggested that modern legal and political institutions were incommensurate with the need for vengeance. Indeed, the Bush administration drew explicitly on the rhetoric of the Western when it promised to "smoke out" Osama bin Laden and al-Qaeda like a latter-day posse in pursuit of outlaws. This cowboy rhetoric was used to legitimate a form of international vigilantism that swept aside the United Nations and the International Criminal Court in the name of swift retribution.[52] Concerns about the strategic efficacy and human costs of spectacular asymmetrical violence in Afghanistan and unilateralist preemptive warfare in Iraq were treated with ridicule by an administration whose canny evocations of lynch law won it massive approval ratings from the American public.

But as events on the ground in Afghanistan and Iraq have demonstrated over the past four years, these belligerent policies are unlikely to gain favor either with the United States' erstwhile allies or with citizens of Middle Eastern countries. Instead, the Bush administration's ham-fisted attempts to restore democracy using high-altitude bombing and military occupation have offered a perfect recruiting tool to al-Qaeda throughout the region. On the other hand, the Bush administration's use of cowboy rhetoric demonstrates that contemporary US imperialism can be understood only through the conjuncture of the specific imperial politics of the present and the various political, religious, racial, and economic practices and rhetoric that have contributed to imperial culture in the past. Without an understanding of the continuity of American exceptionalism, complexly constituted of religious, economic, cultural, political, and racial elements beginning with Puritan theocracy and continuing with the rhetoric of Manifest Destiny and the Monroe Doctrine, for instance, we cannot make sense of the conviction shared by many contemporary politicians and citizens alike that the United States has been and will always remain the provider and protector of world freedom. Similarly, the kind of fundamentalist thinking that many critics of US imperialism see as peculiar to the present moment is a familiar Calvinist typology revived most demonstrably during the Great Awakening of the mid-eighteenth century. Of particular relevance is the Puritan belief in being divinely ordained or settling a New Israel, which later fueled nineteenth-century missionary activity in the Near East. H. Richard Niebuhr famously explained these phenomena as "the kingdom of god in America" in his book bearing that title.[53]

This idea of a self-proclaimed, chosen people pitting itself against a myriad of enemies (feminists, homosexuals, blacks, Arabs, Muslims) both within and without the country thus has a long history in the United States. However, the contemporary alliance of Christian fundamentalism and military machismo received its impetus and intensity through the particular combination of Reagan's Manichaean foreign policy with its uncomplicated patriotism, the evangelical renaissance of the 1980s, the unqualified millennial commitment to hard-line, pro-Israeli and anti-Palestinian politics, and the new military technologies through which millennialism could be concretized. The 1980s witnessed a powerful growth of evangelical Christianity, as well as its political legitimation. Groups like the Moral Majority and the Christian Coalition emerged, with figures such as Jerry Falwell, Pat Robertson, and Jimmy Swaggart using TV, religious programs on radio, and religious bookstores to spread their messages. All these groups supported the Reagan agenda of self-help and privatization; his purported restoration of the American psyche after the humiliations of the Vietnam War and the Iran hostage crisis through images of frontier masculinity (Reagan was most often shown horseback riding); and above all his battle against the evil empire. Falwell's Moral Majority registered around 2 million voters for Reagan both in 1980 and 1984.

Currently, millennial fundamentalists, whose leaders are Falwell, Robertson, and Randall Terry, hold sway over about a quarter of the country's population.[54] The stridently anti-Palestinian and pro-Israeli agenda of these groups today is an updating of the long-standing understanding of the United States as a New Israel beginning with the Puritans. Despite the fundamentalists' deeply conservative criticism of the United States taking on imperial ambitions, Melani McAlister's essay in this volume suggests that the overwhelming popularity of the Left Behind series has placed the evangelicals at the center of the US political map, far from the subcultural status afforded them even in the 1980s. The fundamentalists thus provide the ideological core of a raced, imperial culture even as they criticize imperial politics as a waste of national resources.

POPULAR AUTHORITARIANISM AND THE NEOCON AGENDA

The discourse of American exceptionalism lends itself to peculiarly intense forms of what Stuart Hall calls "popular authoritarianism" in times of crisis such as these.[55] Hall first identified popular authoritarianism during the transition to a post-Fordist economy in the 1970s, when the social compact with the working class was broken in Britain and the United States. In this incendiary context, elites sought to head off popular discontent with economic and social breakdown by scapegoating socially marginalized groups such as blacks. The advent of the neocons in the United States signals an extreme intensification of this strategy. For although the economic policies of neoliberalism were, to an extent, supported by politicians from both ends of the political spectrum, from Reagan to Clinton—with Clinton in fact decreasing domestic spending by ending welfare schemes for hundreds of thousands of the poor through an ill-advised welfare-to-work program, signing into law the North American Free Trade Agreement (NAFTA), and presiding over the WTO—military spending was not increased and an overt rhetoric of empire remained absent among policy makers.

The rise of the neocons to power in the second Bush administration has signaled a major shift in foreign policy. The neocons, whose origins lie in a disaffected liberalism, broke ranks with both liberals and conservatives in advocating direct military confrontation. They comprise a number of people from the military industrial complex of former Reagan and Bush administrations—Dick Cheney, Donald Rumsfeld, and Paul Wolfowitz. Others include the Defense Policy Board member Richard Perle and cultural conservatives such as William J. Bennett, Francis Fukayama, and Norman Podhoretz. Unlike the neoliberals, the neocons want to free the United States of encumbering alliances and compromising organizations like the UN. As the Web site for the Project for the New American Century (PNAC) states, the neocon worldview centers on "a few fundamental propositions: that American leadership is good both for America and for the world; that such leadership requires military strength, diplomatic energy and commitment to moral principle; and that too few political leaders today are making the case for global leadership."[56] Central to neocon thinking is a belief in clear moral principles, the electoral base for which is a special type of Christian fundamentalism—as exemplified by Pat Robertson and Jerry Falwell, who interpreted the events of September 11 as signs of God's wrath but who denounce imperialism as wasted white energy.[57] Notwithstanding their qualms about US intervention abroad, these religious leaders lined up squarely behind President Bush during his campaign for reelection.

A central shift from the neoliberal agenda to that of the neocons is therefore a global intensification of the move from hegemony to dominance, from consent to coercion. This policy derives, of course, from the elitist assumptions of neocon intellectuals such as Paul Wolfowitz, who, influenced by Leo Strauss's obscurantist readings of Plato and Machiavelli, believe that the United States can be united only when confronted by an external threat and that if such a threat does not exist, it must be manufactured.[58] In addition to privatization and the free market agenda at home and abroad, the neocons formulated a vision of US world dominance based on military might and hearkened back to the "Reaganite policy of military strength and moral clarity," in contrast to the dilution of power in the Clinton administration.[59] Key tenets of this contemporary imperialism (including the need to invade Iraq) were formulated by the neocons in the 1990s, but were put into place following 9/11.[60] The neocon philosophy hinges on an unquestioned US dominance to achieve and maintain US power over the world, massive technological supremacy particularly in the military, and control over all new commons such as outer space and cyberspace. Wolfowitz's "Defense Planning Guide," for instance, explicitly proclaims the US intention to maintain "full spectrum dominance" over the other nations of the planet.[61] Much of the philosophy of the neocons, such as the use of global missile defenses to secure a basis for "U.S. power projection round the world" and, more ominously, their support for Harlan Ullman's military strategy of annihilative bombardment, or "shock and awe," sounds like a high-tech and more barbaric version of nineteenth-century European imperialisms shorn of any pretence of a civilizing mission.[62]

And yet the cultural components of the neocon vision are surprisingly familiar. Francis Fukuyama's end-of-history thesis, which bridges the neoliberal vision of capitalist imperialism in the guise of world capitalism and the neocon vision of US dominance, is a contemporary version of American exceptionalism. There are also clear indications that contemporary imperialism is guided by an old Orientalism that has been revived both in foreign policy and in the popular media. Samuel Huntington's *The Clash of Civilizations* (1991), which formulates clear and absolute cultural distinctions between East and West and articulates the need for the West to make its values prevail, has been an influential document for the neocons; Raphael Patai's *The Arab Mind*, originally published in 1973 and excoriated by Edward Said as part of quintessential Orientalism, is now the Bible of the neocons on the Arab world. The book, whose influence Malini Johar Schueller analyzes in her essay in this volume, was reprinted in 2002 and is widely taught at US military institutions.

We thus agree with Harvey, Johnson, Mann, and others that politically, contemporary US imperialism is marked by a shift from various versions of benevolent intervention and economic coercion (combined with covert destabilization of supposedly hostile governments) to overt dominance through brute military force — the shift from neoliberal hegemony to neocon visions of world dominance, although we argue that this vision recycles at least some familiar cultural material. The rise of the neocons has made the arguments put forth by Hardt and Negri in *Empire* that globalization entails a decentered world without insides and outsides, centers and peripheries, seem particularly myopic. For example, although proponents of neoliberal policies called these phenomena globalization, the logic being that all businesses were free to move and that the playing field was leveled (a phenomenon proved to an extent by US deindustrialization and the outsourcing of information technology jobs), the fact that the IMF and the World Bank, the major institutions dictating policy, are controlled by the United States cannot be overlooked.[63] Nor can the uneven cultural coordinates of globalization be ignored. If call centers are outsourced, it is often with the mandate that workers from India, for instance, perform as virtual Americans.[64] Neoliberalism/globalization as a late twentieth-century version of imperialism was different in that its proponents presented the conscious policies of World Bank– and IMF-ordered structural adjustments and the opening up of markets as inevitable. As Manfred Steger points out, globalization theorists have a fondness for using terms such as "irresistible," "inevitable," and "irreversible,"[65] so that globalization as a scenario is presented with the certainty of religious belief. Putatively critical thinkers such as Hardt and Negri help reproduce this mystifying rhetoric through their arguments about the transformation of the US state into a deterritorialized network. The rise of the neocons has made the folly of their poststructuralist stance all too apparent.[66]

As in the realm of foreign policy, however, the advent of the neocons exacerbated trends toward popular authoritarianism in the United States to a significant extent. For 9/11 not only provided the Bush administration with an excuse for unilateral military adventures abroad but the attacks also allowed neocons at the helm of the state to clamp down on civil liberties and dissent at home. Measures such as the USA PATRIOT Act, Secretary of Defense Donald Rumsfeld's denial of prisoner-of-war status to prisoners held in indefinite detention at Guantánamo Bay, and the Justice Department's policy of secret detentions and immigration proceedings all hearken back to the worst moments of bigotry and authoritarian persecution in US history.[67] David Cole argues that the United States is undergoing a spasm of vengeful zeal that parallels the Palmer Raids following World War I, the incarceration of Japanese Americans during World War II, and the McCarthy hearings during the Cold War. Although most of these measures were initially targeted at immigrants after the 9/11 attacks, historical precedent suggests that such draconian measures are always precedents to a clampdown on anyone who questions government power.[68] Heightened domestic surveillance thus combines with rhetoric concerning soldiers abroad protecting "our" civil liberties, making criticism of the war appear not simply unpatriotic but rather a conscious attack on the security of the United States.

This suppression of dissent is accompanied by a heavily gendered discourse that represents Americanism as tolerance and liberty, as opposed to the repressiveness and intolerance of the Arab world, but that is accompanied by a strident celebration of masculinity and compulsory heterosexuality. The rescue of Jessica Lynch, released to the media through the tightly controlled Central Command's media center in Qatar (Al Jazeera's Baghdad office having just been strategically bombed) during Operation Iraqi Freedom, was circulated as two narratives: that of soldier Lynch as female Rambo, fighting to the death; and as the quintessential rescue scene of a captivity narrative in which the superior kind of masculinity prevails, a script well played in US culture since the inception of the genre with *The Narrative of the Captivity and Restoration of Mrs. Mary Rowlandson* in 1682. Although these contrasting images might be taken as symptoms of the mutability of contemporary discourses of gender, the butch but needy Lynch ultimately affirmed the role of masculine military agency. Of course, after the Abu Ghraib photographs became public, standard disciplinary discourses on femininity emerged with the contrasts between the good girl Jessica and the bad girl Lynndie England. Thus despite seeming contradictions deriving from contemporary masculine anxieties, as both Cynthia Enloe and Malini Johar Schueller point out in this volume, the discourse of contemporary imperialism thrives on relatively traditional gender dichotomies that essentially recycle discourses of the colonial period. Similarly, belief in US technological dominance combines with an anxiety about shadowy terrorists breaking through high-tech security systems to legitimate spiraling forms of surveillance such as the Total Information Awareness program.[69] Popular authoritarianism is, in other words, firmly linked to a formation of intersecting markers of identity whose instability must constantly be repressed by strident evocations of patriotism.

To engage in the critique of contemporary US imperialism is therefore to examine and disturb the nexus of raced, gendered, and classed representations of imperial national identity articulated by the Bush regime. The political implications of such scholarly work are clearer today than ever before. The Bush administration explicitly set out to cow critics of its policies by invoking a strident patriotism that viewed all dissent as treason. Scholarly work in the humanities has been particularly targeted for surveillance and disciplining with neocon ideologues such as Lynn Cheney and Daniel Pipes engaged in a project to purge US academia of progressive scholars. Witness Daniel Pipes's Web site Campus Watch, which published dossiers of eight supposedly anti-American Middle East studies faculty in an attempt to discredit their work. The American Council of Trustees and Alumni (ACTA), the group with which Lynne Cheney and Joe Lieberman are associated, issued a report entitled "Defending Civilization: How Our Universities Are Failing America." This report published its blacklist of forty professors and argued that colleges and university faculty were the weak link in America's response to September 11.[70] More ominously, HR 3077 seeks to monitor Middle East studies through a board that includes members from the Department of Homeland Security. Given such repressive moves by the state, including the attempt by the University of Colorado to fire professor Ward Churchill for the remarks he made about 9/11, we believe that we have a responsibility to challenge the seemingly inexorable slide of the United States toward belligerence and authoritarianism at home and abroad. Let us be very clear about one thing: imperial US policies threaten the future of humanity and the planet in the most immediate way. By providing prominent and emerging scholars with a venue to analyze the cultural contradictions of contemporary US imperialism, we intend to highlight and challenge the role of US culture in perpetuating popular authoritarianism. In addition, we believe that *Exceptional State* contributes to the struggle against the new imperialism by delineating strains of anti-authoritarian culture in the United States today that resonate and articulate solidarity with the emerging movement for global social justice. We thus intend our work to provide tools with which to dismantle coercive US power both domestically and internationally. Although the past thirty years have offered scant hope, we believe that there are viable alternatives to a world of indefinite detentions, preemptive strikes, and perpetual warfare.

The collection begins with essays that analyze contemporary technologies of imperialism in the media, politics, and the military. John Carlos Rowe's "Culture, US Imperialism, and Globalization" demonstrates how US cultural production, the work of what Max Horkheimer and Theodor Adorno termed "the culture industry," conditioned American citizens to accept the undisguised militarism and jingoistic nationalism now driving US foreign policy.

Rowe argues that "US imperialism since Vietnam has worked steadily to import the world and to render global differences aspects of the US nation—in short, to internalize and hypernationalize transnational issues." Although this Vietnam effect is a relatively new phenomenon that has gone through several interesting cultural transformations since 1968, it has strong ties with the cultural practices of traditional imperialism, including British and US imperialism in the nineteenth century. Rowe examines several films (*Wag the Dog* and *Three Kings*) and one television program (*Law and Order*) with ostensibly liberal political aims and shows how they represent this tendency toward Americanization as a process specific to the post-Vietnam era (and thus US neoimperialism) and yet still tied to older, more traditional forms of imperialism, especially militarism. Through an analysis of a 2002 episode of *Law and Order*, aired shortly after the arraignment of John Walker Lindh, Rowe demonstrates how the show affirms national values by treating Islam as adolescent rebellion instead of attempting to deal with the realities of the Other. Thus "terrorism" is incorporated into the US itself to strip it of international threat.

While Rowe demonstrates how popular culture facilitated imperial policies, Donald E. Pease turns our attention to the state's use and revision of regulatory national narratives in order to justify its authoritarian policies. In "Between the Homeland and Abu Ghraib: Dwelling in Bush's Biopolitical Settlement," Pease shows how the Bush administration used the mythological theme of the "Virgin Land" as attacked on 9/11 and replaced it with the concepts of the homeland and Ground Zero to mark an insecure emergency state necessitating the violence that the myth of Virgin Land had covered over. Homeland named an unlocatable order that emerged from the dislocation marked by 9/11; the Homeland Security Act, in turn, positioned the population to the state of political minority dependent on the state for its welfare. Pease argues that through Operation Enduring Justice and Operation Iraqi Freedom, the state restaged the colonial settlers' conquest of Native Americans by describing imperial conquest as a form of domestic defense. Whereas the myth of the Virgin Land worked by suppressing the memory of violence, the Bush administration sought to recover the memory of violence and create a new national relationship to violence in order to inaugurate a global homeland in a realm outside the law. Despite its seeming success, Pease suggests that the current biopolitical order can be maintained only as long as the US public remains captivated by spectacles of violence; alternatives will be possible only when the global state of emergency is exposed as the trauma it purports to oppose.

Next, Christian Parenti moves the focus to the present moment, particularly to the technological methods of imperialism. "Planet America: The Revolution in Military Affairs as Fantasy and Fetish" anatomizes the overblown rhetoric surrounding the revolution in military affairs (RMA). Before the conquest of Iraq and the opening of the current guerrilla war there, intellectual circles in the US military establishment, most notably Defense Secretary Donald Rumsfeld and those around him, were engaged in much frenzied talk about the newest high-tech military methodologies of empire. At the heart of the discussion lay the question of replacing military labor — that is, soldiers and politically problematic US casualties — with technology, capital, or dead labor. These efforts to remake the US military into a totally invincible superforce are known among defense geeks and pentagon apparatchiks as the revolution in military affairs, or simply as the transformation. And this military project forms part of a larger policy agenda of global domination, an agenda shared by all three post–Cold War US presidents. Within this framework, the RMA envisions a perpetual global war waged not by human beings who die, rebel, or come home wounded and crazy, but a war waged by labor that is already dead, crystallized into machinery. Future wars are to be the work of zombie armies of swarming robots, armed aerial drones, supersophisticated microwave bombs, over-the-horizon smart artillery, ocean-floated "lily pad" military bases, and space-orbiting offensive weapon systems using lasers, projectiles, and electromagnetic pulses.

Parenti's article argues that the RMA is in many ways simply a recapitulation of capitalism's standard technology fetish. Always the basic equation is the same: replace living labor with capital. But somewhere on the way to frictionless global military dominance the United States found itself stuck in a radically asymmetrical urban guerrilla war, facing exactly the scenario that the Pentagon dissenters from the RMA had warned about for years. Suddenly America's military fantasy had morphed into its military nightmare: a cumbersome high-tech army of soft American kids bogged down in a massive third world city fighting a low-tech and determined local insurgency. Viewed from among the charred remains of blown-up Humvees in the fetid allies of Baghdad, the RMA looks like the last bubble of the nineties to burst. After all, the transformation debate began in earnest in the early 1990s and ran parallel to the new economy and financialization hype, both of which maintained that "everything had changed."

Unlike the first three essays, Omar Dahbour takes seriously the arguments for the United States' leading role in the world. In "Hegemony and Rights: On the Liberal Justification for Empire," Dahbour posits a connection between recent arguments for the hegemonic role of the United States in the international system and advocacy of an international human-rights regime. Tracing these arguments back to the liberal paternalistic imperialism of John Stuart Mill and Lord Acton, Dahbour examines the contemporary rhetoric of humanitarian interventionism. Dahbour concludes that if US hegemony is to be justified in terms other than those of great-power interest and predominance, it has and perhaps must be made in terms of the establishment and enforcement of an international regime of human rights. Dahbour's article examines recent writing by supporters as well as critics of this latter viewpoint such as Lea Brilmayer, Thomas Weiss, and Jack Donnelly. This view is contrasted with the traditional conservative justification of imperial hegemony in terms of great-power interest and predominance — themselves supposedly guarantors of international peace and stability. The liberal argument views hegemony more as an opportunity for the institutionalization of humanitarian norms at the global level — an institutionalization that, however, requires a strong hegemon for its enactment. Dahbour criticizes such views by emphasizing their philosophically problematic conception of human rights. In addition, Dahbour argues, liberal justifications of US interventionism avoid any consideration of the consequences of using hegemonic power to enforce humanitarian norms.

The essays in part 2 of the collection are marked (though not exclusively) by their attention to the dynamics of gender and imperialism. Cynthia Enloe's "Updating the Gendered Empire: Where Are the Women of Occupied Afghanistan and Iraq?" discusses the ways in which militarization continues to operate in what are often thought to be postwar or postconflict societies. In particular, Enloe emphasizes the ways that subtle and not-so-subtle militarizing processes (local and international) serve to privilege certain men and certain forms of masculinity. The trope of saving brown women from oppressive brown men, crucial to liberal justifications of British imperialism in Asia during the nineteenth century, has returned in recent US military adventures in Asia and the Middle East. When no weapons of mass destruction were found in Iraq, the Bush administration quickly seized on the notion of human, and, more specifically, women's rights as justification for American military intervention around the world. Yet as postcolonial theorists have pointed out, the patriarchal rhetoric implicit in this notion of saving women consigns them to completely passive positions. Enloe's article focuses on the impact of American intervention in Afghanistan and Iraq through the lens of women's rights and the militarization of those societies produced by US involvement over the past two decades. In addition to analyzing the impact of US imperial power on these societies, Enloe traces the thinking and strategies of women activists in those societies as they attempt to create cultures and policies that challenge such ongoing militarizations.

Malini Johar Schueller's essay, "Techno-Dominance and Torturegate: The Making of US Imperialism," continues Enloe's focus on militarism and masculinity, extending it to an analysis of the contemporary military strategies of the neocons and the torture photographs from Abu Ghraib prison. In contrast to Parenti, Schueller suggests that the high-tech militaristic dominance has never been disembodied. Through an examination of Harlan K. Ullman and James P. Wade's military strategy document, *Shock and Awe: Achieving Rapid Dominance*, which became the template for the bombing of Iraq, Schueller demonstrates how techno-dominance is articulated through visions of sexual prowess, masculinity, power, and hypermodern precision which, in turn, depend on producing the Other as abject and emasculated. By analyzing the similarities between the dicourses of neocon techno-dominance and those of modern torture, Schueller argues that the tortures at Abu Ghraib prison, which often take the form of sexual othering, need to be seen as microversions of neocon military strategy, cycled through a familiar Orientalism. Denouncing the current reading of the Abu Ghraib photographs as pornography, Schueller suggests that this reading obfuscates the workings of imperial dominance, while ironically supporting neocon imperial visions that often appear as fantasies of D/s. Anticipating Dawson's essay in this volume, Schueller also suggests that despite their seeming inevitability, the very extremes and contradictions of neocon militarism are producing resistances that are contributing to the unmaking of US imperialism.

The final section in the book deals with political and literary imaginings of other cultures, those envisioned as non-Western and/or inimical to US interests. Melani McAlister's "Left Behind and the Politics of Prophecy Talk" examines the cultural and political dynamics of the highly popular Left Behind series published by the evangelist Tim LaHaye and the writer Jerry Jenkins. The Left Behind novels, imperialist fiction in its apocalyptic mode and centering on the Middle East, were already successful before 9/11 spurred even further interest in the books; *Desecration*, released six weeks after 9/11, became the best-selling hardback book of the year. While intellectuals rightly debate whether current US power is imperialist, neo-imperialist, or simply an arrogant exertion of hegemonic power, the Left Behind series offers its readers a way of seeing the militant actions of the United States as part of a divine plan.

Through readings of several novels in the series, McAlister demonstrates the power of the novels as a major cultural phenomenon that has undeniable links with the resurgence of millennialist pro-Israel activism on the Christian Right and the dangerous direction taken by the US war on terrorism in Iraq. McAlister analyzes the Left Behind series as part of a larger project for evangelical mapping, placing evangelicals on the US political map as a modernized political force who have moved beyond the subcultural status that marginalized them even in the heyday of the Moral Majority. By examining the specific ways in which the series maps the Middle East—with Israel as the site of God's action in history, thus rendering Palestine and Palestinians invisible—McAlister argues for a congruence in policy between the evangelists and US policy makers, even though the reasons for policies vary considerably from the sacred intent of the series to the secular (military power, oil, etc.) intents of policy makers.

Although current political attention has been focused on the Middle East, Harilaos Stecopoulos reminds us of the importance of Africa to the US imperial imagination. In "Putting an Old Africa on Our Map: British Imperial Legacies and Contemporary US Culture," Stecopoulos explores the role of contemporary American representations of Africa. What distinguishes the recent vogue of neo-Victorian Africana, Stecopoulos suggests, is a notable disinterest in drawing parallels between the imperial behavior of nineteenth-century Britons and new-millennium Americans. Conservative intellectuals and pundits such as Thomas Donnelly, Niall Ferguson, and Max Boot may construct historical analogies between the British and American empires, but most of the neo-Victorian Africanists do not. Instead, these texts focus on the long-standing British investment in the continent. The US connection to Africa, indeed, the US connection to empire as such, disappears in the face of a historicist focus on Victorian colonial history.

Stecopoulos argues that these neo-Victorian Africanist texts offer contemporary Americans an opportunity to transform sub-Saharan Africa from a shameful reminder of our participation in slavery and neocolonialism to a sign of our innocence of those European crimes: colonialism and imperialism. For all its global power, the United States is consequently not viewed as an empire at all, but rather as a strong nation eager to foster good throughout the world. In short, the historian Niall Ferguson is almost correct when he claims that the United States "is an empire . . . that dare not speak its name"; the US empire is more than willing to say the word, it just likes to say it with a British accent that echoes from the past.

The book concludes with a chapter analyzing alternative discourses of globalization, particularly those emerging in the Americas over the last decade. The essential task for a literature intent on challenging US hegemony, Ashley Dawson argues in "New Modes of Anti-imperialism," is to render visible the transnational networks of power that characterize contemporary American imperialism. For Dawson, the most pervasive of such networks today is that of the handful of US media corporations whose cultural reach spans the globe. Offering an overview of the massive integration that has taken place over the past twenty years in the name of synergy, Dawson's essay delineates the mass-mediated mechanisms of cultural imperialism today. Despite arguments advanced by reception studies concerning the indigenization of the transnational media product, the monopolistic institutional structures that have developed over the past quarter century, Dawson argues, are a central component in eradicating indigenous cultural production and an integral facet of US imperial strategy. An important consequence of this cultural imperialism, of course, is the diminution of alternative voices and visions of the world, helping to make the slogan "There Is No Alternative" a self-fulfilling prophecy.

Despite the sweeping application of media deregulation during the past two decades, the eradication of indigenous media has not taken place without resistance. A vibrant alternative media sphere has been generated by social movements struggling for a just globalization, one that encompasses everything from posters to novels, films, and the Internet. The outlines of a contemporary anti-imperial public sphere are discernable, Dawson argues, in novels such as Robert Newman's *The Fountain at the Center of the World* (2004) and in social movement manifestos such as the texts published in *We Are Everywhere* (2003). Engaging with social movement manifestos, Newman's epic novel focuses on the impact of what David Harvey calls "accumulation by dispossession," the privatization of the global commons that has been one of the primary facets of the neoliberal reconstruction of empire over the past twenty years. While offering a critique of the transnational networked power of institutions such as the WTO that underlie imperial power today, Newman's novel also traces the emergence of an anticapitalist movement of movements that links the dispossessed in the capitalist core and periphery. *The Fountain at the Center of the World* and the movement manifestos discussed by Dawson document the cultural politics of new antisystemic social movements that over the past decade have come to constitute an important internationalist counter-articulation to global imperial power.

NOTES

1. Paul Johnson, for instance, sees nineteenth-century European colonialism as necessitated and sparked by the US intervention against the pirate states of Algiers, Tunis, and Tripoli at the end of the eighteenth century; he commends the colonization of the Philippines as a necessity for pirate hunting and argues that the United States and its allies can suppress criminal states by "administering obdurate terrorist states." Paul Johnson, "The Answer to Terrorism? Colonialism," *Wall Street Journal*, October 9, 2001, A22. Edward Rothstein argues that because the destruction of September 11 calls for a transcendent ethical perspective, hopefully the "relativism of pomo and the obsessive focus of poco will be widely seen as ethically perverse." Edward Rothstein, "Attacks on U.S. Challenge Postmodern True Believers," *New York Times*, September 22, 2001, A17. See also Martin Wolf, "The Need for a New Imperialism," *Financial Times*, October 10, 2001.
2. For a particularly insightful discussion of the neocons' domestic policies, see Frances Fox Piven, *The War at Home: Domestic Consequences of Bush's Militarism* (New York: New Press, 2004), particularly 22–29.
3. For a discussion of the stakes of different fractions of the US business class in globalization, see William Tabb, *Economic Governance in the Age of Globalization* (New York: Columbia University Press, 2004).
4. A typical example in this regard would be Michael Ignatieff, a professor of political

science at Harvard University and a frequent contributor to influential publications, although he was joined by other erstwhile leftists such as Christopher Hitchens. See Michael Ignatieff, "The Year of Living Dangerously: A Liberal Supporter of the War Looks Back," *New York Times Magazine*, March 14, 2004, 13–18.

5. Giorgio Agamben, *State of Exception*, trans. Kevin Attell (Chicago: University of Chicago Press, 2005).
6. Edward Said, *Culture and Imperialism* (New York: Knopf, 1993), 62–63. John Carlos Rowe uses this insight of Said's as central to his study, *Literary Culture and U.S. Imperialism: From the Revolution to World War II* (New York: Oxford University Press, 2000).
7. In 1807, John Adams wrote, "There is nothing, in my little reading, more ancient in my memory than the observation that arts, sciences, and empire had travelled westward; . . . that their next leap would be over the Atlantic into America." Quoted in Loren Baritz, *City on a Hill: A History of Ideas and Myths in America* (New York: Wiley, 1964), 107.
8. Rudyard Kipling, *Complete Verse* (New York: Anchor, 1988), 321.
9. Frank Ninkovich, *The United States and Imperialism* (Malden, MA: Blackwell, 2001), 237–38. Ninkovich writes, "American imperialism was not only a rather frail addition to a family of robust and mature European siblings, but that it died during childhood" (247).
10. Quoted in ibid., 235.
11. Michael H. Hunt, *Ideology and U.S. Foreign Policy* (New Haven, CT: Yale University Press, 1987), 17–18.
12. David Harvey, *The New Imperialism* (New York: Oxford University Press, 2003), 56.
13. J. W. Fulbright, foreword to *The Fourth Dimension of Foreign Policy: Educational and Cultural Affairs*, by Philip H. Coombs (New York: Harper/Council on Foreign Relations, 1964), xi.
14. Tim Watson, "Is the 'Post' in the Postcolonial the US in American Studies? The US Beginnings of Commonwealth Studies," *Ariel* 31, no. 1 (2000): 65. Watson's article is invaluable in tracing the role of American studies in supporting US hegemony.
15. The work of the Birmingham Center for Contemporary Cultural Studies is useful in challenging this facile opposition of culture and politics. Of particular interest in this context is Stuart Hall's careful theorization of the role of culture in securing the hegemony of Thatcherite ideology in Britain during the 1980s. See his *The Hard Road to Renewal: Thatcherism and the Crisis of the Left* (New York: Verso, 1988).
16. See also William Appleman Williams, *The Tragedy of American Diplomacy* (New York: Dell, 1959), and his *Empire as a Way of Life* (New York: Oxford University Press, 1980); and Thomas R. Hietala's *Manifest Design: Anxious Aggrandizement in Late Jacksonian America* (Ithaca, NY: Cornell University Press, 1985).
17. Since 9/11, many works have emerged to theorize what is recognized as US imperialism today, including David Harvey's *The New Imperialism*, Chalmers Johnson's *The Sorrows of Empire: Militarism, Secrecy, and the End of the Republic* (New York: Henry Holt, 2004), Michael Mann's *Incoherent Empire* (New York: Verso, 2003), and Noam Chomsky's

Hegemony or Survival: America's Quest for Global Dominance (New York: Metropolitan, 2003). The United States' aggressive stance after 9/11 has also generated debate in academic journals. For instance, *Public Culture*, a mouthpiece for globalization, devoted a 2003 issue to debating the issue of contemporary US imperialism, as did *Interventions*, a prominent journal of postcolonial studies. The focus of all these works, however, is political rather than cultural.

18. Using the Gulf War as an example of empire being called into being and functioning in the name of global rights, Hardt and Negri suggest that empire is also participatory and called into being. See their *Empire* (Cambridge, MA: Harvard University Press, 2000), 180.
19. Examples include William Crotty, *The Politics of Terror: The US Response to 9/11* (Boston: Northeastern University Press, 2004); Wheeler Dixon, *Film and Television after 9/11* (Carbondale: University of Southern Illinois Press, 2004); and Stanley Hauerwas and Frank Lentricchia, eds., *Dissent from the Homeland: Essays after September 11* (Durham, NC: Duke University Press, 2003).
20. Williams, *The Tragedy of American Diplomacy*.
21. Rowe, *Literary Culture and U.S. Imperialism*, 9. We see Iraq as forming part of the same trajectory. In his contribution to the *Public Culture* volume on imperialism, John D. Kelly argues that because the US military has organized itself for occasional intervention and because US foreign policy has been about holding the door open for capitalism, it is not imperialism. Such arguments suffer from a narrow definition of imperialism and ironically buy into the myth of American exceptionalism. See John D. Kelly, "U.S. Power, after 9/11 and before It: If Not an Empire, Then What?" *Public Culture* 15, no. 2 (2003): 347–69.
22. Naomi Klein, "Baghdad Year Zero: Pillaging Iraq in Pursuit of a Neocon Utopia," *Harper's*, September 2004, 43–53.
23. Chomsky, *Hegemony or Survival*. See also Marilyn Young, "Ground Zero: Enduring War," in *September 11 in History: A Watershed Moment*, ed. Mary L. Dudziak (Durham, NC: Duke University Press, 2003), 10–33. Young argues that different governments have attempted to order the world such that US dominance means limited sovereignty for others. September 11 simply allowed the Bush administration to pursue these policies more aggressively (21).
24. Gabriel Kolko, *Another Century of War?* (New York: New Press, 2002), 93.
25. Elaine Tyler May "Echoes of the Cold War: The Aftermath of September 11 at Home," in Dudziak, *September 11 in History*, 42, 45, 50. Frederic Jameson repudiates the innocence-to-experience narrative that many had used to describe 9/11 and reminds us that similar arguments were made during Watergate. See his "The Dialectics of Disaster," in Hauerwas and Lentricchia, *Dissent from the Homeland*, 57. See also Srinivas Aravamudan's comments about the redeployment of the American jeremiad by the Religious Right in "Ground Zero; or, The Implosion of Church and State," in Hauerwas and Lentricchia, *Dissent from the Homeland*, 199.

26. Leti Volpp, "The Citizen and the Terrorist," in Dudziak, *September 11 in History*, 147.

27. On crises of overaccumulation, see Harvey, *New Imperialism*, 117. Harvey also mentions other ideological contradictions in this stage of US hegemony, such as the tendency to support authoritarian regimes in the name of stability while fostering a rhetoric of democracy to combat Soviet totalitarianism. See ibid., 58–60.

28. For a political economy of the shift to post-Fordism in the United States, see Mike Davis, *Prisoners of the American Dream: Politics and Economy in the History of the US Working Class* (New York: Verso, 1986).

29. For a discussion of the redesign of the international financial system after 1973, see Peter Gowan, *The Global Gamble: Washington's Faustian Bid for World Dominance* (New York: Verso, 1999).

30. Harvey, *New Imperialism*, 68.

31. John Walton and David Seddon, *Free Markets and Food Riots: The Politics of Global Adjustment* (Cambridge, MA: Blackwell, 1994).

32. The most extreme of such assessments was Francis Fukuyama's *The End of History and the Last Man* (New York: Free Press, 1992).

33. Quoted in Thomas Frank, *What's the Matter with Kansas? How Conservatives Won the Heart of America* (New York: Henry Holt, 2004), 17.

34. Ibid., 5.

35. Eddie Yuen, Daniel Burton Rose, and George Katsiaficas, eds., *The Battle of Seattle: The New Challenge to Capitalist Globalization* (New York: Soft Skull, 2002).

36. Joseph E. Stiglitz, *Globalization and Its Discontents* (New York: Norton, 2002).

37. See Harvey, *New Imperialism*, 157; Arundhati Roy, *Power Politics*, 2nd ed. (Cambridge, MA: South End, 2001); and Naomi Klein, *No Logo: Taking Aim at the Brand Bullies* (New York: Picador, 2000).

38. For an excoriating overview of the growth of fundamentalism around the world, see Tariq Ali, *Clash of Fundamentalisms: Crusades, Jihads, Modernity* (New York: Verso, 2002).

39. Chalmers Johnson, *Blowback: The Costs and Consequences of American Empire* (New York: Holt, 2000), 10.

40. David Harvey, *New Imperialism*, 31; Mann, *Incoherent Empire*; Emmanuel Todd, *After the Empire: The Breakdown of the American Order* (New York: Columbia University Press, 2003), xvi–xvii; Immanuel Wallerstein, *The Decline of American Power: The US in a Chaotic World* (New York: New Press, 2003), 24–26.

41. Johnson, *Sorrows of Empire*, 4. Many other critics also see the shift to explicit imperialism and unilateralism as marking the post–9/11 United States. See George Steinmetz, "The State of Emergency and the Revival of Imperialism: Toward an Authoritarian Post-Fordism," *Public Culture* 15, no. 2 (2003): 323–45.

42. Johnson, *Sorrows of Empire*, 25.

43. Ibid., 257.

44. For a very clear, if somewhat dated, discussion of the unsustainability of US economic

policies, see David Calleo, *The Bankrupting of America: How the Federal Budget Is Impoverishing the Nation* (New York: Morrow, 1992).

45. Over a decade ago, Paul Kennedy was already warning of the perils of such overextension in *The Rise and Fall of the Great Powers: Economic Change and Military Conflict* (New York: Random House, 1987).

46. Michael T. Klare, *Resource Wars: The New Landscape of Global Conflict* (New York: Metropolitan, 2001).

47. The need for such an autonomous regional stance on the part of the European Union is set out particularly militantly in Todd, *After the* Empire, 192–202.

48. For a critique of *Fahrenheit 9/11*'s residual racism and its pandering to American patriotism, see Robert Jensen's "What Michael Moore Misses about the Empire," Common Dreams Newscenter, July 21, 2004, commondreams.org/views04/0706–08.htm.

49. Richard Slotkin, *Regeneration through Violence: The Mythology of the American Frontier, 1600–1860* (Middletown, CT: Wesleyan University Press, 1973).

50. A. O. Scott, "Vengeance Is Ours, Says Hollywood," *New York Times*, May 2, 2004.

51. Robert Jensen, *Citizens of Empire: The Struggle to Reclaim Our Humanity* (San Francisco: City Lights, 2004), xxii.

52. The Bush administration's response was also surely affected by Vietnam-revisionist narratives such as *Rambo*, in which the isolated hero must battle not simply foreign foes but also the corrupt and inept forces of the US bureaucracy in order to redeem the nation. See Lynda Boose, "Techno-Muscularity and the 'Boy Eternal': From the Quagmire to the Gulf," in *Cultures of United States Imperialism*, ed. Amy Kaplan and Donald E. Pease (Durham, NC: Duke University Press, 1993), 581–609.

53. Niebuhr wrote: "As the nineteenth century went on, the note of divine favoritism was increasingly sounded. Christianity, democracy, Americanism, the English language and culture, the growth of industry and science, American institutions—these are all confounded and confused. The contemplation of their own righteousness filled Americans with such lofty and enthusiastic sentiments that they readily identified it with the righteousness of God. . . . It is in particular the kingdom of the Anglo-Saxon race, which is destined to bring light to the gentiles by means of lamps manufactured in America." H. Richard Niebuhr, *The Kingdom of God in America* (1937; Middletown, CT: Wesleyan University Press, 1988), 179.

54. Lee Quinby, "Women and the Techno-Millennium," *Review of Education/Pedagogy/Cultural Studies* 21, no. 4 (1999): 284.

55. Stuart Hall et al., *Policing the Crisis: Mugging, the State, and Law and Order* (London: Macmillan, 1978), 217.

56. See the Project for a New American Century Web site, www.newamericancentury.org.

57. Harvey, *New Imperialism*, 190.

58. Anne Norton, *Leo Strauss and the Politics of American Empire* (New Haven, CT: Yale University Press, 2004).

59. As David Harvey has noted, the name PNAC is notable both for its reach and for its

obfuscation of territorial control. It is temporality, a century, that is being named American, rather than space. See Harvey, *New Imperialism*, 91–92.

60. All of this was set out explicitly as long ago as the early 1990s. For a discussion of the history of current national security strategy, see David Armstrong, "Dick Cheney's Song of America: Drafting a Plan for Global Dominance," *Harper's*, October 2002, 76–83.

61. Wolfowitz's draft of the "Defense Planning Guide" was leaked to the press in 1992. Patrick E. Tyler, "U. S. Strategy Plan Calls for Insuring No Rivals Develop," *New York Times* March 8, 1992, 1. In this context, the United States has no interest in resolving smoldering conflicts such as the Israeli-Palestinian one since they legitimate military spending by creating a climate of fear. See Ellen Meiksins Wood, *Empire of Capital* (New York: Verso, 2003), 161.

62. Thomas Donnelly, "Rebuilding America's Defenses: Strategy, Forces, and Resources for a New Century," report of The Project for the New American Century, September 2000, v. See Harlan K. Ullman and James P. Wade Jr., *Shock and Awe: Achieving Rapid Dominance* (National Defense University Press, 1996), www.ndu.edu/inss/books/books% 20-%201996/Shock%20and%Awe%20-%20Dec%2096/intro.html.

63. For an indictment of US control of these institutions, see Stiglitz, *Globalization and Its Discontents*.

64. For Arundhati Roy's scathing criticism of this practice, see her *Power Politics*, 83–84.

65. Manfred B. Steger, *Globalism: The New Market Ideology* (Lanham, MD: Rowan and Littlefield, 2002), 54; quoted in Johnson, *Sorrows of Empire*, 260.

66. Of course, even before 9/11 it should have been apparent that state power was not disseminating itself into a transnational network. As the massive intensification of the policing and carceral apparatuses in the United States over the past thirty years makes clear, state power was simply being redirected from redistributive to punitive ends during the post-Fordist era. For a wide-ranging analysis and indictment of this trend, see Christian Parenti, *Lockdown American: Police and Prisons in the Age of Crisis* (New York: Verso, 1999).

67. For detailed discussion of these various measures, see Cynthia Brown, ed., *Lost Liberties: Ashcroft and the Assault on Personal Freedom* (New York: New Press, 2003).

68. David Cole, *Enemy Aliens: Double Standards and Constitutional Freedoms in the War on Terrorism* (New York: New Press, 2003).

69. See Reg Whitacker, "After 9/11: A Surveillance State?" in Brown, *Lost Liberties*, 52–69.

70. ACTA's Web site is located at www.goacta.org.

1 Technologies of Imperialism

JOHN CARLOS ROWE

☆ ☆ ☆ Culture, US Imperialism, and Globalization

The return of what was once termed gunboat diplomacy in the first decade of the twenty-first century as part of the new global order endorsed repeatedly and abstractly by George H. W. and now George W. Bush's regimes could not have occurred without the prior work of culture. In what follows, I make a simple, important point: US cultural production, the work of what Max Horkheimer and Theodor Adorno termed "the culture industry," conditioned American citizens to accept the undisguised militarism and jingoistic nationalism now driving US foreign policy.[1] In its inevitably globalized forms, the US culture industry continues to produce the deep divisions between local resistance and subaltern imitation so characteristic of colonial conflicts from the age of traditional imperialism to the neo-imperialisms of our postindustrial era. And the culture industry today does its work in ways that encompass a wide range of nominally different political positions, so that in many respects left, liberal, and conservative cultural works often achieve complementary, rather than contested, ends. In this respect, little has changed since Horkheimer and Adorno argued in 1944 that "even the aesthetic activities of political opposites are one in their enthusiastic obedience to the rhythm of the iron system."[2]

As the US military raced toward Baghdad, there was considerable criticism of the embedded reporters allowed to report the war under the special conditions imposed by the Pentagon and Department of Defense. Most of the criticism assumed that such reporting was biased or censored. When a *Newsweek* photographer was caught doctoring on his laptop a photograph of an encounter between Iraqi civilians and US military personnel, his firing seemed to vindicate the news magazine of prejudice. Antiwar activists circulated two photographs of Iraqi demonstrators tearing down a monumental statue of Saddam Hussein in Firdos Square, Baghdad: the first was a familiar photograph in the news of demonstrators beating on the sculpture's foundation and then, with the help of an Abrams tank, toppling the hieratic image of the defeated dictator. In the second photograph, not displayed in the popular press or evening news, the camera provides a wide-angle view of the scene at the square, where access roads have been blocked by the US military and the supposedly populist demolition of the statue has been theatrically staged by US forces. In a third photograph circulated on the Internet, the same Iraqis actively involved in attacking the Baghdad statue are shown "one day earlier" in Basra, where they are preparing to board US military aircraft for transport to Baghdad—identified in this photograph as members of the "Iraqi Free Forces."

Such exposures of US military propaganda during the war have continued in news coverage of the putative rebuilding of the political and economic infrastructure in Iraq. The current debate regarding who was actually responsible for the disinformation regarding weapons of mass destruction used as the principal justification for the invasion of Iraq is the most obvious example of public concern regarding the federal government's veracity. For such propaganda to be successful, there must be a willing audience, one already prepared for certain cultural semantics adaptable to new political circumstances and yet with sufficient regional relevance as to make possible the very widespread confusion between Saddam Hussein and Osama bin Laden, between a secular Iraqi state tyranny and an Islamic fundamentalist guerrilla organization. How was it possible that such a preposterous war could be permitted by Congress and by the US population? The answer is not simply that the Bush administration ignored the numerous international protests against the preparations for war and its eventual conduct. Nor is the answer simply that when the war began, the Bush administration controlled the news and staged symbolic events to fool the public, although there is plenty of evidence to support these claims. The cultural preparations for a supposedly just war and for the United States as global policeman did not occur overnight; they are our cultural legacy from the Vietnam War and integral parts of our emergence as a neo-imperial nation since 1945. Central to this legacy is the conception of the United States as a discrete nation that nonetheless has a global identity and mission. Although traditional imperialism works by way of expansion from a national center, US imperialism since Vietnam has worked steadily to import the world and to render global differences aspects of the US nation—in short, to internalize and hypernationalize transnational issues.

It is commonplace, of course, to criticize the United States as one of the several first world nations to employ cultural media to market its products around the world. Neocolonialism generally connotes some complicity between a "multinational corporation covertly supported by an imperialist power," to borrow Chalmers Johnson's definition, and thus implies some entanglement of economic, political, and military motives.[3] The globalization of consumer capitalism and the commodities of first world economies (often manufactured elsewhere) are identified as specific targets by political movements as different as the slow food movement in Italy, Earth First!, and al-Qaeda. Although the arcades and other defined shopping areas were developed in nineteenth-century Europe—Paris, Milan, Berlin, and other metropoles—the shopping mall is an American spin-off. With its emphasis on the city within a city, the linkage of entertainment and consumption, the faux cosmopolitanism of its international and regionally specific shops (Cartier, Montblanc, Nieman Marcus, Saks Fifth Avenue, Texas Souvenirs) and its ubiquitous, often international food courts, the American shopping mall was developed in the 1960s and refined over the past forty years. Such megamalls as Minneapolis's Mall of America, Houston's Galleria, and Southern California's South Coast Plaza have redefined the public sphere as a site of consumption and commodification both of products and of consumers.

Whether directly exported by US business interests or developed by multinational corporations to look like its US prototypes, the international mall is often traceable back to US funding, design, and marketing sources or models. A PBS *Frontline* report, "In Search of al Qaeda," which aired on November 21, 2002, includes footage of a shopping mall in Riyadh, Saudi Arabia, which is physically indistinguishable from European and American malls and includes many of the same stores. Of course, the reporter calls attention to the presence of the Mu'tawah or religious police, who stroll through this mall looking for unveiled women or illicit liaisons between unmarried men and women. "In Search of al Qaeda" constitutes a fine attempt by *Frontline* to explain the animosity felt by many different groups in the Arab world toward the United States. The mall in Riyadh represents quite clearly one common source of resentment: the rapid Americanization of Saudi Arabia and the tacit demand that everyday Muslim practices be adapted to the demands of the global market. From one perspective, the Mu'tawah operate comfortably within this typical mall, with its long, open corridors and the insistent appeal of its transnational commodities. In another view, the religious police seem already defeated by the cultural rhetoric of the mall, which encourages romance and consumption in the same freewheeling space. As Anne Friedberg has argued, the mall links consumer and psychic desires in ways that depend crucially on "the fluid subjectivity of the spectator-shopper."[4]

Commodities are neither passive nor politically innocent; they are perpetually active in the specific kinds of desires they produce in consumers and work by means of the social psychologies of commodity fetishism analyzed by Karl Marx in *Capital* and the reification elaborated by Georg Lukács in *History and Class Consciousness*.[5] Specific consumer desires can also be traced back to hierarchies of specific kinds of capitalist labor. In modern, industrial economies, stores displaying high-fashion and leisure-class products, such as designer clothing for women and luxury products for successful men, proved central. The traditional display windows with their mannequins of elegantly dressed and sexually alluring women belong to the era of the large department stores and, while still a part of the postmodern mall, are challenged by stores displaying the most elaborate array of computerized bodily extensions and miniaturizations, labor-saving devices, and high-tech tools promising greater access to the primary source of wealth and power: the control and manipulation of information and its assorted hermeneutic and representational protocols. In the crush of the crowds defining the public space of the mall, the consumer is promised some individuality apart from just what forces him or her through the doors of his or her local Circuit City. Such identity depends, of course, on its promise of communication, but not so much *with* other people, especially those who may be different from this consumer, but *apart* from others in the notable privacy of postmodern life. The new laptops and Palm Pilots (PDAS) are prized for allowing us to negotiate the crowd as we travel through it, but then saving from this mob our informational work, which can be stored, sifted, and processed in the privacy of our own homes. Of course, the peculiar desire for representational power and authority fetishized in computer hardware and software is rapidly displacing the public sphere created by the late modern desire for more traditional commodities, such as fashion and luxury items. The mall is morphing into the Internet, an imaginary space so rapidly commercialized as to terrify even the most recalcitrant critic and sometime defender of consumer capitalism.

In spite of the admirable efforts of intellectuals to find emancipatory possibilities in the new technologies — alternatives to traditional social forms and practices certainly do exist today — the speed with which the Internet has been commercialized and hierarchized is symptomatic of the huge inequities dividing corporations that can afford access, individuals who merely use the technology (and are thereby used by it), and the majority of the world's population left entirely out of the new communicative practices. In *What's the Matter with the Internet?* Mark Poster recognizes most of these problems while stressing the "underdetermined" character of new digital technologies and thus their availability for new transnational politics: "The Internet affords an opportunity for a contribution to a new politics [and] . . . may play a significant role in diminishing the hierarchies prevalent in modern society and in clearing a path for new directions of cultural practice."[6] In *Ambient Television*, Anna McCarthy acknowledges the ideological consequences of television's portability and publicity in achieving a culture of surveillance such as Michel Foucault predicted, but she also imagines critical alternatives and interventions capable of disrupting and in some cases even transforming unidirectional television.[7] Such alternatives, however, are pushed increasingly to the margins of the Internet and television. Most television scholars agree that the postnetwork era has reconfigured the industry only by allowing more corporate giants to share the wealth of television programming. Niche television and target audiences have led to a wider variety of television only within certain limits of the liberal-to-conservative political spectrum. Radical television, such as Dee Dee Halleck's Paper Tiger Television, goes virtually unwatched, is financially marginal, and is supported primarily by extramural grants. The networks long ago succeeded in defeating public-access cable as a populist alternative to one-way television, and the short-term future of interactive television, especially when integrated with computers and the Internet, is likely to be little more than an extension of the enormously profitable video-game market.

We yearn for each new electronic device, but the vast majority is finally useless to most consumers either because they do not know *how* to use them or have *no use* for them in the first place. What lures consumers to new digital technologies is the general promise of *social communication*, ironically just the ideal offered by Marx and Friedrich Engels in *The German Ideology*, but it is a false promise that substitutes complex programming and upgrades for socially meaningful communication.[8] Designed to serve business and commercial needs, predicated on the increasing privatization of the public sphere, whereby the illusion of sociability is simulated in the radical alienation and paradoxical exclusivity of the home office, commuter vehicle, or the commercial airline's reserved seat, such devices produce specific desires structured by their ideological motivations. The imperial imaginary thrives on these desires, which once initiated are difficult to reverse or purge. Cultural apologists for the Americanization of the globe, like Francis Fukuyama, imagine that such homogenization will take us to that end of history fantastically dreamt by G. W. F. Hegel and other proto-moderns because such conditions will produce a political consensus.[9] Fukuyama is certainly right that one-way globalization is likely to result in an international consensus, even if it is one we can hardly condone, which we know will be not only excruciatingly tedious but finally inhuman, and will require periods of incredible, unpredictable violence.

Such criticism of what may generally be termed a postmodern economy focused on information, communications, and entertainment products, including their integrated research and development components, may seem strangely anachronistic when applied to the contemporary global situation. Today, we confront the revival of traditional imperialism as the United States towers over all other human communities and exerts its unchallenged power in the most flagrantly militaristic manner. Not since the British Empire ruled the world by force and fear in the late eighteenth and nineteenth centuries has there been such undisguised rule by military power. While recognizing important differences between contemporary US global rule in the twenty-first century and that of the British in the nineteenth century, Chalmers Johnson traces a historical genealogy from British to US imperial policies, especially in such critical regions as the Middle East and Southeast Asia.[10] In Somalia and most of Africa, Kosovo, Serbia, Cuba, Nicaragua, Panama, El Salvador, Colombia, the Philippines, North and South Korea, Afghanistan, Israel and Palestine, Saudi Arabia and the Gulf states, Iraq, and Iran, the United States works by open military action or threats. Such situations hardly appear to have much to do with the postmodern economics analyzed by theorists of postindustrial or late capitalist practices such as Ernest Mandel, Fredric Jameson, and David Harvey.

But there is an important relationship between the emergence of US military power, along with the complementary threats of inequitable and repressive policies toward peoples (especially but not exclusively non-US citizens) at home and abroad, and the capitalization of cultural exports ranging from Hollywood entertainment and television programming to digital technologies and their protocols for communication and work. John Gallagher and Ronald Robinson's theory of "free-trade imperialism" is now half a century old, but the thesis of free-trade imperialism still explains a good deal about how traditional imperial military power should emerge with such prominence and frequency as a foreign policy at the very moment when globalization seems the nearly inevitable consequence of US economic triumphalism. Contemporary critics of US foreign policy like Chalmers Johnson have also recognized that free trade is often used as a rationalization for the conduct of multinational corporations and for the US government's development of so-called client states such as Israel and, until recently, South Korea.[11]

Gallagher and Robinson refute traditional theories that imperialism — their principal example was British imperialism in Africa — proceeded historically from military conquest to consolidation of colonial rule only to be legitimated and transformed slowly through economic development. Gallagher and Robinson argue that free-trade policies generally *preceded* historically the militarization of colonies and that such military force was required only by the failure to negotiate trade agreements between metropolitan and colonial centers. Military force is thus held in reserve, not out of humane considerations, of course, but primarily for reasons of practicality and economy, while the imperial power promotes trade agreements — either for raw materials or finished products — with the appearance of favorable and equitable terms to both colonizer and colonized. It is only when this illusion of free trade is shattered that military force is required to reimpose imperial order, when the appearance of free trade can be resumed, under whose guise what in fact usually occurs is demonstrably inequitable exploitation of natural or human resources of the colony. As they write: "The usual summing up of the policy of the free trade empire as 'trade, not rule' should read 'trade with informal control if possible; trade with rule when necessary.' "[12]

Is this not the situation we are witnessing today in the Gulf and in other strategic locations around the world? One of the assumptions of Fukuyama's approach to globalization is that the end of history will bring an end of warfare and national struggle, that the global village and world peace are inextricably linked. From this perspective, whatever the cost of globalization in the mediocrity and uniformity of personal lives is more than compensated by the security achieved. In view of the everyday fear experienced by the majority of humankind, the sacrifices are well worth the enormous gains achieved by US global hegemony. In his neoliberal defense of the United States exercising power around the world in its own "defense," Robert Kagan reaches a similar conclusion, albeit one that involves his condemnation of both the European Union and the United Nations—the closest competitors for US global hegemony at the present moment.[13]

Late capitalism thrives on fear, even employing fear as a principal marketing strategy. In the depressed US economy of the past few years, one of the rare bright spots has been the booming market for self-defense goods, especially high-tech gadgets, in response to 9/11 and the assorted xenophobic anxieties, such as the mailing of anthrax, it prompted. In his documentary *Bowling for Columbine* (2002), Michael Moore attributes violence in the United States primarily to a culture of fear propagated by the news media and federal government. If we accept the general outlines of his argument, then the globalization of US cultural capital will involve the exportation of precisely this culture of fear, a phenomenon we are witnessing as complementary with the increase in US military actions as the Bush administration takes seriously its role as global policeman of the new world order. I want to propose, then, a dialectical relationship between cultural or free-trade imperialism and military imperialism mediated by way of a culture of fear that helps market late-capitalist products and encourages, rather than diminishes, military conflicts in the place of international diplomacy.

The history of this dialectic is understandably as long as that of modernity itself, especially if we trace modernity back to the voyages of exploration and conquest of the late fifteenth and early sixteenth centuries. Modernization begins not so much with the technologies used to achieve such conquests — no new technology was, in fact, invented just for the voyages of exploration — but with the imagining of other worlds and peoples. It is commonplace to speak of how easily the early explorers substituted one people for another, as Columbus mistook Caribs and Arawaks for "Indians" of the Far East (and the name continues to this day, albeit often contested by Native Americans and First Peoples). But there is a shorter history that tells us a good deal about this dialectic, especially in its present deployment in world politics, and that history begins with the military failure of the United States in Vietnam in the early 1970s. Beginning in that moment, US culture attempted to explain and rationalize the war in a wide range of media and from virtually every possible political perspective. Sorting out these diverse outlooks on the Vietnam War remains crucial work for cultural and political critics, but the general impression this cultural work offers is that of the renarrativization of a military and colonial failure into a foundation for subsequent military ventures in the Caribbean, Central America, the Persian Gulf, Africa, and the warring republics of former Yugoslavia.

What appeared in the mid- to late 1970s to be a series of critical interpretations of US involvement in Vietnam — such films as *Coming Home* (1978), *The Deer Hunter* (1979), and *Apocalypse Now* (1980) — were replaced by films and television programs that appropriated the liberal rhetoric of these predecessors but incorporated it into compensatory narratives intent on imaginatively fighting the war again and winning. Sylvester Stallone's Rambo character is the locus classicus of just such heroic conventions. John Rambo fights the Vietnamese, the Russians, and other foreign enemies in the Rambo films, but he also combats *Americans* in ways that clearly anticipate the contemporary nationalization of global issues in the US mass media. The opening scene of the first film, Ted Kotcheff's *Rambo: First Blood* (1982), establishes Rambo's motivation for fighting the local police department and eventually the National Guard called in to hunt him down. As the opening credits roll, Rambo walks down a charming Northwest dirt road to a modest house on the edge of a lake. The African American woman who is there hanging her wash on a clothesline and who centers a sublime prospect of natural beauty, is the mother of Rambo's best friend in Vietnam, Delmar Berry. In the opening dialogue of the film, Rambo learns from Delmar's mother that his friend has died of cancer, a victim of the

Agent Orange sprayed as a defoliant in Vietnam. I have elsewhere interpreted how Rambo consequently appropriates the civil rights, antiwar, and countercultural movements of the late 1960s and early 1970s to legitimate the militarism he represents in *Rambo: First Blood*.[14]

In the second film, George P. Cosmatos's *Rambo: First Blood, Part 2* (1985), Rambo's rage is directed at the CIA's reliance on high technology rather than human agency. In the concluding scene of the film, Rambo fires the large automatic weapons he has used on his mission into Vietnam to destroy the computer command center of the CIA in Thailand, and then he releases a primal scream to accompany this ritualized destruction of the new automated warfare he clearly condemns as inhuman. Ironically, the Emersonian self-reliance and natural identity of John Rambo in both films is set in explicit contrast to the automated militarism employed by the Department of Defense and Pentagon in the first and second Gulf Wars, which for many people were culturally justified by the revival of militaristic values exemplified by the character of Rambo. There is a direct line from the fictional John Rambo to Brigadier General Vincent Brooks, "the six-foot-plus, Hollywood-handsome African American spokesman for Central Command" during the second Gulf War, who at Camp as-Sayliyah's state of the art, "$ 1.5 million, made-for-TV 'Coalition Media Center,' . . . gave hundreds of journalists his daily edited presentations."[15]

Never very precisely defined as a culture, geopolitical region, history, or people, Vietnam became a flexible term, so that the war refought in cultural fantasy could take place at home in such films as Louis Malle's *Alamo Bay* (1985) and Walter Hill's *Southern Comfort* (1981), or in other global hot spots such as the Grenada in Clint Eastwood's *Heartbreak Ridge* (1986) or Central America in Mark Lester's *Commando* (1985) or Afghanistan in Peter McDonald's *Rambo 3* (1988), where John Rambo fights valiantly with the Afghani mujahideen against the Soviets. Of course, the anticolonial resistance movement in Afghanistan, supported by CIA advisors and US funds and weapons, would in the mid-1990s align itself with the Taliban (Students of Islam), which in turn would host Osama bin Laden and al-Qaeda.[16] Screening *Rambo 3* today in the United States is a bizarre experience, as the viewer watches John Rambo learning and even participating in folk rituals, such as horse racing, of Afghani "freedom fighters" who by 2001 would be our unequivocal enemies in that now nearly forgotten US colonial enterprise in the oil-rich regions southeast of the Caspian Sea, including Uzbekistan, Turkmenistan, and Afghanistan.

Contemporary with these films and such fiction television programs as *China Beach* and *Miami Vice* or documentary series, such as HBO's *Soldiers in Hiding*, were military tie-ins that traded official sites as movie sets and insider information about military procedures for films that promoted military heroism and honor, such as *An Officer and a Gentleman* (1982), *Top Gun* (1986), and the many spin-offs, which together have by now helped establish a cinematic and televisual genre (see, for example, the popular *JAG*, *Judge Adjutants' General*). What came to be termed the Vietnam effect extended its aura to draw parasitically on other wars, so that the recent revival of World War II as a topic in films, television docudramas, and print narratives (fiction, biography, and oral histories) had as much to do with the large-scale revision of the Vietnam War (and US imperialism in Southeast Asia) as it did with such nominal historical markers as the fiftieth anniversary of D-Day or memorials for the end of World War II. Billed as antiwar films, often because of their graphic and thus alienating violence, films like Steven Spielberg's *Saving Private Ryan* (1998), Terrence Malick's *Thin Red Line* (1998), and John Woo's *Wind Talkers* (2002) helped remilitarize the United States not only because they drew on the conventions of World War II heroism and military success but also because each in its own way borrowed liberal, often explicitly pacifist, sentiments for its purposes. Thus the captain (Tom Hanks) leading the soldiers assigned to rescue Private Ryan is a school teacher unwilling to risk human lives unnecessarily and obliged merely to do the unpleasant but necessary job of civilian soldier. Officers in *Thin Red Line* disobey orders from above when they put their troops at unreasonable risk, and the Navajo "wind talkers" in John Woo's film challenge the racism of their fellow soldiers. All end up fighting, however, thereby linking a just-war thesis with liberal and antiwar sentiments. My point that combat films with radically different political perspectives often contribute equally to pro-military sentiments is confirmed by Anthony Swofford in his recent memoir of the Gulf War, *Jarhead*. Describing US soldiers' fascination with antiwar films about the Vietnam War, Swofford concludes: "But actually Vietnam War films are all pro-war, no matter what the supposed message, what Kubrick or Coppola or Stone intended. . . . The magic brutality of the films celebrates the terrible and despicable beauty of their fighting skills.

Fight, rape, war, pillage, burn. Filmic images of death and carnage are pornography for the military man."[17]

Criticized by intellectuals for a variety of reasons—constituting direct efforts to relegitimate US military force, forming part of a general return to supposedly masculine values in reaction to the women's rights movement, functioning as more complex efforts to co-opt and thus defuse the sort of antiwar dissent that did contribute significantly to ending the Vietnam War—the mass media rarely addressed these questions directly. Populist media and documentary filmmakers, including the surprisingly popular Michael Moore and less visible producers of alternative television, such as Paper Tiger Television's Dee Dee Halleck, rarely addressed the subtlety with which the mass media employed the rhetoric of its political opponents. In Moore's *Roger and Me* (1989), the CEO of General Motors is a classic capitalist hypocrite and thief; in *Bowling for Columbine*, the president of the National Rifle Association is the senile, foolish, and contradictory Charlton Heston. Only demystify!

There are important exceptions, of course, such as Barry Levinson's *Wag the Dog* (1998) and David O. Russell's *Three Kings* (1997), both of which criticized the nationalist propaganda and media control that allowed the George H. W. Bush administration to wage the Persian Gulf War with little public scrutiny and the illusion of an international coalition of allied forces. *Wag the Dog* is based on the premise that a war we are waging against Albania is entirely fabricated by a Washington spin doctor (Conrad Bream, played by Robert De Niro) with the help of a Hollywood producer (Sidney Motss, played by Dustin Hoffman) to distract public attention from a sexual harassment charge against the incumbent president two weeks from his reelection. *Wag the Dog* brilliantly satirizes the increasing control the US federal government has exercised over news reporting of its foreign military ventures. In many respects, *Wag the Dog* seems merely to elaborate in Hollywood film satire the claims made by Jean Baudrillard in his deliberately iconoclastic *La guerre du Golfe n'a pas eu lieu* (1991).[18]

In a very different fashion, *Three Kings* attempted to peel away the mask of patriotic dedication in the Gulf War by exposing the greed of the US soldiers for Kuwaiti gold looted by the invading Iraqi army as a metaphor for US self-interest in controlling the oil-rich Gulf. I admit that the pacifist and populist sentiments of *Three Kings* are noteworthy, especially in a period when Hollywood films were targeted increasingly at twelve-to-seventeen-year-old moviegoers, who pay the most dollars per person of any age group in the United States. The grisly scene of an M-16 bullet penetrating human intestines in slow motion and producing the green bile that will slowly and painfully kill the victim is far more effective than the slow-motion melodrama of US troops dying on the beaches of Normandy during the D-Day invasion in *Saving Private Ryan*.

Nevertheless, both *Wag the Dog* and *Three Kings* rely on a narrative of Americanization that plays a significant role in the general public's understanding of globalization and anticipates how post-9/11 film and television would rely on similar processes of nationalizing international problems to "channel the nation back to normalcy—or at least [to] the normal flows of television and consumer culture," as Lynn Spigel puts it.[19] *Wag the Dog* does this cultural work in an obvious manner by locating all of the action of the film in the United States; the imprisoned soldier (Denis Leary), who is picked to simulate an actual US soldier downed by hostile gunfire in Albania and miraculously rescued, has to be picked up by the media team from his maximum-security military prison in Texas. The liberal politics of *Wag the Dog* make what I have termed hypernationalization an explicit theme in the film, so that we are expected to understand immediately the irony of the Hollywood producer Motss and the Washington insider Bream inventing an international crisis to cover a domestic sexual scandal. The film satirizes Americans' chronic ignorance of world events, thanks to news structured around entertainment and commercialism, but it also reinforces the assumption that the United States is the center of the world and that even a fictional war can have meaning and value, as long as it is waged by the United States. Carefully structured news stories about the second Gulf War seem to have followed the example of *Wag the Dog*, despite its satiric and countercultural intentions. The saving of Jessica Lynch, the US soldier wounded and captured by Iraqi troops during the US-British invasion, follows just such a narrative of Americanization, from her heroic rescue by US Special Forces through her medical treatment and debriefing at a US military base near Frankfurt to her triumphant return to her hometown in Palestine, West Virginia. Rather than *Wag the Dog*'s satire overwhelming and thus neutralizing the Jessica Lynch story on the evening news, Lynch's narrative, now made into a television biopic, has undone the irony of Barry Levinson's film, especially its rescued-soldier device.

More conventionally, *Three Kings* challenges self-interested US militarism and foreign policy in the Gulf by condemning the command structure of the US military and countering it with the populist pacifism and humanitarianism of the "three kings," who finally live up to their biblical titles by guiding dissident Iraqis and their families to their promised land across the border in Iran. The familiar imperial narrative of US paternalism, of the white man's burden, plays itself out once again in terms almost identical with those criticized so thoroughly in nineteenth-century imperial narratives. The dissident Iraqis who save Archie Gates (George Clooney), Troy Barlow (Mark Wahlberg), Chief Elgin (Ice Cube), and Conrad Vig (Spike Jonze) from attack by the Republican Guard turn out to be primarily intent on "get[ting] rid of Saddam" in order to "live life and do business," as their leader Amir Abdullah (Cliff Curtis) says.[20]

The film criticizes consumer capitalism and its globalization, but it advocates on the other hand the value of small businesses. When Troy Barlow is captured and tortured by Republican Guards, he is made to drink crude oil poured into his mouth propped open with a CD case. The consumer goods stolen from Kuwait and heaped in poorly guarded Iraqi bunkers exemplify the meretriciousness of multinational globalization—tape and CD players in their unopened boxes, tangled skeins of jewelry, heaps of cell phones, and other consumer junk are visually effective, but the political dissidents these three kings will eventually save are committed to modest but meaningful businesses, such as hairstyling. Following a nearly schematic narrative of education, the three remaining kings (Conrad Vig dies and is prepared for a Muslim burial) use the gold they have stolen from the Iraqis (who have stolen it from the Kuwaitis) to buy safe passage for the political dissidents into the relative safety of Iran. The final scene of the film in which the border crossing is enacted, replete with sentimental waves and sympathetic looks between the dissidents and the enlightened US soldiers, is difficult to watch today as the Bush administration clamors to expand its invasion and occupation of Iraq to include Iran.

The sympathy these US soldiers establish with the Iraqi dissidents is certainly intended by David O. Russell to counter the Orientalist demonization of Arab peoples so common in US mass culture since the nineteenth century, intensified as part of the buildup for the first Gulf War, and driven to near cultural hysteria in the months following the attacks on 9/11.[21] Yet the Iraqi dissidents are represented in what seem to be deliberately ambiguous regional, ethnic, and religious terms. The mercenary US soldiers enter southern Iraq in quest of the stolen Kuwaiti gold, so the political dissidents they encounter in the aftermath of the first Gulf War would most likely be Shiite dissidents, similar to those who appealed to George H. W. Bush for military assistance and staged an unsuccessful rebellion against Saddam Hussein in the weeks following the conclusion of that war. Yet there is considerable cinematic evidence to conclude that the Iraqi dissidents are Kurds. Hairdressing, for example, is a traditionally respected profession among the Kurds, so that one of the dissidents' plans to return to that profession hints at Kurdish affiliations, displaced, of course, from the main Kurdish population centers in northern Iraq to the film's setting in southern Iraq. Saddam Hussein's government did forcibly resettle Kurds in the South (including many who were murdered and buried in mass graves there) during the Anfal, the genocidal ethnic cleansing the Iraqi dictator conducted prior to the first Gulf War.[22]

The deliberate confusion of different dissident groups in Iraq seems intended not only to achieve cinematic economy but also to make these dissidents more accessible to the four US soldiers. These soldiers represented in the film offer a sample of US multiculturalism: Chief Elgin is a devout Christian African American, Conrad Vig is an uneducated southern white racist, Archie Gates is a white career soldier taking early retirement, and Troy Barlow a model WASP. To be sure, the representativeness of this group is very narrow, but their respective sympathies with the Iraqi dissidents perform a narrative of cultural hybridity that unmistakably argues for greater understanding of other peoples as an alternative to unilateral globalization and US militarism. Chief Elgin appears to abandon Christianity for Islam, and he dons the traditional Arab male *kaffieyeh* (head covering) to announce his conversion. Conrad Vig learns about Islamic burial practices, overcomes his racism toward Chief Elgin by way of their shared interest in Islam, and is eventually prepared for an Islamic burial of his own. In fact, when the dissidents cross the border into Iran, they are carrying his body with them for a proper burial on the other side. The protagonists learn to sympathize with and understand not historically and regionally specific groups of Iraqis, but generalized "Arab" and "Muslim" types. In this way, the four Americans act out liberal multiculturalism, which is often criticized for what Lisa Lowe terms its contribution to the "ideological representation of the liberal imperialist state."[23] Thus the cinematic experience of viewing in 2004 the concluding scene of Iraqi dissidents crossing the border into the relative freedom of Iran is not a prophecy from 1997 of how the Bush administration would turn to military power again in 2003 because it failed to follow the humane and politically liberal advice of *Three Kings*. Instead, the liberal ideology, itself deeply invested in US nationalism, helped produce the circumstances that would make the Bush administration's invasion of Iraq a military and colonial reality—and the "logical next step" of this foreign policy covert or military efforts at regime change in Iran.

What has been particularly noteworthy in the US mass media since the terrorists attacks of September 11 and during the invasion of Iraq has been a new twist on these old themes, a turn compatible with them and readable as part of a history stretching from the Vietnam era to the present in the gradual, ineluctable control of the news and entertainment media by the US government. Fiction and nonfiction television has understandably paid great attention to the related events of 9/11 and the justification of US military intervention in Iraq. Lynn Spigel describes in some detail how "traditional forms of entertainment" reinvented "their place in U.S. life and culture" after 9/11, initially by reducing the number of violent films released and replacing them on television with "family fare."[24] Spigel goes on to argue that very quickly after this period of self-censorship, Hollywood and television turned again to familiar historical narratives to stabilize the myths of national cohesion and reaffirm a teleological narrative about the American experience.[25] Spigel's fine study confirms my own sense that Hollywood and television quickly recycled old mythic narratives about America, rather than drawing the opposite conclusion: that the terrorist attacks of 9/11 indicate that Americans need to know far more about the world they are so intent on globalizing. As if in direct response to this promise of greater attention to the other peoples of the world, the media began to incorporate terrorism into the United States and strip it of its international threat. Like President Bush's continuing efforts to link Iraq directly with al-Qaeda, the nationalizing of terror helped defuse its transnational, inchoate, and thus truly terrifying power. The containment of terror on contemporary US television follows the logic of the cultural imperialism I have been tracing thus far, but now with the claim that the best weapons against such terror are those of traditional US democracy: the fairness of the law and the populism of an American people that exceeds party politics.

Since the 1987–88 television season, NBC's *Law and Order*, now the main title for three separate television programs, has worked out fictional solutions to much-publicized cases in criminal law in the United States.[26] Starring Sam Waterston as the lead prosecutor of the district attorney's office in New York, the program makes moral claims specific to the medium of television and distinguishes itself thereby from the continuing spate of police and crime shows, which rely primarily on the urban public's anxieties about living in an increasingly dangerous America and world. The program is structured in two parts: in the first half hour, police detectives investigate a crime, arrest a suspect, and present their case to the district attorney's office; in the second half hour, the chief prosecutor, Jack McCoy (Sam Waterston), and his attractive assistant district attorney, Serena (Elisabeth Röhm), bring the case to trial and judgment. Although the detective and legal work do not always coincide, the errors in the system seem to confirm the overall checks and balances built into the police-judicial system, as it is referred to in the voice-over prologue to the program.

Here I want to digress for a moment to anticipate my larger argument. I disagree with Michael Moore's repeated claim in *Bowling for Columbine* that it is primarily the news media, rather than entertainment television and film, that have shaped the atmosphere of fear in the United States, resulting in more than eleven thousand gun deaths per year. Citing how other societies, like Canada and Japan, where gun deaths are less than one thousand per year, still generate large audiences for violent films, television programs, and video games, Moore contends that in such societies even adolescent viewers can suspend their disbelief in fiction programs and understand the difference between fantasy and reality. But in the United States, there is a long tradition of confusing fiction and reality in the mass media, primarily for the purposes of maximizing the commercial advantages of each mode. We hardly need the examples of recent reality television to remind us that television thrives on what Baudrillard long ago defined as the hyperreal, a phenomenon seemingly explained best by the way television gives us the illusion of heightened knowledge and authority over an otherwise baffling real. *Law and Order* certainly has this effect on its viewers, which may account for its huge success on network television otherwise challenged significantly by cable channels, such as Lifetime and Oxygen, targeting specific market shares and trying to break up network hegemony in the so-called postnetwork era.

I have argued elsewhere that the socially conscious television of the early 1970s, such as that Norman Lear pioneered in *All in the Family*, was transformed in the 1980s into much more conventional moral problem solving within the existing legal and social boundaries of US democracy.[27] *All in the Family* argued that racial and ethnic bigotry could not be overcome entirely by the law, but required changes in personal values. *Sanford and Son* joined that argument to claim that class and racial antipathies were inextricably bound together in psychological habits difficult but still possible to change. But *Law and Order* imagines that equality under the law, despite notable aberrations in US legal history, is our best defense against injustices tied to class, race, ethnicity, gender, or sexuality. The cultural shift is clearly from television committed to political and social reform to television concerned with defending existing institutions, as indeed the title of the program—a slogan of conservative republican campaigns for the past thirty-five years—suggests.

The episode of *Law and Order* I want to analyze focuses on the murder of a popular professor of anthropology, Louise Murdoch, who is also the head of a community advocacy center for Muslim women, and the eventual arrest and trial of a young American male, Greg Landen, who has converted to Islam. Of course, the most infamous American convert to Islam on October 2, 2002, the date this episode was first broadcast, was John Walker Lindh, the so-called American Taliban who had left his upper-middle-class home in Marin, California, to study Arabic and the Koran in Yemen and Pakistan and then to join the Taliban in Afghanistan. Two days after this episode aired, Lindh was sentenced to a twenty-year prison term in a plea bargain that reduced the charges against him to "one count of providing services to the Taliban and one count of carrying explosives during a felony."[28] In his sentencing hearing, Lindh was tearful and apologetic, denying he had any intention of taking up arms against the United States, and his divorced parents stood by him throughout his arrest and trial.

Lindh is certainly the historical model on which the character of Greg Landen in *Law and Order* is based, but very important changes are made to his character and history. First, the young man in *Law and Order* despises his parents, the legal system, and America in general, so that his courtroom tirades as he takes over his own legal defense for purposes of political propaganda remind the viewer of news accounts of Zacarias Moussaoui, the accused twentieth hijacker in the 9/11 attacks, who also insisted on serving as his own legal counsel and used the courtroom as a bully pulpit. Testifying in his own defense, Landen makes some very reasonable connections between al-Qaeda's possible motivations and the historical motivations of oppressed minorities in the United States to resist domination:

> Since 1990, [the United States] has occupied our holy lands. . . . America doesn't respect any culture but its own. . . . America is a country that was born out of the mass murder of native Americans and built on the backs of Africans. If the native Americans could have defended themselves by flying planes into buildings, don't you think they would have? If the slaves could have freed themselves by becoming martyrs, don't you think they would have? And it wouldn't have been terrorism; it would have been self-defense.

In Muslim male dress and beard, Greg Landen is exoticized and Orientalized, even though his testimony echoes reasonable arguments made by many intellectuals in response to 9/11. In addition to his physical appearance, Landen is also alienated by his father, who is shown in the courtroom shaking his head from side to side and mouthing the unheard word, "No," as his son testifies.

The young man's target in *Law and Order* is not the capitalist authority symbolized by the World Trade Center towers in New York City or the military authority of the Pentagon, but a woman professor of anthropology who has devoted her life to liberal social change and exemplifies that work in her diversification of the American university. Equating global terrorist attacks, such as al-Qaeda's on the United States (or Israel, France, or Indonesia), with domestic terrorism within the United States, such as Timothy McVeigh's bombing of the Murragh Building in Oklahoma City, is a common response not only in the United States but in Islamic societies as well. But this episode of *Law and Order* constructs the plot in such a way as to swerve widely from such a conclusion. Instead, we learn that the young man believed his girlfriend, who worked at the professor's Center for Muslim Women, was being drawn away from her responsibilities as a submissive Islamic woman by her feminist work with the professor. In a jealous, but also religiously motivated, rage, he smote his enemy.

Cautious to protect itself against charges of insensitivity to Islamic Americans, *Law and Order* carefully disengages the young man from true Islam, but in much the same fashion al-Qaeda has been distinguished in the popular US news from true Islam: by condemning the fundamentalist irrationality of both, rather than making any substantive claims about the role of women in Islamic societies. In a decisive consultation between the prosecutors and a woman psychologist whom the prosecution will call as an expert witness, the psychologist concludes that Landen's primary motivation for murder was his sexual insecurity, reinforced by his difficult relationship with his parents, and his desperate need to maintain absolute control over his girlfriend. I need hardly comment on how such a conclusion reduces to triviality all of the important ethical questions raised by this episode. To be sure, *Law and Order* does not argue that this young man represents all American Muslims, but it reinforces virtually every convention the West has used to distinguish its supposed civilization from Islamic "barbarism" since Romantic idealist philosophers like Hegel.

Talal Asad has argued in *Genealogies of Religion* that the "West" begins with the "project of modernization (Westernization)" that is inherently colonial and "defines itself, in opposition to all non-Western cultures, by its modern historicity. Despite the disjunctions of modernity (its break with tradition), 'the West' therefore includes within itself its past as an organic continuity: from 'the Greeks and Romans' and 'the Hebrews and Early Christians,' through 'Latin Christendom,' 'the Renaissance,' and 'the Reformation,' to the 'universal civilization' of modern Europeans."[29] Western imperialism, then, is a story told in countless different ways, media, and genres, but with surprisingly few variations when looked at in this light, which allows otherness to be internalized and rationalized, historicized and civilized.

It perhaps should not surprise or even shock us that popular American television contributes to this narrative telelogy in such transparently reductive ways. Islam is for a young American, like John Walker Lindh or the fictional character in *the Law and Order* episode, merely acting out childish rebellion, a confirmation of the supposedly undeveloped features of those "backward cultures," which like Hegel's Africa are without history. In a similar fashion, conservative politicians and the general public accepted antiwar activism in the Vietnam War era as college hijinks, adolescent rebellion, and a rejection of their fathers' America. What each of these historical moments — the Vietnam War and the current inchoate war on terrorism — have in common is a desperate desire to reaffirm national values by repressing utterly the history and reality of supposed enemies in Southeast Asia and the Islamic world. Few today would disagree, including such stubborn old hawks as William Westmoreland, that the Vietnam War marked a historic moment in which the United States needed to change its foreign and domestic policies, its ties between government and corporation, its neglect of public opinion, and the changing political economies affecting these historical crises. If we are to learn the lesson of the Vietnam era, then we must learn to recognize, rather than repress, the complex, intertwined histories of Islam, its influence on the development of US and other Western societies, and our dependence on the economic means it has provided to modernize and thus Westernize, often at its own peril, the world. Before we can even begin to learn this lesson, however, we will have to read critically that other narrative of Western historicity Talal Asad has so cogently interpreted as dependent on a constant assumption:

> To make history, the agent must create the future, remake herself, and help others to do so, where the criteria of successful remaking are seen to be universal. Old universes must be subverted and a new universe created. To that extent, history can be made only on the back of a universal teleology. Actions seeking to maintain the "local" status quo, or to follow local models of social life, do not qualify as history making. From the Cargo Cults of Melanesia to the Islamic Revolution in Iran, they merely attempt (hopelessly) "to resist the future" or "to turn back the clock of history."[30]

It is time for us to think differently about how history is and has been made, to count the local as well as the global, and to develop new institutions, not simply interpretive methods, to negotiate the inevitable conflicts of such histories. Without such critical knowledge, there is likely to be unending terror from all sides in a new era of global warfare, only one stage of which is being enacted in the US occupation of Iraq.

NOTES

1. Max Horkheimer and Theodor Adorno, *Dialectic of Enlightenment*, trans. John Cumming (New York: Continuum, 1988), 122.
2. Ibid., 120

3. Chalmers Johnson, *The Sorrows of Empire: Militarism, Secrecy, and the End of the Republic* (New York: Henry Holt, 2004), 30.
4. Anne Friedberg, *Window Shopping: Cinema and the Postmodern* (Berkeley: University of California Press, 1993), 120.
5. Karl Marx, *Capital: A Critique of Political Economy*, trans. Ben Fowkes, 2 vols. (New York: Random House, 1977), 125–77; Georg Lukács, *History and Class Consciousness: Studies in Marxist Dialectics*, trans. Rodney Livingstone (Cambridge, MA: MIT Press, 1971).
6. Mark Poster, *What's the Matter with the Internet?* (Minneapolis: University of Minnesota Press, 2001), 20.
7. Anna McCarthy, *Ambient Television: Visual Culture and Public Space* (Durham, NC: Duke University Press, 2001), 226–51.
8. Karl Marx and Friedrich Engels, *The German Ideology*, ed. C. J. Arthur (New York: International Publishers, 1988), 47.
9. Francis Fukuyama, *The End of History and the Last Man* (New York: Free Press, 1992), 127.
10. Johnson, *Sorrows of Empire*, 138–39, 217–18.
11. Ibid., 31.
12. Quoted in John Carlos Rowe, *Literary Culture and U.S. Imperialism: From the Revolution to World War II* (New York: Oxford University Press, 2000), 132.
13. Robert Kagan, *Of Paradise and Power: America and Europe in the New World Order* (New York: Random House, 2003), 157–58.
14. John Carlos Rowe, *The New American Studies* (Minneapolis: University of Minnesota Press, 2002), 180–86.
15. Johnson, *Sorrows of Empire*, 249.
16. Ibid., 177.
17. Anthony Swofford, *Jarhead: A Marine's Chronicle of the Gulf War* (New York: Scribner, 2003), 210.
18. Jean Baudrillard, *La guerre du Golfe n'a pas eu lieu* (Paris: Galilée, 1991). The English translation by Paul Patton, *The Gulf War Did Not Take Place*, was published in 1995 by Indiana University Press.
19. Lynn Spigel, "Entertainment Wars: Television Culture after 9/11," *American Quarterly* 56, no. 2 (2004): 239.
20. The screenwriters probably wanted to use the title *Three Kings* for its religious reference to refer specifically to the three officers. Conrad Vig is an enlisted solider, not an officer.
21. One of my points in this essay and in *Literary Culture and U.S. Imperialism* is that when we view US imperialism in its full historical scope, rather than as a recent neo-imperialism dating either from World War II or from the Spanish-American War, we see such features as US Orientalism as relatively unchanged, except for the specific peoples employed. From the Barbary Pirates of nineteenth-century Tripoli to the Philippine revolutionaries led by Aguinaldo in the Philippine-American War (1898–1902) who resisted US annexation to the Vietcong and North Vietnamese Army regulars and,

more recently, to the Libyans, Palestinians, Iraqis, Iranians, and transnational al-Qaeda–style revolutionaries, diverse groups around the globe have been consistently Orientalized by the United States. For an interesting discussion of US Orientalism in these contexts, see Christina Klein, *Cold War Orientalism: Asia in the Middlebrow Imagination, 1945–1961* (Berkeley: University of California Press, 2003), 1–19.

22. I am indebted to Thomas LeClair of the University of Cincinnati for this interpretation of the Kurdish elements in the dissident group represented in *Three Kings*.

23. Lisa Lowe, "Imagining Los Angeles in the Production of Multiculturalism," in *Mapping Multiculturalism*, ed. Avery F. Gordon and Christopher Newfield (Minneapolis: University of Minnesota Press, 1996), 420.

24. Spigel, "Entertainment Wars," 235.

25. Ibid., 240–41.

26. The other two programs are *Law and Order: SVU* (*Special Victims Unit*) and *Law and Order: CI* (*Criminal Intent*).

27. Rowe, *New American Studies*, 170–71.

28. "I Made a Mistake by Joining the Taliban," *Washington Post*, October 5, 2002.

29. Talal Asad, *Genealogies of Religion: Disciplines and Reasons of Power in Christianity and Islam* (Baltimore, MD: Johns Hopkins University Press, 1993), 18.

30. Ibid., 19.

DONALD E. PEASE

Between the Homeland and Abu Ghraib: Dwelling in Bush's Biopolitical Settlement

The following remarks constitute an effort to interpret the current Bush administration's alteration of the regulatory fictions through which government policy makers exercise normative control over the population. They are grounded in the assumption that the state's master fictions are freighted with metaphorical significance and possessed of performative force that characteristically separate "what happened" from the capacity to supply the representations through which what happened becomes meaningful.[1] The mythological tropes—"Virgin Land," "Redeemer Nation," "American Adam," "Nature's Nation," "Errand into the Wilderness"—sedimented within these master narratives supplied the transformational grammar through which the state shaped the people's understanding of contemporary political and historical events. The state's powers of governance depend in part on its recourse to this regulatory intertext that transmits a normative system of values and beliefs from generation to generation. After they subordinate historical events to these mythological themes, the government's policy makers are empowered to fashion imaginary resolutions of actual historical dilemmas.[2]

THE MYTHICAL FOUNDATIONS OF THE BUSH SETTLEMENT

The catastrophic events that took place at the World Trade Center and the Pentagon on September 11, 2001, precipitated a "reality" that the national metanarratives could neither comprehend nor master. In his September 20,

2001, address to the nation, President George W. Bush provided a symbolic reply that inaugurated a symbolic drama partly autonomous of the events that called it forth. The address to the nation was designed to lessen the events' traumatizing power through the provision of an imaginary response to a disaster that could not otherwise be assimilated to the preexisting order of things:

> On September 11, enemies of freedom committed an act of war against our country. Americans have known wars, but for the past 136 years they have been wars on foreign soil, except for one Sunday in 1941. Americans have known the casualties of war, but not at the center of a great city on a peaceful morning. . . . Americans have known surprise attacks, but never before on thousands of civilians. . . . All of this was brought upon us in a single day, and night fell on a different world. . . . I will not forget the wound to our country and those who inflicted it. . . . Our grief has turned to anger and anger to resolution. Whether we bring our enemies to justice or bring justice to our enemies, justice will be done.

As the harbinger for the invariant core beliefs prerequisite to the reordering of reality, the national mythology supplied the master fictions to which Bush appealed to authorize the state's actions. Richard Slotkin has explained how national myths accomplish this reconfiguration of the order of things in terms of their power to assimilate the contingent events of a secular history to "archetypal patterns of growth and decay, salvation and damnation, death and rebirth."[3] As the structural metaphors containing the essential elements of a culture's habits of mind, myths take place in the gap between between a culture's perception of contingent historical events and their assimilation into the nation's traditionalized memory. In supplying the events they retell with timeless cultural value, myths transform historical events into processes of traditionalization that render them central components to the culture they thereby reproduce. It is through their correlation with processes of traditionaliziation that core myths like the Virgin Land acquire the monopoly over a culture's symbolic violence. Their monopolization of the keys to cultural persuasion enables national myths and symbols to constrain a people's thought and behavior by tethering them to paradigms that rationalize and reproduce the traditional order.

The executive phrases in Bush's address alluded to the foundational myths embedded within the national narrative. These phrases also inaugurated a symbolic drama that would transform the primary integers in the narrative the nation had formerly told itself into terms — Ground Zero, homeland, Operation Enduring Justice, Operation Iraqi Freedom — that authorized the Bush administration's state of emergency. Specifically, the state's symbolic response to 9/11 replaced Virgin Land ("Americans have known wars, but for the past 136 years they have been wars on foreign soil") with Ground Zero ("Americans have known the casualties of war, but not at the center of a great city on a peaceful morning") and the homeland ("Americans have known surprise attacks, but never before on thousands of civilians") as the governing metaphors through which to come to terms with the attack. The spectacular military campaigns in Afghanistan and Iraq that followed Bush's September 20 address were in part designed to accomplish the conversion of these metaphors into historical facts.[4]

When George Bush cited the historically accurate fact that "with the exception of a Sunday in 1941," the United States had not been subject to foreign invasion, he linked the public's belief in the myth of Virgin Land with the historical record. But when he did so, Bush did not supply US publics with historical grounds for the collective belief in Virgin Land. The myth that America was a Virgin Land endowed the historical fact that US soil had never before been subjected to foreign violation with a moral rationale: Virgin Land was inviolate because the American people were innocent. In describing the surprise attack as a "wound to our country," Bush interpreted this violation on mythological as well as historical registers.

The wound was directed against the Virgin Land as well as against the US people's myth of themselves as radically innocent. The state of emergency Bush erected at Ground Zero was thereafter endowed with the responsibility to defend the homeland because the foreign violation of Virgin Land had alienated the national people from their imaginary way of inhabiting the nation. This substitution anchored the people to a very different state formation. It also drastically altered the national people's foundational fantasy about their relationship to the national territory, redefining it in terms of the longing of a dislocated population for their lost homeland.

What follows should be understood as a critical itinerary of the discursive strategies through which the Bush administration effected a shift in the nation's governing self-representation — from a secured innocent nation to a wounded, insecure emergency state. At the conclusion of these remarks, I shall also briefly indicate how this newly formed structure of governmentality might be unsettled.

9/11: VIRGIN LAND AT GROUND ZERO

The metaphor of Virgin Land condensed a broad range of historically distinct actions — the uprooting, immigration, and resettlement of European exiles on a newly "discovered" territorial landmass — and it regulated the meanings that should and that should not be assigned to these actions. At its core, the metaphor of Virgin Land was designed to fulfill Europe's wish to start life afresh by relinquishing history on behalf of the secular dream of the construction of a new Eden. The metaphor gratified European emigrants' need to believe that America was an unpopulated space. The belief that the New World was discovered and settled by the Europeans who emigrated there resulted from the coupling of a shared fantasy with historical amnesia.

Virgin Land depopulated the landscape in the imaginary register so that it might be perceived as an unoccupied territory in actuality. The metaphor turned the landscape into a blank page, understood to be the ideal surface onto which to inscribe the history of the nation's so-called Manifest Destiny. Virgin Land narratives placed the movement of the national people across the continent in opposition to the savagery attributed to the wilderness and the native peoples who figured as indistinguishable from the wilderness, and, later, it fostered an understanding of the campaign of Indian Removal as nature's beneficent choice of the Anglo-American settlers over the native inhabitants for its cultivation.

Overall, Virgin Land enabled the American people to replace the fact that the land was already settled by a vast native population with the belief that it was unoccupied. And the substitution of the national fantasy for the historical reality enabled Americans to disavow the resettlement and in some instances the extermination of entire populations. In displacing historical events with the representations through which they became recognizably "American," Virgin Land narratives produced reality as an effect of the imaginary. The fact that this reality could be exposed as unreal did not diminish the control that the national imaginary exerted over the symbolic order; it worked instead to underscore the logic of fetishism as the decisive aspect of its mode of persuasion. US citizens may have known very well that the historical record would not warrant the belief that the colonists who emigrated to America discovered a Virgin Land, but they nevertheless found it expedient to embrace the belief over the historical record. They found it so because the belief that America was a Virgin Land fostered the complementary belief in the radical innocence of the American people.

The belief as well as the disavowal was linked to the historical fact that US civilian populations had not been subject to foreign attack since the war of 1812.[5] The historical fact of the nation's inviolability associated the belief in a Virgin Land with the desire that US soil would remain forever unviolated by foreign aggression. When this fact was conjoined with the belief that the violation of a native people's homeland took place on foreign soil rather than Virgin Land, the composite named what determined US uniqueness.

But the catastrophic events that took place at Ground Zero on September 11, 2001, actualized both of the scenarios that the belief in Virgin Land had been designed to ward off. At Ground Zero, US Virgin Land had not merely been violated by foreign invaders; this violation also assumed the form of the forcible dislocation of a settled population. The buildings erected to symbolize the US rise to world dominance were turned into horrific spectacles of the violent removal of occupants from their site of residence.

The transformation of Virgin Land into Ground Zero brought into visibility an inhuman terrain that the national imaginary had been constructed to conceal. While the term *Ground Zero* was chosen to describe the unimaginable nature of the events that took place on September 11, 2001, the state's association of them with the demand for the securing of the homeland invested them with an uncanny effect. For when it displaced the metaphor of the Virgin Land, the term *homeland* rendered the devastation precipitated at Ground Zero at once utterly unexpected yet weirdly familiar.

After they were figured in relation to the Homeland Security Act, the unprecedented events which took place on 9/11 seemed familiar because they recalled the suppressed historical knowledge of US origins in the devastation of native peoples' homelands. The sites of residence of the Paiutes and the Shoshones had more recently been destroyed as a result of the state's decision to turn their tribal lands into toxic dumps for the disposal of nuclear waste.

The events also appeared familiar, as the signifier Ground Zero attests, because the unimaginable sight of the crumbling twin towers recovered memories of the firebombings of civilian populations over Dresden and Tokyo, as well as the unspeakable aftereffects of the atomic fallout on the inhabitants of Hiroshima and Nagasaki.

With the destruction of the fantasy that the nation was founded on Virgin Land, the violence which it covered over swallowed up the entire field of visibility. Ground Zero evoked the specter of the nation-founding violence out of whose exclusion the fantasy of the Virgin Land had been organized. At Ground Zero, the fantasy of radical innocence on which the nation was founded encountered the violence it had formerly concealed.

THE RETURN OF THE HOMELAND

War might be said to begin when a country becomes a patriotic fiction for its population. A nation is not only a piece of land but a narration about the people's relation to the land. If one of the primary aims of war involves destroying the way an enemy perceives itself, Bush, in his September 20 address to the nation, represented 9/11 as an act of war in the sense that it brought about the destruction of the national people's foundational fantasy concerning their relation to the land.[6]

The foundational fantasy of the United States was organized around a traumatic element that could not be symbolized within the terms of the national narrative. In the United States, the fantasy of the Virgin Land covered over the shameful history of internal violence directed against the native populations. But this historical fact was not utterly effaced. It functioned as an occluded supplement to the nation's view of itself as a redeemer nation whose Manifest Destiny entailed the commission to undertake a providential errand into the wilderness. The disavowed knowledge of the barbarous violence that accompanied this civilizing mission was the unwritten basis for the collective need to embrace Virgin Land as a representative national metaphor.

But George W. Bush turned the enemy's violation of the nation's foundational fantasy into an occasion to fashion exceptions to the rules of law and war, which formally inaugurated a state of emergency. In his September 20 address, Bush designated the "enemies of freedom" as the historical agency responsible for this generalized unsettlement of the national people. But neither Osama bin Laden nor Saddam Hussein was the causative agent responsible for the forcible separation of the national people from their way of life. It was the state of emergency that ensued in the wake of the Homeland Security Act which required the people to depart from the norms and values to which they had become habituated, and that tore to the ground the democratic institutions—freedom of speech, religious tolerance, formal equality, uniform juridical procedures, universal suffrage—that had formerly nurtured and sustained the national people.

With the enemy's violation of the rules of war as rationale, the state suspended the rules to which it was otherwise subject and violated its own rules in the name of protecting them against a force that operated according to different rules. In order to protect the rule of law as such from this illegality, the state declared itself the occupant of a position not subject to the rules it must protect. The Congress's passage of the USA PATRIOT (Proved Appropriate Tools to Intercept and Obstruct Terrorism) Act into law effected the most dramatic abridgment of civil liberties in the nation's history. This emergency legislation subordinated all concerns of ethics, human rights, due process, constitutional hierarchies, and of the division of power to the state's monopoly over the exception.

The emergency state is marked by absolute independence from any juridical control and any reference to the normal political order. It is empowered to suspend the articles of the Constitution protective of personal liberty, freedom of speech and assembly, and the inviolability of the home and postal and telephone and Internet privacy. In designating Afghanistan and Iraq as endangering the homeland, operations Enduring Justice and Iraqi Freedom simply extended the imperatives of the domestic emergency state across the globe.

Following 9/11, the state effected the transition from a normalized political order to a state of emergency by enacting the violence that Virgin Land had normatively covered over. Whereas 9/11 dislocated the national people from the mythology productive of their imaginary relation to the state, Bush linked their generalized dislocation with the vulnerability of the homeland, which thereafter became the target of the security apparatus. Bush endowed the state of emergency that he erected at Ground Zero with the responsibility to defend the homeland because foreign aggressors had violated Virgin Land. The violation of the land's inviolability not only disinhibited the state of its need to mask its history of violence; this act of aggression also required the state to bring the event the public had formerly disavowed — the forcible dispossession of national peoples from their homelands — into spectacular visibility.

But the homeland that emerged as the justification for the state's exercise of excessive violence was not identical with the landmass of the continental United States. The homeland Bush invoked to authorize these emergency actions did not designate either an enclosed territory or an imaginable home. The homeland secured by the emergency state instead referred to the unlocatable order that emerged *through and by way of the people's generalized dislocation from the nation as a shared form of life*. The Homeland Security Act put into place a state of exception that positioned the people in a space included in the homeland through its exclusion from the normal political order.

As the relationship between the state and the population that comes into existence when the state declares a state of emergency, the homeland names a form of governmentality without a recognizable location. As the unlocalizable space the population is ordered to occupy when the state enters the site of the exception to the normative order, the homeland names the structure through which state of emergency is realized normally.

As we have seen, the national mythology turned the nation into a stage for the enactment of particular forms of life. But if the nation designates the arena in which the national peoples enact these ways of life, the homeland names the space that emerges when these peoples are dissociated from their ways of life. The introduction of the signifier of the homeland to capture this experience of generalized dislocation recalled themes from the national narrative, which it significantly altered. But insofar as these themes were antithetical to the range of connotations sedimented within the concept of Virgin Land, the historical antecedents for the homeland surely must give pause.

The homeland originally named the site that the colonial settlers had abandoned in their quest for a newly found land. The homeland also named the country to which the settlers might one day return. In its reference to an archaic land from which the colonial settlers either voluntarily departed or which they were forced to abandon, the homeland represented a prehistoric pastness prior to the founding of the United States. Following 9/11, the homeland became named as the space in which the people were included after acts of terrorism had violently dislocated them from their ways of life. The metaphor of the homeland thereafter evoked the image of a vulnerable population that had become internally estranged from its country of origin and dependent on the protection of the state.

When it was figured within the Homeland Security Act, the homeland engendered an imaginary scenario wherein the national people were encouraged to consider themselves dislocated from their country of origin by foreign aggressors so that they might experience their return from exile in the displaced form of the spectacular unsettling of homelands elsewhere. This imaginary scenario and the spectacles through which it was communicated sustained the dissociation of the people from recognizably American ways of life. Insofar as the homeland named what emerged when the population became dislocated from the conditions of belonging to a territorialized nation, its security required the domestic emergency state to extend its policing authority to the dimension of the globe.

VIRGIN LAND AS GROUND ZERO

The Homeland Security Act regressed the population to a minority condition of dependency on the state for its biopolitical welfare. But the state thereafter correlated this regression in political standing with the reenactment of a formerly suppressed historical event. After the people were regressed to the condition of a political minority, the state produced a series of spectacles that returned the population to the historical moment in which colonial settlers had deployed the illicit use of force against native populations. With the invasion of Afghanistan and Iraq, the figurative meanings associated with Virgin Land were demetaphorized into the actuality of the state's violence. The state's spectacular violation of the rights of the so-called enemies of freedom was thereby made to coincide with the emergency state's radical abridgment of the domestic people's civil rights.

The putative insecurity of the homeland's civilian population and the threat of terrorist attack were coconstituting aspects of the homeland security state. The state's representation of a vulnerable civilian population in need of the protection of the state was fashioned in a relation of opposition to the captured Taliban and Iraqis who were subjected to the power of the state yet lacked the protection of their rights or liberties.

This new settlement required the public to sacrifice its civil liberties in exchange for the enjoyment of the state's spectacular violations of the rights of other sovereign states. For the Bush administration did not exactly represent the military operations that took place in Afghanistan and Iraq as wars conducted between civilized states that respected one another's sovereignty; it constructed them as confrontations between the emergency state apparatus and terrorizing powers that posed a threat to the homeland. If the modern state is construed as the embodiment of Enlightenment reason, and the neoliberal principles of market democracy comprise the means whereby this rationality becomes universalized, neither the Taliban regime in Afghanistan nor the Baathist regime in Iraq could be construed either as modern states or as rational actors in the global economy. In its military operations in Afghanistan and Iraq, the US emergency state apparatus imposed this modern state formation and that market logic on the Afghani and the Iraqi peoples. As a result of these acts of supposedly defensive aggression, Iraq and Afghanistan were relocated within the global order of the homeland security state.

The spectators' enjoyment of them derived from the spectacles' violation of the normative assumptions—that the United States was a redeemer nation rather than an aggressor state, whose manifest errand was civilizing rather than brutalizing, and so on—sedimented within the national imaginary. Because the spectators could not enjoy the state's spectacles without disassociating from the assumptions that would have rendered them unimaginable as *American* spectacles, these spectacles enforced the separation of the state's spectatorial publics from their national forms of life. After these spectacles intermediated between the people and their forms of life, they substituted the lateral linkages with the emergency state apparatus for the people's vertical integration with a democratic way of life.

In Iraq and Afghanistan, the emergency forces of the state openly reperformed the acts of violence that the myth of Virgin Land had formerly covered up. Operation Infinite Justice quite literally depopulated the Afghani landscape so that it might be perceived as a blank page onto which to inscribe a different political order. Operation Iraqi Freedom fostered an understanding of regime change as the Iraqi people's beneficent choice of the political exempla of its Anglo-American occupiers for the institutions of its new political order. As witnesses to the state's colonization of Afghanistan and Iraq, the United States' spectator publics were returned to the prehistoric time of the colonial settlers who had formerly spoliated Indian homelands. By way of "Operation Infinite Justice" and "Operation Iraqi Freedom" the homeland security state restaged the colonial settlers' conquest of Indians and the acquisition of their homelands. The terror and the killing became the homeland state's means of accomplishing anew the already known telos of US history as the inaugural event of America's global rule in the twenty-first century.

These spectacles redescribed imperial conquest as a form of domestic defense in a manner that reversed the relationship between the aggressor and the victim. The homeland security state constructed the preemptive strikes against others' homelands as a spectacular form of domestic defense against foreign aggression. Both spectacles invited their audiences to take scopic pleasure in the return of the traumatic memory of the unprovoked aggression that the colonial settlers had previously exerted against native populations. These massacres, which could not be authorized or legitimated by the Virgin Land narrative, became the foundational acts inaugurating the global homeland as a realm outside the law.

Whereas the myth of Virgin Land produced historical continuity by suppressing the traumatic memory of lawless violence, the events of 9/11 demanded the recovery of this traumatic memory so as to reverse the national people's relation to violence, and to inaugurate a new global order. The spectacles that unfolded in the deserts of Afghanistan and Iraq transformed the US spectatorial population into the perpetrators rather than the victims of foreign aggression. The state's literal recovery of the traumatic memory of barbarous aggression against native peoples thereby overcame the traumatizing experience of aggression at the hands of foreign terrorists.

These spectacles of violence encouraged the public's belief that it participated in the state's power because it shared in the spectacle through which the state gave expression to its power. But the people were also the potential targets of the shows of force they witnessed. In transforming its citizens into spectators, the state interposed a disjunction between the people and the ways of life that the state protected through its exercises of retributive violence. After this new settlement induced the people to suspend their civil liberties in exchange for the enjoyment of the state's spectacular violations of the rights of its enemies, the emergency state transposed the nation and the citizen into dispensable predicates of global rule.

HOMELAND SECURITY AS A GLOBAL BIOPOLITICAL SETTLEMENT

As we have seen, the homeland enacted into law by the Homeland Security Act did not have reference to an enclosed territory. And it was not exactly a political order. The Homeland Security Act was the political instrument on whose authority the state transformed a temporary suspension of order erected on the basis of factual danger into a quasi-permanent biopolitical arrangement that as such remained outside the normal order. After the passage of the Homeland Security Act, the state of exception no longer referred to an external state of factual danger, but instead became identified with the juridical-political order itself. This juridical-political apparatus thereafter authorized a biopolitical settlement that inscribed the body of the people into an order of state power endowing the state with power over the life and death of the population.[7]

This biopolitical sphere emerged with the state's decision to construe the populations it governed as indistinguishable from unprotected biological life. The body of the people as a free and equal citizenry endowed with the capacity to reconstitute itself through recourse to historically venerated social significations was thereby replaced by a biologized population that the state protected from biological terrorism. The biopolitical sphere constructed by the provisions of the Homeland Security Act first subtracted the population from the forms of civic and political life through which it recognized itself as a national people and then positioned these life-forms — the people, their way of life — in nonsynchronous zones of protection, promising that their future synchronization would resuscitate the nation-state.

After undergoing a generalized dislocation from the national imaginary through which their everyday practices were lived as recognizably American forms of life, the national peoples were reconstituted as biological life-forms. Their dislocation from the national imaginary resulted in their mass denationalization. As naked biological life under the state's protection, the biopoliticized population also could play no active political role in the homeland state's reordering of things. The homeland state thereafter represented the population as an unprotected biological formation whose collective vitality must be administered and safeguarded against weapons of biological terrorism. But insofar as the homeland state's biopolitical imperative to regulate the life and death of the population that it governed was irreducible to the denizens of the nation-state, the homeland state's biopolitical regime became potentially global in its extensibility.

It was the state's description of the weapons endangering the aggregated population as biological that in part authorized the state's biopolitical settlement. In representing its biopolitical imperatives in terms of a defense against weapons of biological destruction, the state also produced an indistinction between politics and the war against terrorism. This redescription produced two interrelated effects: it transformed the population's political and civil liberties into life-forms that were to be safeguarded rather than acted on. More important, it turned political opponents of this biopolitical settlement into potential enemies of the ways of life that the state safeguarded.

The homeland security state was the sole beneficiary of the indistinctions thus effected between global and domestic security and between war and politics. But after the Homeland Security Act described the populations under the homeland state's governance as indistinguishable from unprotected biological life, this legislation also produced an indistinction between two distinctly different registers of the population — the People with Rights and the disposable peoples lacking rights.

As the political philosopher Giorgio Agamben has explained, this indistinction is inherent to the concept of the people. "We the People" is an internally antagonized phrase. It contains a dialectical opposition between two opposed poles: the set of the people as an organized political body, on the one hand; and a subset of the people as a fragmentary multiplicity of needy and excluded bodies, on the other. The national people who are the depository of the sovereign will authorizing the policies of a nation-state have been normatively constituted out of the exclusion of the homeless people.[8]

Because the homeland state had separated the sovereign people from the political rights they were understood to bear, it could not depend on this political distinction to sustain their differentiation from the unhomed people. The biopolitical settlement had reduced all of the people to the condition of unprotected *zoe*. In an effort to install a postpolitical distinction, the homeland state invented the category of the detainee.[9]

The detainee is an extralegal fiction that the homeland state constructed to demarcate the limit point that installs a biopolitical (hence postpolitical) distinction between the homeland's peoples and the homeless peoples — in stripping the detainees' biopolitical status of any predication other than mere flesh, the homeland state made the detainee coincide with the state's monopoly over the decision concerning the exception. The detainee's body named the threshold over which the state's exemption from its own rules passes over into fact. Through the construction of detention centers in which the detainees were interned, the homeland state produced a distinction between the people the state protects from injury and the people the state is free to injure and kill.[10] The vulnerable population under the protection of the homeland state forms the counterpart of the disposable population of detainees whose putative endangerment of the protected population requires the state to take them into protective custody.

If the homeland designates the sphere in which the national people are included when they are dislocated from their way of life, it is describable as an order lacking localization within the nation. But the detainment centers and Camp X-Ray are describable as localizations lacking order.[11] If the homeland named the space in which the exception was realized normally, the detainees' unhomed condition of unprotected flesh negatively regulated the dislocatee's relation to the homeland.

DETAINEES: THE STATE'S INJURED

The detention camps were in a realm beyond good and evil where abduction and execution became naturalized by a mythology that rendered them exempt from tests of reality. The fact that the spectacle of the "justice" that "we" brought to our enemies took place in a detention camp that was located on Guantánamo Bay requires some brief explanation. Bush anticipated the state's usage of this space as the staging ground for the state's violation of the Geneva Conventions with the phrase "except for one Sunday in 1941" as the historical location to the sole exception to the United States' exemption from foreign attack. For this attack did not exactly take place on US soil. On December 7, 1941, Hawaii was not a state and Pearl Harbor was, like Guantánamo Bay, Cuba, an unincorporated territory. The exceptional nature of the attacks that took place on this unintegrated territory supplied the state with a metaphoric precedent for its choice of a comparable space to produce its exceptions to the rules of law and war. The Justice Department referred to Guantánamo Bay's exceptional status as an unincorporated territorial possession of the United States in order to justify its contention that as a "foreign territory" it lay outside the jurisdiction of any US court. It was the extraterritorial status of Guantánamo Bay, its exemption from the juridical reach of any state or nation, that enabled the emergency state to demonstrate its monopoly over the exception there.

But the act of transferring these "enemies" to Guantánamo brought about the magical transformation in the condition of the persons interned there. By rendering them at once stateless and countryless, the act of transporting them to Guantánamo Bay set the internees beyond the pale of humanity. The very same gesture that placed them outside the condition of territorial belonging provided the mytho-logic for the deprivation of their human rights. They were interned at Guantánamo Bay because they lacked the protection of human rights, and they lacked human rights because they were displaced onto Guantánamo Bay. The transfer of these unlawful combatants from Afghanistan to Guantánamo Bay rendered what was undecidable in Bush's musing over whether "we bring our enemies to justice or bring justice to our enemies" juridically practicable.

On Guantánamo Bay, the state produced persons who were exceptions to the laws that protected the due process rights of citizens, and exceptions as well to the Geneva Conventions that endowed prisoners of war with the right to refuse to respond to interrogation. Stripped of the rights of citizens *and* prisoners of war, these persons were reduced to the status of unprotected *zoe*. As the embodiments of animated flesh whose lives the state could terminate according to decisions outside juridical regulation, these "unlawful combatants" were invoked by the state to justify its positioning of itself as an exception to the rule of law. The emergency state arrogated to itself its power to operate beyond the jurisdiction of the laws that regulated the world of nations through this production of persons it could hold without due process and whom it could kill without being accused of murder.[12]

The detention camps erected in Guantánamo Bay by the Halliburton Company occupied a realm outside the law in which the emergency state's practices were naturalized by a mythology that rendered them exempt from critical scrutiny. The mythological structures that accompanied the state's fashioning of exceptions to legal categories triggered a recursive operation that reinforced the state's exercise of the power to fashion exceptions to its own rules. The emergency state invoked the terrorists' recourse to unlawful combat as the pretext for the state's violation of the laws regulating due process and the rules regulating the conduct of war. The state violated its own rules, that is to say, in the name of protecting them against a force said to operate according to different rules. In order to protect the rule of law as such from this alien legality, the state declared itself the occupant of a position not subject to the rules it must protect. As Attorney General John Ashcroft explained, in order to protect the entirety of the law against attack, the state had to transgress its own laws. All concerns of ethics, human rights, due process, constitutional hierarchies, and the division of governmental power were subordinated to this urgent eschatological mission.

The vacuum opened up by the vanishing of objective reality into the singularity of Ground Zero was thereby filled in by the mythologized reality in which the emergency state erected its eschatological version of realpolitik and the forcible detention of unlawful combatants made complementary sense. With its undisclosed abductions of persons within the territorial homeland, the Bush administration shifted its war on terrorism from the Afghani desert to the bodies of persons it suspected of domestic terrorism. Ignoring the time-consuming details of due process, the state condensed the juridical-penal process into the moment of abduction wherein accusation, judgment, and punishment coincided. The terrorist may have supplied its official rationale, but the detainee was in fact the cause and effect of the state of emergency.

The state of emergency is not subject to the rules of law that it enforces; it inhabits a realm quite literally beyond good and evil. After September 11, civil rights groups estimated that more than eleven hundred terrorist suspects were disappeared into a juridical maze in which they were denied lawyers, beaten by guards and fellow inmates, subjected to sensory deprivation, and forced to take lie detector tests. Current immigration laws permit indefinite detainment, so no criminal charges were required to warrant the abductees' internment. Their guilt could not be proven, so this "transfer" of detainees to Camp X-Ray constituted a euphemism for extrajudicial measures.

ABU GHRAIB: THE BIOPOLITICAL UNCONSCIOUS OF THE INJURING STATE

The detainees who disappeared into the maze of an unaccountable juridical system and into the cages on Guantánamo Bay represented the Other to and within "We the People." The state proffered this spectacle of sublegal persons stripped of all rights and liberties as a symbolic compensation for the USA PATRIOT Act's drastic abridgment of civil liberties. "We the People" indirectly authorized the state's detainment policies in their dual offices as (1) secondary witnesses to the legality of the governmental operations that accomplished these infernal rites of passage; and as (2) informal signatories to the discourse of legalized illegality crystallized in phrases like *enemy combatants*, *material witness*, and *persons of interest*.

After 9/11, Bush made reference to the vulnerability rather than the sovereignty of the people. Representing the US peoples as exposed to a biopolitical threat, Bush represented "We the People" in the image of vulnerable biological bodies in need of the protection of the homeland state's emergency workers Bush had designated as the people's representatives. In celebrating emergency workers as the representatives of the homeland security state, President Bush produced an equivalence between the nation and the emergency state.

The emergency state expropriated sovereignty from the homeland people so as to establish sovereignty as the rationale for the state's construction of the category of this Other to the people. Bush's declaration of a war on terrorism disrupted the entire social edifice by undermining the mores that regulated the intersubjective relations of the polity. The people were asked to identify with the urgency that expropriated "We the People" from their rights. Lacking the ground from which "we" might respond, "We the People" were made to identify with the security priorities of the emergency state.

But the denizens of the homeland state withdrew their indirect authorization for what went on inside the state's security encampments on April 28, 2004. On that date, *Sixty Minutes II* broadcast a series of photographs that displayed an orgy of penal violence perpetrated by military police guards at Abu Ghraib prison in Iraq. The photographs depicted male and female American soldiers playing various roles in a theater of cruelty that was designed to make the prisoners under their charge feel extraneous to the human condition. In one of the photographs a female guard was depicted holding a leash tethered to a dog collar that had been placed around the neck of an unclothed Iraqi man groveling at her feet; another snapshot represented the same woman locked in melodramatic embrace with a grinning male MP standing behind the naked bodies of Iraqi male prisoners who had been stacked on top of one other; another pictured a guard forcing a hooded prisoner to simulate oral sex with another prisoner; still another photograph represented an Iraqi prisoner precariously perched on a chair with a sandbag over his head, electrical wires attached to his hands.

After they were transmitted globally, the photographs of the abuse at Abu Ghraib prison became the space in which the spectatorial public refused the complicities the security state had solicited. Whereas Bush's biopolitical settlement had set the populations it secured and defended in a relation of opposition to the Muslim extremists imprisoned at Abu Ghraib, the photographs of these vulnerable, unprotected bodies evoked in their viewers the collective desire to shield this unprotected population from continued brutality. Rather than lending the actions represented in these photographs their visual approval, the viewers of these images galvanized a morally authorized, global opposition to the war. World opinion condemned the Bush administration for arrogating to the homeland security state the power to violate internationally agreed on rules of engagement with prisoners of war.[13]

In remaking the internees at Abu Ghraib in the image of what Giorgio Agamben has called *homo sacer* (persons who could be killed without the accusation of murder), the guards had set the images of persons whose lives were not worth living in a relation of opposition to the images of the peoples whose lives must be defended. Through their staging of scenarios designed to terrorize their Iraqi prisoners, the military police at Abu Ghraib prison extracted revenge for the thousands who had lost their lives in the twin towers. In revealing the biopolitical imperatives that informed the guards' optical unconscious, the photographs reproduced Bush's biopolitical settlement reduced to its simplest visual terms.

As we have seen, the Bush administration had defined the homeland state as populated by a vulnerable people whose biopolitical security depended on the state's defending them against a people negatively represented as posing a biopolitical threat. But the Abu Ghraib photographs renegotiated the relationship between these two biologized populations. The photographs represented a way of looking at the prisoners that the guards had staged for the visual pleasure of the members of the homeland society, as well as for one another. The photographs depicted Iraqi prisoners visually cast into subjective positions that the guards had constructed to do violence to their Muslim identities. Their digital cameras transmitted the gaze through which the guards aspired to propagate their extravagant enjoyment of this violation.

The photographs depicted the soldiers deriving spectatorial pleasure from quite literally stripping their prisoners of their human rights, as well as their right to be human. In deriving pleasure from these scenarios of retributive violence, the guards represented the gaze of the spectatorial public for whom the Bush administration had staged its military operations. But instead of identifying with the guards' visual perspective, on bearing witness to the prisoners' suffering, the spectatorial public protested against these obscene acts of state violence. "How can someone grin at the sufferings and humiliations of another human being?" Susan Sontag asked representatively in "Regarding the Torture of Others," an essay she published in the *New York Times Magazine* on May 23, 2004; "is the real issue not the photographs themselves but what the photographs reveal to have happened to 'suspects' in American custody?" "No," Sontag responded; "the horror of what is shown in the photographs cannot be separated from the horror that the photographs were taken — with the perpetrators posing, gloating, over their helpless captives."[14]

But if the Abu Ghraib photographs represented the guards exacting retributive violence against the enemies of American freedom, why did not the homeland population, on whose behalf the guards reputedly acted, share their visual pleasure in these photographs? The military prison guards at Abu Ghraib had not in fact acted against orders, and Abu Ghraib prison was not an anomaly. Abu Ghraib was one of the manifestations of a distinction the Bush administration had introduced between two different biopoliticized populations — a homeland population comprising citizens represented as temporarily dissociated from their civil and political rights, and the subhumans that constituted the prison population at Abu Ghraib, represented as permanently lacking the right to have human rights. The military prison guards' intercultural relations with their Iraqi prisoners at Abu Ghraib followed the regulations spelled out in Bush's biopolitical settlement. The guards' treatment of the Iraqi prisoners at Abu Ghraib established and policed the disjunction between the embodiments of bare-life populations imprisoned at Abu Ghraib and the homeland people.

But the photographs of the horrific means whereby the guards regulated the distinction between these two populations instead opened a space in between the war on terrorism and the inhuman violence it legitimated. The photographs that drew the most notice from the international press were the six photographs taken of a figure that *The Pentagon Report on the Abu Ghraib Prisoner Abuse Scandal* designated as "Detainee Number 15." These photographs depicted a hooded man who was made to stand precariously on the edge of a box, sprouting wires from his hands and from under the poncho that covered his torso.[15]

The voluminous commentary on this hypercanonized photograph positioned the "Man on the Box" within a series of preexisting images from religious and political typologies that memorialized socially sacralized acts of martyrdom. The photographic memories that the Man on the Box recalled—of African Americans lynched during the era of Jim Crow, of Jesus Christ crucified—reactivated traumatic memories of slavery, the violent history of the civil rights movement, and a scene of venerated self-sacrifice. The historical personages with whom the Man on the Box solicited comparison would most likely have been unimaginable to the Abu Ghraib guards who took the photographs. But in discussing the family resemblance between the guards' photographs of their victims at Abu Ghraib prison and the photographs of the victims of lynching taken between the 1880s and 1930s, Sontag characterized both sets of images as "the souvenirs of a collective action whose participants felt perfectly justified in what they had done."[16]

In a lecture he delivered at Dartmouth College on July 21, 2004, the iconologist W. J. T. Mitchell interpreted the Man on the Box in terms of religious rather than political typology. Mitchell described the theatricalization of pain common to both image repertoires as the basis for the comparison he adduced between the guards' photographs of this figure and Christian iconography. Mitchell elaborated on the implications of these shared traits when he interpreted the hooded figure in terms of artistic representations of a devotional image of Christ as he was stationed in between the crucifixion and the resurrection. The box on which the man in the photograph stood resembled a pedestal on which Christ was placed in that both pediments at once mocked yet elevated the figures standing on them. And like the Man on the Box, the devotional image of the Man of Sorrows, too, was either hooded or blindfolded so as ensure the invisibility of his torturers.[17]

The power of Christian iconography may explain why this photograph was reappropriated by Western commentators to fashion their political condemnation of torture. But in turning the hooded Iraqi prisoner into the double of the tortured and sacrificed Christ, these Western commentators utterly ignored the perspective of the Iraqi Muslims who regarded these worshipful comparisons with the Christian Man of Sorrows as culturally demeaning. The photograph's significance to the Iraqis' lived history was brought to an apocalyptic pitch by an Iraqi street artist who placed the photograph of the Man on the Box next to his sketch of the Statue of Liberty caught in the act of pulling the lever that would send a fatal electrical charge coursing through the hooded man's body. To make certain that this pictorial irony was not lost on the viewer, the Iraqi artist added a caption to his portrait that read, "That Freedom for Bush."[18]

When they superimposed this representation of a supposed enemy of American freedom on the photographic memories of persons who had died in their effort to achieve the freedom of the West, the Western commentators on Man on the Box reconstituted it as the limit figure in the homeland state's visual imaginary. Insofar as it brought the United States' official policy of delivering freedom to the Iraqi people into proximity with its unacknowledged technologies of torture, this limit figure brought the spectacle of socially gratifying acts of violence to an abrupt conclusion. They also quite literally short-circuited the media relays through which the Pentagon conducted its war of images. At the site of the short circuit, a very different attitude toward the photographs emerged.

But if the image of the Man on the Box recalled images from Christian iconography as well as from the fraught history of the civil rights movement in America, what about the other photographs? Were the images of the Iraqi prisoners forced to masturbate publicly or simulate oral sex with one another solely informed by the information about Muslim phobias that the guards had learned in their one-week crash course on the culture and history of Iraqi Muslims?[19] The phobias—bodily nudity, homosexual touching of male genitals, appearing naked before a woman — conventionally attributed to Muslim men may have informed some of the staged settings in which the guards conducted their photo shoots. But these scenarios have solicited political decodings in which the guards were accused of having drawn from the image repertoires of feminist and gay liberation for the props and behaviors through which the guards terrorized these suspected Muslim terrorists.

Some of the poses that the guards forced their captors to assume mirrored sexual practices that have in other contexts been represented as possessing an emancipatory social value. Indeed, if they were recontextualized within the manifestos of these social movements, some of these photographs could have been interpreted as expressive of demands for liberation from the recalcitrant order of the male patriarchate, or from the imperatives of a heteronormative social order.[20] The emancipatory value of these alternative sexual practices was premised on the right to self-fashioning and the autonomy of individual choice. On imposing the bodily practice of gays, feminists, and lesbians on Iraqi prisoners who experienced them as painful impositions rather than liberating rights, the guards turned these emancipatory practices into a means of annulling the Iraqis' way of life. But why did they turn these sexual practices into weapons of biopolitical warfare?

Gayatri Spivak has suggested a possible basis for the guards' having correlated the image repertoires of contemporary social movements with their theater of cruelty when she remarked that

> it has seemed increasingly clear to me, that "terror" is the name loosely assigned to the flip side of social movements — extra-state social action — when such movements use physical violence. (When a state is named a "terrorist state," the intent implicit in the naming is to withhold state status from it, so that, technically, it enters the category of *extra*-state collective action.) "Terror" is also, of course, the name of an affect. In the policy-making arena, "terror" as social movement and terror as social affect come together to provide a plausible field for group psychological speculation. The social movement is declared to have psychological identity. In other words, making terror both civil and natural provides a rationale for exercising psychological diagnostics, the most malign ingredient of racism.[21]

With Spivak's observation as warrant, the prison guards in the *theatrum politicum* of Abu Ghraib might be described as having conducted a war of images on two fronts—against Islamic terrorists abroad and against emancipatory social movements at home. After they harnessed the practices and behaviors associated with feminist and gay liberation movement into the instrumentalities of sexual and cultural abuse, the Abu Ghraib photographs voided them of their emancipatory potential. The guards who took these photographs effaced any distinction between the technologies of self-production within emancipatory social movements and the techniques through which they annulled the social ontologies of their Iraqi prisoners. On reversing liberationist technologies of emancipatory social movements into the machines with which they tortured and abused prisoners, the guards turned the prison into an extralegal sphere maintained by the indistinction between law and violence. Moreover, when they directed the terrorism ascribed to these social movements against suspected Muslim terrorists, the military guards intended the annihilation of both forms of terrorism.

The military guards at the Abu Ghraib prison distilled the liberation technology of the various social movements into the biopowers they deployed to terrorize Muslim extremists. After they detached these sexual behaviors from the gay and lesbian bodies through which they were normatively subjectivized as emancipatory legal rights and forcibly imposed them onto Iraqi prisoners, the guards voided these practices of their normativity. But when they alienated these sexual and gendered practices from the human bodies through whom these biopowers had been legalized as civil and human rights, the guards practiced a form of symbolic violence on the civil rights of the persons from whose bodies they had alienated these rights. In reducing gay and feminist rights into the means of stripping Iraqi prisoners of the right to have rights, the guards also practiced a form of symbolic violence on these rights.

The photographs taken by the guards at Abu Ghraib prison recorded forms of violence that remained untethered to law and acknowledged no conventions concerning the rights of prisoners. But the viewers of these photographs interpreted these representations as further evidence of the ways in which the technologies of American freedom had become indistinguishable from American oppression. The images mobilized opposition to the occupation in the name of the Abu Ghraib prisoners who had been victimized by this oppression. The viewers who posed this spontaneous global demonstration on behalf of the human rights of the prisoners at Abu Ghraib transformed their right to human rights into the representative demand of the peoples of the global homeland state.

AFTERWORD: THE PART OF NO PART

Overall, 9/11 brought to the light of day the Other to the normative representation of the United States. It positioned *unheimliche* dislocatees within the homeland in place of the citizens who exercised rights and liberties on the basis of these normalizations. When the signifier of the homeland was substituted for the Virgin Land, the national security state was supplanted by the emergency state. Whereas the Virgin Land enforced the disavowal of the state's destruction of indigenous population's homelands, Ground Zero demanded that spectacle of the destruction of a homeland as compensation for the loss of the land's supposed virginity.

In tracking the radical shift in the governing frames of reference, I have indicated the ways in which the state coordinated the signifiers 9/11, Ground Zero, homeland, and detainee into a relay of significations undergirding the biopolitical settlement of the global homeland state. But in my discussion of the Abu Ghraib photographs, I have also demonstrated the inherent instability of the nodal points constructed to coordinate these newly invented governing representations.

When he inaugurated the prerogatives of the emergency state at Ground Zero, George W. Bush conscripted the traumatic power of the events that took place there to offer preemptive strikes as compensation for the loss. But the events that took place on September 11, 2001, fractured the nation-state's continuist time. As the locus for events lacking a preexisting signification in the social order, 9/11 exists as a sign of what cannot take place within the order of signification. But if it marks the rupture of the time kept by the nation-state, 9/11 is no less discordant with the mode eventuation the Bush administration has inaugurated in its name. Inherently nonsynchronous, 9/11 calls for a time to come.

The Bush administration has attempted to supplant the violence directed against the sacred myth of the Virgin Land that underwrote US exceptionalism with the arrogation of the power to occupy the position of the exception to the laws of the world of nations. But insofar as the homeland state's exceptions to the rules of law and war are themselves instantiations of a force that lacks the grounding support of norms or rules, they resemble the traumatic events on which they depend for their power to rule. Such exceptions could maintain their power to rule only as long as US publics remain captivated by the spectacles of violence the state has erected at the site of Ground Zero. When the photographs of the prison abuse at Abu Ghraib circulated worldwide, the state of the exception was momentarily overruled.

The global homeland erected an order in which the people have no part; that order has positioned the people in a place that lacks a part in the global order. But as the surplus element in the global homeland, the people also occupy the place of an empty universal. This space may have been emptied of any part to play in the homeland's global order. But the very emptiness of that space, the fact that it demarcates the people's part as what is included with no part to play in the existing order, simultaneously empowered it to play the part of articulating an alternative to the existing order.[22] While the people of the global homeland may have lacked a part to play in the governance of the homeland state, they turned Abu Ghraib into the basis for the worldwide demand to an alternative order. After the Abu Ghraib photographs exposed the global state of emergency as the cause of the traumas it purported to oppose, the global homeland state was rendered momentarily indistinguishable from the *punctum* out of which it had emerged.

NOTES

1. This essay builds on but also significantly revises the afterword I contributed to Stanley Hauerwas and Frank Lentricchia, eds., *Dissent from the Homeland: Essays after September 11* (Durham, NC: Duke University Press, 2003).
2. Henry Nash Smith supplied an insight into the mobilizing effects of these collective representations on the US populations throughout history when he observed that "these illustrations point to the conclusion that history cannot happen—that is, men cannot engage in purposive group behavior—without images which simultaneously express collective desires and impulses and impose coherence on the infinitely varied data of experience. These images are never, of course, exact reproductions of the physical and social environment. They cannot motivate and direct action unless they are drastic simplifications." Henry Nash Smith, *Virgin Land: The American West in Symbols and Myth* (Cambridge, MA: Harvard University Press, 1950), ix. But the historian William H. McNeill provided the most cogent description of the role myths played in the articulation

of state governance policies in a 1982 article that he published in *Foreign Affairs*, no. 61 (1982): 1–13, entitled "The Care and Repair of Public Myth." In that article, McNeill argued the indispensable role that myths and symbols played in the manufacturing of the public's consent for domestic and foreign policy. And he admonished revisionist scholars for the propagation of their demythologizing proclivities: "A people without a full quiver of relevant agreed upon statements, accepted in advance through education or less formalized acculturation finds itself in deep trouble, for, in the absence of believable myths, coherent public action becomes difficult to improvise or sustain" (1).

3. Richard Slotkin, "Myth and the Production of History," in *Ideology and Classic American Literature*, ed. Sacvan Bercovitch and Myra Jehlen (New York: Cambridge University Press, 1986), 70.
4. I first began to think of the biopolitical settlement that the Bush administration had constructed out of the relay of signifiers it installed in between 9/11 and the homeland security state while I listened to Amy Kaplan deliver a talk at the Dartmouth American Studies Institute in June of 2001 in which she ruminated over the connotations of the terms *Ground Zero*, *homeland*, and *Guantánamo Bay*. Amy Kaplan has since published those remarks in *Radical History Review*. My indebtedness to, as well as my divergences from, Kaplan's meditation can be discerned from a reading of her "Homeland Insecurities: Reflections on Language and Space," *Radical History Review*, no. 85 (2003): 82–93.
5. When George W. Bush observed that "Americans have known wars, but for the past 136 years they have been wars on foreign soil," he referenced the conclusion of the Civil War in 1865 as the historical benchmark for the figure of 136 years. But the last occasion on which the country was subject to foreign attack was the war of 1812, which took place 189 years earlier. In recalling the Civil War rather than the war of 1812 as the historical precedent for 9/11, Bush also wanted to invoke the South as the symbolic geography that he wished primarily to represent in his crusade against world evil.
6. My understanding of the fantasy structure of war draws on Renata Salecl's discussion of this topic in *Spoils of Freedom: Psychoanalysis and Feminism after the Fall of Socialism* (New York: Routledge, 1994), especially 15–19.
7. My discussion of the biopolitical settlement, as well as my understanding of the state of emergency and the space of the exception, is indebted to Giorgio Agamben's remarkable discussion of the relationship between forms of life and biopolitics, the internally antagonized concept of the people and the Concentration Camp as the *nomos* of modern life in *Means without End: Notes on Politics*, trans. Vincenzo Binetti and Cesare Cassarino (Minneapolis: University of Minnesota Press, 2000), 43–45. Agamben examines the transformation of politics into biopolitics through a reconsideration of Michel Foucault's account of this mutation in the essay "Form-of-Life" (3–14).
8. Giorgio Agamben spelled out the differences between these two peoples with great clarity in the essays "Beyond Human Rights" (in *Means without End*, 15–28) and "What Is a People" (in *Means without End*. 29–36; see especially 30).
9. Agamben has proposed that the modern nation-state was organized out of the nexus that

correlated a determinate localization (the land) with a determinate order (the state) as these are mediated by the state's rules for the inscription of bare life. But the state's localizations necessarily produce dislocated peoples whose disorderly movements exceed the political that would order these errant forms of life in a determinate space by way of juridical rules. See *Means without End*, 19–20.

10. See Agamben's discussion of *homo sacer* in *Means without End*, 3–9.

11. This formulation derives from Agamben's discussion of the state of the exception in "What Is a Camp?" in *Means without End*, 43.

12. Agamben describes the prefigurations of the detainees in the Nazi camps with great eloquence: "Inasmuch as its inhabitants have been stripped of every political status and reduced completely to naked life, the camp is also the most absolute biopolitical space that has ever been realized—a space in which power confronts nothing other than pure biological life without any mediation" (*Means without End*, 40).

13. The standard of acceptability for what counts as cruel, inhuman, and degrading treatment changes in response to changing circumstances. The structure of debate invoked a series of clauses from international treaties and agreements (to which the United States had been a signatory) that valorized the violation of bodily rights negatively. Article 5 of the Universal Declaration of Human Rights reads: "No one shall be subjected to torture, or to cruel inhuman or degrading treatment or punishment." The 1984 Convention against Torture and Other Inhuman or Degrading Treatment or Punishment defines torture as "any act by which severe pain or suffering, whether physical or mental, is intentionally inflicted on another person for such purposes as obtaining from him or a third person information or a confession." The 1984 formulation seemed to address the emergency-state justification head on when it further declared that "no exceptional circumstances whatsoever, whether a state of war or a threat of war, internal political instability or any other public emergency, may be invoked as a justification of torture."

14. Susan Sontag, "Regarding the Torture of Others," *New York Times Magazine*, May 23, 2004, 2, donswaim.com/nytimes.sontag.html.

15. See Steven Strasser, ed., *The Abu Ghraib Investigations: The Official Reports of the Independent Panel on the Shocking Prisoner Abuse in Iraq* (New York: Public Affairs, 2004). "These photographs were taken between 2145 and 2315 on 4 November 2003. Detainee-15 described a female making him stand on the box, telling him if he fell off he would be electrocuted, and a 'tall black man' as putting the wires on his fingers and penis" (132).

16. Sontag, "Regarding the Torture of Others," 2.

17. In his lecture, Tom Mitchell also proposed an imperial theme linking the historical occasion for both figures: "There was no link with weapons of mass destruction, and we have replaced a tyrant with a roman governor who carries out this kind of justice in conflating the United States' official policy of liberating the Iraqi people with technologies that tortured them." MALS Symposium, Dartmouth College, July 21, 2004.

18. A photograph of this piece of Iraqi street art can be found in Meron Benvenisti et al., *Abu Ghraib: The Politics of Torture* (Berkeley, CA: North Atlantic Books, 2004), 143.

19. In his essay "The Logic of Torture," Mark Danner reports that in addition to the week-long course on Iraqi history, the Marine Corps distributed to its troops a pamphlet that spelled out the following codification of prohibited behaviors: "(1) Do not shame or humiliate a man in public. Shaming a man will cause him and his family to be anti-Coalition; (2) The most important qualifier for shame is for a third party to witness the act. If you must do something likely to cause shame, remove the person from the view of others; (3) Shame is given by placing a hood over a detainee's head. Avoid this practice; (4) Placing a detainee on the ground or putting a foot on him implies you are God. This is one of the worst things you can do." Mark Danner, *Torture and Truth: America, Abu Ghraib, and the War on Terror* (New York: New York Review Books, 2004), 18. The manual also explained that Arabs considered feet or soles of feet, as well as using the bathroom around others, unclean.
20. In his talk, Tom Mitchell mentioned that the Berkeley artist Guy Colwell reconfigured several of the Abu Ghraib photographs to reveal their resemblance to gay and lesbian liberationist practices. Barbara Ehrenreich discussed the ways in which the photographs of Lynndie England disfigured feminist prerogatives in "Feminism's Assumptions Upended," in Benvenisti et al., *Abu Ghraib*, 65–70.
21. Gayatri Chakravorty Spivak, "Terror: A Speech after 9/11," *boundary* 2 31, no. 2 (2004): 91.
22. My understanding of the empty or singular universal draws on Slavoj Žižek's discussion of this concept in *The Ticklish Subject: The Absent Centre of Political Ontology* (New York: Verso, 1999), 187–239. Jacques Rancière elaborates on the importance of the phrase "the part of no part" to political contestations in *Disagreement: Politics and Philosophy*, trans. Julie Rosen (Minneapolis: University of Minnesota Press, 1999), 1–60.

CHRISTIAN PARENTI

Planet America: The Revolution in Military Affairs as Fantasy and Fetish

> No longer can areas exist in which life can be lived in safety and tranquility . . . the battlefield will be limited only by the boundaries of the nations at war, and all of their citizens will become combatants, since all of them will be exposed to the aerial offensive of the enemy.—**Giulio Douhet, *The Command of the Air* (1921)**

> The productivity of the machine is therefore measured by the human labour-power it replaces.—**Karl Marx, *Capital, Vol. 1***

Before the conquest of Iraq and the opening of the current guerrilla war there, intellectual circles in the US military establishment, most notably Defense Secretary Donald Rumsfeld and those around him, were engaged in much frenzied talk about the newest high-tech military methodologies of empire. At the heart of the discussion was the question of replacing military labor — that is, soldiers and politically problematic US casualties — with technology, capital, or "dead labor." These efforts to remake the US military into a totally invincible superforce are known among defense geeks and Pentagon apparatchiks as the Revolution in Military Affairs (RMA) or simply "Transformation."

This military restructuring forms part of a larger policy agenda of global domination, structured on planetary policing by the United States, as laid out quite bluntly in the Bush administration's National Security Strategy document of September 2002. Just as policing at the urban or national scale involves the management of excluded and exploited populations within the seemingly neural context of the law, so, too, does the vision of Planet America posit US global policing as a supposedly democratic, moral, neutral, and law-based system for projecting American military violence on a global scale. But just as much order maintenance at the local level is about containing people of color and the poor, so, too, is America's global military project about maintaining a class hierarchy.[1] All three post–Cold War US presidents have in varying forms shared this agenda, though they tend to express their goals in legalistic codes, a discourse of freedom and democracy.

Within this framework, the RMA envisions a perpetual global war waged not by human beings who die, rebel, or come home wounded and crazy, but a war waged by labor that is already dead, crystallized into machinery. Future wars are to be the work of zombie armies of "swarming" robots, armed aerial drones, supersophisticated microwave bombs, "over the horizon" smart artillery, ocean-floated "lily pad" military bases, and space-orbiting offensive weapon systems using lasers, projectiles, and electromagnetic pulses.[2] Early in his tenure, George W. Bush created a "Transformation Czar" within the US military's Joint Chiefs of Staff and has committed many billions to fund the project. In one regard, the project looks very rational, though unfair and brutal. If global domination were the agenda, then long-distance precision weaponry might be the perfect method for policing Planet America.

But in many ways the RMA is anything but rational. It is instead a simple recapitulation of capitalist culture's perennial technology fetish. Always, the basic equation is the same: replace living labor with capital. But somewhere on the way to frictionless global military dominance, the United States found itself stuck in a radically asymmetrical urban guerrilla war, facing exactly the scenario that the Pentagon dissenters from the RMA had warned about for years. Suddenly America's military fantasy had morphed into its military nightmare: a cumbersome high-tech army of soft American kids bogged down in Iraqi cities fighting a low-tech and determined insurgency. Viewed from among the charred remains of blown-up Humvees in the fetid alleys of Baghdad, the RMA looks like the last bubble of the nineties, and Iraq is where it bursts. (After all, the transformation debate began in earnest in the early 1990s and ran parallel to the so-called new economy and financialization hype, both of which maintained that "everything had changed.")[3]

In other words, could the "rising organic composition" of American war making produce declining political returns? Did recent military successes lead to a delusional techno-fetishism among American political leaders and did that techno-hubris prompt a fatal overreach of US imperial power? This essay will attempt to unpack the role of the military technology fetish in shaping the debacle in Iraq, an urban guerrilla warfare in which human intelligence, politics, and cultural knowledge all trump the power of America's mighty military machinery.

HOW THE FANTASY BEGAN

The idea of Planet America — a globe definitively and effectively controlled by the American ruling class, the real Thousand Year Reich — though long imagined and desired only became a feasible project with the fall of the USSR. This removed America's "peer adversary" and the only technomilitary check on US military power. Since then, Pentagon planners have been working out the military components of total global supremacy. As one militarily oriented wonk put it in *The Naval War College Review*: "The end of the Cold War left the United States in a position of power unseen since the Roman Empire. The U.S. economy produces about 25 percent of the world's goods and services; it is more than twice as big as that of Japan, the world's number-two economic power. The United States spends more on defense than the next nine countries combined."[4] Thus runs the common preamble of RMA documents.

The RMA debate is carried on at military confabs and in the pages of numerous armed forces academic journals. The players in the RMA are associated with the Defense Department, the National Defense University, RAND, and the Institute of National Strategic Studies; they populate every level of the officer corps and roost in a plethora of smaller war-oriented think tanks.[5] From the outside often rather dull and technical, its underlying assumptions cover only an obscenely limited spectrum of moral opinion. Nonetheless the RMA debates are worth examining from the left, in part because in reading these doctrinal squabbles we understand the American state, or, more specifically, the officialdom that does "the work of" or makes "the state."

So what do we find in current military planning discourse? First and foremost a vision of total unchallenged American global supremacy — not *nation building* but *planet building*.[6] In service of this we find explicit theorizations of how military power works at a political level: the planners discuss a full spectrum of influence, from nuclear annihilation to friendly "dissuasion." We also find dry discussions of how the Air Force and Army should relate better. There are also the simple bureaucratic turf fights in which every service argues for more of whatever it does. And there is the timbre of a geeky technofetishism, with a whiz-bang vocabulary as wacky as the jargon of the late nineties IT-oriented business revolution. In fact, much of the RMA, at the level of technology and discourse, is taken off the shelf from the private sector.[7] And with the IT gear came a very slaphappy Greenspan-esque discourse of "irrational exuberance"—the RMA would transform everything into frictionless, "weightless," casualty-free war.

Running parallel to this reinvention-of-war line is a different discourse, the voice of old-school military caution marked by a world-weary caution, pessimism, and even *fear*. This is particularly true of publications in which a higher percentage of authors tend to be active-duty officers—like *Parameters* (the academic journal of the Army War College) or *The Naval War College Review* or the more popular but still theoretical *Marine Corp Gazette*. At times the contrarian tone is merely signaled with throwaway lines like, "In theory, at least, the US national security decision making process is rational."[8] At other times the tone verges on an apocalyptic paranoia that fixates on a spectrum of concrete and abstract threats ranging from environmental crisis and mass migration to failed states and rising peer competitors. But the perennial fear is asymmetrical warfare gone bad. As one Marine Corps officer put it:

> Be wary of the signposts and lessons learned from constabulary wars. The Iraqis, Serbs, and the Taliban have not stretched our thinking or tested our mettle in any serious way. We have not yet met an adaptive adversary with the will and capability to compete with us on his or our terms. Western norms or codes may no longer apply, and our technological superiority may prove less resilient than we imagine. These are the cunning enemies whose brutality will shock our system and reintroduce us to the harsh reality of combat.[9]

In this worldview, the technology fix offered by transformation becomes a problem.

Bill Clinton was the first to officially embrace the mission of the RMA to achieve post-Soviet global dominance. He launched a transformation based on new technologies, most important among them information technology. Thus the Joint Chiefs of Staff published *Joint Vision 2010* (1997) and then *Joint Vision 2020* (2002), to guide the military through the information age. Now the armed forces would use "a system of systems" to "concentrate long-range firepower." In short, long distance, high-tech, information-rich blitzkrieg using concurrent rather than sequential strikes would "cause the quick collapse of an enemy's resolve." The emphasis here was speed and information.[10]

Joint Vision 2010 aimed to be "the conceptual template for how America's Armed Forces will channel the vitality and innovation of our people and leverage technological opportunities to achieve new levels of effectiveness in joint warfighting [*sic*]."[11] The overarching strategic goal that eventually emerged was "Full Spectrum Dominance," defined as superiority on land and sea, in cyberspace, over communications, in the air and even in orbital space. Key to this was the quest to eliminate the Clausewitzian fog and friction of war through informational dominance.

The surrounding literature of policy papers, strategy documents, and articles frequently invokes characters like Alfred Mahan, who theorized American naval power in the age of the Great White Fleet, and the Italian air strategist Giulio Douhet. Now, with the RMA well underway, the literature is full of heady prognostications. One general-cum-historian writing in 1998 described the Army's transformation goals as follows: "The Army of 2025 will differ from today's Army in two distinct ways. First, it will achieve unprecedented strategic and operational speed by exploiting information technologies to create a knowledge-based organization. Second, it will exhibit tremendous flexibility and physical agility through streamlined, seamlessly integrated organizations that use new tactics and procedures. The collective result will be a versatile, full spectrum, capabilities-based force that can decisively respond to any future global contingency."[12] This reeks of new economy pabulum to be sure, but the central point is clear: full spectrum dominance means having a military that can fight anyone, anywhere, anytime. In other words, beneath the language of quality is the issue of quantity. They want more, much more.

The retired general Anthony Zinni—now a senior advisor at the Center for Strategic and International Studies and formerly commander in chief of Central Command and one of the key architects of Clinton's RMA—described the same thing:

> Our security interests will require that we have a military prepared to respond to:
>
> - a global power with sophisticated military capabilities
> - regional hegemons with asymmetric capabilities, such as weapons of mass destruction and missiles, designed to deny us access to vital areas and regional allies
> - transnational threats that include terrorist groups, international criminal and drug organizations, warlords, environmental security issues, health and disease problems, and illegal migrations
> - problems of failed or incapable states that require peacekeeping, humanitarian assistance, disaster relief, or national reconstruction
> - overseas crises that threaten U.S. citizens and property
> - domestic emergencies that exceed the capacity of other Federal and local government agencies to handle
> - threats to our key repositories of information and our systems for moving information.[13]

The right-wing intellectual Robert Kagan, who has also been instrumental in shaping the RMA and current Bush foreign policy, describes America's military mission with equally massive scope. Kagan wants the military to control or prevent the "rise of militant anti-American Muslim fundamentalism in North Africa and the Middle East, a rearmed Germany in a chaotic Europe, a revitalized Russia, [and] a rearmed Japan in a scramble for power with China in a volatile East Asia."[14]

At the heart of this strategy, as mentioned above, is technology, or the machine fetish endemic to the capitalist mode of production. Also fueling this fixation are the politics of casualty aversion. Though not often mentioned in RMA doctrine, the fear of Vietnam-style casualties is ever present. As one study noted: "Since the Vietnam War it has been a political imperative for the U.S. to keep casualties to its soldiers minimal in foreign interventions. The extraordinarily low casualties in the . . . Gulf War has reinforced this requirement and set a new standard. With this precedent now set, the political consequences of likely combat casualties much above a few hundred in a foreign intervention will be considered a grave risk."[15] All of this has spawned an amazing array of new weaponry. There are the plans for swarming robots, armed drones, microwave bombs, space-based ordinances, and network-centric warfare that would use information technologies to digitally and horizontally link forces and give all soldiers in the field a real-time overview of the battle. The idea is to create, within the ultimate hierarchical bureaucracy, an environment rich in horizontally distributed information. Remarkably, the model for this is Wal-Mart, because the retailer has perfected a "self-synchronized distributed network" with "real-time transactional awareness."[16]

Then there are the "smart bombs," often referred to as joint direct action munitions (JDAMS) or just precision guided munitions. These bombs have been getting smarter and smarter since their major debut in the Gulf War of 1991 (though even in Vietnam the military used various smart munitions). According to one report, only about 7 percent of bombs dropped in the first Gulf War were precision guided, in Yugoslavia about 35 percent were precision munitions, and roughly 60 percent were in Afghanistan. In the current war, it is likely that 80 percent of bombs will be new and improved in this fashion. Central to both smart bombing and troop deployment are the real-time mapping capabilities of small, portable Global Positioning System (GPS) units that transmit their geographic coordinates to twenty-four Pentagon-maintained satellites. These tracking devices are used to guide everything from bombs to containers of spare parts.

Added to this are the various bunker-busting ordinances and new versions of the Predator Drone. The Predator-B, for example, is equipped with eight Hellfire missiles. Other remote-control aircraft include reconnaissance drones like the Global Hawk, which can operate virtually undetected and accurately from altitudes of sixty-five thousand feet and can travel many thousands of miles in a single mission. As for launchpads, there is even discussion of "New Basing Concepts" that would involve "mobile offshore basing" so as to "eliminate the ability of any regional state to veto U.S. operations by blocking access to command facilities."[17] General Richard Myers, chairman of the Joint Chiefs, imagines the synergies of all this mechanized killing combined could "have the potential to change significantly the way we fight and perhaps even the nature of warfare itself."[18]

CONNECTED DOCTRINES

The RMA has impact beyond actual war making. Crucially, it contributes to what some call a "diplomacy of violence," best summed up in the doctrine of dissuasion. Here again military superiority—rather than cooperation, assurance, and alliance—is increasingly seen as the key for controlling allies. A crass example of this was offered by former national security advisor Zbigniew Brzezinski, in his widely read book, *The Grand Chessboard.* Sounding more like Peter Gowan than himself, Brzezinski refers to America's allies and friends as "vassals and tributaries." For him, geostrategy should aim to "to prevent collusion and maintain security dependence among the vassals, to keep tributaries pliant and protected, and to keep the barbarians from coming together."[19]

By this logic, friends are dissuaded, that is, vaguely intimidated. An important National Defense University position paper called "Dissuasion as a Strategic Concept," written by the civilian wonk Richard Kugler, describes the difference between deterrence and dissuasion as follows:

> Dissuasion arises in a different, less confrontational place along the spectrum from peace to war. It applies to situations in which the relationship between the United States and another country has not yet descended into intense political-military rivalry but has the potential to do so if events take a wrong turn. Thus, the United States is dealing not with a full-fledged adversary but with a country with which it has a mixed relationship of cool peace, mutual suspicions, and common incentives to avoid violence. War is not in the air, but deep trouble could arise if that country begins misbehaving in ways that threaten U.S. interests.[20]

The rest of Kugler's paper goes on to spell out how dissuasion can work with more or less military muscle in different zones, but in doing so, he makes the point that increased basing, particularly in Asia and the Gulf, is central to US power on the Eurasian land mass. As regards China: "The United States will need to think in terms of dissuading China from assertive, menacing political-military conduct that rising geopolitical powers often have pursued before."[21]

THE PRIZE AND THE DEEPER LOGIC

Technofetishism and the momentum of already existing military advantage are not the only factors driving the RMA. Underlying the imperative to seize the unipolar opportunity is the *class* ideology of the American state. In other words, the project of capitalist accumulation, or, more specifically, American-led neoliberal economic restructuring, is also driving US political elites.

As Thomas Friedman succinctly put it: "The hidden hand of the market will never work without the hidden fist—McDonald's cannot flourish without McDonnell-Douglas, the designer of the F-15. And the hidden fist that keeps the world safe for Silicon Valley's technologies is called the United States Army, Air Force, Navy and Marines."[22] President Bush made this same point, though more delicately, in his "National Security Strategy of the United States." For example:

> We will promote economic growth and economic freedom beyond America's shores. . . . We will use our economic engagement with other countries to underscore the benefits of policies that generate higher productivity and sustained economic growth, including: pro-growth legal and regulatory policies to encourage business investment, innovation, and entrepreneurial activity; tax policies—particularly lower marginal tax rates—that improve incentives for work and investment . . . strong financial systems that allow capital to be put to its most efficient use; sound fiscal policies to support business activity . . . and free trade that provides new avenues for growth and fosters the diffusion of technologies and ideas that increase productivity and opportunity.
>
> The lessons of history are clear: market economies, not command-and-control economies with the heavy hand of government, are the best way to promote prosperity and reduce poverty. Policies that further strengthen market incentives and market institutions are relevant for all economies—industrialized countries, emerging markets, and the developing world.[23]

Likewise, military planning documents make *constant* reference to "trade liberalization," "economic reform," and "free markets"—the hallmark euphemisms of neoliberal-style capitalist accumulation. For example, from an Institute for National Strategic Studies special report on the Gulf, we get: "It is therefore in the interest of the United States to encourage political pluralism, good governance, transparency in decision making, and economic liberalization."[24] Or from a report written for the Strategic Studies Institute of the US Army War

College comes the argument that economic policy, in fact, *determines* military strategy. The logic is such that it is worth quoting at length:

> Macro-level strategic objectives fall on a spectrum of engagement. At one end is creation of a global system composed exclusively of stable, prosperous, free-market democracies. At the other end is political and military disengagement. . . . Where future U.S. strategy falls on this spectrum has tremendous implications for the sort of military force the nation needs. The more the United States stresses active engagement and the promulgation of open economies and political systems, the more the U.S. military must be able to project power and sustain protracted operations.[25]

Obviously, the United States is not experimenting with any sort of economic disengagement, and the intellectuals of the RMA know this. Thus globalization, or unfettered private accumulation, compels them to create a strategy, infrastructure, and menu of weaponry and tactics commensurate with the task; and it drives the security planners to believe in the lethal technological promise of the RMA.

Nicolas Lehmann linked this sort of thinking to accumulation American style in an amazing but rather overlooked *New Yorker* piece, in which he canvassed Bush administration insiders on America's new global doctrine. Richard Haas, director of policy and planning at the State Department, provided the most coherent overview when describing America's global project:

> Is there a successor idea to [the Cold War doctrine of] containment? I think there is. . . . It is the idea of integration. The goal of U.S. foreign policy should be to persuade the other major powers to sign on to certain key ideas as to how the world should operate: opposition to terrorism and weapons of mass destruction, support for free trade, democracy, markets. Integration is about locking them into these policies and then building institutions that lock them in even more.[26]

What a tantalizing vision for politicians and military strategists alike—Planet America, the earth remade for capital by the threat of high-tech violence. But can the empire run on intimidation and dead labor alone? Or does it require *dead workers*, that is, soldiers sent from the metropole to control the wild zones and perhaps come home in body bags?

MEET THE CRITICS

Despite the smell of victory, there is a pessimistic strand of thinking within the RMA debates. As mentioned in the opening section of this essay, some maintain that the US military is woefully unprepared for the real wars it will face if it is to control the planet. Perhaps the best way to understand the dissident voices within the RMA is to focus on a few of the leading critics.

There is the famously worried Marine Corps Lieutenant Colonel Francis G. Hoffman, who has been speaking and writing against the RMA in military journals of all sorts. He has even written a book-length critique. Here is a typical slab of his spleen:

> From a Marine perspective, the key to this capability [Full Spectrum Dominance] lies more in doctrine and training than in hardware and computer technology. JV 2010 suggests that information superiority is generated by technology alone and underestimates the basic contribution of trained and properly educated leaders who have been immersed in tactical decision making environments over many years. . . . JV 2010 makes a few references to high quality people, professional training, and the need for physical presence in the form of "boots on the ground," but it has a clear technological focus. We must avoid the illusion of attempting to impose certainty on the battlefield.[27]

While the *Joint Vision 2010* wants "informational dominance," Hoffman wants soldiers who can make decisions even when they do not have information. Connected to this concern is the general decline of front-line troops as a percentage of military personnel. Today, infantry forces are less than half their Vietnam-era strength. As the military becomes more capital intensive, soldiers become technicians who sit in air-conditioned tents. And elite Special Forces are stretched thin; one report found that "two-thirds of the Army's Special Forces are currently spread out over eighty-five countries."[28]

Even more scathing are Hoffman's comments when crossing swords with RMA cheerleaders and technology boosters like James Blaker. Hoffman's concern is that the US military is understaffed and undertrained: "Readiness strains throughout the U.S. armed forces are evident already. None of the investments Dr. Blaker advocates represent solutions to the current crisis in operational tempo, readiness, and maintenance. They make great profits for a defense industry scrambling for Department of Defense (DOD) business, but some—though certainly not all—make poor investments today. Defense planners must inoculate themselves from military-industrialists shilling for high-end systems that are inappropriate for tomorrow's more diverse and asymmetric threats."[29] Hoffman's occasional coauthor, the retired Marine Corps Lieutenant General Paul K. Van Riper, is even more hostile to RMA nostrums. He made international news when he was hired to command the "opposition" (meaning Iraqi) forces in the Millennium Challenge 2002 war games, the largest such training in US history. This 250 million–dollar exercise involved virtual maneuvers in cyberspace, as well as massive real-life troop, ship, and air deployments, all designed to test the joint fighting capabilities of the US military.

To the total shock and awe of the US side of the game, Van Riper attacked first! Though outnumbered, outgunned, and scheduled to lose, he unleashed a swarm of explosives-laden pleasure boats and prop planes on suicide attacks. This and some outmoded Silkworm antiship missiles from China sank sixteen US ships—"including the fleet's aircraft carrier and other vessels carrying thousands of marines." When the boats were unsunk and the game restarted, Van Riper avoided US satellite and radar surveillance by using motorcycle couriers and audio messages broadcast from the mosques of his fictitious country. When this was disallowed halfway through the game because the real brass were suddenly unable to target enemy communications, Van Riper quit, calling the exercise rigged.[30]

Officers like these and their less numerous civilian allies insist that the empire requires a real military, not robots and drones. The defense policy analyst William Hawkins sums it up as follows: "War is about politics, and politics is about the governing of land and people. Enhanced sensors and precision-guided weapons may have greatly improved 'search and destroy' operations, but technology is not strategy." In his view, "it still takes 'boots on the ground' to consolidate a victory that really matters. In that respect, two millennia of scientific progress has not made the cruise missile a more effective tool of high politics than the Roman legionnaire."[31] The same author went on to deride the very base assumptions of Clinton's National Security Council (NSC), which helped launch the RMA:

> What gives [NSC document] authors confidence that the United States can assume the role of world policeman at an acceptable cost is a belief in the power of stand-off aerial weapons to break the will of adversaries without risking the lives of American personnel. This, in turn, is apparently based on the notion that the "diplomacy of violence" has worked. Yet, the survival of rogue regimes against which this strategy has been applied, and the perceived need to maintain substantial troops and airpower assets on their doorsteps, call the basic assumptions of this strategy into question.[32]

Another dissident argued, "the age of large-scale conventional interstate warfare . . . is drawing to a close, and with it the relevance of Clausewitz's postulation of total war among states." For this group, the future wars facing the empire will likely "erupt across ethnic and cultural rather than state boundaries." The methods on these fronts will be "predominantly unconventional" and small scale. But

> The Department of Defense, however, continues to prepare precisely for big conventional wars, and not for just one at a time but rather for two. . . . In fact, the Weinberger-Powell Doctrine has little relevance in a post-Soviet world in which a modern-day version of imperial policing is likely to consume much of U.S. military energy. The Pentagon, concludes Eliot Cohen, has yet to recognize "the reality of an America that now acts as a global empire, rather than as one of two rival superpowers, or a normal state."[33]

The end result of all this, in the critics' view, could be inadequate preparation: "Confidence that unfolding RMA technologies will evaporate the 'fog of war' is dangerously misplaced."[34]

In this regard the RMA threatens to deliver the very quagmire it originally sought to escape. And if one concurs with Bill Tabb—who has noted that America's domineering military and economic capacities are immiserating millions, destroying the environment, and aiding awful tyrants worldwide—one could argue that "the central issue of our time is what to do about the United States."[35] In the long run, a quagmire might be the only way for an anti-imperial resistance to be sustained within the otherwise narcotic and repressive culture of the American metropole, though to be clear, I do not wish war on myself or anyone else.[36]

POST-FORDIST WARFARE?

Cut to Oakland, California, 1999; the Marines have landed. Their mission: separate the warring "Furzians" and "Booleans" and restore democracy in an imaginary war-torn third world country. The deep thinkers from the Marine Corps Warfighting Laboratory at Quantico have turned the grounds of a decommissioned military hospital on the San Francisco Bay into a "city" where they are practicing the theory of the "Three Block War."[37]

Here a different part of capital's rhetoric has been taken up by soldiers; it is the idea of the flattened hierarchy, where decision-making power and responsibility are pushed down to front-line workers. The Marines in these games were expected to move seamlessly from managing refugees and doling out aid to keeping the peace between warring factions, arresting fugitives, and, when necessary, switch to storming into an old fifteen-story tall hospital to fight militiamen.

As an observer, I watched the young Marines pour out of the high-rise hospital after several hours of fighting. They lined up and checked the electronic gear strapped to their bodies. According to the computers, designed to catch the light beams of enemy guns, between 30 and 70 percent of the young jarheads were "dead" or "wounded." This had the adult supervision, the Marine leadership at the war game, very worried.

Call it limited war, occupation, low-intensity conflict, or, as is now fashionable, Military Operations Other Than War (MOOTW), but the future looks grim because empire will involve urban combat, and that is the military's worst nightmare.

A DENOUEMENT?

Having seen occupied Iraq up close and on the ground throughout 2003 and 2004, I can report this: Rumsfeld's dreamy RMA starship has crash-landed in the desert. The US military will try to retreat to maximum-security bases in which its soldiers are essentially prisoners serving support roles to Iraqi proxies. But it looks doubtful that this plan will work. The Iraqi resistance has made the decimation of US-backed proxies one of its top priorities. Likewise, the UN has been driven out, along with the entire nation-building industry, the NGO mop-up crews.

The cost of this war and the transformation-oriented military budget are not enough to break the bank. This is a point the RMA hawks like William Kristol love to point out. But technically speaking, they are correct. According to the economic journalist Doug Henwood, current military spending, which reached $396.1 billion for the fiscal year 2003, is not all that high measured against GDP. "We've got a long way to go before we even get back to 1980s levels, much less 1950s levels," says Henwood. "In Clinton's last budget, the military share of GDP was 4.0%; Bush is proposing to raise this to about 4.3% (leaving aside the cost of an Iraq war, which could be another 1% at the high end). The late-1970s low was 5.7%, which Carter, then Reagan, pushed up to a high of 7.5% in 1986. But that was still a lot less than 1967's 10.3%, or 1953's 14.7%."[38] The war is massively expensive, but if the Bush tax cuts were rescinded there would be plenty of cash on hand. Likewise, the US right wing likes the deficit created by the war because it justifies belt-tightening cuts in social services.

In other words, military spending could double if the rich would pay taxes. And raising taxes on the wealthy is not as impossible as many believe: both Bush Senior and Clinton raised taxes (slightly) on higher income groups. Future presidents saddled with George W. Bush's war debt will inevitability have to do the same. In the meantime, social services are gutted.

Shockingly, the neocon hawks entrenched in the DC war-and-policy apparatus still seem intoxicated by and confident in their vision of Planet America ruled by the high-tech might of the RMA's diplomacy of violence. This hubris fuels the downward spiral in Iraq and could lead to RMA-style missile-strike warfare against Iran.

But Iraq is clearly the place where the post-Vietnam American imperial machine first faltered. In Baghdad and Falluja, military labor—boots on the ground—is clearly what the empire needs and does not have. Slowly, this crisis will shake the ideological and cultural power of both the state and capital, offering political openings in which movements and critical opinion makers can link war to capitalism and thus delegitimize both.

NOTES

1. David Garland, *Punishment and Modern Society: A Study in Social Theory* (Chicago: University of Chicago Press, 1990); Phil Scraton, "The Politics of Morality," in *Beyond September 11: An Anthology of Dissent*, ed. Scraton (London: Pluto, 2002), 40–46.
2. For Marx on "dead labor," see *Capital: A Critique of Political Economy*, vol. 1 (London: Penguin Books, 1976), 342: "Capital is dead labour which, vampire-like, lives only by sucking living labour and lives the more, the more it sucks." On RMA technology, see Mark Williams and Andrew P. Madden, "New Technologies May Revolutionize War," *Red Herring*, August 14, 2001.
3. On the 1990s hype, see Doug Henwood, *After the New Economy* (New York: New Press, 2003). The Soviets, lead by a Marshall Ogarkov, were the first to write about a military technical revolution.
4. Stephen M. Walt, "American Primacy: Its Prospects and Pitfalls," *Naval War College Review* 55, no. 2 (2002): 9–29.
5. For a discussion of the state, state officials, and the politics of their discourse, see Stefano Harney, *State Work: Public Administration and Mass Intellectuality* (Durham, NC: Duke University Press, 2002).
6. The phrase *planet building* comes from George Monbiot, "Wilful Blindness," *Manchester Guardian Weekly*, March 11, 2003, 21.
7. Tom Frank, *One Market under God: Extreme Capitalism, Market Populism, and the End of Economic Democracy* (New York: Doubleday, 2000).
8. P. H. Liotta, "Chaos as Strategy," *Parameters* 32, no. 2 (2002): 47–56.
9. F. G. Hoffman, "Transforming for the Chaordic Age," *Marine Corps Gazette* 86, no. 11 (2002): 47.
10. Hans Binnendijk, introduction to *Transforming America's Military* (Washington, DC: NDU Press/U.S. Government Printing Office, 2002), xix.
11. Joint Chiefs of Staff, *Joint Vision 2010*, 1.
12. Robert H. Scales Jr., "America's Army: Preparing for Tomorrow's Security Challenges" (Carlisle Barracks, PA: Strategic Studies Institute of the US Army War College, December 1998), 10.
13. Anthony C. Zinni, "A Military for the Twenty-first Century: Lessons from the Recent Past," *Strategic Forum*, no. 181 (2001): 3.
14. Quoted in Charles William Maynes, "The Perils of (and for) an Imperial America," *Foreign Policy* 111 (1998): 41.
15. Charles Knight, Lutz Unterseher, and Carl Conetta, "Reflections on Information War, Casualty Aversion, and Military Research and Development after the Gulf War and the Demise of the Soviet Union," in *Military Technological Innovation and Stability in a Changing World*, ed. Smit, Grin, and Veronkov (Amsterdam: VU University Press, 1992).
16. Binnendijk, introduction, xix; Mike Davis, "Slouching towards Baghdad," ZNET, February 28, 2003.

17. Richard D. Sokolsky, "Beyond Containment: Defending U.S. Interests in the Persian Gulf," *Strategic Forum*, special report (September 2002), 1–8.
18. Peter Goodspeed, "New Empire: Tomorrow's Army Today," *National Post*, January 24, 2003.
19. Quoted in Charles William Maynes, "The Perils of (and for) an Imperial America," 36; Peter Gowan, *The Global Gamble: Washington's Faustian Bid for Global Dominance* (London: Verso, 1999); Kori N. Schake, "Do European Union Defense Initiatives Threaten NATO?" *Strategic Forum*, no. 184 (2001): 1–6.
20. Richard Kugler, "Dissuasion as a Strategic Concept," *Strategic Forum*, no. 196 (2002): 3–4.
21. Ibid., 4.
22. Quoted in William K. Tabb, "The Face of Empire," *Monthly Review* 54, no.6 (2002). And as Bill Tabb has argued, "Given this [military] capacity it can be argued the central issue of our time is what to do about the United States."
23. White House Web site: www.whitehouse.gov/nsc/nss6.html.
24. Sokolsky, "Beyond Containment."
25. Steven Metz and James Kievit, "Strategy and the Revolution in Military Affairs: From Theory to Policy" (paper presented at the Strategic Studies Institute of the US Army War College, Carlisle Barracks, June 27, 1995).
26. Nicolas Lemann, "The Next World Order," *New Yorker*, March 21, 2003, 48.
27. F. G. Hoffman, "Joint Vision 2010: A Marine Perspective," *Joint Force Quarterly* 17 (1997): 37–38; Hoffman, "Transforming for the Chaordic Age," 44–56.
28. Jason Vest, "The Army's Empire Skeptics: Officers Are Raising Serious Questions about Manpower, Morale, and Technology," *Nation*, March 3, 2003, 28.
29. F. G. Hoffman, "Why the Critique? An Author's Response," *National Security Studies Quarterly* 4, no.1 (1999): 90.
30. Norman Friedman, "War Game Raises Questions," *United States Naval Institute: Proceedings* 128, no. 10 (2002): 2; Otis Port and Stan Crock, "Guerrilla Ships for a New Kind of War," *Business Week*, January 27, 2003, 102.
31. William R. Hawkins, "Imposing Peace: Total versus Limited Wars, and the Need to Put Boots on the Ground," *Parameters* 30, no. 2 (2000): 79.
32. Ibid., 81.
33. Jeffrey Record, "The Creeping Irrelevance of US Force Planning" (Carlisle Barracks, PA: Strategic Studies Institute of the US Army War College, May 19, 1998), 1.
34. Ibid., 12.
35. Tabb, "The Face of Empire."
36. I am obviously opening myself to charges of "fight the previous war," but these things do have a way of repeating themselves.
37. Gary Anderson, interview by the author, Oakland, March 1999; Frank L. Jones, "Marine Corps Civil Affairs and the Three Block War," *Marine Corps Gazette* 86, no. 3 (2002): 33.
38. Doug Henwood, private e-mail communication.

OMAR DAHBOUR

☆ ☆ ☆ **Hegemony and Rights:** On the Liberal Justification for Empire

Just as the "civilizing mission" of bringing Christianity to the heathen provided a justifying pretext for the imperialist conquest of Asia and Africa in the past, today the protection of "human rights" may be the cloak for a new type of imperialist military intervention worldwide. . . . [It] also distracts from active criticism of global economic structures that favor the basic human rights abuse of a world split between staggering wealth and dire poverty.—**Diana Johnstone, "Seeing Yugoslavia Through a Dark Glass"**

Violations of human rights are indeed all too common, and if it were permissible to remedy them by external use of force, there would be no law to forbid the use of force by almost any state against almost any other. Human rights . . . will have to be vindicated . . . by other, peaceful means, not by opening the door to aggression and destroying the principal advance of international law, the outlawing of war and the prohibition of force.—**Louis Henkin, *How Nations Behave***

Throughout much of the twentieth century, the idea of a liberal imperialism, or of a liberal argument for neo-imperial hegemony, would have seemed absurd. The reason for this is that twentieth-century liberalism developed during the same period in which so-called national liberation movements emerged in the third world, so that liberal theorists largely accepted some version of a principle of self-determination, a core idea for those movements. The suggestion that a state might legitimately play a hegemonic, imperial, or, above all, colonial role in the world was anathema to those who espoused liberal ideas.

Yet in the nineteenth century, liberalism had been closely associated with empires, particularly the British Empire. Key liberal philosophers such as John Stuart Mill and Lord Acton explicitly endorsed some version of imperialism. At the beginning of the twenty-first century, there seems to be a guarded renewal of this liberal espousal of imperial goals. This is most apparent in Great Britain, where Prime Minister Tony Blair—and more explicitly the British diplomat Robert Cooper—have advocated a global interventionism by the United Kingdom and the United States (i.e., "the West") reminiscent of the nineteenth-century British Empire.[1] Perhaps this historical legacy has enabled politicians there to be more open about the nature of contemporary imperialism than is the case in the United States.

In any event, as Niall Ferguson has emphasized, the contemporary world seems to have witnessed a new (US) imperialism that is comparable to empires from the past.[2] But can it be justified in liberal terms—or is it, as some might contend, just a feature of the overweening power of a globally dominant state? In this essay, I seek to show that there is indeed a (contemporary) liberal argument to be made for empire—though only if both liberalism and imperialism are understood in certain ways. This argument can be found *in part* in a number of contemporary thinkers; but I am more interested in examining the best possible version of such an argument, whether or not it has been made in its entirety by any one philosopher or politician. Furthermore, I want also, having constructed such an argument, to criticize it—to show why empire is ultimately not justifiable in liberal terms. What the implications of this are—whether imperialism or liberalism or both are to be abandoned—I leave for the conclusion.

The liberal argument consists of four steps; I will examine them in the next four sections, leading up to an assessment of the practical consequences of the argument and a consideration of alternatives to it. First, the term *hegemony* must be substituted for *empire* in order to make the latter palatable for contemporary liberal sensibilities. Second, liberalism must be defined as entailing a political project to be realized on a global scale. Third, this project is to be equated with a new concept of human rights that replaces the traditional practice of emergency humanitarian relief. Fourth, this human-rights agenda is viewed as realizable only through a scheme of global governance, that is, of governmental institutions capable of the global enforcement of norms. A conclusion is reached when the hegemonic state is appealed to as a stand-in for the (unrealizable) project of establishing such effective global governing institutions.

The question to ask about this line of argument is whether it is a necessary progression, or whether there is nothing inherently imperialistic about liberal ideas. I will argue that there is such a conceptual logic embedded within liberalism (or at least a currently dominant version of it) and that avoiding the conclusion to which this reasoning leads requires either drastically restricting or abandoning liberal theory as it is generally understood. But a prior contextual question needs brief consideration: what is the importance of a liberal argument for empires when liberalism seems to have been decisively abandoned by the very empire under consideration?

In the era of wars on terrorism and dictatorship, does liberal imperialism—even if it could be said to exist—have any relevance? Here, the political shift at the end of the 1990s in the United States seems to have ended whatever liberal hegemony there might have been. The discourse of (economic) globalization that marked much of the Clinton era in the United States has been replaced by the more militaristic discourse of the Bush administration's war on terrorism. This shift looks like a fundamental one; yet it may not be. Has the liberal rhetoric of democratization and human rights really been abandoned? And how different is the neoliberal agenda of the Clinton years from the neoconservative project of the current administration?

As Neil Smith argues in his book *The Endgame of Globalization*, there has been a fundamental continuity of goals in US governments over the past several decades (including the present one). Whether these goals are stated in the internationalist language of rights and liberties or the nationalist language of state interests, "both are the fruit of the classical liberal tradition."[3] There is less difference than may at first be apparent between the Clinton-era policies that emphasized international agreements—often engineered through global agencies such as the World Trade Organization (backed by US diplomacy when necessary)—and the current policies of military threats and interventions, from Afghanistan to Iraq (and beyond).

Certainly, this is true at least ideologically (and that is my main concern here): recent US interventions have been justified by much the same discourse of human rights, democracy, and freedom that was used in the 1990s to argue for everything from trade liberalization to sanctions (and eventually interventions) against recalcitrant regimes from Iraq (again) to Yugoslavia. This point has been documented by Julie Mertus, who shows that after the initial rhetorical use of terms such as *terrorism* and *weapons of mass destruction* to argue for an intervention in Afghanistan and Iraq, the Bush administration has resorted to the same liberal justifications (particularly utilizing the concept of human rights) voiced by the Clinton administration in previous years.[4]

EMPIRE OR HEGEMONY?

It seems that liberal arguments for US actions abroad are not so easily discarded. So we need to consider how such arguments might be employed in an *explicit* (and general) justification of empires, rather than in just defending specific actions that a globally dominant state such as the United States has taken. The first step, as previously mentioned, is to replace talk of empires with that of hegemonic states. These terms need not be synonymous and have at times denoted importantly distinct entities. Michael Doyle, for instance, contrasts the ancient Greek states of Athens and Sparta, with Athens regarded as explicitly imperialistic and Sparta as hegemonic only.[5] The difference lies in the degree of interference that the imperial or hegemonic power exercises on subordinate countries. The imperial power will be involved in ordering the internal social institutions of subject peoples (tax policy, property law, religious practices), while the hegemonic power will simply dictate external policy (diplomatic alliances, trade pacts, military deployments). Today, liberal schemes of global governance *in theory* are at most hegemonic, attempting to influence states (or more strongly, force them) to abide by certain international standards of rights, development, governance, and so on. In practice, however, such attempts often become more intrusive, breaking down any distinction between internal and external policies.

Furthermore, a burgeoning historical literature has shown how the United States, in replacing the colonial empires of England and France, developed an innovative set of institutions designed to establish an "informal empire," that is, one without colonies.[6] The uniqueness of this informal empire—what historians have more traditionally referred to as hegemony—should not, however, be exaggerated. As Ferguson has mentioned, the hundreds of US military bases around the world today—what Chalmers Johnson has called an "empire of bases"—are remarkably similar, in both geographical location and political purpose, to the system of British Royal Navy stations a century ago.[7]

But even if the United States had become in the twentieth century, as did England in the century before, an (informal) imperial power, why is this not simply a fact of modern history or geopolitics, without ideological or philosophical significance? After all, does not the US reluctance to take on the trappings of a formal empire itself indicate an embarrassment about the nature of imperialism that was all but universal by the mid-twentieth century? As indicated above, if this embarrassment existed in the immediate postcolonial era, it now shows signs of waning in the years following the end of the Cold War (i.e., after 1990). There is increasingly a confluence between this historical watershed and a coterminous change in the political philosophy of liberalism, and it is this confluence that has led to the renewed possibility of a future for liberal imperialism.

Before turning to this new version of liberal theory, a moment should be devoted to recalling the prior life of liberal imperialism at the height of the British Empire in the nineteenth century. The leading advocates for imperialism at this time—John Stuart Mill and Lord Acton—made similar arguments in their writings from the 1860s, though with different emphases.

Acton regarded empires as examples of what we would today call multicultural communities—states in which different peoples could live in relative harmony (his examples were the Austrian and the British Empires).[8] To advocate empires as a form of rule was to be freed from a dangerous delusion of the age—that peoples could find self-determination within nation-states. Rather, they ought to accept an imperial framework that gave them material benefits while protecting them from the civil wars and ethnic cleansing entailed by conflicts between national groups.

Mill, in contrast, seemed to view empires as temporary institutions, ones designed to help backward peoples in their progress toward civilization, that is, toward the creation of institutions of representative government.[9] As Uday Mehta has emphasized, it is the belief in the desirability—and the possibility—of progress toward civilization that informs Mill's (and other liberals') advocacy of empire.[10] Empires have a crucial role to play in tutoring peoples without progressive political institutions in the knowledge of what is required to establish them.

Today, Acton's view of empires has few adherents, among other reasons because such multinational empires as he favored (Great Britain and Austria, but also perhaps the Soviet Union and Yugoslavia) have seemed either actually oppressive themselves, or, when not, unable to quiet the ethnonational strife to which they have often been subject. Mill's concept, however, may be more relevant to the so-called new imperialism. The rhetoric of democracy and freedom (e.g., in US-occupied Iraq) is again playing a role in justifying interventions and occupations by the United States. But how can imperialism be regarded as liberal in view of its obviously oppressive features? Understanding this requires a brief consideration of what liberalism has come to mean in the current context.

IS IMPERIALISM NECESSARILY ENTAILED BY CONTEMPORARY LIBERALISM?

One way to get at the connections between liberal theory and imperial politics is to ask whether contemporary liberalism still embodies a concept of progress that might entail state intervention in and administration of nonprogressive countries, as Mill thought was sometimes necessary. There are actually two questions here: is the concept of progress still implicit in contemporary liberalism, and, if so, does liberalism mandate foreign interventions (and perhaps occupations) to achieve this progress? Here the concept of hegemony, and its divergence from empires as such, is important. Liberal imperialists seek to justify not a colonial regime, or even a strictly imperial one, but one that is hegemonic, *provided* this hegemony is used to institutionalize liberal values. The fact that in a postcolonial world, direct justifications of empires are largely discredited does not mean that an indirect justification might not be considered legitimate when viewed as a last resort. If empire is not considered a fully legitimate form of political authority, due to its inherently undemocratic character, it may still be viewed as a means, under certain conditions, of creating a liberal society when such a society does not exist in a given country (i.e., one ruled by an oppressive and/or dictatorial regime).

Turning to the first question, it is true that there has been much recent discussion about whether core liberal values are supposedly Western or transcultural. This debate, especially as it is focused on the nature of human rights, suggests that contemporary liberalism may have distanced itself from the nineteenth-century progressivism of Mill. But in fact the debate has shown a surprising resilience in affirmations of the universality of liberal values (above all, human rights), even in the face of skeptical or relativist doubts.[11]

What has actually been more up for debate is how to justify and categorize human rights. In the first case, constructivist theories that refer to a historical project of universalizing the legal rights recognized in European countries have tended to predominate over naturalist theories that identify rights as features of human agency.[12] In the second case, there has been contention between minimalist and maximalist interpretations of rights, with the former emphasizing basic rights and the latter maintaining the existence of socioeconomic rights, as well as the less controversial (basic) rights to life, liberty, personal property, and legal equality.[13]

These debates need not detain us from adopting a basic definition of human rights that can be instrumentalized internationally, and this is the goal of most liberal theorists today. It is crucial to note that traditional definitions of liberalism — emphasizing, for example, personal liberties, private property, or religious toleration — have been largely folded into the idea of human rights by late twentieth-century liberals. Human rights, on this view, can be defined as *high-priority claims to the conditions for personal moral agency*.[14]

Two features of this definition are noteworthy and get us to the second question of whether liberal theory does still mandate international interventions to realize its conception of social progress. First, human rights are applicable primarily in those places where a legal system does not already recognize rights as just defined. Elsewhere, the human-rights doctrine of contemporary liberalism functions as an attempt to establish the "right to have rights."[15] Second, there is an ambiguity built into the idea of rights, which originated, after all, as a *legal* concept. Are human rights essentially moral or political entitlements? The difference lies in whether human rights are foundational (ethical) norms, ones that do not mandate any particular actions — or are norms of political behavior that can be instrumentalized by states or other agents (e.g., international or nongovernmental organizations).

This brings us to the second question of whether liberalism *requires* state actions globally in the name of progress, that is, the realization of human rights. Since the universalistic nature of liberalism virtually makes all liberals cosmopolitans—that is, believers in the idea that all persons have equal value (and therefore, rights)—the difference adumbrated above is one between *moral* and *political* cosmopolitans. Moral cosmopolitans are those who, while they espouse liberal values such as human rights, resist the temptation (as they would see it) to use the diplomatic or military power of states or other international actors to realize these values directly. Political cosmopolitans, in contrast, disagree with the idea that the state—including hegemonic states—should not be utilized to realize these values.

It is political cosmopolitanism, in my view, that opens the way to a liberal justification of empires. More is required for such an argument to be made. But the initial step involves a commitment to some political scheme—for instance, a more robust form of international organization—that can instantiate cosmopolitan values (in particular, human rights). Some philosophers, such as Thomas Pogge, use the concept of a global social contract to argue that the values of liberalism (distributive justice, representative democracy, and especially human rights) should be institutionalized globally through the acceptance of universally agreed on norms by existing states or peoples.[16] Others, such as Peter Singer, who argues from a quasi-utilitarian position, argue that cosmopolitan values—which are conducive to the interests of mankind generally—will remain unrealized until some more equitable scheme of "global governance" is established.[17] But the idea that a moral scheme of human rights requires *some* institutional embodiment is essential to the political cosmopolitan view—contractualist, utilitarian, or otherwise. *What sort* of institutions will do the trick? Certainly, most political cosmopolitans would reject the idea of using an imperial-hegemonic state as a means of realizing their ideals; few liberals would openly endorse a scheme that traduced the principle of self-government.

But they need not do so. For once the question is asked of how to institutionalize the enforcement of human rights, the achievement of democratic constitutions, or a global redistribution of income, the answer must be that it is done through the actions of some political entity greater or stronger or more authoritative than most states existing today. Of course, such an institution must be committed to cosmopolitan ideals, or at least potentially committed to them. At first, talk of states need not occur—the United Nations or some less compromised ideal international organization is sufficient. But before long, in the face of the manifest unrealizability of all such entities, the state—that is, the hegemonic state—will become the second (or last) choice of political cosmopolitans. I want to look at this conceptual slide toward empire in some more detail with regard to the problem of human rights in particular. A similar process could be seen in discussions of cosmopolitan democracy or of international distributive justice; but the human rights context is a particularly fraught one since it has been invoked in a number of recent international conflicts (Yugoslavia, Central Africa, the Middle East), either where interventions by hegemonic states have occurred or where various philosophers think they ought to have occurred.

FROM HUMANITARIANISM TO HUMAN RIGHTS

Recent discussions of the politics of human rights have been caught up by terminological confusions over the difference between humanitarianism and human rights, the "old" versus the "new" humanitarianism, and so on. Underlying this confusion are differing interpretations of the history of the idea of human rights. The crucial moment was that of the creation of the United Nations and the writing of the Universal Declaration of Human Rights in the late 1940s. From this point, human rights definitively entered the discourse of international relations; yet the meaning and significance of such rights remained unclear. The key issue was the relation between human-rights claims and state sovereignty. Yet as Michael Ignatieff, among others, has noted, the relation between these has never been worked out in international law and in fact embodies a clear contradiction between different principles: "The human rights covenants that states have signed since 1945 have implied that state sovereignty is conditional . . . yet this conditionality has never been made explicit in international law."[18]

In the three to four decades after 1950, human rights tended to be subordinate to humanitarian actions such as famine relief that did not challenge the sovereignty doctrine. This humanitarianism opted for a stance of neutrality in relation to warring or tyrannical states and was aimed primarily at the amelioration of suffering in emergencies. While human rights remained a regulative ideal within international law, it did not have—as humanitarianism seemed to—any readily available embodiment other than moral exhortation.

Starting in the 1980s, however, and gathering strength in the 1990s with the end of the Cold War, a new view of humanitarian emergencies arose that regarded them as violations of human rights, justifying political remedies, possibly including military actions.[19] Advocates of this view sometimes saw the concept of human rights as further humanizing international law, including the part dealing with humanitarian actions in wartime. As Theodor Meron has written, to genuinely humanize international law, including the law of war, would be to "put an end to all kinds of armed conflict."[20] Failing this, human rights could be used to extend and potentially universalize the humanitarian impulse, including, crucially, in intrastate conflicts (i.e., civil wars).

Other advocates of extending the human-rights doctrine have viewed this extension as a return to a perspective they saw embodied in the UN and the Universal Declaration of Human Rights—an antitotalitarian perspective that regarded human rights as a weapon in the fight against, first, fascism, and then other forms of antihumanitarian ideologies (communism, nationalism, fundamentalism, and so on). Alain Destexhe, for instance, attacked what he called the "new humanitarianism" for forgetting that "the construction of a world order and the development of the UN after the Second World War have been guided by a principle: never again. The Nazis' unprecedented crime against the Jews became a benchmark for an international community founded on certain basic values: opposition to genocide, the search for world peace and respect for human rights."[21] Instead, "today, from Bosnia to Rwanda, the new humanitarianism or the emergency ethic has rebounded on the victims. They are now seen in terms of their immediate suffering rather than as fellow human beings."[22]

The task, for these critics of humanitarianism, is to get back to a political advocacy of human rights in general, not just for the victims of tyrannical regimes but for all persons. Humanitarian emergencies, in this view, are the result of more deep-seated problems that can only be successfully addressed by an aggressive human rights–oriented international community. Humanitarian problems, in other words, "cannot be solved by humanitarian means alone."[23]

Another view, by contrast, sees consistency between the Universal Declaration and more recent ("new humanitarian") measures to redress emergency suffering. This consistency is embodied by the paramount value of peace in international law—a paramountcy only reinforced by the development of the UN and the adoption of the Universal Declaration.[24] The great departure in practice was not perpetrated by the humanitarian relief agencies that worked in the decades following World War II, but by the nongovernmental organizations dedicated to human rights that now seek to use political means to address humanitarian emergencies. This, as David Rieff, for instance, has written, is the real new humanitarianism — relief policies predicated on taking sides, getting politically involved with one or another state or movement that is willing to sponsor relief.

The most illustrative case of the turn away from humanitarianism to a militant human-rights approach is that of Bernard Kouchner. At one time head of one of the most respected humanitarian nongovernmental organizations, Doctors without Borders (DWB), Kouchner eventually resigned because of DWB's refusal to breach its long-standing policy of neutrality between actors in political conflicts (in this case, Yugoslavia). Kouchner ended up as head of the UN-sponsored administration of Kosovo, overseeing a NATO/US occupation of that region after the withdrawal of the Yugoslav army.[25]

Two issues are central to an assessment of these differing perspectives on humanitarianism and human rights activism: (1) the value of neutrality for humanitarian organizations; and (2) the relation between humanitarian emergencies and military interventions. The view of the new human rights activists is that humanitarian organizations can never be neutral. In fact, they argue, attempts at neutrality actually play into the hands of the perpetrators of emergencies by giving them an excuse to act with impunity — since someone else (the NGOs) will deal with the consequences.[26] Furthermore, humanitarian work can only be effective if it becomes politically savvy — takes sides, condemns the perpetrators of atrocities, and fights for a political solution to the conflict. Otherwise, the aid workers (for instance) find themselves to be pawns in the hands of other political agents in conflicts — and willingly so, in order to gain access to the worst-off victims of these conflicts.

The solution: become *willing* pawns in the hands of the international community (e.g., Kouchner and the US protectorate in Kosovo)! If neutrality is a hard policy to maintain, partisanship sacrifices any ability to ameliorate the situation other than through the clear victory and dominance of one or another party to the conflict. For NGOs that forego neutrality, all their efforts are now dependent on the success, usually military, of one side. So war and occupation are now the solution to humanitarian emergencies.

This brings us to the second issue: how can war be a humanitarian solution when it is the greatest humanitarian disaster conceivable? Only a consequentialist willing to weigh the relative costs of life and death for scores of victims and potential victims of such wars or interventions could claim such a thing. Yet such calculations must be long-term ones since interventions end, while wars and their sequels can continue almost indefinitely. How can anyone calculate with confidence that some wrongdoing now will definitely result in lives saved later? Alternatively, interventions may not end (for a long time, anyway), and the new humanitarians may find themselves administering a colony of the international community that in turn must repress those within it—sometimes violating their human rights—in order to maintain control.

These quandaries suggest what the more traditional human-rights advocates view as a truism—that war is the chief cause of the loss of people's human rights in the long term and the greatest of humanitarian disasters in the short term. This is why Louis Henkin writes that

> clearly, it was the original intent of the [UN] Charter to forbid the use of force even to promote human rights. . . . Nothing has happened to justify deviations from that commitment. Human rights are indeed violated in every country. . . . But the use of force remains itself . . . the most serious . . . violation of human rights. It should not be justified by any claim that it is necessary to safeguard other human rights.[27]

The connection of the new humanitarian/human-rights activism to a renascent imperialism should now begin to come clear. It is, of course, in some sense, an old story, recalling the connection between nineteenth-century colonialism and the missionaries and abolitionists active at that time.[28] But there is a new aspect to the contemporary dilemmas of humanitarianism, having to do with a widely shared commitment to democratic legitimacy in the twentieth century. If human rights are going to be a partisan political project of states, it ought to have the assent of the peoples in whose name such states act. Yet this is rarely the case. The most important instance of such assent seems to be the European Union, which has institutionalized human rights commitments.[29] But this is largely beside the point, since such commitments apply only to member peoples and are not the basis for actions taken toward (or on) other peoples—something for which the EU has been criticized by interventionist human rights activists.

Almost by definition, *international* (or, if you prefer, universal) human rights cannot have political legitimacy in any straightforward sense—either through some form of democratic consent or by way of constitutional ratification. In either case, they cease to be international or universal, applying only to that people or peoples who have consented to or ratified them. But the point is to apply them to others who do not have such rights—or the chance to adopt them. We therefore get the unrepresentative, unaccountable agencies of NGOs and the international community attempting to represent those lacking such rights as they supposedly have. This raises problems with the very idea of human rights that we need not go into here.[30] But even such an advocate of politicized human rights as Michael Ignatieff acknowledges the contradiction with attempting to provide human rights for those who lack them: "If human rights principles exist to validate individual agency and collective rights of self-rule, then human rights practice is obliged to seek consent for its norms and to abstain from interference when consent is not freely given."[31]

Another way to put this is that if human rights are to have legitimacy—in other words, to become positive law within countries—they must be institutionalized by peoples themselves, not imposed by the international community. Such impositions, however cloaked in the language of human equality, violate a fundamental political right—that of self-determination—just as surely as military interventions to achieve these results violate the fundamental right to life of the victims of such interventions. How, we might ask, do human-rights activists avoid the obvious link between their rights advocacy and the imperial implications of utilizing hegemonic states to realize their goals?

In the case of Ignatieff, who has advocated military interventions for humanitarian purposes, it is done by acceding *some* legitimacy to sovereignty as a principle in international law. But it is of course a conditional principle—conditional on respecting human rights. Once violated, state sovereignty may be overridden if certain criteria are met. These criteria, which I will examine in more detail below, play the role of protecting interventions from the *immediate* suspicion of imperial designs. It turns out that humanitarian interventions are acceptable—are not imperialist, despite their appearances—if they are *temporary*. For instance, the intervention(s) by NATO into Yugoslavia are not imperialist if they do not result in permanent occupation (protectorates).[32]

But, as David Chandler has pointed out, the reason that such interventions occur in the first place is that the human-rights activists regard the indigenous states as untrustworthy or worse. The "humanitarian impulse" is therefore "transformed into a framework of long-term involvement, assistance, and capacity-building." As a result, humanitarian interventions end up "subordinating universal humanitarian needs to selective political ends."[33] Furthermore, denying that such interventions by the international community are imperialist is to overlook the changes in the nature of empire that have resulted from twentieth-century developments in law, communication, and warfare. These developments have altered the debate about empires and their legitimacy, not in terms of underlying principles, but in terms of the forms such empires might take.

LIBERAL IMPERIALISM AS GLOBAL GOVERNANCE

Today, it is the belief not in permanent colonies or even protectorates that is imperialist, but in the necessity of a system of global governance by which the international community enforces its norms. Advocates of global governance come in at least two varieties — the so-called cosmopolitan democracy school of David Held and Daniele Archibugi, among others, and the "one-worlders" such as Peter Singer and Thomas Pogge. Critics of global-governance schemes tend to want to reform international law in such a way as to leave intact, though modified, some principle of state sovereignty. This is the view both of some human-rights jurists such as Louis Henkin, and of political philosophers, of whom John Rawls, in his work on the "law of peoples," is the best known. The debate between these two positions reconstitutes the debate over the meaning of cosmopolitanism (whether it is moral only or also has political forms) in more concrete terms.

The views of the critics suggest that any modification of international law that opens the door to military interventions in sovereign states (except perhaps in dire emergencies) has gone too far along the road toward undermining the primary desideratum of international law — world peace. Henkin, for instance, has argued that the primary purpose (and achievement) of international law in the twentieth century has been to circumscribe the right of states to wage war for their own purposes. Allowing states to make their own judgments about whether others have violated human rights opens the door to justifying conflicts between states, rather than rendering them illegitimate.

This is so even in the case of states sponsoring terrorism against others—military interventions or attacks against such states are not acceptable.[34]

International law, in this view, is a system of norms to be acted on through persuasion and exhortation, not instrumentalized through enforcement mechanisms that inevitably will involve the discretionary determination of reasons for war by self-interested states. The history of claims of rights violations by others inevitably includes not only supposedly enlightened or civilized states that have enshrined such rights in their own constitutions but also states—notoriously including Nazi Germany in the 1930s—with long-standing territorial and other designs on neighboring countries.[35] In such cases, the idea that rights violations provided sufficient reason for military actions against other states also provided a rationale for imperialist expansion, the establishment of puppet states, colonies, protectorates, and so forth.

Even when international law is deemed ripe for reform, if it is to be kept as the primary instantiation of human-rights doctrines, the actions permissible on the basis of failure to fulfill such doctrines must be strictly circumscribed. This is one reason why Rawls's *Law of Peoples* has met with such skepticism or criticism from other liberal philosophers—because Rawls does advocate such limits, and it is these limits that make it hard for the international community to force states to conform to liberal (especially human-rights) doctrines. Rawls uses the idea of "decent" societies as ones that, while not liberal—and perhaps not abiding by an expanded list of human rights—nevertheless are legitimate actors in international relations and worthy of respect under international law.[36] Such societies may not be democratic—they may even be theocratic. But as long as they do not commit the most egregious violations of basic rights, they are considered legitimate, at least *internationally*.[37] This distinction is quite out of favor with many liberals today because they want to extend their doctrines and schemes universally, by virtually any means necessary. It is this matter of how to institutionalize liberal doctrines, especially those of human rights, that makes liberal internationalists at least potential imperialists.

There are two ways in which such a view gets expressed. On the one hand, there are those who advocate comprehensive, universal schemes of global justice, often including some notion of human rights, and that therefore need to provide some idea as to how such schemes might be actualized. On the other hand, there are those who advocate a global governance scheme for its own sake, that is, so that certain specifically political values may be realized on a global scale.

In the first case, the idea is that conceptions of human rights (for instance) are essentially universal and therefore require universal political institutions to realize them across the globe. This is a popular idea with those who in particular advocate schemes of global resource or income redistribution, often based on a right to a minimum income. For them, global governance may begin with a "value overlap" (embodied in "ethical dialogue") between different, like-minded countries.[38] These can serve as a nucleus for an ever-expanding array of states that have endorsed such rights. Of course, this immediately raises a question about the relation of these countries to those who do not endorse such rights — a question these liberal theorists are sometimes reluctant to answer.

Alternatively, global governance may take the form of revised and strengthened international institutions, above all the UN. These institutions would then be in a position to enforce global norms. This view takes it for granted that the weakened role of the UN and other international institutions in recent years — and their increasing subservience to US foreign policy objectives — is a fact of no essential importance. What, then, remains is to ask how much progress could be made to create such institutions of global governance. The answer is that though, to date, there is little evidence of their practicability or probability, such institutions are not impossible and, in any case, are morally mandated.[39]

But perhaps the good of global governance lies not in its instrumental value but in its basis as itself a human right, for instance, to self-rule. This is the view of the cosmopolitan democrats who advocate democratizing institutions such as the UN.[40] The chief problem with this view is that it avoids facing the primary fact about such institutions — not their undemocratic nature, but their weakness in the face of the hegemonic dominance of the United States. Democratizing an already weak institution will not have the effect of providing a new means of realizing human-rights claims. Rather, it may have no discernible effect at all. The outcome of cosmopolitan democracy will not be an international regime of human rights — though it may provide a more attractive facade for the absence of such a regime.

As Michael Walzer, a more realistic commentator on — yet still an advocate of — schemes of global governance, has written, there just are no useful precedents for how such schemes will come about. As he puts it, "the kinds of governmental agencies that are needed in an age of globalization haven't yet been developed; the level of participation in international civil society is much too low; regional federations are still in their beginning stages."[41] Yet the willingness of liberals to advocate such schemes continues. What, we may ask, is their ultimate import, if not to justify *substitutes* for such schemes? And what better substitute than a benevolent (or potentially benevolent) hegemonic state that is willing, at least occasionally, to intervene in the ostensible pursuit of human-rights goals?

FROM HEGEMONY TO EMPIRES, INFORMAL OR FORMAL

The liberal case for empire is not a straightforward one, by any means. Rather, it proceeds by a series of steps from a commitment to human rights (or other liberal values) to advocacy of its international enforcement to justification for interventions to do this and finally to authorization for the political agents capable of so intervening and enforcing these liberal norms. It is the last step that we have still to consider. Two aspects of political agency are important here: who is to be so authorized to act to enforce liberal norms globally, and what exactly should they be authorized to do?

Let's take the second aspect—that of the ends or goals of liberal interventions—first. Returning to Ignatieff and his advocacy of humanitarian interventions, he notes the following criteria that he asserts must apply in order to justify them: (1) the existence of human rights abuses; (2) their constituting a threat to international peace and security (in the region); (3) the possibility that military action *can* end the abuses; and, in addition, a de facto fourth criterion, "the region in question must be of vital interest . . . to one of the powerful nations of the world and another powerful nation does not oppose the exercise of force."[42] About these criteria in general Ignatieff makes the point that, without them, and without a mechanism to act on them, those who wish to intervene will go ahead and do so anyway. But this will make interventions less legitimate and, therefore, less successful.[43] Success is obviously essential here, for if the third criterion cannot be met, intervention would not be justified. How this criterion could be met I will discuss in a moment. But the fourth de facto criterion is the crucial one: even given the intent to utilize the UN, at least as an authorizing body, for legitimate interventions, intervention still requires the agency of a hegemonic power to go forward. This is the imperialist criterion: if it is only pursuant to the interest of powerful states that interventions can be successful, then such actions are essentially, however liberals may otherwise view them, equivalent to imperialist actions.

Ignatieff certainly does not see them this way. For him, it is very much how the interventions *end* that determines their imperialistic or nonimperialistic character. Discussing NATO's Kosovo intervention, he writes that "an indefinite protectorate amounts to imperialism, and this violates the anti-imperial ethos of our human rights commitment."[44] But this comes at the end of a passage in which he reflects that such a protectorate is probably the necessary element to making such intervention a success. Otherwise, withdrawal would amount to leaving the region in worse shape than before the intervention, with all the attendant conflicts reappearing, perhaps inflamed by the violence done by the intervention itself, plus the existence of a power vacuum and the anarchy and further violence resulting from that. As Ignatieff himself puts it, "Today . . . the chief threat to human rights comes not from tyranny alone, but from civil war and anarchy." And he adds, "It can be said with certainty that the liberties of citizens are better protected by their own institutions than by the well-meaning interventions of outsiders."[45]

Given this candid assessment, why then do Ignatieff and other liberals insist on the legitimacy of interventions? Because "something must be done" — the very idea of human rights suggests, for them, its universalization by any means necessary. The only problem is the one of the endgame — are the means employed *ultimately* inconsistent with the ends sought? Not if self-government is the end result, so that peoples can protect their own rights. So we enter on the murky ground of regime change and state building, to use the current jargon. Military interventions and UN protectorates are legitimate if they are used as means to reconstruct governments into liberal states. We have now come full circle to the nineteenth-century Millian argument for empires.

Is there any way out of this dilemma for liberal theory? Current attempts focus on the first aspect of the problem of political agency to enact global, liberal norms, the question of who is to be authorized to act. Two approaches have been used to try and solve this problem — one is that of establishing a legitimate hegemony, and the other is that of using a collective form of authorization. The first has been argued for by Lea Brilmayer in her book *American*

Hegemony, the second most recently by Allen Buchanan in his work *Justice, Legitimacy, and Self-Determination*.

Brilmayer contends that despite the obvious asymmetries and abuses of power that hegemonic states such as the United States exercise, it is still the case that "hegemony also creates the *opportunity* for political morality."[46] Great powers have their own goals; but to the extent that they are truly hegemonic, they also increasingly become susceptible to appeals from subordinate parties and peoples. Great powers can allow for benevolence in a way that contested and beleaguered powers cannot.

But beyond this psychological insight, if it is that, is Brilmayer's assertion that international relations are not best understood as relations between equal (and equally legitimate) states. They consist not of horizontal relations between (formally) equal states, but of vertical (and unequal) relations between hegemonic and subordinate entities. In this respect, international relations are similar to relations between governments and citizens within states. The important consequence of this view is that just as we can make ethical judgments about the responsibilities of a government to its citizens, so we can make similar judgments about the responsibilities of hegemonic powers toward their subordinates in the international system. Some hegemons may be legitimate and others not, in other words — as Brilmayer puts it, all political philosophies (except anarchism) include concepts of "justified hierarchy."[47] Hegemonic states can be held to standards and expected to take actions that are ethically legitimate, just as governments can be.

While this may be true, it is also the case that providing hegemonic states with *additional* opportunities for mischief (as well as morality) seems to be a bad move. Rather, the actions of hegemons ought to be restricted so that the opportunities they have to act morally or otherwise will be tested as little as possible. This is, in fact, the purpose of adherence to international law, which seeks to restrict such opportunities for power to be exercised (whether for good or bad). Yet this is the conservative view that has so disturbed liberals intent on realizing their global agenda. Liberalism seems to entail the hope that the powerful can be persuaded to use their power for liberal ends — but in any case, that if they do not in one or another instance, this is no reason for restricting that power. Better to have an empire that *could* be used for good ends than to have no means of directly achieving these ends at all.

But if we cannot reasonably expect hegemons to act morally, yet cannot give up on a global human-rights regime, perhaps hegemonic power can be tamed through the medium of collective agency. Allen Buchanan has given the most recent argument for this widely held hope—that there ought to be criteria for intervention in cases of human rights abuse, criteria that can either be acted on by international agencies or, failing that, by states collectively authorized by such agencies. This view has also been given expression in the widely read report *The Responsibility to Protect*, written by an international commission supported by the Canadian government.[48]

Buchanan's argument is that if appropriate international institutions and regulations are in place and operating, then sanctioning interventions will be procedurally legitimate and not subject to the dictates of hegemonic powers. Conversely, refusing to sanction interventions at all will actually allow greater discretion for states, especially hegemonic ones, to intervene at will.[49] But there are obvious problems with such a view of collective authorization for interventions. What guarantee of impartiality do we have for international organizations that have historically been more or less willing to sanction any actions that hegemonic powers undertake? There just is no procedural guarantee that collectively authorizing interventions will be any less imperialist than the unilateral actions that have been taken. Furthermore, institutionalizing authorization for interventions risks turning organizations officially committed to pursuing peace and security into war-making entities who sanction hegemonic powers in pursuit of their own ends. As Lori Damrosch has written of the effect of such a change, "international law would ironically be transformed from a system of restraints on transboundary projections of military power into a system of affirmative approval for achieving political objectives through forcible means."[50]

Historians have noted that the nineteenth-century colonial empires were not for the most part created according to a well-defined plan for imperial domination of the non-European world.[51] European powers gradually, for a variety of reasons, and in a variety of ways, acquired in some ways unprecedented power over peoples and countries well removed from their traditional spheres of political influence and even from their areas of interest. That this could happen again—and may be happening today—suggests that a justification for empire need not be an explicit one. Rather, it can be put together from a number of related notions that imply the possible, conditional desirability of imperial administration and control of other countries. It is instructive to note that recent tendencies in liberal political philosophy, itself hegemonic intellectually since the end of the Cold War, may be contributing, however unintentionally, to just such an eventuality.

IS THERE AN ALTERNATIVE TO LIBERAL IMPERIALISM?

Is there any way to avoid this eventuality? Of course, empires fall as well as rise. Furthermore, as I have hoped to show, the liberal justification for empires —and it is the chief one used historically and at present—is problematic due to its contradictory attempt to use humanitarian considerations as an argument for what are essentially antihumanitarian actions. The political cosmopolitanism that leads, as I have suggested, to a liberal defense of empires becomes either a failed project—due to the unrealizability of the global institutions that it advocates—or an opportunistic accommodation to the designs of hegemonic states.

So the first possible alternative to liberal imperialism lies in rejecting cosmopolitanism as a political project and reconstituting liberalism as a *moral* philosophy.[52] We may just all be *moral* cosmopolitans now, in the sense that the idea of a universal claim of all human beings to equal respect is a bedrock principle for conservative, liberal, and radical thinkers alike (one exception would no doubt be avowed theocrats, who would privilege members of their own faith over others). But realizing such a bedrock principle politically is where the controversies really begin.

If liberalism is worth maintaining as a *political* philosophy as well, it would be as a much more circumscribed one than the globalists and nascent liberal imperialists would consider acceptable. This is the interest of Rawls's late work on international ethics, work that has angered so many of his followers, as well as others not already committed to a Rawlsian contractualism. While Rawls still voices the principles of a liberal philosophy that he had characterized earlier as a political liberalism, he deliberately refuses to apply the contractual apparatus of his early theory to the global scale, or indeed to advocate global institutions that could realize the robust program of distributive justice and maximalist human rights many of his former followers espouse. While remaining a liberal constitutionalist and moral cosmopolitan, Rawls is a conservative internationally, because he continues to accept a conditional principle of state sovereignty and rejects grandiose schemes for global governance and redistribution.

But this conservatism is at the same time the only philosophy consistent with a real commitment to the principle of political self-determination that underlay the anticolonial movements of the early twentieth century. It is this principle of political or popular self-determination — of a continuing advocacy of the idea of rule by the people, both internally and externally — that has been and remains the true basis of antihegemonic politics. Of course, the liberal imperialist might argue that a benign neo-imperial imposition of liberal values (i.e., human rights) is preferable to the toleration of dictatorial and illiberal regimes — Baathist Iraq being the current paradigmatic example of such a regime.[53] In fact, as Jack Donnelly has candidly affirmed, human rights themselves serve not only as a means of arguing for the satisfaction of important human needs but also as a standard of political legitimacy that can be used against illiberal states.[54]

But state building by foreign military occupation is a notoriously difficult, if not impossible, enterprise; and in any case, it is contradictory to the principle of self-determination that it is ostensibly designed to serve. As we saw above, liberals such as Ignatieff attempt to avoid this contradiction by arguing, as Mill did before them, for a quick invasion, a brief occupation, and so on. But, as David Chandler noted, if the existing state is so bankrupt that it merits violent overthrow, what assurance is there that it could be replaced with a more liberal one with any ease or speed, especially given the decimation of civil society that such a state may have caused? So if liberalism is to eschew the imperialist temptation, it must also give up on the project of creating liberal states by force, accepting the modest principles of solidarity with and (mutual) aid between peoples.

But what about the protection of human rights, a principle that seems to be essential to liberal philosophy? If liberalism is to be rescued, it must accept the limitations of the minimalist interpretation of human rights — the bare or basic set of rights that could be said to be most inextricably linked with the material survival of persons and peoples (for instance, rights to the preservation of life, liberty of thought, security of personal property, and the prevention of discriminatory treatment). But even here, with this basic list, it is important that the traditional humanitarian philosophy of emergency aid and relief again be recognized as the appropriate response in all but perhaps the most egregious cases of rights violation (in other words, while still leaving room for what might be called a genocide exception).

Just as with the political cosmopolitan belief that justice can be done globally if only an appropriate agent could be found (and why not a hegemonic state with the power to do this?), so it is with the human rights activists' belief that all wrongs can be righted. The approaches of solidarity with the oppressed and aid to the suffering are the true methods of the moral cosmopolitan. The Faustian bargains with hegemonic states that some hope might break the grip of dictatorial regimes and neglectful societies only lead to other forms of dictatorship (imperial rather than local) or neglect of human needs (capitalist rather than neofeudal).

It is likely, however, that, with the lonely exception of Rawls and a few others, liberalism has gone too far down the road of globalist and maximalist temptations to retreat from its flirtation with empire. It may well be that only a new radical philosophy of needs, rather than a liberal philosophy of rights, however circumscribed, can address the tremendous problems of a world growing more oppressive and inequitable. As Chandler mentions in relation to humanitarianism, it is the substitution of an *ideal*, that of human rights, for a material reality, that of unmet needs, that is the real meaning of the shift away from the old humanitarian emphasis on emergency relief and to a neo-imperial politics of state building.

It is a task for the future to recreate such a radical philosophy of needs satisfaction that does not get lost in the contradictions of liberal rights theory —and to embody this philosophy in a new form of political action. After all, it may have been that the collapse of the Soviet Union signaled not only the end of a state that occasionally played a counterhegemonic role to US global dominance but also to the patent absence of any concrete form of international solidarity, socialist or otherwise. The belief of many formerly radical activists that first NGOs, then international organizations such as the UN, and finally, a hegemonic state bent on overthrowing local tyrannies could serve as a vehicle for their emancipatory hopes must surely have been a reaction to this collapse and absence. If we cannot yet discern the shape of new forms of global solidarity and activism (though there may be some indications of it in the current global justice movements), we can at least insist on the ethically stringent position of defending the independence and integrity of peoples. However unpalatable certain regimes or societies may be at times, finding the means to express solidarity with and give aid to their peoples is preferable to acquiescing in the politics of war making and empire building, even when given a liberal veneer of progress and enlightenment.

NOTES

1. See Niall Ferguson, *Empire: The Rise and Demise of the British World Order* (New York: Basic Books, 2002), 364–67.
2. Ibid., 370.
3. Neil Smith, *The Endgame of Globalization* (New York: Routledge, 2005), 29.
4. Julie Mertus, *Bait and Switch: Human Rights and U.S. Foreign Policy* (New York: Routledge, 2004), 121–24.
5. See Michael W. Doyle, *Empires* (Ithaca, NY: Cornell University Press, 1986), 54–81.
6. See especially, Emily Rosenberg, *Financial Missionaries to the World: The Politics and Culture of Dollar Diplomacy, 1900–1930* (Cambridge, MA: Harvard University Press, 1999), as well as Neil Smith, *American Empire: Roosevelt's Geographer and the Prelude to Globalization* (Berkeley: University of California Press, 2003).
7. Ferguson, *Empire*, 368; about the "empire of bases," see Chalmers Johnson, *The Sorrows of Empire: Militarism, Secrecy, and the End of the Republic* (New York: Metropolitan Books, 2004), especially ch. 6.
8. Lord Acton, "Nationality," in *History of Freedom and Other Essays* (Salem, NH: Ayer, 1907), reprinted in Omar Dahbour and Micheline R. Ishay, eds., *The Nationalism Reader* (Atlantic Highlands, NJ: Humanities Press, 1995), 108–18.
9. John Stuart Mill, *Considerations on Representative Government* (Amherst, NY: Prometheus, [1861] 1991), chaps. 16, 18.
10. Uday Singh Mehta, *Liberalism and Empire: A Study in Nineteenth-Century British Liberal Thought* (Chicago: University of Chicago Press, 1999), 81, 105.
11. For a recent statement of the critique, see Chris Brown, "Universal Human Rights: A Critique," in *Human Rights in Global Politics*, ed. Tim Dunne and Nicholas J. Wheeler (Cambridge: Cambridge University Press, 1999), 103–27; for an early response to the relativist challenge, see James W. Nickel, *Making Sense of Human Rights: Philosophical Reflections on the "Universal Declaration of Human Rights"* (Berkeley: University of California Press, 1987), ch. 4; and for a more thorough rejoinder, see Jack Donnelly, *Universal Human Rights in Theory and Practice* (Ithaca, NY: Cornell University Press, 1989), part 3.
12. For the constructivist view, see Donnelly, *Universal Human Rights*, part 1; for the naturalist view, see Alan Gewirth, *The Community of Rights* (Chicago: University of Chicago Press, 1996).
13. Nickel, Donnelly, and Gewirth, among many others, advocate a maximalist view. Henry

Shue and John Rawls, on the other hand, emphasize the basic rights; see Henry Shue, *Basic Rights: Subsistence, Affluence, and U.S. Foreign Policy* (Princeton, NJ: Princeton University Press, 1980); and John Rawls, *The Law of Peoples* (Cambridge, MA: Harvard University Press, 1999), especially 65.

14. Donnelly, *Universal Human Rights*, 18.

15. On this idea, see Hannah Arendt, *The Origins of Totalitarianism*, new ed. (New York: Harcourt Brace Jovanovich, 1973), 290–99, especially 296.

16. Thomas W. Pogge, *Realizing Rawls* (Ithaca, NY: Cornell University Press, 1989), part 3.

17. Peter Singer, *One World: The Ethics of Globalization* (New Haven, CT: Yale University Press, 2002), especially chaps. 4, 5.

18. Michael Ignatieff, *Human Rights as Politics and Idolatry* (Princeton, NJ: Princeton University Press, 2001), 37.

19. See, for example, Jarat Chopra and Thomas G. Weiss, "Sovereignty Is No Longer Sacrosanct: Codifying Humanitarian Intervention," *Ethics and International Affairs* 6 (1992): 95–118; and David J. Scheffer, "Toward a Modern Doctrine of Humanitarian Intervention," *University of Toledo Law Review* 23, no.2 (1992): 253–93.

20. Theodor Meron, "The Humanization of Humanitarian Law," *American Journal of International Law* 94, no. 2 (2000): 240.

21. Alain Destexhe, "The Shortcomings of the 'New Humanitarianism,'" in *Between Sovereignty and Good Governance: The United Nations, the State, and Civil Society*, ed. Albert Paolini, Anthony Jarvis, and Christian Reus-Smit (New York: St. Martin's, 1998), 85.

22. Ibid., 86.

23. Ibid., 98.

24. Louis Henkin, "The Use of Force: Law and U.S. Policy," in *Right v. Might: International Law and the Use of Force*, by Henkin et al. (New York: Council on Foreign Relations Press, 1989), 38.

25. See David Rieff, *A Bed for the Night: Humanitarianism in Crisis* (New York: Simon and Schuster, 2002), 97–100, 216–17.

26. Ibid., ch. 3.

27. Henkin, "Use of Force," 61.

28. See Rieff, *Bed for the Night*, ch. 2.

29. See Louis Henkin, *The Age of Rights* (New York: Columbia University Press, 1990), 23–24.

30. See, for example, Douglas N. Husak, "Why There Are No Human Rights," *Social Theory and Practice* 10, no. 2 (1984): 125–41.

31. Ignatieff, *Human Rights*, 18.

32. Ibid., 46.

33. David Chandler, "The Road to Military Humanitarianism: How the Human Rights NGOs Shaped a New Humanitarian Agenda," *Human Rights Quarterly* 21, no. 3 (2001): 693–94.

34. Henkin, "Use of Force," 62.

35. See John Rosenthal, "Kosovo and 'the Jewish Question,'" *Monthly Review* 51, no. 9 (2000): 36–39.

36. See Rawls, *Law of Peoples*, 59–88, on this distinction between decent and liberal peoples.

37. Rawls uses a distinction between external (international) and internal sovereignty that may not be familiar to many. Internal sovereignty or legitimacy is a separate matter from whether states are recognized members of international society, and therefore able to claim the rights of territorial integrity and sovereignty that such members are accorded. On this distinction, see M. H. Hinsley, *Sovereignty*, 2nd ed. (Cambridge: Cambridge University Press, 1986), especially 158.

38. Thomas Pogge, "Moral Progress," in *Problems of International Justice*, ed. Steven Luper-Foy (Boulder, CO: Westview, 1988), 290–91.

39. Singer, *One World*, 196–99; Thomas Pogge, "The Moral Demands of Global Justice," *Dissent* 47, no. 4 (2000): 42.

40. See Daniele Archibugi, David Held, and Martin Köhler, eds., *Re-imagining Political Community: Studies in Cosmopolitan Democracy* (Stanford, CA: Stanford University Press, 1998).

41. Michael Walzer, "Governing the Globe: What Is the Best We Can Do?" *Dissent* 47, no. 4 (2000): 52.

42. Ignatieff, *Human Rights*, 40.

43. Ibid., 43.

44. Ibid., 46.

45. Ibid., 35.

46. Lea Brilmayer, *American Hegemony: Political Morality in a One-Superpower World* (New Haven, CT: Yale University Press, 1994), 224; emphasis added.

47. Ibid., 26.

48. International Commission on Intervention and State Sovereignty, *The Responsibility to Protect* (Ottawa: International Development Research Centre, 2001).

49. Allen Buchanan, *Justice, Legitimacy, and Self-Determination: Moral Foundations for International Law* (Oxford: Oxford University Press, 2004), 180.

50. Lori Fisler Damrosch, "Commentary on Collective Military Intervention to Enforce Human Rights," in *Law and Force in the New International Order*, ed. Damrosch and David J. Scheffer (Boulder, CO: Westview, 1991), 220.

51. Ferguson, *Empire*, 368.

52. Two recent books may be seen as attempts to reformulate liberalism in just this way: Charles Taylor, *The Ethics of Ambiguity* (Cambridge, MA: Harvard University Press, 1991); and Anthony Appiah, *The Ethics of Identity* (Princeton, NJ: Princeton University Press, 2005).

53. Thomas M. Franck, "Intervention against Illegitimate Regimes," in Damrosch and Scheffer, *Law and Force*, 159–76.

54. Jack Donnelly, *Universal Human Rights*, 43.

2 Engendering Imperialism

CYNTHIA ENLOE

Updating the Gendered Empire: Where Are the Women of Occupied Afghanistan and Iraq?

Empire. Until not long ago, the study of empires was the purview of academic historians. Some historians, though, especially male historians, recently managed to draw considerable attention from thoughtful magazines and television's serious talk shows for their hefty new and reissued books on empire.[1] Sales figures began to rise and media invitations rolled in. Readers and viewers were beginning to look for parallels to contemporary international affairs. We often try to sort out puzzles by thinking through analogies. Analogies are powerful. If we get our analogies wrong, our explanations are likely to be askew. In the wake of the US military invasions of Afghanistan in 2001 and of Iraq in 2003, those experts invited to speak in the public arena began to summon British and even Roman history in order to ask: Are we today seeing the emergence of a new empire?

As the US-led wars in Afghanistan and Iraq dragged on, there were good reasons not only for media commentators and political decision makers but also for ordinary citizens to become curious about past experiences of empire. History teachers began to feel vindicated. Victorian wasn't just stuffy furniture. Caesar wasn't just a salad dressing.

Does the global reach of the present United States military, political, cultural, and economic influence have the cohesiveness, the expansiveness and the sustainability to amount to an empire? Or, to put it more concretely: If we compare the US role in the world today—its invasions and political occupations of Afghanistan and Iraq; its diplomatic roles in the former Yugoslavia and Liberia; its global network of military bases stretching from North Carolina and San Diego to Guam, South Korea, Okinawa, Uzbekistan, Kuwait, Iraq, Turkey, Bosnia, Germany, and Britain; its refusal to ratify a host of new international treaties; its manufacturing, trading, and banking practices from Poland to Indonesia—with those military, cultural, economic, and diplomatic practices of earlier Roman, Persian, Habsburg, Ottoman, British, Belgian, Russian, Chinese, Japanese, US, French, Spanish, and Dutch empires, do we risk comparing an orange with apples? Or are we perhaps on firmer ground, comparing a new apple with a host of earlier apples?

Despite their remarkable absence from interview shows and op-ed pages, scores of feminist historians have given us fresh and detailed accounts of how women and notions of femininity, both, were pressed into service by earlier empire builders. Where were the women? Thanks to three decades of sleuthing by feminist historians, we now know where to point our analytical binoculars. We know not to look just at the gilded diplomatic halls, the bloody battlefields, and the floors of stock exchanges. We have been taught by these pioneering feminist historians to point our glasses further afield. If groundbreaking feminist historians—Philippa Levine, Piya Chatterjee, Kumari Jaywaradena, and others—were invited to submit feature articles and to give mainstream media interviews, they would urge us to look instead inside brothels, to peer into respectable parlors, to press our noses against the sooty windows of factories, and to keep an eye on sexual relations on rubber plantations.[2] All of these sites, it turns out, though far from the official centers of imperial power, have been sites of empire making. That is, empires are built in parlors. Empires are built in brothels. Empires are built in allegedly private places. If this is so, then we have to examine the current possibility of a US imperial enterprise from the vantage points of parlors and brothels too. To make sense of putative American empire building, we will have to become much more curious. We will have to become curious about the marriage aspirations of factory women, about the household dynamics inside soldiers' families, about the sexual policies of the US occupying forces based in Afghanistan, Uzbekistan, Iraq, and Kuwait. And that is just the beginning. Reports now labeled human-interest stories will have to be considered serious commentaries on foreign policy.

These thoughtful, worldly feminist investigators have also shown us how diverse and complex women's actions and feelings have been within empires. Women as tea pickers, women as nannies, women as teachers, women as wives, women as explorers, women as missionaries, women as activist reformers, women as mothers, women as educators, women as mistresses, women as prostitutes, women as textile factory workers, women as writers, women as overseas settlers, women as anticolonial nationalists—each in their own way played crucial, yet overlooked, roles in greasing (or clogging) the wheels of an imperial enterprise. The roles each of these groups of women played were crucial because so many empire builders designed international power-extension strategies that relied on particular ideas about where different sorts of women were "naturally" meant to be. The imperial strategists may have been men, but they were men who thought (and worried) a lot about women. The imperial strategists—and their male opponents too—may constantly have weighed varieties of masculinity, but they could only do so by trying to rank and manipulate the varieties of femininity.[3]

By their not asking about women in this current possibly imperial enterprise—except, that is, for the Western media's seeming addiction to the visual image of the veiled Muslim woman—the commentators capturing the current public limelight are making themselves as men inside empires, as well as other men and masculinities in empires, virtually invisible. Feminists all over the world have learned how risky *those* sins of omission can be.

WILL THE WOMEN STAND UP?

In the 1980s, at a meeting up in Happy Valley, Labrador, a group of Native Canadian women of the Innu community brought together several dozen women, mostly from other parts of Canada, to discuss the effects that a NATO air force base was having on their lives. The term *empire* was not used. Yet fueling this collective conversation was a shared feminist curiosity about how unequal international power relations between allied masculinized governments depend not only on certain relationships between men but also on global presumptions about where women will be—and where they should stay. The Innu women were helping us to "unpack" NATO.

One morning the Innu organizers cleared the meeting hall of chairs and asked each of us to imagine ourselves being a particular woman playing a role, maybe even unconsciously, in sustaining, questioning, or resisting this NATO air force base. As each of us thought of a woman, we took on her persona, spoke to the group in the first person as that woman, and joined others sitting on the floor. The floor soon became a complex world of militarized relationships between diverse women. Within an hour that late winter morning—it was April, but the ice was just receding on the nearby lake—we had populated the wooden floor with women from Canada, the United States, Britain, and Germany, with women married to air force officers, local Innu girls dating young fliers, other Innu women camping on the NATO runways to protest low-flying training flights, Canadian feminists in Toronto unaware of the Canadian government's alliance policies in supposedly remote Labrador, women from the Philippines eager to share their own experiences of foreign military bases, and more.

More recently in Tokyo and Okinawa, groups of us tried a similar feminist exercise, one inspired by the Innu activists' innovation. Our aim also was to make women visible in international power politics. We sought to piece together a map of where women are in sustaining, questioning, and resisting the unequal United States–Japan military alliance. Any assessment of American empire building today must look closely at the dynamics sustaining this unequal alliance. This time we could not move the furniture, since we were in a lecture hall at Ochanomizu University, so we stood up. Women and men in the audience, one by one, imagined themselves a particular woman living her life inside this alliance. As we took on the persona of a particular woman, we got onto her feet and spoke to the rest of us:

> I am an African American young woman proud to be serving in the US Marines stationed in Okinawa; thank God, I didn't take that job at Wal-Mart.
>
> I am an Okinawan woman, and I think I'm becoming what you might call an Okinawan nationalist because I'm growing more resentful of officials in Tokyo government who routinely override our Okinawan concerns when they agree to allow so many US bases to operate here on our land.
>
> I am a Japanese mainland young college graduate. As a woman, I've decided that enlisting in the Japanese Self-Defense Force will offer me more career opportunities than a dead-end job of working as a corporate office lady.

As some people stood up, others in the audience began to think of more women whose feelings, ideas, and actions were shaping—though scarcely controlling — the current US-Japanese military alliance, a government-to-government agreement that was projecting American military dominance throughout Asia and the Pacific and as far away as Afghanistan. Our "map" was becoming bigger and more complicated with every person who stood up:

> I am a Yokohama high school student; my friends and I are dating American sailors to improve our English.
>
> I am a dairy farmer in Kyushu. I care personally about Article 9, the peace article of the Japanese Constitution, so, in between my daily milkings and stall muckings, I write a small newsletter to tell other Japanese what it means to live next to a fighter air base. One Friday a month, I go sit outside the gates of the SDF [Self-Defense Force] fighter plane base; sometimes a dozen people come to join me; other times, I'm sitting there all alone.

Over on the other side of the hall another Japanese young woman then stood up: "I am an American white woman married to a US Navy officer. I'm surprised that the Navy's family housing here in Japan is so much nicer than what I had to endure at the base back in the US. Maybe I'll urge my husband to reenlist after all." Then another: "I'm one of those guides you see up in the front of tourist buses all over Okinawa; but recently I've retrained myself to become what's called a 'peace guide.' Now as my tourist bus travels around the countryside, I point out to visitors all the good farmland and beautiful coastal beaches that have been taken over by American military bases." Way in the back a young man stood up: "I'm just a housewife. My husband runs a small construction company, which makes me feel so nervous because the Japanese economy has been in recession now for over a decade. I don't like our government offering to send Japanese soldiers to help the Americans occupy Iraq, but I feel relieved that my husband's company just won a government contract to build a new road leading to a US base. How should I reconcile my mixed feelings?" A graduate student at a Tokyo university was sitting toward the front of the room. She waited until the end and then stood up. She turned around to look at others in the large lecture hall:

> I'm just starting my doctoral dissertation in political science. There aren't many Japanese women teaching international relations, so to get a university job, I'll need to have the full support of my dissertation super-

visor. He's quite well known in the field. Listening to everyone talk here tonight, I now want to change my dissertation research focus so I can look at the lives of Japanese girls and women living near a military base. I want to find out how they relate to the base and what that means for how they imagine themselves in Japanese political life. But my faculty supervisor won't think that asking these questions amounts to doing "real" international politics. How can I persuade him?

These collective acts of Innu, Okinawan, and Tokyo feminist imaginations revealed to all of us who took part several important political realities. Each revelation is relevant to our current thinking about where women are in the pursuing—or subverting—of any imperial enterprise. First, women are intimately engaged in the little-noticed daily workings of those unequal international military alliances that form the backbone of nascent or mature empire building. Second, women's roles in these large structures of international power are far from uniform. In fact, some of these women might view some of the other women engaged in the same global structure as too remote or too unsympathetic due to their class, ethnic, national, and ideological locations, or even just due to their jobs, to be potential partners. This despite the fact that some of these women live their daily lives within just a mile of each other. Third, every one of these women, nonetheless, are where they are on the globalized political map because of dominant notions about femininity and ideas about how they, as women or girls, should relate to men and to masculinized foreign policies. Fourth, many women are privately ambivalent about the complicit roles they play in these unequal international power structures; some of them are actively self-conscious about their ambivalence. Fifth, while most of these women never make the headlines, they are counted on by foreign policy makers to keep playing their supportive, or at least passive, roles: today's international unequal alliances depend on that.

AFGHAN WOMEN STAND UP

While spending several months at Tokyo's Ochanomizu University in early 2003, as the Bush administration mobilized to invade Iraq, I had the good fortune to meet and listen to one of the handful of Afghan women appointed to a senior post in the interim government created in the wake of the US-led military invasion of Afghanistan. She herself was not a cabinet minister; only two of the twenty-seven members chosen for cabinet posts in the interim administration of president Hamid Karzai were women. But she was a deputy minister, with considerable responsibility for shaping the policies and institutions of the post-Taliban state. She was now in her fifties and had been a professional woman before the Taliban's ascendancy. Before that she had fought with the insurgent Afghan mujahideen forces against the occupying Soviet army. As this story will suggest, it seems wise even today not to mention her name or even her precise post. She was in Tokyo at the invitation of the Japanese government, especially of Japanese women working inside the government's overseas aid program, a program coordinated with the United Nations relief efforts in the postinvasion, post-Taliban Afghanistan.

While passionate about the need to invest in girls' and women's training and empowerment, this Afghan woman official did not see herself as a natural ally of the Afghan women's organization best known outside of the country, the Revolutionary Association of the Women of Afghanistan, or RAWA.[4] Afghans (like the Vietnamese, Filipinos, and Tanzanians) have experienced not just one but several waves of imperialist occupation: Persian, British, Russian, and now American. Creating a sense of national identity in countries such as Afghanistan has meant for many women advocates crafting comparative judgments about both past and present foreign rulers and about rival male-led local parties, each claiming to represent the nation, each claiming to know what is best for the nation's women.

One activist woman's savvy use of openings created by the latest occupying power looks to another activist woman like collaboration with the enemy, betrayal of the nation. Neither woman controls the masculinized political contest. Having to make such choices, often in the midst of war, displacement, and confusion, does not breed trust among women. Thus this woman as a deputy minister, so eager for support in her efforts on behalf of girls' and women's empowerment in the midst of the US-led occupation, voiced distrust of the women active in RAWA. She doubted their local and international politics, even though RAWA's women activists had taken risks to do this work, as she also had, both inside Afghanistan during the Taliban's rule and in the increasingly politicized male-run refugee camps over the border in Pakistan.[5] She imagined, nevertheless, that the women active in RAWA had been too sympathetic to Kabul's 1980s Soviet-backed secular regime. So today, during the current US-backed regime, this woman was not only seething with frustration at the patriarchal resistance she encounters daily from the men at the top of the Karzai regime; she is simultaneously keeping an arm's length distance from the activist women of RAWA. Imperialism does this. It can send out fissures among the advocates of women's rights.

During one of the Tokyo discussions, the Japanese woman who hosted this Afghan deputy minister whispered, "In all the times I have met with her in Kabul, I have never seen her smile." Now, after two weeks in secure Tokyo, enjoying daily conversations with Japanese specialists on women's and girls' health, economy, politics, and education, she seemed to be letting down her guard. She dared to smile. She even made a joke. She had good reason, though, to maintain her deadpan game face when she did her risky work in Kabul. Not long before, her son had been beaten severely on a street in Kabul by a group of unidentified men. Before he lost consciousness, his assailants warned him, "Tell your mother to get out of the place where she doesn't belong." The message was clear: a year and a half after the US military's and their Northern Alliance partners' toppling of the Taliban regime, any woman who dared to take on a modicum of political authority was still endangering not only herself but members of her family as well. This woman was not easily cowed. Following her son's beating, she became angrier, and even more committed. But smiling was a luxury that an activist woman still could ill afford in Kabul.

Security

Security — how to measure it, who gets to define it — has been a major issue during the US-led occupation of Afghanistan. It was in the name of what it called the pursuit of national security that the Bush administration had mounted its invasion of Afghanistan in 2001. In the months following the invasion, now in the name of concentrating its own military forces on combat missions to eliminate the remnants of both the Taliban's and al-Qaeda's armed forces, the US government rejected repeated requests by the UN secretary-general, international relief agencies, the Karzai administration, and local Afghan women's groups to extend the reach of the international peacekeeping force — a NATO force, though nominally operating under a UN mandate — beyond the city limits of Kabul. The woman deputy minister told her Japanese hosts that one reason it was proving so difficult to achieve genuine parity between newly recruited male and female teachers was that many men in government claimed that the school districts outside of the capital remained too dangerous for women teachers and principals to be appointed.

Danger

When governments claim danger, the deepening of masculinized authority typically follows.

Combat

Combat as an allegedly distinct mission has always trumped peacekeeping and policing in the hierarchical game of competing masculinities. For the first two years of the US military operation in Afghanistan, it appeared as though the American military's civilian superiors in Washington wanted to ensure that American soldiers in Afghanistan stayed firmly in control of the hallowed "combat" mission. The supposedly softer masculinized missions of policing and peacekeeping seemingly were best left the responsibility of German, Canadian, and Dutch men.

The story of the rarely smiling Afghan woman official might be taken by some Americans as a vindication of the Bush administration's militarized, expansionist foreign policy; that is, the violence perpetrated against women by the Taliban local regime in the late 1990s was so extreme that only a foreign-led militarized response and foreign occupation appeared proportionate. In fact, many Americans had only the vaguest notion of where Afghanistan was, of what had been the longtime US government involvement in its twenty-year civil war, and how its Taliban-controlled government was related to the clandestine operations of the insurgent movement led by Osama bin Laden. Consequently, for these American voters, forging a link between the geopolitics of counterterrorism and the liberation of benighted women proved especially helpful in constructing their own informal narratives of the causes for 2001 US invasion of Afghanistan. The fact that there were *any* women in the postinvasion Karzai interim government and that those women remained under threat only served to entrench many Americans' justifying narrative.

But an alternative interpretation exists. To explore this alternative, we need to ask another Afghan woman to "stand up." This is a young woman living in the Afghan province of Herat. Her mother is literate, having attended school in the 1970s, during a time when the regime then in power cited the education of girls as a primary strategy for national modernization. Thus she is eager for her daughter to now attend school. But mother and daughter remain subject to public intimidation here in Herat if they voice such aspirations. This young woman's life two years after the US invasion is not governed by the American, UN, and Afghan officials working in Kabul. Her life—her sense of security, physical mobility, personal identity, public identity, educational and economic opportunities—is governed by the self-proclaimed provincial governor of Herat, Ismail Khan.

English-language commentators have called Khan a warlord. The label makes him sound archaic. It is a label that dampens our political curiosity. In reality, the power Khan and other Afghan regional "warlords" wield in post-invasion Afghanistan derives from two very modern resources: first, Ismail Khan commands a sizeable army of his own, equipped with modern weaponry; second, he is deemed an ally by the US military.[6]

Herat's Khan had contributed his troops to a loose amalgam of Afghan militarized opponents first of the Soviet Army in the 1980s and then of the Taliban regime. His and the other so-called warlords' forces are now called the Northern Alliance, a name that makes the group sound akin to NATO. These Afghan regional commanders proved useful to the US government in its own rivalry with the Soviet Union during the Cold War, and they became useful again to the US government when it decided to wage war against the Taliban and al-Qaeda. In October 2001, the Northern Alliance's commanders and all-male militias—despite their interethnic tensions, they share a history of opposition to the modernizing, secularizing reforms of the 1970s Kabul government—were selected by Washington's war planners as their most trusted, effective military allies on the ground when they devised their US-led invasion of Afghanistan in the aftermath of the attack on New York's twin towers.

Which men foreign elite expansionist men choose to become their trusted local allies will almost certainly have repercussions for local women. Moreover, which men an invading force selects as its local allies will either enhance or, more commonly, undermine the viability of those foreign expansionists' use of women's emancipation as a moral justification for their expansionist enterprise. When US policy makers in Washington selected Ismail Khan and his fellow Northern Alliance antimodernist regional commanders as their most promising allies, they did not employ the empowerment of Afghan women as their chief criterion. Instead, the Washington strategists chose ground-level military capability and previous experience of cooperation with the United States as their principal criteria for choosing their Afghan allies.

The criteria that any expansionist government uses when it chooses its local allies are a much better predictor of the expansionists' postinvasion commitment to women's advancement than is any post hoc discourse of moral justification. Furthermore, which men the invading force chooses as its primary local allies will also privilege certain forms of local masculinity over others. This was true in earlier imperial enterprises, and it is true in any putative imperial enterprises today. Internationally ambitious governments have typically sought local allies as they expanded the reach of their power and authority. Stories of the Spanish expansion into Mexico, the Dutch expansion into what is now Indonesia, the British expansions into Malaya, India, and Egypt, the US expansion into the Philippines, and the French expansion into Vietnam—each testify to this common expansionist strategy of forging unequal local alliances of convenience. Empires, that is, are crafted out of unequal alliances between the ambitious imperialists and those local actors who calculate, often mistakenly, that they will be able to extract strategic gains for themselves even out of a clearly imbalanced alliance. Bedfellows are not all equal. All masculinities are not equal.

Virtually every one of the imperializing alliances mentioned above were between men. This fact is not trivial. Today in Afghanistan, the likelihood of the young Herat woman experiencing meaningful liberation of the sort wishfully imagined by so many Americans who lent their moral support to the US invasion of Afghanistan has been made dependent on a deeply masculinized local provincial regime whose power is ensured by its deeply masculinized foreign institution, the US military.

Several independent human rights researchers have investigated what happened to Afghan girls and women between 2001 and 2003. What these researchers discovered—not only in Khan's Herat but in many other provinces outside of Kabul where Northern Alliance commanders have used their militias and their intimate ties with American soldiers on the ground to consolidate their grasp on the levers of local power (and money)—was that the military strategy the Bush administration officials adopted to conduct the invasion constituted a strategy that hobbled, rather than facilitated, the genuine liberation of most of Afghanistan's women and girls. These observers noted the apparently easy rapport that had developed between the American Special Forces male soldiers—the Special Forces being perhaps the most masculinized of all US military units—and the local governor's militiamen, perhaps due to their shared identity as combat-tested men. The investigators also noted that despite their opposition to the Taliban regime, Khan and Northern Alliance commanders were committed to a very patriarchal form of post-Taliban social order. Khan thus shared with the Taliban's and al-Qaeda's male leaders a belief that controlling women's marital and sexual relations was important for sustaining their hold on power.[7]

The Northern Alliance and its relationships with the US military each warrant feminist-informed investigations for several reasons. First, we need to know in precisely which ways shared masculinity has facilitated the sustaining of this alliance between Herat's warlord Ismail Khan and the US field commanders. Second, we need to know in exactly which ways, other differences notwithstanding, shared masculinities created an easy rapport between the American and Afghan Northern Alliance commanders' rank-and-file men, assisting each to consolidate their authority in their respective daily operations. Third, we need to explore the ways in which this two-layered masculinization served to entrench the Northern Alliance regional commanders' own notions of subordinate femininity. Fourth, in our investigation of contemporary American expansionism, we need to pay serious attention to the rivalry between the Northern Alliance commanders' model of masculinity and the models of masculinity projected by the Kabul-based senior civilian officials in Hamid Karzai's cabinet. Some Afghans have declared this to be a contest between the warlords and "the neckties." Men such as Khan can claim that the neckties sitting in Kabul have become the lackeys of the United States and other foreign donors (the UN, the European Union, and Japan). Khan and the other warlords, despite their intense ethnicized mutual distrust of each other, on the other hand, can claim to be combat-tested veterans, commanders of men, men who have wielded manly violence and risked their lives to defend the nation. The warlords thus can drape over their patriarchal shoulders the mantel of masculinized nationalism. Their ability to control the women in their provinces and to act as the guardians of "true" Afghan femininity constitutes a crucial component of their ability to mobilize their own armies and collect their own tax revenues.

On the other hand, the neckties — represented especially by Dr. Ashraf Ghani, Karzai's minister of finance — can claim to be men of reason. *Reason* and *combat* — both have been used repeatedly by men of myriad cultures to compete with other men for the political brass ring: being recognized as the manliest of public men. The neckties see themselves as builders of a new centralized constitutional state, a political order based on laws and budgets, not on artillery and armed roadblocks. The neckties can portray themselves as being able to represent the nation's interests where it counts, not on some desolate battlefield, but in the corridors of the most important masculinized international arenas, the United Nations Security Council, the US State Department, the World Bank, and the European Commission.[8]

One might think that any form of dominant masculinity might be better for most women than is the warlord variety. In practice, however, women hoping for the education, public voice, and economic opportunities that US officials promised for them commonly find that there is little space left for autonomous women in such a masculinized contest. In such a contest, women are deemed crucial by the rivals, but merely as symbols, subordinates, admirers, or spectators. Men rivaling each other in the arena of politicized masculinity have always needed to ensure that "their" women will play those politically salient feminized roles. That is not liberation. That is not authentic citizenship.

Wait. Now another Afghan woman is standing up. She is Suraya Parlika. Trained as a lawyer, she has led the Afghan Women Lawyers' Association based in Kabul, one of several nongovernmental organizations founded by women in the wake of the fall of the Taliban regime. Parlika has decided to monitor the commission assigned to draft Afghanistan's new constitution.[9] In September 2003, she attended a small, unofficial conference in the southern city of Kandahar along with other women — lawyers, human rights specialists, and civil society leaders. They represented groups such as Women for Afghan Women and the Afghan Women Lawyers' Association. Although an estimated 80 percent of Afghan women (compared to 53 percent of men) remained unable to gain access to the tools that would allow them to learn how to read and write, these Kandahar women conferees were literate.[10] They were thus prepared to read the fine print of the newly drafted Afghan constitution.

Moreover, they were prepared to write constitutional proposals of their own. Coming to the meeting, Parlika and her colleagues each had chosen to defy intimidating personal threats made by opponents of reforms against those Afghans daring to introduce the discourse of human rights into local politics.[11]

Parlika and her co-organizers took the unusual step of inviting to join them — and persuading the Karzai government to temporarily release just for this purpose — three women prisoners. Eqlima had been jailed on charges of running away from an abusive uncle's home; Mina was arrested for running away from a husband to whom she had been sold; Rosia had been imprisoned for fleeing her father-in-law's house after being forced to marry her brother-in-law after her own husband's death. Parlika and the other activist women had invited these three prisoners because they had come to the conclusion that a country's constitution could not be fairly and realistically drafted unless its provisions flowed from an understanding of the actual life experiences of debilitating gender-power imbalance that shaped the daily lives of women and girls.

With her co-organizers, Parlika was going far beyond the American Abigail Adams's much-quoted eighteenth-century modest admonition to John, her constitution-drafting husband: "Do not forget the ladies." These Afghan women activists were drawing lessons from their own twentieth-century Afghan experiences of living with constitutions written, constitutions amended, constitutions partially implemented, and constitutions left unimplemented. Like women activists recently in South Africa, Cambodia, Palestine, Rwanda, and East Timor, and like feminists active in UN peacekeeping operations around the world, these Afghan women meeting in postinvasion Kandahar had become convinced that the writing of a new constitution must become women's business. Any constitution, after all, is a blueprint for a state's power and authority, a design for distributing of power and responsibilities within the state's own institutions and a map of citizens' limitations, rights, and responsibilities.

Consequently, every stroke of the pen could empower women as full citizens or turn them into marginalized dependents of male citizens and a patriarchal state. Thus constitution drafting and constitution ratifying had to be a process that included politically conscious women, preferably in equal numbers with men around the drafting table and in the ratifying assembly. If that fair representation proved impossible to achieve, then, these women concluded, women must be on the alert, mobilized right outside the drafting-room door. In fact, the Afghan constitution-drafting commission in 2003 did include seven women among its appointed members, a significant presence if still a minority. Men remained a decisive majority. Thus Parlika and her colleagues used their four days to listen to the stories of Eqlima, Rosia, and Mina and then to draw up their own constitutional proposal.

Here are the provisions Parlika and her colleagues concluded had to be explicitly included in the new Afghan state's constitution if it were to ensure women's participation in public life as fully autonomous and effective citizens: (1) mandatory education for girls through secondary school; (2) a guarantee that women had freedom of speech; (3) a provision ensuring that every woman was free to cast her own ballot and to run for elected office; (4) insurance that women had equal representation with men in the government's new legislature; (5) the appointment of women in the same number as men to judgeships; (6) the legal entitlement of women to rates of pay equal to those of men; and (7) a constitutional guarantee that women had the right to exert control over their own finances and to inherit property.[12]

All of these provisions, individually and taken together, would not only upset political convention but would fundamentally rearrange the relationships between women and men in the sphere commonly imagined to be private. But the women conferees were not yet finished. After listening carefully to the stories of Rosia, Eqlima, and Mina, Parlika and the other activists included additional provisions that they would press to be spelled out in the new Afghanistan constitution: (8) a constitutional permission for women to bring criminal charges against men for domestic violence and sexual harassment, whether those violations occur in a public place or inside a home; (9) a ban on the common practice of family members handing over girls and women to another family as compensation for crimes committed by the former against the latter; (10) the raising of the legal age of marriage from the present sixteen years to eighteen years; (11) the right of all women to marry and divorce "in accordance with Islam"; and (12) a reduction of the time that women must wait to remarry if their husbands abandon them or disappear.[13]

These twelve provisions do not add up to a constitutional vision of a post-Taliban "good society" for which most Northern Alliance male commanders, the US government's close military allies, have been waging their wars. Those

Northern Alliance commanders, several of whom serve as governors and cabinet ministers in the interim government, would be among the influential men who would be ready to try to wield influence over the next large national council, the *loya jirga*, that was to due to convene in December 2003. This was the national assembly designated to consider—and amend—the draft constitution. The success of Parlika and her own allies in pressing for the sort of a new constitutional state that was structurally and ideologically designed to fulfill the promise of women's liberation would depend in large part on whether the US government still then imagined the Northern Alliance commanders to be its chief partners in expanding its global reach. As the *loya jirga* opened its constitutional debate under the watchful eye of the US occupation officials, who would those American officials and American voters choose as their own best allies in achieving American and global security: the warlords, the neckties, or the Afghan women constitutional activists?

WHERE ARE THE WOMEN IN THE US-DOMINATED OCCUPATION OF IRAQ?

Three women who might help us better understand the US-British military invasion of Iraq and its drawn-out militarized occupation are Raja Habib Khuzai, one of three Iraqi women members of the US-anointed Governing Council; Nimo Din'Kha Skander, a woman who operates a small hair salon in Baghdad; and Kwakab Jahil, one of the woman activists who have begun organizing independently to advocate for women's participation in the US occupation era's emerging political system. Between them, these three women do not represent all of the women in Iraq. None would make such a claim. But by starting to take seriously at least these three distinct, complex, and thinking women, we are likely to make visible where women and femininities are in the consolidation or, alternatively, the subversion of the US expansionist enterprise. That, in turn, should shine a bright light on where the men and rival masculinities are in Iraqis' postinvasion, US-dominated lives.

Raja Habib Khuzai takes the floor. She is a medical doctor and maternity hospital director, a skilled professional. Until September 2003, Khuzai was one of three women on the twenty-five-member Iraqi Governing Council. After September, she was one of only two. On September 20, 2003, her colleague, Akila al-Hashimi, was gunned down by unknown assailants in broad daylight as she was leaving her Baghdad home.[14] Al-Hashimi, then fifty, had been a career Iraqi diplomat. She was described by journalists as a "member of a prominent family of Shiite clerics" and a "force for peace and tolerance."[15] Just two months before being assassinated and shortly after being appointed to the Governing Council, al-Hashimi had been one of three members of the council to represent the interim government on a trip to New York to lobby members of the United Nations.[16]

Both al-Hashimi and Khuzai had been selected to serve on the US-approved Governing Council in early July 2003 as a result of what was reportedly intense behind-the-scenes bargaining, bargaining not unlike the sort which produced Afghanistan's interim cabinet of Hamid Karzai a year earlier. The need to use the maddening passive tense — "had been selected" — in the previous sentence is telling. To date, we do not know precisely the dynamics that shaped this Baghdad bargaining and its eventual outcome. But in virtually every political system we know about, the less transparent any process of political bargaining is, the more likely it is to be governed by presumptions of masculinized politics.

The cause for this masculinization is this: closed-door bargaining is less vulnerable to popular pressure and popular scrutiny. Those who wield the most influence in such backroom political transactions are those individuals who come into the process with resources that can be converted into political currency. First are those who have organized public support — based on religion, ethnicity, or political party affiliation. As in Afghanistan, where rivalries between self-declared male leaders of the Pashtun majority and Uzbek and Tajik minorities became central in the bargaining, so, too, in Iraq, it appeared that the ethnicized and sectarian male-led organizations of Shiite and Sunni Muslim sects and Kurdish ethnic communities and Kurdish rival political parties were imagined to create the salient divisions that required juggling on the Governing Council. That is, organized ethnic, religious, and ideological divisions were thought by the crafters of the new Afghan and Iraqi governments to be the salient bases for representation. Gender was deemed by these same men to be simply symbolic, a step above trivial. Second among the individuals enjoying an advantage in closed-door bargaining sessions are those who have ready access to weapons and armed men. Third are those with economic resources — companies of their own, trading connections, open lines to donors, bank accounts abroad. And fourth among the advantaged bargainers are those who have earned credibility in the eyes of those foreign men orchestrating the bargaining. In the case of the makeup of the new Iraqi Governing Council, that meant credibility in the eyes of the American occupation officials and their superiors in Washington. Some players in any backroom bargaining possess all four convertible resources. In most political systems all of these bargaining chips are kept out of the hands of women.

The bargaining process that produced the 2003 Iraqi Governing Council had been going on among a virtually all-male cast of characters in various forums since December 2002, months before the Bush administration and its British allies launched their actual military invasion. Sixty Iraqis were invited to the December 2002 London meeting convened by the Bush administration. They were deemed by Washington strategists to be key players in the opposition to Saddam Hussein's regime. Of the sixty, three were women. In May 2003, with the Americans now in military control of Baghdad (though scarcely having a firm grasp on the country's postwar politics), the Bush administration called a second meeting to map out a post-Saddam political system. This time American officials invited three hundred Iraqis. Now the number of women included rose to five.[17]

Eventually the three women who were two months later selected for membership in the Iraqi Governing Council were notable for not having access to the four crucial bargaining chips that could be converted into effective political influence. That is, Khuzai and the other two women each entered the Governing Council without their own political parties, without their own militias, without their own treasuries, and without their own direct lines of communication to Washington.

Looking down the list of the twenty-five members of the Governing Council, what stands out is how the women's twenty-two male colleagues are identified. These men were identified not as individuals with their own professional credentials, but, instead, as leaders of this or that political party or public organization. Perhaps these three women were selected by the bargainers precisely because they could make the council look minimally legitimate to the world, while not possessing the political resources needed to shape the council's agenda. Maybe the three women would not even make common cause with each other. The masculinization of the new Governing Council's internal culture could thus proceed undisturbed. Maybe.

It most likely became difficult for any of the three (now two) women on the council to wield effective influence with either their fellow council members or with the US occupation authorities. Thus when the question arose about what steps should be taken to draft a new constitution for Iraq and reporters tried to figure out who among the Governing Council's members seemed to be wielding the most influence in that debate, the names of the power brokers mentioned were all male.[18]

Now an Iraqi beautician stands up. Dressed in snug-fitting pants and a flower-patterned top, she is Nimo Din'Kha Skander.[19] She describes her small business, the Nimo Beauty Salon, as a lively place. Just a single room in the busy Karrada neighborhood of Baghdad, the salon attracts women of several generations for haircuts, facials, and hair dying. Some of her customers wear headscarves, many do not. The Nimo Beauty Salon is also a place where political affairs are regularly analyzed. Skander could be seen as presiding over a political forum.

While choosing hair colors, she and her customers talk about where the country is heading, whether religious male clerics could ever win a majority of Iraqis' votes, what the American occupiers ultimately intend. Like other Iraqi women and girls, these women have heard the harrowing stories of abductions and rapes of women since the lawlessness escalated after the collapse of the regime. They talk about the rapes in whispers. Stories of sexual assaults make many of them afraid to go about the city. They know of some women and girls who have become afraid to leave their homes at all. There is no sign that the new US-recruited and US-trained police force is being taught to take seriously violence against women. The police recruits selected by the US occupation officials, furthermore, appear to be only men. The militias still controlled by some clerics and certain political parties also seem to be exclusively male.[20] This combination of masculinized minimalist security forces and a lack of gender security planning consciousness deprives Iraqi women of opportunities to emerge as effective participants in the emerging new political system. It is no wonder that only men appear at street demonstrations.[21]

Despite the political character of their conversations at the Nimo Beauty Salon, these women see politics as happening somewhere else, somewhere they are not. In this perception, Skander and her customers share a view commonly held by more influential political commentators. A beauty parlor is imagined by them all as a feminized space, a private place. Politics could not, therefore, be going on here. It takes a feminist curiosity to see a beauty salon as a political forum—and to pay attention. Here is where the relationship between public and private power is being sorted out. Here the nature of the past's influence on the present is being weighed. Here the implications of sexual violence for enacting effective citizenship are being exposed. A feminized space is not the opposite of a political place. For many women—especially in a time of foreign military occupation, governmental flux, masculinized rivalries, and increasing sexualized violence—a feminized space in fact may be the most secure political place to trade analyses and strategies.

Baghdad of the 1990s was not Kabul of the 1990s. The Nimo Beauty Salon was never shut down by the regime of Saddam Hussein. In fact, Skander takes pride in Saddam's second wife having been a customer. Yet there have been changes in the constrictions faced and internalized by many women over the past decade. The regime headed by Saddam Hussein had been built on the strength of the Baathist Party, a political party despised by both the young Afghan men who joined the Taliban and the Arab men who became followers of Osama bin Laden. The Baathist Party was a secular, nationalist political party. Iraqi women first voted in 1980. Women's education, women's paid work, women's votes all were encouraged by the Baathist-run government, though not for the sake of democratization, but for the sake of economic growth, to earn the status of being a modern nation and to maximize wartime mobilization. By 2000, 78 percent of school-aged Iraqi girls were enrolled in primary schools.[22] However, after the regime's 1991 wartime defeat in the first Gulf War and during the subsequent decade of international economic sanctions, Saddam's regime sought to garner more regional aid by diluting its secular ideology and vaguely courting Islamic support. During the 1980s war with Iran, the Iraqi regime sought to attract more women into paid government civil service jobs in order to replace the thousands of men it was drafting into its army. By contrast, during the 1990s, the regime, worried about dents in men's sense of manly esteem after two devastating wartime defeats, embraced a more conservative brand of femininity. At the same time, many younger Iraqi women, now enduring greater hardships and cut off from the outside world, not free to travel as their mothers and aunts had been before them, began to adopt a more literal interpretation of Islamic femininity. To the dismay of many older urban Iraqi women who had fought in earlier decades for a woman's right to live her life as an autonomous individual, it became more common among young Iraqi women to adopt a headscarf.[23]

Women's liberation in any country rarely follows a simple path of onward and upward. Women's status and political participation can vary surprisingly from one decade to another, from one generation to another. One's feminist curiosity, consequently, needs to have staying power. One cannot afford the luxury of turning away to follow the next new thing as soon as women in a country have won the vote, or as soon as a handful of women have been awarded a cabinet portfolio, or even as soon as many women have gained access to reproductive rights.

Progress can all prove stunningly ephemeral. Older women are sometimes more literate, more worldly, and more economically autonomous than their daughters and nieces. Some wars and postwar times will widen women's spheres of economic, social, and even political influence. Other wars and postwar times will cause those spheres to dramatically shrink. The key causal factor here is whether the war-waging and postwar-coping government is masculinist. If the government remains one that privileges masculinity, then even those policies it may enact to widen women's spheres of activity can be reversed as soon as that same masculinist government decides that such a reversal proves politically convenient. This is a lesson that both Afghan and Iraqi women have learned. The broadening of women's autonomy will be secure only when that broadening actually rolls back the masculinization of both local and foreign interventionist political culture and government power.

Kwakab Jahil now rises to her feet. She is dressed in a fashionably tailored, long black dress.[24] Her fingernails are hennaed. Her dark hair is uncovered. Jahil, who is forty-six, explains that she only donned the scarf a year earlier due to social pressure, but recently put it aside when she decided that she did not have to prove her feminine respectability to strangers. She did not remove her headscarf to make Americans feel satisfied in their roles as liberators. Jahil had stayed in Iraq during the eight-year war with Iran, the years of international sanctions, the era of increasing intimidation wielded by the Baathist regime. She stayed even after she had been forced out of her long-standing job with the state electrical company when she refused to join the ruling party. In the wake of the fall of the Baathist regime and the confusion set off by the US military conquest, Jahil says, "We need more courage, further boldness. We must reflect a bright future of Iraqi women. Not be oppressed, weak people who have no power."[25]

Jahil was not a participant in the backroom bargaining sessions that produced the US-appointed Governing Council. She has, instead, joined a small number of Iraqi women in activating independent women's advocacy organizations designed to put pressure on both the Governing Council's disparate Iraqi political leaders and the US occupation authorities. Jahil herself has become a member of the Iraqi Women's League leadership committee. The league was founded back in the 1950s, but it was forced underground during Saddam Hussein's era. By August 2003, four months after the American and British invasion, league membership had risen to five hundred women, though Jahil and other women of the older generation noticed that many of the younger women now becoming active remained tentative. It was not a matter of age, but rather one of historical generation. These younger Iraqi women had grown up with little chance to speak out or learn organizational skills.[26]

Among the conditions that Jahil and other Iraqi activist women have tried to transform into political issues are the escalating violence against women. In August 2003, another women's group, the Organization of Women's Freedom in Iraq (OWFI), led a public demonstration in Baghdad to call for official action to stop the abduction of, and assaults on, women. Sixty people came out to demonstrate. One middle-aged woman who attended said, "This is my first demonstration for thirty-five years . . . I came out here all by myself today to raise my voice, but where are all the women?"[27] A majority of the demonstrators, even on this issue so crucial to women, indeed were men. The attendance gender profile says less about women's political consciousness than it does about how far—in any society—the threat of violence suppresses women's capacity to act as fully participant political actors.

Insofar as the American occupation officials and their handpicked Iraqi male advisors treat violence against women as a secondary matter, as something that can be dealt with later, the emerging Iraqi political system will become masculinized. Violence against women, as so many feminists—from Congo to Kosovo to East Timor—have taught us, must be accorded urgent political attention if women are to gain the status of genuinely autonomous citizens.[28]

About the three women chosen behind closed doors to serve on the twenty-five-member Iraqi Governing Council, activist women such as Kwakab Jahil have expressed skepticism. At one strategy meeting, women kept telling an American reporter, "We do not know them. . . . Who are they?"[29] They noted that not one of the then-three women on the council seemed to have an influential organizational support base of her own and thus was unlikely to carry much political weight either in the council's own deliberations or in lobbying the American authorities. Warned a school teacher, "And if they're going to fail, that's it. They won't give this chance to women again."[30]

Then there is the serious matter of drafting Iraq's new constitution. Iraqi women activists, just like Afghanistan's women's rights advocates, have decided that who is chosen to draft and, thereafter, to amend and ratify the new constitution will wield the kind of political influence that will shape women's lives for years to come. Thus one young woman at the same political gathering expressed her activist colleagues' general dismay at the composition of the committee chosen to draft the new constitution: it contained twenty-five members; all of them were men.[31] It appeared that in the eyes of the US occupation authorities, their superiors in Washington, and the members of the Iraqi Governing Council, women's future relationships to state power, to law, and to male citizens were deemed well cared for in the hands of a small group of ethnically, religiously, and ideologically competitive men. This was, these Iraqi activist women argued, a highly questionable supposition.

To bolster their weakened political position, some Iraqi activist women therefore began to foster alliances with women activists outside Iraq. A group of Iraqi exiled women in Britain created the Iraqi Women's Rights Coalition (IWRC), which began to publish its own newsletter, *Equality Rights Now!* These British-based Iraqi women lent support to women in Iraq who in June 2003, two months after the US-British invasion, founded the OWFI.[32] One of the group's first efforts was to establish in Baghdad a shelter for Iraqi women suffering from several forms of domestic violence, including from threats of so-called honor killings by their own brothers, fathers, and uncles.[33] In August, members of the OWFI wrote a formal letter to Paul Bremer, the chief US occupation administrator in Baghdad, calling on him to use his authority to address the "unprecedented violence against women." He did not reply.[34]

Two months later, one of the founders of the OWFI, Yanar Mohammed, also sought to raise the consciousness of Americans by travelling to New York. Mohammed, once active in Iraq's Communist Party, a group banned by the Baathist regime, had spent her exile years in Canada. She returned in the wake of the invasion to contribute to the new mobilization of women. Sponsoring her visit was a group of New York women who had created the Working Committee in Support of Iraq's Women.[35]

CONCLUSION

Women in colonized countries, women in militarily occupied countries, and women under local authoritarian rulers all have a long history of seeking alliances with those women abroad who seem sympathetic to their causes. The internationalization of women-to-women political alliances is not new. It began in the mid-1800s. There is plenty of evidence, garnered by feminist historians, to suggest that sustaining such alliances is hard political work.[36] There are the pulls and pushes of local women's own nonfeminist compatriot male potential allies. Men who oppose foreign occupation or foreign domination are not necessarily men who see the sovereign nation as composed of women and men living as equals in the family, the market, the courts, the universities, and the state's policy-making circles. Yet it is precisely those nonfeminist, even outright patriarchal, men with whom some women believe they must make common cause, at least tactically. This can prove hard to explain to overseas feminist partners. Then there are the pitfalls of miscommunication. Mail now travels in a cybernetic flash, rather than weeks of ocean voyage, but speed does not assure a shared understanding of the terms and phrases. In fact, today any miscommunication can be spread far and wide with alarming quickness and so prove harder to undo. And there is burnout. Doing alliance building among women, none of whom control abundant resources of time or money, can tax the most dedicated of internationally minded feminists.

In addition, as we have painfully learned, there is the perpetual temptation for women outside to imagine that by dint of their access to media and financial resources, those women residing in the affluent country may also have a superior understanding of what should be prioritized in the local women's struggle. And there is the complementary temptation by local women activists to tailor their strategies and discourses to reassure the seemingly well-endowed overseas supporters. On the other hand, the step-by-step building of such dynamic cross-national alliances among women holds out the possibility that women in the imperially minded country will themselves gain a new understanding of their own government's policies and actions overseas, and that this will prompt them to publicly question their government's official justifications for the expansionist maneuvers carried out in their names. Moreover, if women pursue a genuine cross-national alliance of equals, it will involve a lot of intense listening, questioning, and rethinking. Together, such efforts, in turn, can sharpen activists' feminist understandings of what causes the perpetuation of masculinization in public life, not only "over there" but here at home as well.

The intensity and variety of cross-national feminist interactions today is beyond anything seen before in the history of international politics. These feminist interactions are producing fresh analyses of what is causing and perpetuating unequal international power and strategies to expose those causes and subvert them. Thus it would be a mistake, I think, to imagine that the latest version of empire building—in the name of world order or global security or civilization—constitutes an unstoppable steamroller.

Crafting a system of expansive, cohesive political influence, an empire, has always proven a tricky enterprise. Only in retrospect do the earlier British, Ottoman, or Spanish empires look deceptively unavoidable. In practice, there were doubters and critics to persuade or silence at home; there were rebels and recalcitrants to co-opt or suppress in the occupied society. Silencing, suppressing, persuading, co-opting—those make for imperial activities not guaranteed success over the long term. In large part each of these imperializing activities depends on certain gender ideologies. And those ideologies, we have seen, are vulnerable to contradiction and challenge.

Masculinity has always been an essential tool wielded in this many-pronged process of empire building. At home, not only men but women as well have had to be convinced that a militarized manliness (especially when allied with a manly sort of reason and a manly brand of commercial competitiveness) constituted a superior form of humanity. That is, not only men but women, too, have had to be persuaded that such a particular construction of privileged masculinity endowed those actors who claimed to possess it with unique capacities to bring security and a sense of moral well-being to citizens at home, while it simultaneously conferred enlightenment, progress, and "civilization" on those abroad over whom they held sway. All of these—security, moral satisfaction, progress, civilization—are gendered. Subtract the politics of masculinity and the politics of femininity from the investigation, and it is likely one will produce an unreliable explanation of how empire building proceeds, or falters.

For such militarized expansionism does falter, does lose its protective glow at home and among the co-opted and daunted abroad. It falters if the supposedly civilizing rewards promised turn out to fuel not the blessings of technocracy, order, and peace but, instead, violence, corruption, and demoralization. Ambitious expansionism also stumbles if the performers of privileged masculinity turn out to appear self-serving or naive, or both.

The privileging of masculinity in general, and of certain forms of masculinity in particular, thus needs to be investigated. Making sense of the masculinized political cultures and masculinized political processes that legitimize and energize global expansionism, however, cannot be accomplished just by paying attention to varieties of men. Paying serious attention to women—their experiences, their actions, their ideas, in all their diversity—that is, wielding a feminist curiosity, is the only way to ensure that men as men and masculinity as an ideology are made sufficiently visible to be seen with political clarity.

No sustained curiosity about women means no discussion of the politics of femininity. No serious analysis of the politics of women and femininity converts into no concentrated public thinking about men and masculinities. No focused investigation of men and masculinities means no understanding of the genderings of international affairs. No curiosity about how and why international affairs (in both their local and global manifestations) have become reliant on particular ideas about femininity and masculinity produces little chance, then, to make the current workings of unequal power fully visible. No visible rendering of internationalized gender means no possibility of instituting genuine and lasting change in those unequal power arrangements at home and abroad.

NOTES

1. Among the most talked about have been Niall Ferguson, *Empire: The Rise and Demise of the British World Order* (New York: Basic Books, 2003); Paul Kennedy, *The Rise and Fall*

of Great Powers: Economic Change and Military Conflict (New York: Random House, 1987); Eric Hobsbaum, *The Age of Empire, 1875–1914* (New York: Vintage, 1987); Simon Schama, *The Embarrassment of Riches* (New York: Vintage, 1987).

2. Phillipa Levine, *Prostitution, Race and Politics: Policing Venereal Disease in the British Empire* (New York: Routledge, 2003); Piya Chatterjee, *A Time for Tea: Women, Labor, and Post/Colonial Politics on an Indian Plantation* (Durham, NC: Duke University Press, 2001); Kumari Jayawardena, *The White Women's Other Burden: Western Women and South Asia during British Rule* (New York: Routledge, 1995).

3. See Insook Kwon, "'The New Women's Movement' in 1920s Korea: Rethinking the Relationship between Imperialism and Women," *Gender and History* 10, no. 3 (1998): 358–80; Vron Ware, *Beyond the Pale: White Women, Racism, and History* (London, Verso, 1991); Laura Wexler, *Tender Violence: Domestic Visions in an Age of U.S. Imperialism* (Chapel Hill: University of North Carolina Press, 2000); Amy Kaplan and Donald E. Pease, eds., *Cultures of United States Imperialism* (Durham, NC: Duke University Press, 1993); Lora Wildenthal, *German Women for Empire, 1884–1945* (Durham, NC: Duke University Press, 2001); Kristin L. Hoganson, *Fighting for American Manhood: How Gender Politics Provoked the Spanish-American and Philippine-American Wars* (New Haven, CT: Yale University Press, 1998); Nupur Chaudhuri and Margaret Strobel, eds., *Western Women and Imperialism: Complicity and Resistance* (Bloomington: Indiana University Press, 1992); Louise Young, *Japan's Total Empire: Manchuria and the Cultrue of Wartime Imperialism* (Berkeley: University of California Press, 1998); Mona Etienne and Eleanor Leacock, eds., *Women and Colonization* (New York: Praeger, 1980); Clare Midgley, ed., *Gender and Imperialism* (Manchester: Manchester University Press, 1998). See also two critically insightful novels by the prewar Dutch writer Madelon H. Lulofs, set in 1930s colonial Indonesia: *Rubber* (New York: Oxford University Press, 1987); and *Coolie* (New York: Oxford University Press, 1987).

4. Anne E. Brodsky, *With All Our Strength: The Revolutionary Association of the Women of Afghanistan* (New York: Routledge, 2003).

5. For a feminist analysis of how Pakistani government officials, Afghan male party leaders in exile, and complying international agencies and donors together have colluded to deepen the masculinization of the political, economic, and cultural power inside the refugee camps during the period from 1990 to 2003, despite women and children comprising a majority of the camps' residents, see Saba Gul Khattak, "In/Security: Afghan Refugees and Politics in Pakistan," *Critical Asian Studies* 35, no. 2 (2003): 195–208.

6. A detailed account of Ismail Khan's mode of provincial rule is contained in Barry Bearak, "Unreconstructed," *New York Times Magazine*, June 1, 2003, 40–47, 62–101.

7. For information on women and girls in Herat, see Human Rights Watch Report, *We Want to Live as Humans: Repression of Women and Girls in Western Afghanistan* (New York: Human Rights Watch Report,, 2002); Amnesty International report, "Afghanistan: No One Listens to Us and No One Treats Us as Human Beings: Justice Denied to Women,"

October 5, 2003. For a detailed journalistic account of the Taliban's and al-Qaeda's marriage politics, see Amy Waldman, "Kabul Brides Married Taliban for Better, Then for Worse," *New York Times*, December 31, 2001.

8. Bearak, "Unreconstructed," 62.
9. This account is derived from Carlotta Gall, "Women Gather in Afghanistan to Compose a Bill of Rights," *New York Times*, September 28, 2003.
10. Joni Seager, *The Penguin Atlas of Women in the World* (New York: Penguin, 2003), 113.
11. Preeta D. Bansal and Felice D. Gaer, "Silenced Again in Kabul," *New York Times*, October 1, 2003.
12. Gall, "Women Gather in Afghanistan."
13. Ibid.
14. Patrick E. Tyler, "Attackers Wound an Iraqi Official in a Baghdad Raid," *New York Times*, September 21, 2003.
15. Alex Berenson, "U.N. Chief Orders Further Reduction of Staff in Baghdad," *New York Times*, September 26, 2003.
16. Felicity Barringer, "U.N. Gives Iraqi Governing Council Qualified Welcome," *New York Times*, July 23, 2003.
17. Zainab Al-Suwaij, "Iraq's Silenced Majority," *New York Times*, May 23, 2003.
18. Patrick Tyler, "Iraqi Groups Badly Divided Over How to Draft a Charter," *New York Times*, September 30, 2003.
19. Much of the following derives from Sabrina Tavernise, "Iraqi Women Wary of New Upheavals," *New York Times*, May 5, 2003.
20. Amy Waldman, "US Struggles to Transform a Tainted Iraqi Police Force," *New York Times*, June 30, 2003.
21. Human Rights Watch Report, "Climate of Fear: Sexual Violence and Abduction of Women and Girls in Baghdad," New York, July, 2003; Neela Banerjee, "Rape (and Silence about It) Haunts Baghdad," *New York Times*, July 16, 2003.
22. Seager, *The Penguin Atlas of Women in the World*, 114–15.
23. Tavernise, "Iraqi Women Wary."
24. Most of the following is derived from Sharon Waxman, "Facing the Future," *Washington Post*, June 17, 2003.
25. Ibid.
26. Lauren Sandler, "Veiled Interests," *Boston Globe*, August 31, 2003.
27. Ibid.
28. The women inside the United Nations and their allies in feminist nongovernmental organizations have been most influential in pressing all international agencies and donor countries to take seriously the political implications of violence against women in war zones and in postwar reconstruction efforts. One of the closest monitors of these efforts is *PeaceWomen*, an electronically distributed newsletter published by the Women's International League for Peace and Freedom (www.peacewomen.org). See also UNIFEM's report on the chief conditions and official attitudes that obstruct women's effective

participation in postconflict political life, Elisabeth Rehnand and Ellen Johnson Sirleaf, *World Progress of Women 2002*, vol. 1, *Women, War, and Peace* (Bloomfield, CT: Kumarian, 2003).

29. Sandler, "Veiled Interests."
30. Ibid.
31. Ibid.
32. See *PeaceWomen*, www.peacewomen.org (accessed September 12, 2003).
33. E-mail announcement circulated by the New York–headquartered National Council for Research on Women (www.ncrw.org), October 10, 2003.
34. Lauren Sandler, "Veiled and Worried in Baghdad," *New York Times*, September 16, 2003.
35. National Council for Research on Women, e-mail announcement.
36. See, for example, Claire Midgley, *Women against Slavery: The British Campaigns 1780–1870* (New York: Routledge, 1992); Lila Rupp, *Worlds of Women: The Making of an International Women's Movement* (Princeton, NJ: Princeton University Press, 1997); Margot Badran, *Feminists, Islam, and Nation: Gender and the Making of Modern Egypt* (Princeton, NJ: Princeton University Press, 1995). For case studies of contemporary efforts at creating genuine alliances of women across national boundaries, see Felicity Hill, Mikele Abotiz, and Sara Poehlman-Doumbouya, "Non-governmental Organizations' Role in the Buildup and Implementation of Security Council Resolution 1325," *Signs* 28, no. 4 (2003): 1255–70; Pam Spees, "Women's Advocacy in the Creation of the International Criminal Court," *Signs* 28, no. 4 (2003): 1233–54; Sherrill Whittington, "Gender and Peacekeeping: The United Nations Transitional Administration in East Timor," *Signs* 28, no. 4 (2003): 1283–88; Mrinalini Sinha, Donna J. Guy, and Angela Woolacott, eds., "Feminisms and Internationalism," special issue, *Gender and History* 10, no. 3 (1998).

MALINI JOHAR SCHUELLER

☆ ☆ ☆ Techno-Dominance and Torturegate: The Making of US Imperialism

American leadership is good both for America and for the world.
—Project for the New American Century

You know, I don't think a photo inspires murderers. I think they're inspired by an ideology that is so barbaric and backwards that it's hard for many in the Western world to comprehend how they think.
—George W. Bush, May 2005

A day after Saddam Hussein's capture on a remote farm near Tikrit on December 13, 2003, newspapers and television networks throughout the world printed and broadcast images of the former dictator being examined by US army doctors. Released by the Department of Defense, these videos and photographs overshadowed the reportage of jubilant Iraqis taking to the streets. One of the most popularly reproduced pictures was that of a disheveled and dirty-looking Saddam with a long, unkempt beard, his head tilted back and mouth open to allow the physician to shine a torch into it. Saddam's scraggly, disheveled hair, the unfocused, bewildered look in his eyes, and his disoriented expression bespeak a defeat so unmistakable that one can understand why this would make a trophy picture for the Department of Defense. But of course there is more to the picture than Saddam. Indeed, the power of the image rests on the sharp differences between Saddam and the physician. While Saddam exudes disorder, incoherence, and bestiality (Saddam's hideout was often called a "rat hole" or a "spider hole"), the physician's actions are marked by science, technology, and precision. Whereas the bestial and infantilized Saddam obediently opens his mouth to the bidding of the US physician, the latter uses the spatula to extract an exact marker of human identity, a DNA sample.

Obviously the Defense Department footage capitalizes on the humiliation of the erstwhile dictator. The video clips most incessantly replayed dramatized the dinginess of Saddam's hideout and his meek acquiescence to the doctor who with his latex gloves searched his captive's hair for lice and examined his mouth. If we remember that prior to the AIDS outbreak, latex gloves were used by physicians only for vaginal and anal examinations and that they are still rarely used for routine throat or mouth exams, Saddam's body is suggestive of, and produced as, an abject body, one signifying leaky boundaries and contagion, a body marked not so much as feminine as Julia Kristeva has argued, but as one demasculinized and aberrant in its difference from the bounded, masculinized body of the physician.[1] My purpose here is not to generate sympathy for Saddam as an abjected body but rather to point to imperialist, indeed Manichaean, self-representation in the video footage released by the Department of Defense: US power, control, technological mastery, and masculinity triumphing over, yet humanely tending to—as is the obligation of good empires—an incoherent, demasculinized, and bestialized adversary (the footage not released included photos of Saddam being kicked by soldiers). The photo spelled the triumph of the United States as empire because Saddam constituted a metonym for the dictatorial nation that had to be occupied in order to be liberated, bombed in order to be cleansed of weapons. Indeed, the point of the footage was not lost on even the most strident of Saddam's critics. As a forty-four-year-old Iraqi engineer remarked, "I hate this man to the core of my bones. Just seeing him sitting there makes the hairs on my arms stand up. And yet, I can't tell you why, I feel sorry for him, to be so humiliated. It is as if he and Iraq have become the same thing."[2]

Ostensibly, there seems to be no connection between the photograph and the video footage of Saddam's capture, on the one hand, and the torture photographs of Abu Ghraib on the other. While the Saddam photograph is perfectly "respectable," the Abu Ghraib photographs blatantly cash in on ideas of sexual aberrance. Saddam is being inspected, the prisoners are being tortured. One is a propaganda photograph meant for national and international consumption; the others are photographs initially intended for limited circulation. Yet I would argue that there is a continuity between these sets of photographs and their construction of abjection that becomes clear once we examine the techno-dominance vision of the neocons, from *Shock and Awe* (1996) to the Project for the New American Century, which provides the context for Abu Ghraib. These neocons envision the body politic as masculinist, a powerful empire by right and undergirded by technological supremacy. Both the photographs of Saddam's capture and those of Abu Ghraib metaphorically encapsulate techno-dominance, a vision of coercion, yet one with echoes of a D/s (dominance/submission) fantasy.[3] If my analysis gives the neocon vision too much credence, it is so because I consider it important at the current moment to analyze this version of imperialism in all its brutality and am skeptical of the value of postcolonial studies scholars who seem determined to read the archives of imperialism as hybrid and incoherent alone.[4] On the other hand, as I will suggest at the end of this essay, dominance is never absolute or final;[5] the reception and circulation of the photographs points to ways in which the extremes of the neocon project and its reliance on a fantasy of submission might well contain the seeds of the (un) making of US imperialism.

What is new about the neocon vision? In many ways, the idea of technological superiority as a means of sustaining imperialism is not novel if we remember Lenin's argument about imperialism as the highest stage of capitalism, or world systems theorists' articulations of capitalism's dependence on systems of unequal development between core and periphery.[6] As the introduction points out, although there has been a ratcheting up of this process, there has also occurred a shift from capitalist imperialism to sheer militarism and unilateralism, the empire now constituted through a spectacular display of military power.[7] My reading of contemporary US imperialism follows the directions of this militaristic empire but suggests that this imperialism also needs to be read in all its cultural complexity, through its racial and sexual components. Thus I argue that the particular conception of absolute dominance defined in the mid-1990s by the neocons through a masculinized vision of technological supremacy makes for a definition of the national body politic as force, power, precision, and control—a hypermodern, punitive empire—both causing and dependant on the paralysis and destruction of the Other.

Generalized formulations such as *the society of surveillance*, *biopower*, and *gov-*

ernmentality prove inadequate for encapsulating this imperial culture because they cannot explain racial differences, or the fact that particularly after 9/11, highly visible forms of disciplining—something Michel Foucault deemed disappearing forms of exceptional disciplining—coexist with surveillance.[8] Such forms of disciplining (i.e., punishment) have always proven integral to colonial power and have been deployed in the suppression of minorities in the United States from antimiscegenation laws, exclusion acts, and Jim Crow legislation to now the prison industrial complex. As Darius Rejali argues, the very fact of scientific modern torture suggests the need to rethink the Foucauldian argument that modern societies have moved from torture to disciplining; indeed, torture forms an integral part of modern disciplinary society.[9] The current US imperial vision is both punitively technomilitaristic and masculinist, imbricated in colonialist discourses of race, gender, and sexuality that crystallized in an Orientalism refashioned for the current moment and of which the Abu Ghraib photographs partake.

The refashioning I speak of is that of Edward Said's explanation of Orientalism as a colonial discourse through which gendered categories of the West and the Orient were normalized: the Orient promised unlimited sexuality, was gendered as woman, and invited penetration.[10] Following the mind-body logic of gender construction, the Orient was seen as "aberrant, undeveloped, inferior" and given to irrationality.[11] Although criticized for perpetuating gender binaries and being bound to heterosexuality, this concept of Orientalism articulated a central dynamic, namely, that the symbology of sexual dominance formed an integral part of colonial power. Similarly, theorists such as Klaus Theweleit have demonstrated how raced Others (here, Jews) were constructed through markers of abjection, leaky boundaries, and deviant sexuality in contrast to the bounded, masculine Germanic body.[12] Although it is an oversimplification to argue that colonialism and imperialism are all about gender and sexuality because that negates factors such as racism, economic control, and sheer human greed, sexuality was and is an important form of imperial control. Sexuality might not explain the "why," but it does crucially explain the "how" of imperial power.[13]

In the United States, sexuality has been a long-standing technology of racial governance, from the oversexualization of African American women to lynching. Similarly, US imperialism has been constructed through sexuality, although the specific forms of sexual demarcation vary historically and geopolitically.[14] The Middle East, constructed through Orientalist categories in the nineteenth century, is once again being seen through the prism of classic Orientalism with its gender and sexual categories intact.[15] September 11 simply reworked the categories of Oriental degeneracy to now characterize the supposed terrorism of the Middle East.[16] The unveiling of Afghan women and the need to save them from Islamic fundamentalism were stated by both George W. Bush and his wife Laura as reasons for going to war with Afghanistan after 9/11. Similarly, homophobia was invoked in popular culture to do the work of political domination. Just as Saddam was depicted as sodomized during the Gulf War, fliers circulating in New York City after 9/11 with the caption "You like skyscrapers, bitch?" showed Osama bin Laden sodomized by the World Trade Center.[17] These fliers evoked masculinity and heteronormativity, compensating the castration of the nation by symbolically using the twin towers as phallic emblems sodomizing the homosexual pervert, while the word *bitch* invoked both racism as bestiality and sexism as normative masculinity.

Although the induction of women into the military, particularly in combat positions, might seem to undermine the gender dynamics of Orientalism, I suggest that in relation to the Iraqi Other, imperialism still works through the logic of gender construction and normative sexuality. Thus the rescue of Jessica Lynch, released to the media through the tightly controlled Central Command's media center in Qatar, was circulated as either the narrative of Lynch as female Rambo, fighting until death, or conversely, as a colonial captivity narrative demonstrating the true manliness of US soldiers. Indeed, the woman soldier might represent all that the oppressed Iraqi woman might lack; and homophobia continues to structure the matrices of domination whereby the Other is deemed aberrant.[18] The current torture of Iraqi prisoners can be explained through these familiar matrices. However, while the current occupation of Iraq draws on earlier imperial discourses, it has been significantly affected by the imperial policy outlined by the neocons that I described above as techno-dominance, power, and control, premised on the complete destruction of the will and mind of the Other.

This imperial policy draws on an existent techno-culture, emblematic of Cold War fervor, in which nation and masculinity intersect to constitute a new network of regulatory power relations.[19] Part of the Gulf War reporting was, for instance, that of a masculinist triumph of technology in which messy bodies remained offscreen.[20] The military itself is aware of the lure of techno-machismo for recruiting purposes. The military's free computer game, "America's Army," five hundred thousand copies of which had been downloaded by the fall 2002, includes "clean" combat scenes against enemies, most of whom are unshaven. Since 1999, the Army has entered its own car in drag-racing events at which it also sets up recruiting booths.[21] In the policies of the neocons, which we might well see as the ultimate D/s fantasy, technology and military might constitute the nation as hyperdominant and sadistic. It is a technosexual dominance marked by order, control, and precision, one which seeks to reduce the Other to disorder, chaos, and destruction through discourses of homophobia and masculinity.[22]

FORMS OF TECHNO-DOMINANT IMPERIALISM

Of the many papers and policy statements produced by the neocons and their military pundits, I want to focus here on Harlan K. Ullman and James P. Wade's *Shock and Awe: Achieving Rapid Dominance* and a key paper from the Project for the New American Century. *Shock and Awe*, published by the National Defense University, is both a policy document and a cultural text, one widely discussed in the Bush administration prior to the invasion of Iraq, with officials confirming that the war would rely on the concepts propounded in the book. Ullman was repeatedly interviewed on TV in early 2003, so that by the time the war began, all major news channels referred to the bombardment of Baghdad as "shock and awe," which had, by then, become a household phrase. *Shock and Awe* outlines a military strategy, but more important, it identifies the psychosexual and social coordinates of US imperialism.

Ullman and Wade write as military hawks, yet with a post–Cold War anxiety about techno-masculinity — clear about US global supremacy yet eager to display its military might. Spectacularization and masculinist values of dominance are central here:[23] "The military posture and capability of the United States of America are, today, dominant. Simply put, there is no external adversary in the world that can successfully challenge the extraordinary power of the American military."[24] Ironically, military supremacy requires constant validation through the use of force, which Ullman and Wade argue the United States should be prepared to use. Integral to the deployment of force is high-tech weaponry, near-perfect knowledge enabled by information technology, and a colonizing of channels of information. In a sense, Ullman and Wade's prescriptions respond to what globalization theorists see as diffused networks of power in the information age, where the nation state has lost much of its sovereignty and the boundaries of information have become leaky.[25] In Ullman and Wade's vision, information technology needs to be controlled and channeled for military use: "This drive is needed to translate this technology into military hardware. . . . The largest challenges may be to shape and exploit this commercial potential and then to ensure that its enduring advantages become fundamental in the makeup of our military forces."[26] Diffuse techno-culture, in other words, needs to be translated to militaristic techno-dominance.

The key strategies of US warfare outlined in *Shock and Awe* are notable for their invocation of a hypermasculine, virile destruction based on technological precision and mastery, categories dependent on an oppressive logic of gender construction that have worked in colonialism and imperialism as techniques of domination. By associating techno-dominance with masculinity, I am not valorizing a reification of essentialist gender constructions such as male/female, mind/body, culture/nature, or technology/primitivism; rather, I am arguing that such categories continue to be invoked for purposes of domination.[27] *Shock and Awe* is remarkable for the images of virility and sexual power it incessantly summons to describe imperial domination. No more older George Bush wimp factor here: "Physical dominance includes the ability to destroy, disarm, disrupt, neutralize, and to render impotent. Psychological dominance means the ability to destroy, defeat and neuter the will of an adversary."[28] Despite the key difference Ullman and Wade articulate between physical and psychological dominance, the emasculization signaled by words such as *impotent* and *neuter* proves central to both. The adversary is constantly figured as sexually disempowered and effeminized: "The key objective of Rapid Dominance is to impose this overwhelming level of Shock and Awe against an adversary. . . . An adversary would be rendered totally impotent and vulnerable to our actions" (introduction). Or again, "The aims of this doctrine are to apply massive or overwhelming force as quickly as possibly on an adversary in order to disarm, incapacitate, or render the enemy militarily impotent" (chapter. 2). The nation, figured through techno-dominance as a virile, masculine body, renders the body of the adversary emasculated and vulnerable.

The dominance outlined in *Shock and Awe* also rests on a regime of hypermodernity marked by precision, order, and control, which mirrors the ordering of the disciplinary society within the nation through the prison industrial complex and the management of the population through the so-called war on drugs and the war on crime. The fundamental strategy of "rapid dominance" is the "control and management of everything that is significant to the operations bearing on the particular Area of Interest (AOI). And we mean everything! . . . Through virtual reality, movement in three-dimensional grids over hundreds of square kilometers, offer precise location and movement control" chapter 1).

But more important, the authors explain rapid dominance through the new, modern technologies of the power to punish theorized by Foucault in which the object of punishment shifts from the body to the mind: "Punishment has to make use not of the body, but of representation. Or rather, if it does make use of the body, it is not so much as the subject of a pain as the object of a representation: the memory of pain must prevent repetition of the crime."[29] While Foucault diagnoses this shift from body to mind as the transition from torture to punishment, Darius Rejali analyzes the shift as part of the apparatus of modern torture in which punishment is directed at a point beyond the body. Unlike Foucault, that is, Rejali suggests (1) that torture is very much part of modernity; and (2) that it involves both body and consciousness. Based on Reza Baraheni's analysis of torture in Iran, Rejali writes, "A new quality of pain was necessary, a pain that gripped the 'consciousness,' . . . The prisoner was grasped from within, through electric shocks, injections, internal pressure and sensory deprivation. The marks of punishment were seen not merely on the body but also in the 'eyes, [which] become frenzied out of fear, morbid dread, and insomnia.' "[30] The object of punishment was mnemonic, one designed to "locate, isolate, and cripple the prisoner's 'soul.' "[31]

Modern torture is thus distinguished by the fact that its perpetrators attempt to and do control the victim's consciousness. Ullman and Wade's explanation of shock and awe offers a macroversion of the technologies of modern torture. They write: "Rapid Dominance is aimed at influencing the will, perception, and understanding of an adversary rather than simply destroying military capability."[32] For historical precedents, the authors excavate examples of massive destruction: the impact of the use of atomic weapons in Hiroshima and Nagasaki, where the display of US technological might generated in the Japanese populace the equivalent of the trauma experienced by victims of modern torture; or, as another, Hitler's brutal bombing of civilians in Guernica. As Ullman and Wade explain, "The impact of those weapons was sufficient to transform both the mindset of the average Japanese citizen and the outlook of the leadership through this condition of Shock and Awe. The Japanese simply could not comprehend the destructive power carried by a single airplane. This incomprehension produced a state of awe" (introduction). Similarly, the authors describe the German blitzkrieg in the language of modernity, as the application of "precise, surgical amounts of tightly focused force to achieve maximum leverage" (chapter 2). What fascinates Ullman and Wade are representations of mental paralysis: "One recalls from old photographs and movie or television screens, the comatose and glazed expressions of survivors of the great bombardments of World War I. . . . These images and expressions of shock transcend race, culture, and history" (chapter 2).

Shock and Awe makes for a fascinating military document, demonstrating the imbrication of discourses of modernity, technology, and masculinity in the making of US imperialism. By invoking fascism as the precursor of a triumph of phallic power next embodied in the United States, the document writes US history through a teleology of successful dominance that erases the symbolic castration of Vietnam, a historical fact tellingly absent here. Was there not enough shock and therefore not enough awe? Most important, in the translation of terror and pain to awestruck wonder and amazement lies a misguided fantasy of domination as D/s. It also marks the sheer brutality of contemporary imperialism, based on a model of modern torture and shorn of all pretenses of the civilizing missions of eighteenth- and nineteenth-century colonialism. That the US invasion of Iraq followed the ruthless prescriptions of Ullman and Wade should not surprise us, however, given the vision of empire in the Project for the New American Century (PNAC), established in 1997 as a think tank with the express purpose of promoting a global US militaristic empire. Many of the founding members of PNAC were representatives of the military industrial complex of the former Reagan and Bush administrations—Dick Cheney, Donald Rumsfeld, and Paul Wolfowitz. Others included cultural conservatives such as William J. Bennett, Francis Fukuyama, and Norman Podhoretz. The central proposition of the PNAC is based on a contradictory imagining of empire by invitation: "American leadership is good both for America and for the world." In its statement of principles, the PNAC looks back to a muscular "Reaganite policy of military strength and moral clarity," in contrast to the dissipation of the Clinton administration.[33]

In a key PNAC paper, "Rebuilding America's Defenses," published in September 2000, technological supremacy and global power are indissolubly linked. Lamenting Bill Clinton's brakes on military spending and urging a militaristic definition of the body politic, the paper argues unequivocally for the need of a US empire. It does so, however, by euphemizing empire as "leadership." Thus the paper is scattered with phrases such as "global technological leadership," "American leadership around the world," "American global leadership," and "American geopolitical leadership," the latter hauntingly recalling the fascist use of the term *geopolitics*. Yet the paper also makes abundantly clear the imbrications of military-techno might, imperial power, and world dominance. Of the four core missions the paper outlines for US military forces, two clearly spell the imperatives of territorial control: to fight and win "multiple, simultaneous major theater wars" and to undertake "constabulary" duties for the "security environment in critical regions."[34] The paper recommends the deployment of global missile defenses not simply for protection but also "to provide a secure basis for U.S. power projection around the world."[35] Conscious of their new articulation of imperialism, the authors envision the role of the United States as one creating a new enclosure of the commons analogous to that of seventeenth-century Britain, except that the enclosure is now to "control the new 'international commons' of space and 'cyberspace,' and pave the way for the creation of a new military service—U.S. Space Forces."[36]

TECHNO-DOMINANCE, SEXUALITY, AND ORIENTALISM

The techno-dominance articulated by the neocons prior to 9/11 and put into practice thereafter bespeak a particularly ruthless militaristic imperialism, but one that became normalized in popular culture through a melodramatic narrative of the fight between oppositional forces of good and evil, civilization and barbarity. George Bush's address to the nation on September 20, 2001, presented the case for global militarism by invoking these binaries and turning the ambivalent question "Why do they hate us?" into a dichotomous freedom-versus-despotism issue by arguing that "they hate our freedoms."[37] This Manichaean landscape enabled Bush to assume a cowboy masculinity and issue a threat: "Every nation in every region has a decision to make: Either you are with us, or you are with the terrorists."[38] Bush's decision to invade Iraq in March 2003 (an act recommended by the PNAC in 2000),[39] rationalized through a fabricated link with al-Qaeda and scripted through Manichaeanism, was readily supported by the majority of the US public.[40]

What is new about the current ideology of techno-militarist dominance is its unilateralism and advocacy of heightened levels of destruction and the suppression of the populace. However, this ideology is familiar in its harnessing of sexuality for the purposes of domination, as well as in its deployment of an old Orientalism, now directed at the Iraqi terrorist. Commensurate with the idea of the Orient as a site of barbarity and backwardness, US occupation forces did nothing to stop the lootings of Iraq's national museums despite prior warnings from civilian advisors.[41] And even as the Bush administration was ostensibly differentiating good Iraqis from terrorists, tolerant Muslims from murderous fundamentalists, the neocons' favorite book about the Arabs in the months leading up to the Iraqi invasion was Raphael Patai's *The Arab Mind*, first published in 1973. The title itself, reducing to homogeneity over 200 million people from Morocco to the Gulf, speaks volumes about the essentialized constructions of Orientalism. In its obsession with veiled women and its reduction of so diverse a geopolitical space as "the Arab world" to an undifferentiated, presocial sexual drive, Patai's book is consistent with Orientalist representations of the oversexed, irrational, traditional Arab male.[42] Patai argues that resultant on gender segregation and veiling, sex became a "prime mental preoccupation in the Arab world." At the same time, all sexual activity and sexual expressions, including homosexuality, were never made public: "These are private affairs and remain private."[43] From Patai's book the neocons concluded that the major weakness of the Arabs was sexual shame and humiliation.[44] The neocons' fascination with Patai's work, as with Samuel Huntington's equally static conception of cultural differences and clashes, says more about the hierarchical binaries necessary for imperialism's functioning than any interest in "the Arabs." More disturbingly, despite the thorough condemnation of the book by scholars of Middle East studies, it is used as the definitive text on "the Arabs" for the military. Republished in 2002, it now has an enthusiastic introduction by Norvell "Tex" De Atkine, former US army colonel and head of Middle East studies at Fort Bragg who touts it as "essential reading." "At the institution where I teach military officers, *The Arab Mind* forms the basis of my cultural instruction."[45] A clearer statement about the mutual imbrication of stereotypes and foreign policy can hardly be found.

The normalization of massive destruction (and consequent suffering) as a spectacle of awe and the scripting of the war with Iraq as a battle against barbarity, necessary for homeland security, provide the context for the now infamous torture photographs from Abu Ghraib prison in which the techno-dominance and Orientalism of the neocons reverberate.[46] After 9/11, as the introduction points out, when American exceptionalism was rewritten both in popular culture and official discourse as the revenge of victimhood, the well-being of the body politic was presented as dependent on the surveillance and incarceration of Arab Others. It is not surprising, therefore, that the torture of prisoners at Abu Ghraib was seen as part of a patriotic machismo. Indeed, techno-masculinity as racism was in operation in the reportage of the shock and awe bombings which excluded any mention of the physical misery of Iraqis. At home, techno-masculinity governs the coverage of US casualties. While most newspapers faithfully report the number of US soldiers killed in combat, the decision of some to print photographs of flag-draped coffins—thus gesturing to the body (indicative of messiness, physicality, and the unnational) beneath—caused an uproar and was condemned by the White House. Only Al Jazeera, Michael Moore's *Fahrenheit 9/11* (2004), and Jehane Noujaim's *Control Room* (2004) have shown bodies of wounded/crippled soldiers. George W. Bush has yet to attend a funeral for a slain soldier.

Physicality, the body, irrationality, and loss of control mark the Other, who can be constituted as a woman through the vector of gender, and as homosexual through the vector of sexuality. In both cases, the Other is abject. Thus, despite the acknowledgment of gays in the military during the early days of Clinton's first term, the "don't ask don't tell" rule legislates as forbidden any performance of homosexuality and defines soldiers through a compulsory heterosexuality that upholds the codes of normative nationhood. If homophobia is the official policy of the military, it is not surprising that the homosexual is marked as the aberrant, uncontrolled, sexualized, and unnational Other, or, in Abu Ghraib, the Iraqi Other.

Of the dozens of torture photographs released by the media and seared into public memory, three predominant features stand out: the obvious pride of the US soldiers posing in some of the photos; the vulnerability and often undefinability of the prisoners' bodies; and the homosexual content of many of them. All these features illustrate the brutal techno-sexual dominance that characterizes contemporary US imperialism. What immediately strikes the viewer in all of the photographs is the power of the soldiers, heightened in contrast to the pathetic bodies of the prisoners. All of the photos are taken inside the Abu Ghraib prison, where the stark walls and iron bars serve as grim reminders of carceral force. While the prisoners' bodies are naked and vulnerable, their heads covered with plastic bags to delimit definition, the soldiers' bodies are defined and marked. They appear dressed, often armed with assault rifles, with full camouflage gear, boots, and helmets. When not armed, as in the picture of Private Lynndie England, cigarette in mouth, pointing to the genitals of a masturbating man, arming is simulated through gestures. Sometimes several ready-to-kill army dogs, snarling and barely restrained by the already armed soldiers, stand poised to attack and terrorize the prisoners. And again, as in the photo of Saddam Hussein, we have the circulation of the ubiquitous surgical gloves bespeaking precision and control. Specialists Charles Graner and Sabrina Harman both wear gloves while giving triumphant thumbs-up signs as they pose behind the carefully ice-packed and cellophane-wrapped body of a battered prisoner. The gloves appear again on the hands of Graner as he, in an embodiment of violent masculinity, pummels the body of a hooded prisoner while several other bound and shackled prisoners lie on the floor.

Perhaps no photograph illustrates better the idea of techno-dominance than the pathetic body of the prisoner standing, arms outstretched, atop what looks like a wooden crate, his fingers attached to an electric wire. With a blanket over his body and bare feet with scarcely enough room to move, the hooded prisoner with outstretched arms resembles Christ on the cross or a mendicant in supplication. Wired for torture, ready to undergo shock at the bidding of soldiers, the prisoner becomes at once a metonym for the Iraqi populace who need to be "awed," as well as for the nonbeing being whose incipient cyborg status speaks more to brutalization than subversion. As Specialist Harman testified about the prisoner who was nicknamed Gilligan, "He was just standing on the box with the sandbag over his head for about an hour. I put the wires on his hands. I do not recall how. I was joking with him and told him if he fell off he would get electrocuted."[47]

What the photographs capture dramatically is the illustration of imperial power through the rendering of Iraqi bodies as abject, undefinable, or vulnerable, or all of these. If the abject is that which disturbs identity, system, and order and which gets symbolized through forms of bodily waste such as feces or urine — that which the bounded body separates itself from — imperial power formulates itself through the symbolic or real abjection of the conquered, raced Other, as Klaus Theweleit argues.[48] The natives who symbolize abjection and whose bodies invite loathing also confirm the power and masculinity of the carriers of imperial power. In what might seem like a classic illustration of both Kristeva's and Theweleit's analyses of abjection, there is a photograph of a naked male prisoner, his back toward the camera, his feet shackled and legs uncomfortably crossed. His naked body is covered with sand and either dirt or feces as he stands with arms outstretched facing a soldier. The prisoner is in the classic position of being looked at. He is viewed from all sides — from that of the soldier whom he faces, and from either side of the hallway from the prisoners whose hands dangle outside the prison cells. The symmetrical rigidity of the prison cells and walls, and the glare of the lights, call attention to the body of the prisoner marked as filth and deviance. In stark contrast to the order of the prison, his body suggests disorder. The soldier facing him embodies power and dominance through almost symmetrical opposition to him. The soldier is dressed in uniform and boots, his legs aggressively apart as he stands grim-faced, brandishing a phallic baton. And yet, this is also where the paradigm of dominance begins to be visually undermined. The prisoner's body appears almost sculpted and visually dwarfs that of the soldier.

And then we have the numerous group photographs of abjected bodies of male prisoners, uncomfortably stacked on top of each other, forming naked human pyramids as if simulating a cheerleading squad. One photograph, with a frontal body view, depicts a tangle of arms, legs, and torsos as naked men, legs spread apart, sandbagged heads bowed, pile atop each other. Another, taken from behind, shows the word *rapist* compensatorily marked on the buttock of a prisoner. Of course, as we know, the prisoners were raped and sodomized by soldiers and translators. Bodily contours virtually disappear in these photos of masses of humans reduced to their bodily parts—much as women often are in voyeuristic images, with the difference that it is difficult to even visualize a complete body or tell how many bodies there are unless one starts counting heads or buttocks. Again, behind two of the human pyramids stands a triumphant Charles Garner with his ubiquitous green rubber-gloved hands, giving a thumbs-up sign. In contrast to the tangled mass of male bodies in front of him, Garner poses with women—once with Lynddie England and once with Sabrina Harman.

If I seem to be describing these photographs as conscious representation, it is because, despite the fact that they were intended for limited circulation among a group of friends, there is the obvious posed nature of most of them. Just as Saddam's photo constituted a trophy for the Defense Department, these photos served as private trophies. It is this latter aspect that has shocked many people, the fact that not only were the soldiers conducting inhumane acts but that they also thought these worth recording, remembering, and circulating as praiseworthy. The soldiers themselves are subjects in the photographs and appear proud of their heinous acts. Such photographs, both Susan Sontag and Sarah Boxer suggest, have virtually no precedents even in the heaps of bodies photographed by the Nazis because the perpetrators themselves did not pose with the bodies of their victims. While Boxer argues that the shock of the Abu Ghraib pictures lies in their structuration as tourist photos, Sontag argues that the only analogue lies in the post-Reconstruction photographs of black lynching victims, which show white Americans grinning beneath the dangling, mutilated bodies of (mostly) black men. Such photographs suggest the complete moral justification white Americans felt concerning their actions.[49] Sontag's analogy seems particularly appropriate because it suggests how racial othering and legally mandated structures of domination create an internalization of the righteousness of racial violence. In the case of Iraq, as I have suggested, if we examine the confluence of a public touting of a brutal techno-dominance, unilateral militarisitic imperialism, and the reintroduction of the Orientalist thematics, the photographs do not appear at all surprising. They form part of the archives of imperialism, much like, for instance, the famous US military souvenir photograph in the Philippines showing US soldiers grinning over the decapitated corpses of Muslim insurgents whose unrest they had helped subdue.[50] The soldiers, no ideological putties, appropriate the techno-dominance torture paradigm but map the scenario as individual mastery.

IMPERIALISM IS NOT PORNOGRAPHY

Of course it is the sexual content of most of the photographs that has generated the greatest interest and outcry; and the reportage of this content has followed its own sexist logic in its disproportionate attention given to Lynddie England, referred to as the "leasher-gal" by the *New York Post*.[51] England's family has sought to discredit her participation in torture by publicly describing her as a tomboy with a tender heart, unable to kill animals while hunting.[52] Those of us who are students of colonialism and imperialism know well, however, that sexuality is the most common trope of imperial domination and that phallic power defines imperialism (Teddy Roosevelt's "speak softly and carry a big stick" comes to mind), of which soldiers like England form a part. In the case of Iraq, the confluence of practices of imperial domination and the gender dynamics of Orientalism created the conditions for sexual torture through humiliation and othering. The "typical Arab male," viewed simultaneously as sex-obsessed yet not quite manly enough, was prime fodder for sexual humiliation meted out by women and would, according to a US Army official interviewed by *Time*, do anything to avoid being so dominated.[53] Indeed, England's role in the torture photos illustrates vividly the sex/gender dissociation in the operation of imperial power. As England herself told reporters, she was told to participate in some of the torture in order to pry information from the prisoners because the ultimate insult for an Arab male was to be seen naked in front of a woman. And if imperial violence mimics violence at home, Garner's participation in acts of sexual humiliation needs to be seen in continuity with, although not a complete extension of, the domestic violence he participated in at home and which his wife reported to the police.

An obvious feature of many of the pictures is their implied homosexual content. Naked males are made to pile up on top of each other, genitalia touching, as in the human-pyramid photos, or are made to stand in a row and masturbate together. In most of these photographs, the prisoners are hooded. One photograph shows a naked hooded prisoner standing legs apart, while his putative partner is on his knees giving him oral sex. Another shows a prisoner —fingers crossed behind his neck, his sandbagged head bent in submission—

as he leans on another naked prisoner. Clearly, both homophobia and Orientalism are in operation in these photographs in which Iraqi prisoners are being coerced into homosexual acts, unable to see through the sandbags over their heads, and in the presence of threatening soldiers/intelligence officers. If the Arab male is indeed a sex-obsessed being, these mass sex acts can confirm it. If he (most of the photographs are those of men) is the aberrant Other, the abject that needs to be demarcated from the masculinist, heterosexual body politic, homosexuality is a confirmation of it. In contrast, the grinning faces of the major US protagonists—Garner and England or Garner and Harman—signal the normative heterosexuality of the nation. Whether or not the male and female soldiers are indeed heterosexual (as is in fact the case with England who has since given birth to Garner's and her child) is beside the point. The issue is that of representation and domination through sexual othering. Although one could argue that women soldiers function as representatives of the patriarchal nation, and that as such they have a predictable position within that representation, in the service of US militarist imperialism today, women soldiers are bearers of empire. Just as Bush's imperial agenda seeks to unite the races with the nation through a tokenism that suppresses exclusions and inequalities, so, too, does the imperial narrative unify men and women soldiers as techno-dominant in the service of empire, suppressing the constant erosion of women's reproductive rights, among other things. In the cases of the photographs in which a male and female US soldier give a victorious thumbs-up sign, discourses of masculinity and heterosexuality function to designate the deviancy and uncertain masculinity of the Iraqis. The markers between normal (heterosexual) and aberrant (homosexual) sexuality—which are also central to the armed services and, as the reelection of George W. Bush indicates, remain central to the idea of the social body—are policed and exploited for the purposes of imperial domination.

What has surprised me is how people on both ends of the political spectrum, from Susan Sontag to Rush Limbaugh, have characterized the Iraqi torture photographs as pornography. The right-wing columnist George Will (who must, in this instance, at least be lauded for acknowledging that imperialism, including that of the United States, concerns domination) writes, for instance, that "pornography is, almost inevitably, part of what empire looks like. It does not always look like that, and does not only look like that. But empire is always about domination. Domination for self-defense, perhaps. Domination for the good of the dominated, arguably. But domination."[54] Sontag's and filmmaker Alessandro Camon's diagnoses of the photographs as pornography are not far from Will's. Sontag attributes the "confluence of torture and pornography" to the evils of readily available Internet pornography (another conservative line);[55] Camon similarly reads the readiness of female soldiers to participate in sexual torture as a consequence of women having been co-opted into watching porn and seeing "porn star" as a label of cool.[56] In addition, Camon also presents a more aesthetic reasoning to argue why the torture photographs are pornographic. Spectacularity, he suggests, forms an integral part of both porn and torture, S/M constituting the shared territory. This is a reasoning shared by Jean Baudrillard, who deems the pictures pornographic in their visibility and has titled his essay on Abu Ghraib "War Porn."[57] It is important, however, to question these porn arguments because they seriously obfuscate the sheer brutality of imperialism, its colonial antecedents and racial counterparts, shifting the focus instead to degraded cultural values, a shift that feeds the interests of the Right; they also blind us to the ideological continuities between neocon policy documents and Abu Ghraib.

At the outset, let me concede that the argument about the photos being pornographic, that is, exciting pleasurable/sexual feelings in viewers, appears perfectly valid (although not particularly useful), but this is not the same as calling the pictures pornography. No doubt, the fact that the pictures have popped up on porn Web sites and that they had to be suitably doctored for publication in magazines suggests a pornographic consumption. Obviously viewers find pleasure in the confluence of violence and sex, but in the United States, this pleasure has never been restricted to pornography alone. As Monique Guillory, who recently coordinated an exhibit on lynching, suggests, these photos would not have been made available if it were not for the murderers' desire to revel in the act.[58] Why are the Abu Ghraib photos not compared more to lynching photos than to porn? Is it the repression of lynching and its confluence of violence, racism, and sex, which, as the faces of smiling women and children in these pictures suggest, was particularly enjoyable, that the culture would rather forget?

Camon's argument for the oneness of porn and torture because of their spectacularity again begs the question of audience and intended effect. Of course, as museums of torture testify, torture is spectacular, but as Ullman and Wade have argued, both shock and awe and the bombings of Hiroshima were spectacular too. However, to analyze the bombings through the lens of porn would be to shield ourselves from the functionings of techno-dominance and the sheer human misery generated. As Foucault's description of the quartering of a prisoner in the public square at the opening of *Discipline and Punish* makes clear, torture demands a certain regime of visibility.[59] While Western societies have ostensibly abolished the use of torture as public spectacle (hence the discomfort of viewers for whom the United States denotes progress), torture has continued to be practiced under US directives overseas in countries such as Bolivia, Guatemala, and Chile, and at home in our vast network of prisons in which, as Angela Davis argues, sexual abuse is an institutionalized component.[60] Both at home and abroad, limited spectacularity has always been part of torture. Indeed, I would argue that torture cannot fulfill its purpose without being an open secret, something at once closeted and exhibited. Unlike in porn, however, spectacularity within torture serves the purpose of intimidation.

Here we come to the major problem of viewing the photos as pornography. They are pornography only if we assume—like Catharine MacKinnon, Andrea Dworkin, and a host of ultraconservatives in both Bush administrations—that pornography is only about domination and violence, and certainly about humiliation (although MacKinnon and Dworkin justifiably critique only what they see as the subjugation of women in pornography). At the very minimum, pornography has to be a representation of simulated sexual desire between or among participants. Even the corporal punishment scene of D/s functions through pleasurable desires, and pornographic simulations of these scenes attempt to represent that desire.[61] But in none of the pictures do the prisoners seem to be "into" it, whatever that it may be. In fact, we do not know what the prisoners are feeling because in the majority of the pictures—completely unlike porn where, when the face is part of the picture, facial expressions are clearly recorded to suggest a variety of pleasures—the prisoners have sandbags on their heads. When we are shown faces, as in the photographs of men facing vicious, snarling dogs, they are terror stricken, registering more the shock and terror Ullman and Wade recommended generating than anything approximating sexual desire/pleasure. This should, of course, come as no surprise given the different determinants of porn and torture. Even if one argues that pornographic actors and actresses play their roles through necessity, their participation in porn is still consensual, if highly bracketed and overdetermined; to a lesser degree, the same applies to the comparison of the torture pictures with hazing rituals.[62] The victims of hazing consent to certain rituals (which often get abused) in order to enter a certain community. Thus although the photograph of England holding a prisoner on a leash comes from a familiar repertoire of dominatrix imagery, neither the prisoner nor England seem to be deriving/simulating pleasure from the kitten-with-a-whip fantasy.[63] To call the photographs porn, then, is to completely equate porn and torture and thus deny the brutality of the latter.

More important, to make the porn argument as a cultural statement that sees sexual torture as an extension of a cultural proclivity to violence is to delink it from the machinery of imperialism and, to an extent, absolve the administration's explicit sanctioning of a masculinist techno-dominance. Instead of comparing the pictures to hazing (in a uniquely American manner, as Žižek suggests) or to porn, we are better positioned for critique when we compare them to colonial forms of torture throughout the world—that of the French in Algeria, the Japanese in Korea, and so on. The photographs, I suggest, constitute classic pictures of imperialism's sexualization of violence, humiliation, and domination, or to use Ranajit Guha's classic phrase, the sexual equivalent of "dominance without hegemony."[64] The line between porn and sexual torture meted out to prisoners by an occupying force needs to be maintained.

Finally, the discussion of the Abu Ghraib tortures as pornography can insidiously function as a means of rerouting discourses on the sexual hierarchies of the nation. By displacing their vested interest in maintaining normalized categories of gender and sexuality onto Abu Ghraib, conservatives like George Will can continue to pursue their agendas of sexual policing, albeit under a new garb. The reelection of George W. Bush through discourses of masculinity and in explicit opposition to gays speaks volumes about the national investment in sexual hierarchies supported by the antiporn decency rhetoric. Needless to say, this decency rhetoric again functions to deflect attention away from the disturbing nexus of empire, sexuality, and race that the photographs foreground.

If we accept, momentarily, Chalmers Johnson's argument that the new face of US imperialism is the proliferation of its numerous army bases in which soldiers are often provided amenities comparable to those available to colonial British administrators and in which they are not subject to the laws of the outlying nation, Abu Ghraib appears simply as part of the disciplinary apparatus of imperialism. The fact that Geoffrey Miller, then commander of the interrogation center at Guantánamo Bay (a site where the United States has stated that no prisoners' rights apply) visited Abu Ghraib and urged the commanders in Iraq to "Gitmoize" the prison system there should not be surprising. Not only have Afghanistan and Iraq been presented to the public as major threats to the well-being of the nation but as disciplinary apparatuses of the new techno-dominant empire, they also require the display of brute power, which in Abu Ghraib intersected with the raced, gendered, and sexual imperatives of Orientalism to produce the tortures that made headlines.

Thus far, I have stressed the continuity between neocon visions of techno-dominance and the photographs of torture from Abu Ghraib. However, as I pointed out early in this essay, domination is never final or, as Guha eloquently puts it, "there can be no ideal structure of power that is not subject to and modified by the contingencies of history."[65] The very excesses and contradictions of techno-dominance are now generating a dialectical undermining of US imperialism. While the soldiers at Abu Ghraib were arguably enacting a form of well-sanctioned techno-dominant imperialism, the neocon equivalent of fantasizing consent to dominance, the reception of the photographs has generated a fierce public questioning of the occupation of Iraq in the United States, as well as having generated more contempt in the Arab world about the supposed values of Americanism. What might have been clandestinely circulated as a spectacle of conquest, as was, for instance, the footage of Saddam's capture, became, after national and international publication, a spectacle of the nation's degradation in the theater of empire. (Of course, following sexist logic, the narrative of declension has been cast in terms of the opposition between good girl Jessica Lynch and bad girl Lynndie England.) The Cubans' use of the photographs as murals facing the US embassy, as a response to US condemnation of Cuba's political prisoners, speaks to the need to confront the photos as part of national policy, rather than as evidence of the abuses by a few perverted, porn-struck rotten apples. On May 17, 2004, *Time* ran on its cover a photograph of four Iraqi men reacting to a television broadcast of the torture photograph of "The Man on the Box" (the prisoner being threatened with electrocution). Vigorously engaged in conversation, they gesticulate at the television, expressing a variety of emotions. The mixture of disgust, outrage, incredulity, and anger in the reactions of four Arab men depicted in this photograph has become part of the narrative of US imperialism that must be forced to incorporate its raced Other as subjectified agent rather than as de-subjectified body. International condemnation is subjecting to scrutiny the state of exception under which prisoners, supposed terrorists, become unclassifiable "detainees," like Agamben's *homo sacer*, to be tortured with impunity.[66] Of course, pundits in the administration, as well as other conservatives, have buried the Abu Ghraib tortures as the supposedly aberrant and misguided actions of the few who have received sentences, but as colonial history teaches us, mimicry of the imperial project is never more subversive than when it magnifies and accentuates the barbarities of the original.

NOTES

1. Julia Kristeva, *Powers of Horror: An Essay on Abjection*, trans. Leon S. Roudiez (New York: Columbia University Press, 1982), 54. Kristeva identifies abjection with the fear of the maternal and the merging it represents.
2. John F. Burns, "In the Streets, a Shadow Lifts," *New York Times International*, December 15, 2003.
3. The term *domination-submission*, or D/s, denotes a variety of practices including S/M.
4. Ella Shohat, Benita Parry, and Edward Said have all commented eloquently on this turn in postcolonial studies. Parry writes how the privileging of language alone results in the colonial encounter being "rewritten as an exercise of authority that is agonistic rather than antagonistic." She continues, "If the purpose of displacing an oppositional structure is to construct colonialism as a complicated, overlapping and entangled event, then this should not imply that its operations are to be understood as necessarily conducted in a negotiatory or interstitial space. Rather, it counsels us to recognize borders as ground that is policed as well as transgressed." Benita Parry, "The Postcolonial: Conceptual Category or Chimera?" *Yearbook of English Studies*, no. 27 (1997): 13. Edward Said similarly denounced the effects of a globalized, postmodern consciousness on the field: "Anticolonial liberation theory and the real history of empire, with its massacres and exploitation, have turned into a focus on the anxieties and ambivalences of the colonizer, the silent thereby colonized and displaced somehow." Edward Said, "Globalizing Literary Study," *PMLA* 116, no. 1 (2001): 66. See also Ella Shohat, "Notes on the Post-Colonial," *Social Text* 31/32 (1992): 99–113.
5. Of the many theorists who have analyzed power, I find Ranajit Guha the most useful

because his model is complex and locally contingent. Thus while he demonstrates that power can be neither absolute nor complete, he also suggests that the specific conditions under which coercion or persuasion predominate can vary. The condition of colonialism, for instance, is a domination without hegemony or a condition in which persuasion does not predominate. See his "Domination without Hegemony and Its Historiography," in *Subaltern Studies 6* (Delhi: Oxford University Press, 1989), 229–32.

6. See V. I. Lenin, *Imperialism, the Highest Stage of Capitalism: A Popular Outline*, new rev. trans. (New York: International Publishers, 1939), 79; Immanuel Wallerstein *The Capitalist World-Economy: Essays* (New York: Cambridge University Press, 1979).
7. Today's "accumulation through dispossession," David Harvey argues, has created conditions similar to the enclosing of the commons in seventeenth-century Britain, a perspective Harvey derives from antiglobalization activists such as Arundhati Roy and Naomi Klein. See David Harvey, *The New Imperialism* (New York: Oxford University Press, 2003), 190–212; Arundhati Roy, *Power Politics*, 2nd ed. (Cambridge, MA: South End, 2001); and Naomi Klein, *No Logo: Taking Aim at the Brand Bullies* (New York: Picador, 2000). Chalmers Johnson, *The Sorrows of Empire: Militarism, Secrecy, and the End of the Republic* (New York: Henry Holt, 2004), 23.
8. Michel Foucault, *Discipline and Punish: The Birth of the Prison*, trans. Alan Sheridan (New York: Vintage, 1979), 209.
9. There have been a number of critiques of Foucault's inattention to race and colonization including Ann Laura Stoler's *Race and the Education of Desire: Foucault's* History of Sexuality *and the Colonial Order of Things* (Durham, NC: Duke University Press, 1995); Abdul JanMohamed's "Sexuality on/of the Racial Border: Foucault, Wright, and the Articulation of 'Racialized Sexuality,'" in *Discourses of Sexuality: From Aristotle to AIDS*, ed. Domna C. Stanton (Ann Arbor: University of Michigan Press, 1992), 94–116. Darius M. Rejali, *Torture and Modernity: Self, Society, and State in Modern Iran* (Boulder, CO: Westview, 1994), 8, 13–14.
10. Edward Said, *Orientalism* (New York: Vintage, 1978), 309.
11. Ibid., 300.
12. Klaus Theweleit, *Male Fantasies*, trans. Stephen Conway (Minneapolis: University of Minnesota Press, 1987). George Mosse has also demonstrated how modern European nationalism was allied with respectability, marked through its difference from forms of sexual aberrance such as masturbation and homosexuality. See George L. Mosse, *Nationalism and Sexuality: Middle-Class Morality and Sexual Norms in Modern Europe* (Madison: University of Wisconsin Press, 1985), 1, 3, 16.
13. See Ronald Hyam, *Empire and Sexuality: The British Experience* (Manchester: Manchester University Press, 1990), 2. More recently, Ann Laura Stoler has argued that sexual control constituted more than a metaphor for colonial dominance in that the very categories of colonizer and colonized were defined through forms of sexual control. See Ann Laura Stoler, *Carnal Knowledge and Imperial Power: Race and the Intimate in Colonial Rule* (Berkeley: University of California Press, 2002), 42, 45.

14. See Malini Johar Schueller, *U.S. Orientalisms: Race, Nation, and Gender in Literature, 1790–1890* (Ann Arbor: University of Michigan Press, 1998), for an examination of the different kinds of constructions of nation and sexuality through the various Orientalisms of the so-called barbary wars, Egyptology, and Indology.

15. Melani McAlister argues that the nineteenth-century construction underwent more flexibility between the end of World War II and the turn of the century, influenced, for instance, by the politics of the Nation of Islam, but that these constructions have been revived at the turn of the new century. See her *Epic Encounters: Culture, Media, and U.S. Interests in the Middle East since 1945*, rev. ed. (Berkeley: University of California Press, 2005), 2, 11, 270.

16. See also Leti Volpp, "The Citizen and the Terrorist," in *September 11 in History: A Watershed Moment*, ed. Mary L. Dudziak (Durham, NC: Duke University Press, 2000), 153.

17. Ibid., 153–54. Jonathan Goldberg's *Sodometries*, although about Renaissance England, begins with an analysis of the poster depicting Saddam being sodomized. Jonathan Goldberg, *Sodometries: Renaissace Text, Modern Sexualities* (Stanford: Stanford Univeristy Press, 1992).

18. Melani McAlister suggests the change in gender dynamics during the Gulf War, when the most popular pinup for soldiers was a white, jean-clad policewoman. Soldiers in Saudi Arabia saw her as a representation of why they were at war: because they served in a country where women received ill treatment. While McAlister rightly points to the contradiction between the pinup girl and the officer, she neglects to note that the colonial narrative of "saving" the native woman remains unchanged. See her *Epic Encounters*, 256.

19. Lee Quinby, "Women and the Techno-Millennium," *Review of Education/Pedagogy/Cultural Studies*, no. 21 (1999): 283, 287.

20. For an interesting analysis of the contradictory representations of masculinity as both public and private in the Gulf War, see Robyn Wiegman, "Missiles and Melodrama (Masculinity and the Televisual War)," in *Seeing through the Media: The Persian Gulf War*, ed. Susan Jeffords and Lauren Rabinovitz (New Brunswick, NJ: Rutgers University Press, 1994), 171–87.

21. Johnson, *The Sorrows of Empire*, 98.

22. This imperial techno-dominance also colludes with the surveillance of the domestic population through sharply increased incarceration levels since the 1980s and the introduction of various forms of disciplining of the populace since 9/11.

23. For an analysis of the relationship between masculinity and dominance, particularly in the context of war, see Susan Jeffords, *The Remasculinization of America: Gender and the Vietnam War* (Bloomington: Indiana University Press, 1989).

24. Harlan K. Ullman and James P. Wade Jr., *Shock and Awe: Achieving Rapid Dominance* (National Defense University Press, 1996).

25. See Manuel Castells, *The Power of Identity* (Malden, MA: Blackwell, 1997), 354. Although I disagree with such theorists about the loss of power for the nation-state, which

I contend has enormous disciplinary powers, as well as control of bodies and borders, there is some merit in the argument that these new technologies, such as the Internet, also escape the power of the nation-state. New, virtual, and other technologies are both part of, and can pose a resistance to, imperialism.

26. Ullman and Wade, *Shock and Awe*, chapter 1.
27. However, resistance to such categorization will not necessarily come from a postmodern feminist technomania, which might well support the necessities of multinational capitalism, or even from the confusion of the boundaries of machine and organism through cyborg bodies as articulated by Donna Haraway. While under certain conditions this confusion might well undermine gender binaries, these conditions change drastically from the Western context to that of anticolonial struggle. Can we, for instance, read cyborg disruption as functioning analogously in the body/suit of the astronaut and in the ultimate cyborg body of the suicide bomber in Palestine and Iraq? What is needed is an attention to local context and to racial-colonial difference. See Rosemary Hennessey, *Materialist Feminism and the Politics of Discourse* (New York: Routledge, 1993), 47; and Donna J. Haraway, "A Cyborg Manifesto: Science, Technology, and Socialist-Feminism in the Late Twentieth Century," in *Simians, Cyborgs, and Women: The Reinvention of Nature* (New York: Routledge, 1991), 150. Haraway writes, "By the late twentieth century, our time, a mythic time, we are all chimeras, theorized and fabricated hybrids of machine and organism; in short, we are all cyborgs. . . . This chapter is an argument for *pleasure* in the confusion of boundaries and for *responsibility* in their construction" (150).
28. Ullman and Wade, *Shock and Awe*, introduction, 3.
29. Foucault, *Discipline and Punish*, 94.
30. Rejali, *Torture and Modernity*, 14.
31. Ibid., 14.
32. Ullman and Wade, *Shock and Awe*, ch. 1, 1.
33. As David Harvey has noted, the name PNAC is notable both for its reach and for its obfuscation of territorial control. It is temporality, a century, that is being named American, rather than space. See Harvey, *The New Imperialism*, 91–92.
34. Thomas Donnelly, "Rebuilding America's Defenses: Strategy, Forces, and Resources for a New Century," report of the Project for the New American Century, September 2000, iv.
35. Ibid., v.
36. Ibid., v. The document also states that such control includes the ability to ensure the United States access to space, as well as to deny others such use (55).
37. Presidential address to the nation, September 20, 2001, 2, www.angelsharleyevents.com/presidentialaddress.html. Bush made the case for global militarism by stating, "Our war on terror begins with al-Qaeda, but it does not end there."
38. Ibid.
39. The report, "Rebuilding America's Defenses," asserts the importance of the Gulf region to the United States. Donnelly writes, "While the unresolved conflict with Iraq provides

the immediate justification, the need for a substantial American force presence in the Gulf transcends the issue of the regime of Saddam Hussein" (14).

40. Bush argued that "the regime has a history of reckless aggression in the Middle East. It has a deep hatred of America and our friends. And it has aided, trained, and harbored terrorists, including operatives of al-Qaeda." Presidential address to the nation, March 17, 2003.
41. Paul Martin, Ed Vulliamy, and Gaby Hinsliff, "US Army Was Told to Protect Looted Museum," *Guardian*, April 20, 2003.
42. Said, *Orientalism*, 287. Indeed, in *Orientalism* Said critiqued Patai for his construction of the Oriental as fixed, stable, and in need of investigation (308–9).
43. Quoted in Seymour M. Hersh, "The Gray Zone," *New Yorker*, May 24, 2004, 1.
44. Ibid., 5.
45. Quoted in Brian Whitaker, "Its Best Use Is as a Doorstop," *Guardian*, May 24, 2004.
46. These photographs were first reported to the administration by Joseph Darby, a military policeman, and to the public through CBS's airing of them on *Sixty Minutes II* at the end of April 2004. It is also important to remember that Abu Ghraib prison forms part of the hypermodern machinery of violence, the prison industrial complex, that has become central to the disciplining of the population, particularly of minorities. See Fox Butterfield, "Mistreatment of Prisoners Is Called Routine in U.S.," *New York Times International*, May 8, 2004. Abu Ghraib was refurbished under the direction of Lane McCotter, the director of a Utah-based private prison company who was forced to resign from the Utah Department of Corrections in 1997 following the death of an inmate from inhuman treatment. Just as in Abu Ghraib, physical deprivation and physical abuse of prisoners is rampant in US jails; indeed, it is codified and normalized under practices such as the strip search and forced vaginal and rectal exams. Although some prison abuse gets public attention — such as the case of the privately run Brazoria Detention Center where prisoners were bitten by dogs, kicked in the groin, and stepped on by guards — much of it remains unreported. See Angela Y. Davis, *Are Prisons Obsolete?* (New York: Seven Stories, 2003), 95–96.
47. Josh White and Christian Davenport, "Soldiers and Detainees Tell Stories behind the Pictures," *Washington Post*, May 22, 2004.
48. Kristeva, *Powers of Horror*, 4, 71.
49. Susan Sontag, "Regarding the Torture of Others," *New York Times*, May 23, 2004; and Sarah Boxer, "Humiliating Photographs as Trophies of War," *New York Times*, May 20, 2004.
50. Mike Greenwood, letter to the *Guardian*, May 25, 2004.
51. Cited in Richard Goldstein, "Bitch Bites Man!" *Village Voice*, May 10, 2004.
52. James Dao, "W.Va. Soldier Finds Herself at Center of Prison Scandal," *Gainesville Sun*, May 7, 2004.
53. Johanna McGeary, "The Scandal's Growing Stain," *Time*, May 17, 2004, 34.
54. George F. Will, "No Flinching from the Facts," *Washington Post*, May 11, 2004.

55. Sontag, "Regarding the Torture of Others."

56. Alessandro Camon, "American Torture, American Porn," salon.com, www.salon.com/opinion/feature/2004/06/07/torture/index.html.

57. Jean Baudrillard, "War Porn," trans. Paul A. Taylor, *International Journal of Baudrillard Studies* 2, no. 1 (2005),

58. Salim Muwakkil, "Dungeons and Demons," *In These Times*, May 21, 2004.

59. Foucault, *Discipline and Punish*, 3–6.

60. Davis, *Are Prisons Obsolete?* 77.

61. Dossie Easton and Catherine A. Liszt, *The Topping Book; or, Getting Good at Being Bad* (San Francisco: Greenery, 1995), 31. See also Mistress Lorelei, *The Mistress Manual: The Good Girl's Guide to Female Dominance* (Emeryville, CA: Greenery, 2000), 70.

62. See Slavoj Žižek, "What Rumsfeld Doesn't Know That He Knows about Abu Ghraib," *In These Times*, May 21, 2004.

63. Richard Goldstein in "Bitch Bites Man!" suggests that the dominatrix imagery works and is a means of allaying homosexual anxiety for the viewer. Like many others, Goldstein sees the photographs as pornographic.

64. Guha, "Dominance without Hegemony and Its Historiography," 210–310.

65. Ibid., 231.

66. On the detainees as unclassifiable, see Giorgio Agamben, *State of Exception*, trans. Kevin Attell (Chicago: University of Chicago Press, 2005), 3–4.

3 Imagining Others

MELANI MCALISTER

☆ ☆ ☆ Left Behind and the Politics of Prophecy Talk

"I have never had such a bad feeling about a war ever before," wrote Sha Twa Nee in April 2003 on the message boards for the popular evangelical Left Behind novels. The war, she said, "has given me such a 'heaviness' in my heart, knowing that it is only the beginning of more to come . . . . I do believe we are living in the end times and that this war with Iraq is the precursor war to Armageddon . . . never has there been so many signs as now in history." For a fan of the Left Behind series, Sha Twa Nee's convictions about the end times were entirely orthodox. The pathbreaking fiction series, written by the conservative evangelist Tim LaHaye and the writer Jerry Jenkins, has energized one wing of evangelical culture with a strong sense of the religious significance of events in the Middle East. The novels describe the "end of times," the rise of the Antichrist and the final battle of Armageddon, all of which figure prominently in Christian apocalyptic theory. When the twelve-book series ended in 2004, the last five releases had all debuted at number one on the *New York Times* and other best-seller lists. In total, the works have sold more than 60 million copies (including graphic novels and children's versions) since the first book appeared in 1995.[1] (In 2005, LaHaye and Jenkins published the first of three prequels to the series, which also went to number one on the *New York Times* list for a few weeks.)[2] In addition, the series has spawned two movies, no fewer than five soundtracks, calendars, mugs, an impressive line of screensavers and e-greetings, and, in early 2006, an action computer game, "Left Behind: Eternal Force."[3] Until relatively recently, the series was all but invisible in the mainstream of American culture. In the past few years, however, LaHaye and Jenkins have been at the center of friendly articles and interviews on CNN, ABC, NPR, CBS, CNBC, in *Newsweek* and *Time* magazines, and on *Sixty Minutes*, among others, and the topic of several scholarly books and articles.[4]

The Left Behind novels are unabashedly fundamentalist fictions, based on literalist interpretations of the end time as understood through the prophetic books of the Bible. They describe a group of tough-minded, action-oriented Christians who live through those events, including the rise of the Antichrist and the final battle of Armageddon. The books are not popular with all evangelicals, many of whom are not particularly interested in prophecy interpretation and do not consider it essential to their faith (though a belief in the perhaps imminent Second Coming of Jesus is nearly universal among those who call themselves evangelical). But the series has a broad and deep appeal for a substantial subset of Protestant Christians who, for the past thirty years, have made prophecy talk central to their religious practice.[5]

Although the series was already quite popular well before September 11, 2001, the events of that day spurred a new interest in the books and the larger field of biblical prophecy. For many evangelical prophecy watchers in the United States, the terrorist attacks were more than simply a horrific political crisis or personal loss; they also constituted further proof that the end of times predicted in biblical prophecy was imminent. Those who mine the apocalyptic books of the Bible for signs of the Second Coming of Christ often argue that "wars and rumors of wars," as well as great sorrow and tribulation, are key indicators of the quickening of God's plan.[6] Although there are many disagreements—schools within schools of prophecy interpretation—the overall framework is not up for debate: the end of times has been predicted in detail in the Bible, and as events unfold, the Middle East will be the stage and Israel at the heart of the story. At the battle of Armageddon, Jesus Christ himself returns to fight on the side of his chosen people against the Antichrist.

The popularity of Left Behind is no doubt connected to the much broader growth in the sales of religious-themed cultural products in the United States, which have increased by over a third in the past six or seven years. These days, one can buy anything from books on New Age spirituality and Jewish dating to Christian T-shirts and Hindi lunch boxes. Sales of religious items have blossomed in the past ten years, and religious-themed books have become by far the fastest-growing genre in the book market. There has been particularly impressive growth in Christian products, a great many of which are specifically aimed at evangelicals rather than mainline Protestants or Catholics. The evangelical culture industry includes a rapidly expanding book market that has major publishing houses like Warner Books and Bertelsmann rushing to sign up evangelical authors for their new Christian imprints. It also includes contemporary Christian music, films, videos, radio, and national conferences, all of which act as sites for talking about evangelical concerns, from family life to weight loss to global missionary work.[7]

As the United States prepared to invade Iraq in the spring of 2003, fans of Left Behind joined other Christian evangelicals in a broad-ranging discussion about foreign policy, one that traversed the Internet, Christian radio, church sermons, and various forms of popular culture. That discussion was remarkably complex, theologically and politically speaking, drawing, among other things, on notions of biblical prophecy, more general opinions about international politics, views about Islam, and debates about the application of just-war theory. Somewhere between 25 and 40 percent of Americans claim to be born again or evangelical (the exact percentage depends on how you ask the question).[8]

It is hard to determine just what percentage of evangelicals actually engage enthusiastically with prophecy; many are not particularly interested in the subject, and liberal evangelicals tend to be caustically critical. Evangelicals make up a diverse group, and their responses are marked by tensions of race, class, political values, and theology.[9] The community includes not only white evangelicals of the South and Midwest but also many African Americans (most of whom are doctrinally evangelical, though some eschew the label), some Asian Americans, and increasing numbers of Latinos, not to mention some Arabs and some converted Jews.[10] They are also theologically and politically divided, ranging from right-wing conspiracy-minded prophecy watchers to African American social conservatives who vote Democratic to the left-leaning pro-life peaceniks at *Sojourners*. Interest in prophecy is much higher among conservative white evangelicals than among the other groupings, and that subgroup has made itself into a potent cultural force, entering the public sphere not only through specific political activism but through the production and consumption of culture. (Even here, the lay of the land is complex: the Christian rapper and pop singer Toby McKeehan, formerly of DC Talk, is deeply committed to antiracism and to fighting hunger, even as he also plays at Jerry Falwell's Liberty University and as DC Talk is featured on one of the Left Behind CDs.)[11]

The Left Behind novels constitute imperialist fiction in its apocalyptic mode. Scholars rightly debate whether the post–Cold War exercise of US global power is best described as imperialist, neo-imperialist, or just an arrogant and unilateral hegemony. Whatever the case, the series offers its readers a way to see the aggressive actions of the United States (and those of terrorists or other actors in the region) as part of a divine plan. Wars, peace treaties, terrorism: these constitute secular horrors but godly promises. Certainly, the novels seem to support US expansion in the Middle East at the level of plot and characters, though that has its own complexities, given the lack of importance given to the United States as a state, as I will discuss. More important, perhaps, they present the political events of the Middle East as supernatural, literally God-given, and thus, in their overall outlines, beyond any human agency to effect — or to judge. Despite the fact that the characters fly all over the world, engage in military battles, and rescue those in need, they are acting as participants in a set of events they never imagine themselves to control. When the Antichrist uses his platform to support an Arab peace treaty with Israel, the members of the Tribulation Force know that such peace really serves as a stepping stone to his global dictatorship. They are appalled and angry, but they also realize that every step in the Antichrist's evil plan takes them one bit closer to the Second Coming of Jesus, which they wait and watch for with enthusiastic devotion. The interweaving of secular and sacred interests here is profound, and the role of such imperialist literature is not only to support US policies but to reframe those policies in ways that most US policy makers probably never imagined. As a group, however, evangelicals in general have been reliable foreign policy allies: they supported the Iraq war more enthusiastically than any other subset of the population, with 77 percent describing themselves as in favor at the onset of the conflict.

These days, conservative Christian interest in the Middle East is certainly not expressed or experienced only in novelistic form. As the conflict in Israel/Palestine escalated after the beginning of the second Palestinian intifada in 2001, evangelical preachers and their communities have rushed to Stand for Israel — organizing support rallies, letter-writing campaigns, and tours of the Holy Land linked directly to the Israeli Right.[12] These Christian Zionists seem to be having a very real influence on the Bush administration's policies as they fire off e-mails, hold lobbying days, and organize rallies to insist that the United States take the strongest stance in favor of right-wing Israeli policies to fully subjugate Palestine. LaHaye tells interviewers repeatedly that Israel's existence is one of the "super signs" signaling the coming of the end times, and he refers inevitably to the biblical injunction, so frequently cited by evangelicals, that "God promised he will bless those who bless Israel and curse those who curse Israel."[13] (Thus the question of whether President Bush's own evangelical convictions or end-times beliefs have played a role in his Middle East policies is something of a red herring. There is no question that the president's advisors have made securing and maintaining the loyalty of conservative evangelicals a primary political commitment.)

The link between political ideology and cultural consumption is of course never simple or direct, but in the past five years, and especially since September 11, the power of Left Behind as a major cultural phenomenon has an undeniable link with the resurgence of millennialist pro-Israel activism on the Christian Right and the extraordinarily dangerous directions taken by the US so-called war on terror in the Middle East. Although it is appropriate to connect Left Behind to Christian activism in support of Israel, media discussions of the issue often make one of two mistakes: either they present the novels as examples of a Christian fascination that is entirely new, and which somehow emerged full blown in recent years; or they suggest that the revitalized Christian Right is simply a return of the repressed—a new Moral Majority. Neither view is correct, and both approaches can lead to mistaken analyses of the current situation. If, for example, we fail to understand the long and deep history of the prophecy tradition in US evangelical culture (and, to a lesser but still significant degree, its power in mainstream popular culture), we will fail to see the emotional and intellectual force of current trends. Yet we also must not fail to appreciate what is new. The worldview embraced and exemplified by the Left Behind novels links biblical literalism and a traditional Christian Zionist interest in prophecy to what is in many ways a broader, even liberalizing sensibility—more sophisticated, more multicultural, and certainly more consciously modern than anything that has come before. These transformations have helped to bring what was once a culturally marginal branch of old-time religion into the mainstream of postmodern American life.[14]

This essay will explore the Left Behind series as an exemplary cultural text, one that is simultaneously a symptom of and a strategy for the renewed politicization of conservative evangelicals on issues of US foreign policy in the Middle East and the revitalization of Christian Zionism. I will analyze the novels as part of a larger project of evangelical mapping, that is, the intertwined process of making sense of the evangelical community in the United States and the United States in the world. First, the novels work to place evangelicals on the US political map as a modernized and mainstreamed political force that has moved far beyond the subcultural status marginalizing it even in the heyday of the Moral Majority. Second, the works also map the Middle East in highly specific ways. Looking to biblical passages as support for the "restoration" of Jews to Palestine, and marking Israel as the site of God's action in history, the conservative evangelical vision of Left Behind renders Palestine and Palestinians literally invisible. And as Palestine is wiped off the prophecy interpreters' map, it is also removed to the dustbin of history for a sizeable audience of American readers.

THE FUTURE IS COMING

The first novel of the Left Behind series begins when, without warning, a large group of people from all over the world suddenly and mysteriously disappear, leaving clothes and jewelry behind. The disappeared are committed Christians who have been taken up bodily into heaven—an event that evangelicals call the Rapture. Having been left behind, one small group of Americans comes to realize what has happened and, armed with the knowledge, they are then converted into committed believers. Then, in accordance with biblical prophecies, these believers must face the rise of the Antichrist, a Romanian national named Nicholae Carpathia who rose to power as the head of the United Nations and now is a global dictator. He will persecute Christians and Jews and lead a global crusade against Israel. Carpathia builds himself a gleaming capital city from which to rule the world—a shining symbol of the totalitarian one-world order—in New Babylon, Iraq. The Antichrist's rule will coincide with the Tribulation, seven years of suffering marked by a terrifying and devastating series of plagues in which millions of people are killed. The plagues include earthquakes, water turning to blood, drought, and the invasion by death-dealing horsemen of the air who kill with fire, sulfur, and smoke.

The group of believers quickly forms itself into an anti-Antichrist underground dubbed the Tribulation Force. Over the course of several novels, the membership of the force evolves, but the key players are four: Raymond Steele, an expert pilot in his forties who becomes the official leader of the group; his daughter Chloe, recently a college student; Chloe's husband, Buck, a crack journalist; and, eventually, Tsion Ben-Judah, an Israeli Jew who, after carefully studying the prophecies in the Bible, converts to believing that Jesus of Nazareth was the predicted Jewish Messiah. By stating his newfound conviction to the world, Tsion becomes one of the first of the 144,000 "witnesses" —Jewish converts who testify to the world that they accept Christ as their Messiah. Tsion becomes the spiritual mentor of the Tribulation Force and, eventually, of the new believers who begin to spring up around the world.

LaHaye and Jenkins have constructed fast-paced and plot-driven stories that are also generic hybrids, combining traditional evangelical homily with science fiction–like threats and action adventure thrills, complete with plenty of male bonding and high-flying action. The Christians who form the core of the stories are tough and modern people, strong and resourceful. Several of them are professional pilots and can thus zip around the world in Gulfstreams or old Egyptian fighter planes. They face the dramatic plagues and terrible dangers of the end times as well-equipped international travelers, with access to private jets, untraceable cell phones, untouchable bugging devices, and advanced laptop computers described in loving detail. The novels thus gesture toward Tom Clancy in their style, Stephen King in their sensibility, and Ian Fleming in their plot structures. Laced with wry humor and yet also featuring frequent, detailed statements of theological doctrine, they are worlds away from an older, didactic terrain of prophecy exegesis. Instead, they exhibit what can best be described as evangelical worldliness—a melding of traditional subcultural views with a mass-culture style and a broad, mainstreamed appeal.

The Left Behind series is deeply embedded in a long-established tradition of evangelical thought that looks to the books of Ezekiel, Daniel, and Revelation for information about the end times and the Second Coming of Christ. Evangelicals generally regard the Bible as literal truth, but, in the face of the allusive and elusive texts of the prophecies, they must become hermeneutic experts, unpacking highly metaphorical passages for their predictive value. Drawing on the interpretations developed by John Darby in the nineteenth century and popularized in the 1909 Scofield Reference Bible, generations of evangelicals have held that the Bible's accuracy can be tested and confirmed by political developments, especially those concerning Israel.[15] While the doctrinal specifics vary among different groups, all agree that in the Bible one important signal of the approach of the Second Coming of Christ is the return of Jews to the Holy Land. Then, according to prophecy, as the end times approach, an Antichrist will arise, claiming to bring peace. During the tribulations under the Antichrist, both Jews and Christian believers will be persecuted. (Various groups disagree about whether the Rapture of believers will happen before or after the tribulation. The Left Behind novels are exemplars of the theory of pre-Tribulation Rapture. Pat Robertson is a well-known proponent of the belief that the Rapture will happen *after* the Tribulation.) All agree that as God shows his hand and the truth of the Christian Bible's prophecies are revealed, a mass conversion of Jews to the recognition that Jesus was their Messiah will occur. At the end of seven years, Israel, threatened by a confederacy of most of the nations of the world, will face down her enemies at a final, terrible battle of Armageddon, during which Christ himself will return to do battle for Israel. After Christ's return, the millennial reign of one thousand years of peace begins.[16]

Evangelical enthusiasm for prophecy study quickened after the founding of Israel in 1948, but it was mobilized to a near frenzy when, after the 1967 Arab-Israeli war, the Israelis occupied all of Jerusalem, just in time for the revival of fundamentalism in the United States. For many, Israeli control of the Holy City was a crucial indication — perhaps *the* indication — that "this generation" will see the coming of Christ. In 1970, Hal Lindsey published *The Late Great Planet Earth*, a popularization of evangelical doctrines of the end times that used accessible language and a pseudohip writing style to target worried baby boomers on the edge of the counterculture. It went on to become the best-selling nonfiction book of the 1970s.[17]

Lindsey, like others before and after him, highlighted the *political* significance of his interpretations of biblical prophecy: the Middle East wars that had happened, and those that were coming, were predicted and explained in the Bible. Lindsey also aimed to bring the study of prophecy a new kind of panache: he wanted to reach audiences, particularly young audiences, who might be interested in politics first, and convinced of Christian revelation as a result.

At the same time, he also pushed hard against traditional evangelical opposition to worldliness: Christians *must* begin to pay attention to politics, he argued, and in particular to foreign policy, because the Middle East, particularly the nation of Israel (and its allies and enemies), would be central to the greatest *religious* test of all time. In this context, political events become important because of how they fit into a biblical scheme, and interpreting that scheme makes for a complex and politically saturated process.[18]

These general views about prophecy, politics, and Israel explicitly formed part of the conservative evangelical activism of the late 1970s, when the community began making itself felt as a political force. In 1978, Jerry Falwell told reporters, and later repeated in his preaching, that he believed that Christians must involve themselves politically in such a way as to guarantee that the United States would support Israel: "I believe that if we fail to protect Israel, we will cease to be important to God. . . . We can and must be involved in guiding America towards a biblical position regarding her stand on Israel."[19] When the Moral Majority was founded in 1979, one of its founding principles read: "We support the state of Israel and the Jewish people everywhere."[20]

The writers of the Left Behind novels hail from that earlier era, the 1970s and 1980s, when evangelicalism's political power was on the rise. LaHaye, who provides the biblical commentary and prophecy interpretation that structures each novel, was active in the Moral Majority and in 1987 was deposed as cochairman of Jack Kemp's presidential campaign for having called Catholicism a "false religion" and blaming Jewish suffering on the Jewish rejection of Jesus.[21] Jenkins, who does all of the actual writing, was a staff writer for the evangelical powerhouse the Moody Bible Institute, as well as the collaborator on Billy Graham's autobiography and a ghostwriter for several sports autobiographies before he turned to the series. Although LaHaye has until recently enjoyed less visibility than television preachers like Falwell and Robertson, his intellectual and cultural influence has been tremendous. He is one of the founding members of the deeply conservative and secretive Council on National Policy. He is also married to Beverly LaHaye, the founder of the conservative Concerned Women for America, the antigay, antifeminist, antiabortion and pro-creationist enterprise that currently claims to be "the largest public policy women's organization" in the country.[22] Even before the Left Behind series, he had published more than forty books on marriage and family, "sexual adjustment," and, of course, biblical prophecy. Recently, Jerry Falwell established the Tim LaHaye School of Prophecy at Liberty University in Lynchburg, Virginia.[23]

The fascination with end-times theology is inevitably political, but it is not always, or at least only, ideologically driven. Left Behind uses images, character types, and even whole scenes from the subcultural industry of novels and movies that since the early 1970s, have been making prophecy, the Rapture, and Armageddon staples of evangelical popular culture.[24] As one scholar of evangelicalism has pointed out, prophecy interpretation can be *fun*. Unpacking obscure biblical passages, evangelicals debate what the founding of the European Union signifies, or how the oil crisis or Operation Desert Storm fit into the prophetic scheme. By providing avenues for meditating on the future, both politics and religion get energized by their relationship to each other.[25] Many mainline Protestant leaders have spoken out against end-times theology in general, and even evangelicals have strong theological disagreements with an approach that focuses heavily on the possibility of an imminent Second Coming.[26] Yet the appeal remains, bringing the distinct passions and proclivities of politics junkies, sci-fi fans, horror aficionados, and spy-novel readers to the world of prophecy watching.

If some popular analyses of Left Behind and/or current evangelical culture fail to appreciate the depth of this history, it is perhaps not surprising that the other major response of secular commentators has been to see the novels as the vanguard for a revival of 1980s-style political fundamentalism. At one level, this view is entirely justified. As Michelle Goldberg argued on salon.com, it is surely significant that "the most popular fiction in the country creates a gripping narrative that pits American Christians against a conspiracy of Satan-worshipping, abortion-promoting, gun-controlling globalists—all of it revolving around the sovereignty of Israel."[27] The on-the-ground political power of Christian Zionism is undeniable. Representative Jim Inhofe (R-OK), as well as his former colleagues Dick Armey (R-TX) and Tom DeLay (R-TX), positioned themselves as highly visible and hard-line congressional supporters of Israel: In an MSNBC interview, Armey called for the transfer of the Palestinian population out of the West Bank, before offering a halfhearted retraction the next day; Inhofe has said on the House floor that Israel should keep the West Bank, "because God said so."[28] Grassroots churches are increasingly in the mix, raising money to fund Jewish immigrants to populate Israeli settlements, for example, or joining the estimated sixteen thousand congregations who participated in the so-called Pray for Israel day in October 2002.[29] When President Bush called for Ariel Sharon to withdraw Israeli tanks from Palestinian territory in the spring of 2002, Falwell and others organized the Religious Right to send nearly a hundred thousand e-mails to the White House to protest the request.[30] When the Christian Coalition held its Rally for Israel in October 2002, President Bush sent a videotaped message, while Tom DeLay and the mayor of Jersualem both gave speeches.[31]

In fact, the enthusiastic embrace of Israeli "security" and Israeli settlements includes not only a strong push in Congress but also a close alliance with Israeli leadership—an alliance that goes back to the Israel Labor Party's embrace of fundamentalism in the 1970s, when the Israeli government began courting evangelical leaders and hosting Holy Land tours for well-known preachers (including Falwell and Bailey Smith of the Southern Baptist Convention), and which only intensified under the right-wing Likud government elected in 1978.[32] In January 2002, the Israeli embassy in Washington held the first of a series of meetings with conservative Christian leaders and launched a drive to encourage Christian tourism to Israel; later that year, Sharon spoke to an enthusiastic crowd of thousands of evangelicals in Jerusalem.[33] Observers argue that these activities are making a real difference, for quite pragmatic political reasons. While of course it cannot be ignored that President Bush has every reason to want to secure the position of Jeb Bush in Florida, where his strong support for Israel is also winning him increasing support from Jewish voters, this is only a small part of the story.[34] Many congressional Republicans have few Jewish constituents but a large number of conservative Christian ones, and their support has been seen as instrumental in pushing Congress to more hawkish positions.[35] One recent poll showed that 44 percent of Americans believe that God gave the land that is now Israel to the Jewish people, while 36 percent—almost exactly the number of declared evangelicals—believe that "the state of Israel is a fulfillment of the biblical prophecy of the second coming of Jesus."[36] As one commentator in the *Jerusalem Post* put it: "The US is Israel's best friend largely because the American Christian community wills it to be so."[37]

To the degree that critics of the Christian Right see these actions *only* as a revitalizing version of Reagan-era Christian activism, however, they are likely to miss the important ways in which the political culture of fundamentalism is changing—maintaining deeply conservative views on Israel and US foreign policy generally, but otherwise revamping its cultural politics. In the Left Behind novels, we see not only what one reviewer has called the "conspiratorial balderdash" of some conservative evangelicals' political ideology but also a significant outward reach in terms of both style and content.[38] The Left Behind novels claim to be about the future—"prophecy is history written in advance," LaHaye once said—but they are also very much about the present and about a new kind of evangelical self-fashioning that self-consciously reaches out to the larger world—in part to evangelize that world, certainly, but also in part to construct a complex set of connections to it. As evangelical performance, these novels struggle to enact modernity and to establish both for their protagonists and, implicitly, for their readers the kind of broad cultural reach that might authorize evangelical mappings of American global politics.

NOT YOUR FATHER'S FUNDAMENTALISM

Chang Wong is seventeen years old, cocky and tough, a new convert to Jesus. He is also the technical czar for Nicholae Carpathia's Global Community government, working out of the headquarters in New Babylon. Carpathia and his team fully trust Chang since he appears to have the Antichrist's "mark of loyalty" on his forehead. The young Chang is a computer whiz, and from his position in the belly of the beast, he controls the computers and surveillance system through which the Antichrist keeps track of the population and tries to hunt down those who oppose his rule: Christian converts and Orthodox Jews. Chang is able to thwart the system at every turn. At a key moment, as the Antichrist prepares to interdict the Jews who have retreated to Petra (where they will be protected by God), Chang is able to force the simultaneous broadcast of the spiritual leader Tsion Ben-Judah's sermon over every television channel, radio station, and Web site on the Internet. While he is doing that, Chang is also listening to the plotting of Carpathia and his henchmen via the absolutely secure bugging device that the Tribulation Force has installed on the Antichrist's personal plane. As he listens, automatic filters provide the simultaneous translation of conversations held in languages other than English. When Chang hears that the security team is about to track down some key members of the Tribulation Force, he immediately enters the computer system and erases all trace of them in the database. He is not worried about being caught because his system is so thoroughly encrypted — it has a "revolving encoder" — that it is impenetrable even by the forces of the one-world government.

In this scene, and literally hundreds of others like it over the course of the series, LaHaye and Jenkins establish their characters as highly competent and hypermodern. Making the most of the fact that the events they describe must necessarily take place in the future (though a rather near-term future, in their view), the novels present a world in which our Tribulation Force members are unfailingly knowledgeable about, and outfitted with, an impressive array of the best possible equipment, from guns to high-end SUVs, from Gulfstream jets to the "computer without limitations" ordered by the Tribulation Force from an underground dealer. Leaving aside the ways in which the novels' various fantasies about the power of perfect gear actually expose a certain technological naïevete, the embrace of matériel is not simply decorative; it performs important cultural work. If evangelicals at the turn of the century still carry a residual reputation as old-fashioned and unsophisticated, *these* characters leave no doubt about their up-to-dateness. They are unflappable globetrotters, as comfortable whipping out their cell phones during a rescue mission as they are in witnessing to an unconverted colleague while piloting the most advanced aircraft in the world.

This technological savvy is present not only within the novels but in the marketing of the series as well. Though Left Behind sales have a strong base in Christian bookstores and superstore chains centered in the heartland, like Wal-Mart, the series is also supported by a highly sophisticated Web page that its managers claim receives sixty thousand visitors a day. Leftbehind.com has a younger, hipper presence far less apparent in the other marketing efforts for the series (such as NASCAR promotions). It includes visual images that can be downloaded as screensavers and e-cards, message boards and discussion groups, online polls, advertising for products, an e-mail newsletter, and so on.[39] The message boards on leftbehind.com have many active threads at once, with several threads posting hundreds of entries at any given time. The sections designed to promote the graphic novel versions of the books, or the separate series for children, Left Behind: The Kids, are visually arresting, with the pulsating text and moving images that characterize video games.

On the official site, and on several nonofficial fan pages, there is a great deal of the fan accoutrement that the Internet has made routine: quizzes, games based on the characters, chat rooms for fans who want to meet each other on the Internet, and, perhaps most important, postings of fan fiction. The fiction entries are generally short stories, usually penned by people in their teens and twenties, and they often add new, younger characters to the series. Yet despite this impressive Web presence, the use of the Web sites makes for a more complicated question; as with many fan-based sites, the vast majority of posters constitute a rather small group (probably no more than three thousand) of participants, almost all of whom are under thirty.[40] Tyndale publishers has said that the average buyer of the books is a Southern, white, married female between the ages of twenty-five and fifty-four.[41] It is easy to imagine that many of those buyers pick up the books at Wal-Mart, read them, and perhaps even share them with friends, without ever going so far as to visit a Web site. This opens the question of how much the impressive Internet presence functions, like the "untraceable" Internet connections of the books' protagonists, to promote a particular image of evangelical Christianity—rather than serve the needs of Internet-savvy fans.

Such worldliness and ease with modernity is doubly striking in that it frames, and perhaps in some sense even cushions, the uncompromising religious views propounded in the novels. At the level of evangelical doctrine, the Left Behind series is unreconstructed and proud of it: there is only Jesus Christ, Christianity is the only truth, and winning converts is the primary moral duty of the characters (and, one presumes, of the novels themselves). This purity is contrasted with the evil One World faith propounded by the Antichrist and led by a pompous, ritual-obsessed fraud priest who, before the Rapture, was a Catholic archbishop. The One World faith defines itself as eclectic and open to all beliefs, but in fact, it does little more that provide a platform for the eventual worship of the Antichrist while encouraging decadence and immorality. Thus when, in one of the early novels, the leader of this syncretic abomination calls our Tribulation Force members a "right-wing, fanatic, evangelical faction," we as readers are invited to consider the source and take it as a compliment.[42] It is not despite but *because of* this doctrinal conservatism that the novels also insist throughout on a certain kind of secular situatedness for their characters: with their high-powered jobs and their impressive access to the best computers and the fastest planes, these end-times Christians speak the high-tech language of the unbelieving world around them.

Speaking that language also means operating in its preferred generic registers, and nothing is more striking about the Left Behind series than formal intersections with — even slavish devotion to — the conventions of popular science fiction and horror. The evangelical world, at least during the years of the Tribulation, is littered with lower-level supernatural creatures: demons and angels in the flesh, ghostly horsemen in the sky who can be seen only by believers, and of course Satan incarnate in the person of the Antichrist. Here, for example, is the description of the first demonic invaders of the Tribulation, called Apollyon: "Buck stared out the window, and his heart thundered against his ribs. From out of the smoke came flying creatures — hideous, ugly, brown and black and yellow flying monsters. Swarming like locusts, they looked like miniature horses five or six inches long with tails like those of scorpions. Most horrifying, the creatures were attacking, trying to get in."[43] In addition, we learn that these creatures also have a man's face, long flowing hair, and a golden crown. The locusts attack nonbelievers in a swarm, attaching themselves to the body, stinging and biting their victims. Christian believers are immune. In one scene, a loyal but unconverted household employee is caught outside, attacked, and felled by the creatures. He lies screaming and writhing until Buck, fearful but protected, rushes outside to combat the invaders and rescue him. The debt to science fiction tales of alien attack, or sci-fi/horror narratives of monstrous invasion, is obvious here, right down to the hero who must leave the safe house to rescue his buddy from the creatures. In the tribulations faced by those left behind, the invaders who torment nonbelievers are satanic forces that are nonetheless in the service of god. The Christian heroes of the novels face them with the mix of awe and fear and yet hope that has so often attended accounts of alien abduction: the superior beings, with their nightmarish bodily invasions and probings, leave the vivid impression that this encounter indicates malevolent intent and perhaps future destruction.

The science fiction address of the series is even more apparent on the Web page images designed to accompany each book, which draw on the look and feel of popular action and sci-fi movies: weapons, anxious people fleeing a scene, or nightmarish post–nuclear war–style devastation familiar to anyone who has seen *Terminator* or *Mad Max*. The e-card/screensaver for *Apollyon* works as a perfect apocalyptic cliché: in the background, a destroyed building, with only the half-standing outline of the structure left. Strangely orangish clouds dominate the sky; fires burn on the street. In the foreground, a large, almost distended image of a man's face; he is middle-aged, probably white, and his eyes are bulging, fearful. The image for *The Mark*, the eighth book in the series, shows a futuristic urban skyline—tall, streamlined buildings against a darkening sky. In the middle of the scene is a harshly lit building guarded by men in suits with machine guns, with lines of people streaming into it. For those who have read the book, this is the "loyalty mark enforcement center," where people are forced to apply the mark of loyalty to the Antichrist or face execution. For those who might not have read Left Behind, the building is nonetheless easy to recognize: it is any of those station stops in the world after *1984* where unwitting victims go to face a lobotomy, the alien takeover of their minds, or a mandatory execution at age thirty.

In terms of plot, the science fiction connection makes sense. The dramatic nature of the events is plausible only in the sense that the entire end-times scenario is *supposed* to be otherworldly—it is, after all, the story of the judgments of God and the rise to power of supernatural evil. So when the Antichrist takes over the United Nations and then takes control of the world's military, police forces, and finances, the level of his power and the extent of his malice are credible precisely either to the degree that the reader believes in the general outlines of the evangelical interpretation of the prophetic books of the Bible or to the degree one is willing to suspend disbelief in order to enjoy the pleasures of a story of conflict between great evil and great good. The science fiction tie also works at the level of form, functioning much like the technology fetish within the stories, with invading demons, narrow escapes, flawed but brave heroes, and the race to get the fancy technology to do the bidding—always just in time. Science fiction fans can recognize not only the futuristic plot elements but the emotional language of a favored genre as well.

RACIAL LIBERALISM, RACIST CONSERVATISM

The voice of the Left Behind series is distinctly modern in another way as well: it suggests that while the chosen believers at the end of times may be doctrinally narrow, they are culturally and racially expansive. In the world of the evangelical future, there is little room for discrimination among God's people.

The rather striking racial liberalism in the books has both a domestic politics and a global reach, and it is linked to both kinds of maps that structure the cultural politics of the novels. That is, race politics works both to map conservative evangelicalism into the mainstream of US domestic politics *and* to mainstream within US foreign policy the evangelical mapping of a Holy Land without Palestine or Palestinians.

Domestically, the history of white evangelicalism in the United States has often been one of racial exclusivity and prejudice. In the 1960s, the largely Southern base for white evangelicals helped to establish their firm opposition to racial integration.[44] And into the 1980s, the Moral Majority and then the Christian Coalition did little more than pay lip service to issues of race, despite the fact that the beliefs of many black Christians were clearly evangelical in doctrine. But in the 1990s, with the rise of the Promise Keepers and other new parachurch organizations, evangelicals of all races began to talk more extensively about crossing racial barriers, and they did so in ways that brought discussions of racism into the heart of white evangelism.[45] It perhaps should not be so surprising, then, that LaHaye and Jenkins put the white characters who form the core of the Tribulation Force through their multicultural paces: at various times, they work closely with at least two African American male characters, one set of Chinese Christians, a Native American woman, two Muslim Arab converts, and uncountable numbers of Israeli Jews. The plot consistently presents racial liberalism as the norm for the characters, and implicitly for the readers as well.

In the fourth book, for example, the first of two important African American characters is introduced into the plot. Dr. Floyd Charles is a young physician who helps save Buck's wife Chloe when she is pregnant, injured, and on the run from the forces of the Antichrist. Floyd is soon making regular visits to the Tribulation Force's safe house; he eventually ends up living there and, in the process, falling in love with a woman in the group, Hattie. When Floyd reveals his feelings for Hattie to Rayford, who functions as the Tribulation Force's leader, the latter expresses deep concern. This concern, however, is not framed as an issue of race; the fact that Floyd is black and Hattie is white goes unmentioned in their discussion. Instead, Rayford is worried that Hattie is simply not a good enough person for Floyd since she is both unconverted and remarkably selfish. Though Floyd conveniently dies before he can even de-clare his love to Hattie, much less act on it, it is nonetheless remarkable that the Left Behind series would present an interracial relationship as so utterly noncontroversial (what *is* controversial is falling in love with a nonbeliever). It says volumes about the ways in which white conservative evangelicalism has changed its self-presentation, both within the community itself and in terms of its public voice on issues of race.

In *Divided by Faith*, Michael Emerson and Christian Smith have argued that despite white evangelicals' expressed desire to overcome racism, the extreme individualism of evangelical culture and theology make it all but impossible for many of them to perceive and acknowledge systemic racial injustice. White evangelicals concerned about racial issues focus on activities that are piecemeal and interpersonal, such as socializing with a person of another race or working at a soup kitchen, rather than approaching problems of structural inequality.[46] One sees a particularly awkward instantiation of that problem in the Left Behind series. Although LaHaye and Jenkins have obviously made a conscious decision to bring African Americans into close proximity with the core characters, the novels nonetheless register a particular self-consciousness about this fact—one that at times borders on self-parody. On several occasions, for example, Buck or Rayford make what the authors seem to think are rather cute jokes playing off of the parallels between the concept of brothers in Christ and the trope of African American men as brothers. At another point, an older and uglier stereotype appears: when Rayford and Floyd find themselves in trouble, Rayford asks the other African American male character, T. M. Delanty ("T"), to help him by trading cars with Floyd. T has never met Floyd, and Rayford explains that he can recognize Floyd because of the vehicle he is driving—and the fact that he "looks a lot like you."[47] A few pages later, LaHaye and Jenkins have T refer back to this apparent reality—that black men basically look alike—as useful in carrying out an escape plan. This character is forced, in other words, to testify in favor of the quiet racial presumptions that defy the overt embrace of Christian diversity.

The global racial and religious politics of the novels are even more complex, and equally problematic. As the Tribulation Force expands its global reach—over the course of the series, more and more of the action is set in New Babylon, Iraq, where the Antichrist has set up his headquarters—the white American members run into diverse believers all over the world. In one novel, an Israeli Jew who has also converted to Christianity gets a friendly lesson on avoiding stereotypes from a Native American woman named Hannah Palemoon.[48] Later in the series, the young Chinese man, Chang, moves to the forefront of the action as he battles with his father over his Christian beliefs. And soon Chang's sister Ming becomes a leading character, and her emerging romance with a Korean believer is followed enthusiastically.

These international characters are among the most popular on the fan sites, and it is here that one gets the strongest sense of a worldview in which multiculturalism, albeit of a rather limited type, is the presumptive norm. One female fan, for example, has written a series of stories on a fan Web site about a young man named Jonathan Palemoon, who she describes as Hannah Palemoon's younger brother. On the story site, she listed among her character's strengths his "family and his heritage," as well as his martial arts skills.[49] Early in the series, T, the African American man, was frequently listed by contributors to the message boards as their favorite; since the last few books were released, Chang, the young computer hack with parent problems, has been widely embraced.[50]

The internationalism of this multiculturalist vision is precisely of a piece with the stark doctrinal narrowness of the stories: *anyone* can convert, but conversion to (born-again) Christianity is of course necessary to be recognized by God. This has been the source of concern for a good many Jewish and Israeli commentators, who have pointed out that the evangelical love of Israel comes at the price of a belief in the massive conversion of Jews at the end of time—144,000 Jewish "witnesses" recognize Jesus as the Messiah and join with the non-Jewish believers to fight the Antichrist. As Gershom Gorenberg has argued, this seeming embrace of Jews and Israel is merely instrumental, at best. At worst, it is vicious: Israeli Jews exist to testify, in the end, to the truth of Christianity.[51] On the other hand, the views about conversion are entirely consonant with the larger evangelical view of the "narrow road" to heaven. When conservative Christians insist that Jews, Muslims, and all others must convert in order to see God, this is perhaps best understood less as racism or anti-Semitism per se than as simple doctrinal conservatism. (There are, of course, other examples of conservative evangelical anti-Semitism, including the LaHaye statements I mentioned above. My argument here is that the requirement of, and enthusiasm for, Jewish conversion is not, in itself, anti-

Jewish.) However, and this is surely not incidental, there are no American Jews in Left Behind: either American Jews are of little interest in a novelistic world focused on the scriptural importance of Israel, or, perhaps more likely, LaHaye and Jenkins are intensely conscious of recent controversies about attempts to evangelize American Jews and would rather not stir up that debate. In either case, the omission is telling: not only are Jews instrumental *when* they matter but they do not matter at all unless they make themselves of interest to God by becoming Israelis.

Arabs and Muslims, however, fare much worse, though they are also subject to a version of the deadly love offered to Jews. In 2002, the news media reported a rather extraordinary series of anti-Muslim slurs by evangelical leaders. Jerry Falwell, for example, made an infamous declaration on *Sixty Minutes* that "Muhammad was a terrorist," and Pat Robertson warned on his Christian Broadcasting Network that Muslims are "worse than the Nazis."[52] Yet in the Left Behind series, Arabs and Muslims are woven into a much more complicated cultural tapestry. The evil characters include Muslims, preeminently Suhail Akbar, the demonic Pakistani who serves as the Antichrist's head of security. But Akbar is just one member of what is a virtual rainbow coalition of evil, including the Antichrist himself, a Romanian; his right-hand man, the Italian American Leon Fortunato; the leader of the abominable One World faith, the former Catholic US (presumably white) bishop Peter Matthews; and, later, the Chinese security expert Walter Moon. In addition, there have been, over the course of the series, several moments in which Islam and/or Arabs were positioned ambivalently. In *Remnant*, for example, there is a fairly long scene in which a group of Chinese Muslims prove themselves to be holdouts against the Antichrist and are thus about to be executed. The views of Islam are summarized briefly but respectfully. Just before they are about to die, a group of the Muslims convert to Christianity and thus assure their assent to heaven.[53] In the earlier novels, two key Arab characters emerged, both of whom are Muslims who convert after the Rapture. Both are presented as highly positive individuals. One, Al-B, or "Albie" (described as a native of Al Basrah, Iraq, which in later novels is glossed as simply "north of Kuwait"), plays a key role in many of the novels' most daring rescues and escapes. The second is Abdullah Smith — "the name looks weird," his friend Mac explains, "but he has his reasons."[54] Abdullah is a Jordanian pilot and is almost always named as a favorite character on the fan sites: one young person has even taken his name as her *nom de Web*, and he is often featured in fan fiction as well.

In fact, Abdullah emerges as one of the central characters of the entire last half of the series. As one of the pilots who can ferry the Tribulation Force members back and forth between the United States and the Middle East, he is key to the plot. But he is also figured as a good friend to several of the important male characters at the heart of the story, particularly the Tribulation Force leader Rayford, another pilot. Abdullah is one of the tough men of action who provide the story's emotional center; he is laconic but has a rough and earthy sense of humor that allows him to trade friendly insults with another pilot, a white American named Mac. When Abdullah first appears, his broken English is presented as the source of "friendly" amusement for other characters, as well as, presumably, for readers.[55] Later, as he becomes more central to the Tribulation Force, he and Mac trade the kind of ethnic jokes that are supposed to be the staple of locker-room and battlefield bonding: Abdullah makes fun of Mac's "Texan" talk and calls him a "cowboy"; Mac returns by calling him a "camel jockey."[56] Here, as with the African American characters in the earlier novels, LaHaye and Jenkins exhibit a genuine but awkward embrace of diversity and yet a none-too-subtle racism: Abdullah is warmly welcomed into the fraternity of Christian believers, but he must consistently perform as a (racially) marked man.

The more subtle but perhaps more important signifier within the world of Left Behind is the fact that Abdullah is located as Jordanian, not Palestinian. In fact, there are *no* Palestinian Arabs ever mentioned in a series that has much of the action take place in Jerusalem and the surrounding areas. There are Arabs, presumably, in the masses who gather to hear the Antichrist when he speaks in Jerusalem, but in those moments, it is Jews and Israel that actually matter: Israeli Jews are key doctrinally, and they are central characters in the novels as they convert, provide leadership to other believers, and, in one of the recent novels, find themselves gathered and protected in the city of Petra as the Antichrist marshals his forces.

So it is that the mapping of characters' identities is also a mapping of the space of Palestine/Israel, precisely because the very notion of Palestinian is made invisible, impossible. There are Muslims and there are Arabs in Left Behind, but there are no Arab Christians (except those who convert), and there are no Palestinians. Within the logic of the series, Palestinians cannot convert like Abdullah or Albie, and they cannot resist like the righteous Chinese Muslims, because they are simply outside the representational possibilities of the Left Behind world. Dick Armey's suggestion that Palestinians should be removed from the West Bank and Gaza, and Pat Robertson's insistence that Israel should never compromise one bit of land, are enacted within the novels as wish fulfillment: there is no Palestinian problem on the evangelical map.

CONCLUSION

In the summer of 2002, *Time* magazine featured the Left Behind series on its cover, just in time to usher in the release of *The Remnant*. With several closely related stories, including a flattering portrait of LaHaye, *Time* explained the popularity of the novels as a sign of the times: in a post–September 11 world, the stories provided hope, a certainty about the future, and a promise that the good guys won in the end. There might be *some* problems with the series: *Time* pointed out that there was a sense of unease among some religious scholars about the books' enthusiasm for the violence and devastation afflicted during the end times. As the theologian Harvey Cox suggested, it is impossible to read the series without getting the impression that a certain "lip-licking anticipation of all the blood" is involved.[57]

What mattered most about the *Time* story was not its ideological slant—it carried the requisite combination of reporting balance, slightly snide tone, and empty summations that are *Time*'s standard for most stories—but the fact that it was there at all. Left Behind had reached the very heart of mainstream media and had been received both as a doctrinal juggernaut—evangelical views on the apocalypse were reported in impressive detail—and as a popular culture sensation. The sense was that evangelical culture was not only tapping into the mainstream of American life but might indeed *be* the mainstream of American life. After all, *Time* reported, its own poll with CNN showed that 59 percent of Americans believed that the events in Revelation are going to come true.[58]

After September 11, fighting in Israel and Palestine escalated considerably. The Oslo process was all but over, and there were increasing numbers of suicide bombings by Palestinians against Israeli civilians, followed by Israeli ground incursions and then missile attacks on Palestinian refugee camps. The death toll rose, anger and despair became heightened all around, and the US media feverishly recounted each new atrocity. With the US war on terrorism stalled and the occupation of Iraq a disaster, American policy had provided remarkably little in the way of satisfying vengeance or morally righteous certainties. The Israeli-Palestinian conflict, on the other hand, remained a repository of longings for righteous battle.

In this context, righteous Israeli Jews, fighting an Antichrist located in New Babylon, might well begin to look like "history written in advance." In fact, in the Web discussion in which Sha Twa Nee expressed her anxiety about the impending war in Iraq, another poster told her not to worry so much: "Relax! Enjoy watching the Bible come to life!" Another Left Behind fan suggested as much to a *Time* reporter, when he explained that he was sure the Antichrist was already among us: "He's probably a good-looking man," he said. "I'm sure he's in politics right now and probably in the public eye a little bit." Left Behind, he explained, "helped me to look at the news that's going on about Israel and Palestine" and to understand that it "is just ushering in the End Times, and it's exciting for me."[59] If that view seems like a nightmare for secular politics, in the context of prophecy interpretation, such excitement makes sense: Israel is fulfilling its biblical destiny in its conflict with the Palestinians, and those battles, along with the current struggle in Iraq, are necessary conditions for the Second Coming of Jesus.

Mobilizing and organizing such views, Left Behind participates in the larger project of evangelical mapping, both domestically and internationally. That mapping positions evangelical cultural styles within the US mainstream, through an embrace of popular culture genres, expressions of high-tech savvy, and a self-conscious embrace of multiculturalism. And it marks — and markets — a particular vision of the Middle East, one that sees Iraq as the home of the Antichrist and Israel as a nation chosen by God as an instrument of his plan. This moral geography of the Middle East is not new; the enthusiastic embrace of the region's politics as religious revelation has a long tradition in evangelical thought and popular culture. In the current wave, however, it has reached a much broader audience and has played a role in mainstreaming the Manichaean views that see Christianity in a conflict with Islam and the United States in a battle with evil. On those maps, conservative prophecy-watching evangelicals define the terrain; Israel controls all of Palestine; and a US empire is the path toward democratizing the Middle East. Left Behind constitutes a literature well fitted for a new era in which the United States defines itself as a frankly imperialist power engaged in a long-term battle for control of the Middle East.

NOTES

1. The first book is Tim LaHaye and Jerry Jenkins, *Left Behind: A Novel of the Earth's Last Days* (Wheaton, IL: Tyndale House, 1995). Further books in the series appear in the following order: *Tribulation Force* (1996); *Nicolae* (1997); *Soul Harvest* (1998); *Apollyon* (1998); *Assassins* (1999); *The Indwelling* (2000); *The Mark* (2000); *Desecration* (2001); *The Remnant* (2002); *Armaggedon* (2003); *Glorious Appearing* (2004).
2. Tim LaHaye and Jerry Jenkins, *The Rising: Before They Were Left Behind* Wheaton, IL: Tyndale House, 2005). *The Regime: Evil Advances* was published in November 2005.
3. Jonathan Dee, "Playstations of the Cross," *New York Times Magazine*, May 1, 2005, 48; "Blockbuster Left Behind Series in Development as a Real Time Strategy Computer Game," *Business Wire*, June 29, 2005; Benjamin Golze, "Spot On: Christian Game Makers Rise to New Heights," July 6, 2004,www.gamespot.com. The movies are *Left Behind* (dir. Vic Sarin, 2000) and *Left Behind II: Tribulation Force* (dir. Bill Corcoran, 2002), both produced by Cloud Ten Pictures, a small evangelical production company. LaHaye and Jenkins were very unhappy with the low-budget, straight-to-video approach of the films and unsuccessfully litigated to regain rights to the films.
4. News reports include CNN's *American Morning*, November 8, 2002; NPR's *Fresh Air*, October 28, 2002; ABC's *Up Close*, July 30, 2002; the CBS *Saturday Early Show*, July 13, 2002. The *Time* cover story by Nancy Gibbs, "The Bible and the Apocalypse," ran on June 23, 2002, with several accompanying stories and an interview with LaHaye. The two appeared on *Sixty Minutes* on Februrary 8, 2004. Several good scholarly works that engage the cultural phenomenon of Left Behind have also appeared in recent years. These include Amy Johnson Frykholm, *Rapture Culture: Left Behind in Evangelical America* (New York: Oxford University Press, 2004), which looks at the responses of a group of readers in North Carolina; and Bruce David Forbes and Jeanne Halgren Kilde, eds., *Rapture, Revelation, and the End Times: Exploring the Left Behind Series* (New York: Palgrave Macmillan, 2004), which is a collection of essays aimed at a general audience and encouraging critical discussion about the books. Other authors critique the Left Behind series in terms of its ideology and theology: Lee Quinby's *Millennial Seduction: A Skeptic Confronts Apocalyptic Culture* (Ithaca, NY: Cornell University Press, 1999), argues that the appeal of apocalyptic thought in general is its embrace of reinforcing doses of both fear and hope, and its commitment to absolutist thought. Barbara Rossing's *The Rapture Exposed: The Message of Hope in the Book of Revelation* (Boulder, CO: Westview, 2004), is a liberal theologian's response to premillennial dispensationalism.
5. A good discussion of varied religious groups' responses to Left Behind is Bruce David Forbes, "How Popular Are the Left Behind Books, and Why?" in Forbes and Kilde, *Rapture, Revelation, and the End Times*, 5–32.

6. Kevin Sack, "Apocalyptic Theology Revitalized by Attacks," *New York Times*, November 23, 2001.
7. An excellent overview of evangelical media culture, including a discussion of the Left Behind movies, is Heather Hendershot's *Shaking the World for Jesus: Media and Conservative Evangelical Culture* (Chicago: University of Chicago Press, 2004). For more recent market data, see Sheila Jacobs, "Religious Items Sell: Demand Grows in Particular for Christian Theme," *Arizona Daily Star*, January 27, 2004; "New Study Predicts Robust Growth in the Religious and Elhi Market Segments," Book Industry Study Group press release, May 16, 2005; Eric Noe, "Why Hasn't Boom in Religious Merchandise Helped Retailers?" ABC News, June 27, 2005. See also Martha MacNeil Hamilton, "Retailing's New Testament Faith; Sales of Items Tied to Spirituality Are Booming, and Not Just through Traditional Religious Venues," *Washington Post*, October 15, 2001. I discuss Christian evangelical culture in my "Empire of Their Own," *Nation*, September 4, 2003.
8. In an ABC News/BeliefNet poll in June 2004, 37 percent of Americans described themselves as born-again or evangelical; that included about half of all Protestants and 14 percent of all Catholics. Gary Langer, "Poll: Most Americans Say They're Christian," ABCNews.com, July 18, 2004.
9. According to a *Newsweek* poll, approximately 45 percent of US Christians believe that the world will end in Armageddon. Caryle Murphy, "At Millennium, Finding Salvation: Popular Series by Evangelical Christian Authors Retells Book of Revelation," *Washington Post*, November 28, 1999.
10. A number of recent surverys provide overviews of this diversity. See "Evangelicals in America" released by the Greenberg Research on April 5, 2004; "The American Religious Identification Survey 2001" released by CUNY Graduate Center; and, for a more qualitative analysis, Diana Eck, *A New Religious America: How a "Christian Country" Has Become The World's Most Religiously Diverse Nation* (San Francisco: HarperSanFrancisco, 2002).
11. I am currently writing a book that traces the racial liberalism and social justice activism among evengelicals. One study that focuses on human rights issues among conservative evangelicals in particular is Alan Hertzke, *Freeing God's Children: The Unlikely Alliance for Global Human Rights* (New York: Rowman and Littlefield, 2004).
12. Stand for Israel (www.standforisrael.com) is a project of the International Fellowship of Christians and Jews, which is led jointly by Rabbi Yechial Eckstein and Ralph Reed, formerly of the Christian Coalition. Eckstein also heads the Jerusalem Friendship Fund, which last year funneled more than $15 million in evangelical contributions to support Jewish immigration to Israel. Yair Sheleg, "Christian Generosity Becomes Rabbinical Nightmare," from *Ha'aretz*, October 16, 2002, translated and reposted at www.bintjbeil.com/articles/en/021016_sheleg.html. See Yaacov Ariel, "How Are Jews and Israel Portrayed in the Left Behind Series?" in Forbes and Kilde, *Rapture, Revelation, and the End Times*, 131–66.
13. This is LaHaye's paraphrase in one of many similar interviews; Sandi Dolbbe, "Second-

Coming Attraction; Best-Selling, Apocalypse Author Is Drawn to the End Times," *San Diego Union-Tribune*, November 15, 2002. The biblical verse is Genesis 12:1–3. See also CNN's *American Morning*, with Paula Zahn, November 8, 2002, transcript #110814CN.V74.

14. For an informative discussion of apocalyptic religious views of all kinds as organized on the Internet, see Brenda Basher, *Give Me That Online Religion* (San Francisco: Jossey-Bass, 2001).

15. For a good discussion of the basics of this theology, see Paul Boyer, *When Time Shall Be No More: Prophecy Belief in Modern American Culture* (Cambridge, MA: Harvard University Press, 1992).

16. James Hunter, "The Evangelical Worldview since 1890," in *Piety and Politics: Evangelicals and Fundamentalists Confront the World*, ed. Richard John Neuhaus and Michael Cromartie (Washington, DC: Ethics and Public Policy Center, 1987), 19–53; Nancy Ammerman, "North American Protestant Fundamentalism," in *Media, Culture, and the Religious Right*, ed. Linda Kintz and Julie Lesage (Minneapolis: University of Minnesota Press, 1998), 55–114.

17. Hal Lindsey, with C. C. Carlson, *The Late Great Planet Earth* (Grand Rapids, MI: Zondervan, 1970). I discuss Lindsey in some detail in *Epic Encounters: Culture, Media, and U.S. Interests in the Middle East, 1945–2000* (Berkeley: University of California Press, 2001), 165–78.

18. The Presbyterian Gary DeMar has written a debunking treatise, *End Time Fiction: A Biblical Consideration of the Left Behind Theology* (Nashville, TN: Thomas Nelson Publishers, 2001). There are also multiple Web pages devoted to various arguments with the theology, though these are often from the perspective of those who disagree over the timing of the Rapture.

19. Jerry Strober and Ruth Tomczak, *Jerry Falwell: Aflame for God* (Nashville, TN: Thomas Nelson, 1979), 167.

20. David Snowball, *Continuity and Change in the Rhetoric of the Moral Majority* (New York: Praeger, 16). See also my discussion in *Epic Encounters*, 193–97.

21. Ann Rodgers-Melnick, "Evangelical Fiction Cracks the Best-Seller List," *Pittsburgh Post-Gazette*, May 6, 2000.

22. For more information on this organization, see the "Right Wing Watch" section of the People for the American Way Web site, www.pfaw.org.

23. David Mehegan, "Appeal Spreads for Series That Spreads the Word," *Boston Globe*, February 27, 2002.

24. See, for example, films like *A Thief in the Night* (dir. Donald W. Thompson, 1972), which was a sensation in churches throughout the 1970s. See Hendershot's *Shaking the World for Jesus*, especially 176–209.

25. Randall Balmer and Lauren F. Winner, *Protestantism in America* (New York: Columbia University Press, 2002), quoted in David Van Biema, "The End: How It Got That Way," *Time*, June 23, 2002.

26. Karen Long, "*Left Behind* and the Rupture over the Rapture," *Washington Post*, May 5, 2001. In December 2000, the Office of the President of the Lutheran Church, Missouri Synod, released a statement, "The Left Behind View Is Out of Left Field," www.cms .org/predient/statements/leftbehind.asp.
27. Michelle Goldberg, "Fundamentally Unsound," www.salon.com, July 29, 2002.
28. For a discussion of Armey's statements from a moderate conservative who nonetheless fears the influence of the Christian Right on pro-Israel policy, see Peter Beinart, "Bad Move," *New Republic*, May 20, 2002, 6. Inhofe's statement is quoted by Gershom Gorenberg, "Unorthodox Alliance: Israeli and Jewish Interests Are Better Served by Keeping a Polite Distance from the Christian Right," *Washington Post*, October 11, 2002. In May 2002, the House passed 352 to 21 a resolution supporting Israel "as she wages war against terrorists who would mercilessly kill her citizens." Bruce Alpert, "Support for Israel Bridges Old Divides," *Times-Picayune* (New Orleans), May 3, 2002.
29. Jason Keyser, "Hundreds of Americans Move to Israel: Mass Immigration Is Paid for in Part by Evangelical Christian Groups," *Seattle Post-Intelligencer*, July 20, 2002. Ken Ellingwood, "A Christian Day of Prayer for Israel," *Los Angeles Times*, October 21, 2002. Other groups that support Jewish immigration to Israel (i.e., the "ingathering" of Jews they believe to be predicted in the Bible) are Christians for Israel, which operates a project called Exobus, and John Hagee Ministries of Texas.
30. Tatsha Robertson, "Evangelicals Flock to Israel's Banner: Christian Zionists See Jewish State Bringing Messiah," *Boston Globe*, October 21, 2002.
31. Avram Goldstein, "Christian Coalition Rallies for Israel in Comeback Bid," *Washington Post*, October 12, 2002.
32. I discuss these connections from the 1970s and 1980s in some detail in chapter 4 of *Epic Encounters*. See also Don Wagner, "For Zion's Sake," *Middle East Report*, 22, no. 4 (2002): 52–58. Currently, there are dozens of groups linking conservative Christians and conservative Jews, both American and Israeli, including the International Fellowship of Christians and Jews (IFCJ), headed by the former Christian Coalition leader Ralph Reed and Rabbi Yechiel Ekstein. The IFCJ claims to have raised more than $60 million for Israel; see Wagner, "For Zion's Sake." In April 2002, the *New York Times* touted the alliance between the former Republican presidential candidate Gary Bauer and William Kristol, the editor of the *Weekly Standard*; see Alison Mitchell, "Mideast Turmoil: The Conservatives; Israel Winning Broad Support from the US Right," *New York Times*, April 21, 2002. Bauer is also the cochair of the American Alliance of Jews and Christians, alongside Rabbi Daniel Lapin. Other Christian Zionist organizations include Friends of Israel, based in New Jersey; Bridges for Peace, which has contributed more than $20 million to programs in Israel in the past five years; and the International Christian Chamber of Commerce, which actively promotes Israeli businesses.
33. On the meetings at the Israeli embassy, see Roberston, "Evangelicals Flock to Israel's Banner." Mark O'Keefe, "Israel's Evangelical Approach: U.S. Christian Zionists Nurtured as Political, Tourism Force," *Washington Post*, January 26, 2002, discusses both the

meetings and the push for tourism. Sharon's talk is mentioned by Roberston, as well as on "God and Country," ABC *Nightline*, November 26, 2002.

34. Katty Kay and Roland Watson, "Influential US Jews Like What They Hear," *Times* (London), June 26, 2002.

35. Marshall Whitmann of the Hudson Institute,a former lobbyist for the Christian Coalition, quoted by Abraham McLaughlin and Gail Russell Chaddock, "Christian Right Steps in on Mideast," *Christian Science Monitor*, April 16, 2001. In April 2002, President Bush called Ariel Sharon a "man of peace"; several observers have seen Bush's pro-Israeli policies, which differ significantly from his father's, as motivated by a combination of political pressure and true belief. Gay Alcorn, "Bush Follows His Conservative Heart Back to Israel," *Age* (Melbourne), April 20, 2002. Gary Bauer also makes claims for the Right's success in pressuring Bush, and Pat Buchanan, who is very critical of the conservative tilt toward Israel, concurs; Alpert, "Support for Israel Bridges Old Divides."

36. Pew Forum on Religion and Public Life, "Religion and Politics: Contention and Consensus," July 24, 2003.

37. David Klinghoffer, "Just Be Gracious," *Jerusalem Post*, August 16, 2002.

38. Andew Gumbel, "The Profits of Doom: In Five Years as a Religious Thriller Writer, Tim LaHaye Has Sold 30 Million Copies; Andrew Gumbel Meets the Moral Majority's Answer to J. K. Rowling," *Independent*, November 12, 2000.

39. On how the series has affected Tyndale, see Corrie Cutrer, "Left Behind Has Been Very, Very Good to Tyndale," ChristianityToday.com, October 17, 2000.

40. In terms of the self-representation of posters, I am aware of the arguments about the performativity of age and gender on the Internet, but other research suggests that the vast majority of people present themselves realistically, at least on these basics, and there is reason to suspect that most people who join an evangelical community would be inclined to self-represent accurately. In fact, there is some evidence for that precisely because there are clearly demarcated ways in which participants *do* perform across gender, ethnicity, and age via the handles that people take when they sign onto the message boards. In these situations, performance is allowed and even encouraged via character identification—participants often take versions of the name of a favorite character— which thus clears the profiles as a space for authenticity. See David Gauntlett, "Web Studies: What's New," in *Web Studies*, ed. Gauntlett and Ross Horsley (New York: Oxford University Press, 2004), 3–23; and Kevin Robbins, "Cyberspace and the World We Live In," in *The Cybercultures Reader*, ed. David Bell and Barbara M. Kennedy (London: Routledge, 2000).

41. In *Rapture Culture*, Amy Frykholm interviews a group of Left Behind fans in North Carolina. She determines that these fans, most of whom fit Tyndale's profile, use the novels as a way of negotiating relationships and coming to terms with the complexities of politics in general. Frykholm pays little attention to the Middle East specifically. See also Mehegan, "Appeal Spreads."

42. LaHaye and Jenkins, *Soul Harvest*, 359.

43. LaHaye and Jenkins, *Apollyon*, 305.

44. Among the many histories of conservative Christianity that trace this legacy, see William Martin, *With God on Our Side: The Rise of the Religious Right in America* (New York: Broadway Books, 1996).

45. Here my interpretation disagrees with that of Lee Quinby in *Millennial Seduction* in that she sees a direct and necessary link between apocalyptic thought and racism, misogyny, and homophobia. While homophobia is rampant, and sexism, if not misogyny, is frequent in the novels, the engagement with the politics of race is far more complicated, reflecting the impressive changes in race politics among white evangelicals in the United States, which, albeit far from complete, is of great significance. See here also Philip Jenkins, *The Next Christendom: The Coming of Global Christianity* (New York: Oxford University Press, 2002).

46. Michael Emerson and Christian Smith, *Divided by Faith: Evangelical Religion and the Problem of Race in America* (New York: Oxford University Press, 2002).

47. LaHaye and Jenkins, *Apollyon*, 371.

48. LaHaye and Jenkins, *The Mark*, 215.

49. These stories were originally posted at www.tribforcehq.com/fiction, under the series SpiritWalker's Song, but the Web site is no longer functioning.

50. While the leftbehind.com site once hosted fan fiction, it no longer does. Before the fiction was removed in 2002, one of the popular threads of fan fiction featured Chang as the protagonist, and in an earlier, 2001 discussion board thread (now unavailable; discussion boards are not archived at leftbehind.com), Chang was often mentioned as a favorite character. When I posted a query about Chang on the message boards on August 12, 2002, I received several replies, most of which said Chang was one of their favorite characters (often running behind Buck, or, interestingly, David Hassid, the converted East European Jew who preceded Chang as the new mole inside New Babylon). Remembering that there are literally dozens of characters in the series, and that each book introduces at least three or four new ones, it is no small thing for a character to be more of a favorite than the central four characters of the Tribulation Force.

51. Gershom Gorenberg, *The End of Days: Fundamentalism and the Struggle for the Temple Mount* (New York: Free Press, 2000). See also Ariel, "How Are Jews and Israel Portrayed in the Left Behind Series?" in Forbes and Kilde, *Rapture, Revelation, and the End Times*, 131–66.

52. Bob Simon, "Zion's Christian Soldiers," CBS *Sixty Minutes*, October 6, 2002. Pat Robertson's statement was reported by Matthew Lee, "US Evangelist Says Muslims 'Worse Than Nazis,' Urges Jews to Know Enemy," Agence France Press, November 12, 2002.

53. LaHaye and Jenkins, *Remnant*, 282–97.

54. LaHaye and Jenkins, *Apollyon*, 333.

55. Ibid., 353; and LaHaye and Jenkins, *Assassins*, 136.

56. LaHaye and Jenkins, *Remnant*, 350–53.

57. John Cloud, "Meet the Prophet: How an Evangelist and Conservative Activist Turned Prophecy into a Fiction Juggernaut," *Time*, July 23, 2002. (*Time* also mentioned controversy over the fact that LaHaye and Jenkins are reported to have both made about $50 million, with more to come. Both authors have been asked repeatedly in interviews about their newfound wealth, and both insist that the money brings with it an enormous responsibility to stewardship and to giving a good deal of it away. There have been few suggestions that either of them has embarked on an extravagant lifestyle.)
58. Gibbs, "The Bible and the Apocalypse," 2.
59. Kelly Sellers, interviewed and quoted in ibid.

HARILAOS STECOPOULOS

Putting an Old Africa on Our Map: British Imperial Legacies and Contemporary US Culture

It is time for Americans to put a new Africa on our map.

—William Jefferson Clinton, March 23, 1999

If, as Henry Louis Gates Jr. has argued recently, Africa has proved of interest to the US public as never before, it is above all the "dark continent" experienced by white Brits from the nineteenth century onward that fascinates contemporary Americans.[1] The list of recent US-published books that engage with this sprawling historical topic is rich and varied: Carrie Perloff's play *The Colossus of Rhodes* (2003), offers an engaging portrait of Cecil Rhodes (as does the 1998 PBS broadcast of *Rhodes*, a BBC biopic of the same subject); Jeffrey Tayler follows Sir Henry Morton Stanley down the Congo in *Facing the Congo: A Modern Journey Into the Heart of Darkness* (2001), a journey also chronicled by Martin Dugard in *Into Africa* (2002) and David Liebowitz and Charles Peason in *The Last Expedition* (2005); Richard Bausch incorporates the story of the explorer Mary Kingsley into his novel *Hello to the Cannibals* (2002), while Giles Foden documents the true tale of the African Queen in *Mimi and Toutou's Big Adventure* (2005). Memoirs and histories that engage with the British colonial legacy during the twentieth century—Owen Sheer's *The Dust Diaries* (2003), Alexandra Fuller's *Don't Let's Go the Dogs Tonight* (2001), Aidan Hartley's *The Zanzibar Chest* (2003)—have proliferated, as have books that comment on the contemporary impact of British (neo)colonialism: Alexander McCall Smith's *The No. 1 Ladies' Detective Agency* (2003) and Daniel Bergner's *In the Land of*

Magic Soldiers (2004). From Robert Kaplan's comment that "West Africa is reverting to the Africa of the Victorian atlas" in his notorious article "The Coming Anarchy" (1994) to McCall Smith's sentimental evocation of former British rule in his popular Botswana mysteries, cultural producers have invited Americans to put an *old* Africa on their map.[2]

Why Victorian Africa now? Why not an outpouring of books on the history of the European experience in the Middle East and Central Asia, a portion of the world that has grown important to the US public ever since the attacks of September 11, 2001? In what follows, I demonstrate how the appeal of these representations of old Africa lies in their peculiar capacity to offer a historical justification for US geopolitical power. The allure of Victorian Africa for our public culture has less to do with US interest in exploiting a poor part of the world, although such exploitation certainly goes on, than it does with the way the bankrupt state of the continent renders Africa an exemplary signifier for Western intervention.[3] If much of our public culture depicts postcolonial Africa as disastrous, that image of the continent tends to provoke American fascination with the virtues of the old colonial regimes. In this fantasy, the lethal chaos of contemporary Africa cannot help but remind us that Victorian Africa was a stable, if somewhat savage, place, a sepia-tinged world emblematic of an era in which our anglophone predecessors (and current allies) disciplined people of color for their own good. Affirming the British mission as an extended example of colonial tough love, recent invocations of Victorian Africa have suggested to new-millennium Americans that empire can be altruistic, indeed, civilized—that invasion and conquest, whether in the nineteenth-century dark continent or in twenty-first-century Iraq, might be the best thing that ever happened to supposedly backward peoples.[4] In the age of Darfur, such positive representations of Victorian Africa lend historical gravitas to the argument that the United States now bears the responsibility of reforming the unstable parts of the world.

There is little doubt that Washington has proven willing to exploit the image of an unstable Africa for its own purposes. The Bush administration may offer the world inspiring pronouncements on its future plans for the continent, but the claim that the West African nation of Niger provided Saddam Hussein with an opportunity to purchase yellowcake uranium has proven far more integral to its legitimization of the war on Iraq and thus to its foreign policy than any attempt to defeat African hunger. In the Niger affair, the United States sought to use the darkness long ascribed to Africa as a means of rendering Hussein even more frightening than he already appeared. After all, who in the United States would doubt the possibility of such a fearful transaction on a continent that had been represented as particularly demonic in recent mass-market journalism? Who can doubt the capacity of Africa to infect the rest of the world? The tragedies of Ebola and HIV/AIDS epidemics segue seamlessly into the horror of nuclear proliferation and radiation poisoning.[5] If the United States and its major ally Great Britain cannot eliminate the threat of the continent altogether, they can block any attempt by rogue states to claim it as their own. Fear-inspiring Africa might not warrant a major US intervention in and of itself, but tales of the heart of darkness help dramatize the need to combat evil in the world. Or, as the journalist Sebastian Junger warns his readers in a recent essay on Liberia, "If there ever was a nightmare vision of a future world — overpopulated, overarmed, and run by gangster states — Monrovia is it."[6]

Needless to say, most contemporary cultural representations of the British experience in Africa do not pursue as strategic an invocation of African dangers as the Bush administration. But they do offer readers an opportunity to read about the difficulties encountered by white British colonialists attempting to explore, control, and "civilize" Africa.[7] The vogue for tales of the dark continent suggests that the US public is in its time-honored fashion attempting to understand and justify a new imperial identity by turning to the all-too-familiar problem of blackness; the fact that these narratives concern the experience of another white people allows the US public to indulge in feelings of innocence where Africa is concerned — after all, we never held African colonies — and attempt to learn from the British record at the same time. For once, raced history comes with no guilt attached! That most of these narratives testify to the extraordinary challenges the British faced and conquered in Africa goes without saying; that these texts also applaud the imperialists' pluck and tenacity, their willingness to do what it takes to drag the continent into supposed civilization, suggests that for all its problems and all its costs, the imperial project may have its human, as well as its financial, rewards.

The pervasiveness of contemporary interest in British Africa extends even to those texts that purport to represent late twentieth-century and new-millennium Africa from an avowedly liberal perspective. And it is these texts, more than any other, that reveal how US fascination with old Africa has less to do with ethical historicism than with a need to generate a usable past for the American imperial present. In what follows, I examine three highly acclaimed nonfiction works that testify to the seductiveness of this dynamic: Paul Theroux's *Dark Star Safari* (2003), Alexandra Fuller's *Don't Let's Go to the Dogs Tonight* (2002), and Daniel Bergner's *In the Land of Magic Soldiers* (2003).[8] These writers either have established themselves as award-winning public writers (Theroux) or are in the process of doing so: Fuller has published work in the *New Yorker* and won the 2003 Books Sense Award for *Dogs*; Bergner writes regularly for the *New York Times Magazine* and *Harper's*; *Magic Soldiers* received the Overseas Press Club Award. These writers' status as recognized or burgeoning public intellectuals stems in large part from their respective claims to offer a sympathetic perspective on mysterious, dangerous, and misunderstood parts of the world. Theroux's travel writing, Fuller's family memoir, and Bergner's literary reportage present themselves as unvarnished examinations of particular white encounters with darkest Africa — candid accounts that urge a reconsideration of many stereotypes about the continent. These revisionary texts invite readers to reevaluate their usual image of black Africans and Western aid workers, to take the two most prominent examples; more disturbingly, they ask their readers to reconsider the usual critique of the white imperialist and colonist. Theroux, Fuller, and Bergner push in different ways for recognition of what the British have contributed to Africa; and, in the process, they insist on a qualified revaluation of the British Empire itself. It should come as no surprise that an affirmation of US imperial power lurks in the wings.

When the historian Paul Johnson published "Colonialism's Back — and Not a Moment Too Soon" in the *New York Times Magazine* twelve years ago, he inadvertently helped popularize the strategy of citing older imperial examples to incite and legitimate contemporary exercises of US power.[9] Rumor has it that Donald Rumsfeld has received tutorials on the Roman Empire from the Yale classicist Donald Kagan — father of the neoconservative pundit Robert Kagan. And with good reason, the "warrior" journalist Robert D. Kaplan would no doubt claim. According to Kaplan, the contemporary US empire must emulate second-century Rome in its pagan ruthlessness in order to survive.[10] Yet the Roman Empire has its limits as a historical exemplum when compared with the far more proximate British imperial experience. Kaplan ends his recent *Atlantic Monthly* essay, "Supremacy by Stealth," by invoking Winston Churchill's hope that the United States would prove "a worthy successor to the British empire": a plea he has reiterated in his introduction to the new Modern Library edition of Joseph Conrad's *Nostromo* and *Lord Jim*.[11] Kaplan's celebration of the British Empire has been forcefully seconded by such figures as the *Wall Street Journal*'s Max Boot, the Project for a New American Century's Thomas Donnelly, and, most visibly, Niall Ferguson, the Harvard historian whose recent books have earned him the dubious title of empire-booster extraordinaire.[12]

This intellectual fascination with the British Empire has found its popular analogue in recent Hollywood productions. From the heroic representation of British naval officers at the end of *Amistad* to Russell Crowe's charismatic performance as Jack Aubrey in *Master and Commander* to affirmations of empire in the latest version of *The Four Feathers* to the British-led coalition of the willing in *The League of Extraordinary Gentlemen*, the legacy of British expansion has received the blessing of the film industry. Indeed, even the remake of *The Quiet American* enshrines the idea of the savvy British veteran of empire as it highlights the idealistic follies of the gung-ho American. Such anglophilic discourse has a fairly long history in the United States. Ever since Rudyard Kipling published his poem "The White Man's Burden" in *McClure's Magazine* in 1899, many white Americans and, more surprisingly, more than a few black Americans have identified the British civilizing mission as worthy of emulation.[13] Yet there exists a countervailing tradition in our popular and political culture that has denounced the idea of following the British imperial example. From African American protests over the treatment of India to President Dwight D. Eisenhower's forceful objection to the attempt to reclaim the Suez Canal, Americans have found much wanting when it comes to the British imperium. As Mark Twain reminded his American auditors in 1901, when we follow our anglophone relations down the imperial road, we do not so much demonstrate the superiority of whiteness as remind all the world that we are "kin in sin."[14]

While one would expect today's avowedly centrist or conservative intellectuals and filmmakers to follow in the former tradition and idealize the British Empire, one would hardly predict that more liberal anglophone writers would commemorate the British Empire and celebrate its relevance in the age of George W. Bush and US expansion. Yet the likes of Kaplan, Ferguson, and Donnelly have been joined by figures one would have expected to find on the other side of the ideological debate—Joseph Nye, dean of the Kennedy School of Government, Christopher Hitchens, a radical journalist, and, most visibly, the acclaimed human rights scholar and *New York Times* contributor Michael Ignatieff. Now, to be sure, the latter three figures hardly subscribe to the chest-thumping rhetoric exemplified by Robert Kaplan; one does not find enthusiastic affirmations of imperial brutality in Ignatieff's comments on US power.[15] Yet Nye, Hitchens, and Ignatieff have each opined that the United States should use "its preponderance of power" to intervene in and civilize the world—and that it may learn a thing or two about this process from its illustrious forebear, the United Kingdom.[16] Thus Nye claims that "the U.S. can learn a . . . useful lesson from the period when Britain," "the leading country, pursued its interests in a manner that provided benefits to many countries outside its empire"; Hitchens suggests that today's US imperialists should heed the example of their more courageous British predecessors and demonstrate a willingness to sacrifice themselves for the civilizing mission; and Ignatieff invokes Kipling's fin de siècle affirmation of white imperial identity in his essay "The Burden."[17] What the new literature of Africa offers US public culture is a sustained narration of such ideas—a more engaging, if not to say grounded, version of the pro-imperial anglophilia proffered by the pundits, conservative and liberal, noted above. Attempts to reappraise Stanley and David Livingstone, Rhodes, and other Victorian imperialists constitute one aspect of this engagement; but so do less obvious inscriptions of the British colonial project in narratives that purport to examine the predicament of individuals—American, British, and African, white and black—confronting contemporary manifestations of African poverty and violence. What Renato Rosaldo dubbed imperial nostalgia when discussing the Raj revival of the 1980s emerges in these texts as an imperative directing Americans toward the example of the British Empire and its disciplinary strategies.[18] The new imperial nostalgia speaks to more than the global range of white American racism; it speaks to a growing desire to reconsider and, if possible, relegitimate empire through recourse to "dark" Africanist fictions.

Paul Theroux's recent travel book *Dark Star Safari* — the author's first work on Africa in over thirty years — offers us a provocative example of this phenomenon. Over the past several decades, Theroux has earned a reputation for a contrarian, not to say revanchist, political perspective, and the new book does not disappoint. The chronicle of his overland journey from Cairo to Capetown, *Dark Star Safari* offers the reader a scathing assessment of contemporary Africa that also affirms the value of the former British colonial system in backhanded and subtle ways. Theroux accomplishes this feat by engaging in a critique of Western aid organizations and their workers that serves, however inadvertently, to highlight what he sees as the qualified but undeniable accomplishments of the British colonialists.

To be sure, Theroux's indictment of the NGOs, while less insightful than the work of such scholars as James Petras, contains many home truths and offers a useful corrective to our sentimental notions of aid.[19] The charity workers Theroux encounters are, "in general, oafish self-dramatizing prigs, and often complete bastards" (146); they travel in African-chauffeured Land Rovers and stay in far better accommodations than those inhabited by Africans; they strictly regulate the dispensation of food, technology, and medical aid in a self-aggrandizing manner. Like Graham Hancock and Michael Maren, Theroux comes to believe that in contemporary Africa, "all aid is self-serving, large-scale famines are welcome as a 'growth opportunity,' and the advertising to stimulate donations for charities is little more than 'hunger porn' " (193). And even as he reserves his greatest fury for Western aid workers, Theroux sees the African themselves, from the "big men" to ordinary citizens, as complicit with the calamitous effect NGOs have had on the continent. Indeed, if Theroux's trip teaches him anything, it teaches him that "only Africans were capable of making a difference in Africa. Everyone else, donors and volunteers and bankers, however idealistic, were simply agents of subversion" (327).

Yet even as Theroux indicts Western aid workers and African aid recipients alike, he has little, if anything, to say about the crippling effects of colonialism and neocolonialism on African society. The expropriation of natural resources, the brutalization of plantation labor, the degradation of Africans by white supremacist regimes: these historical facts do not provoke the same sort of attention as do the failures of contemporary Western charity. To the contrary, Theroux implies that the citation of colonial and neocolonial abuses found in so many works on Africa constitutes a crippling obsession with the past. Not for him the historical preoccupations of an Adam Hochschild or a Howard French! In Theroux's view, nothing less than willed historical amnesia will allow one to view the poverty and violence of contemporary Africa in a truthful manner. And yet for all his desire to confront Africa's problems in the present tense, Theroux cannot resist the urge to represent what is in his view a long tradition of British contributions to the continent. Even as we forget the crimes of colonialism we must remember its good works. Selectively engaging with the historical past, Theroux places his travel text in the service of a subtle affirmation of the British and their presence in Africa.

Some of these British good works appear not in Africa at all, but in the English literary tradition and its capacity for instructive critique. Theroux turns repeatedly to Charles Dickens and Joseph Conrad for their cutting satires of nineteenth-century Western charitable efforts in Africa, citing moments from *Bleak House* and *Heart of Darkness* on a regular basis; Dickens's missionary-minded and child-endangering Mrs. Jellyby thus makes three extended appearances in Theroux's narrative. To be sure, the object of Dickens's and Conrad's critiques are invariably fellow citizens; yet the frequent association of British culture with a self-consciousness about the white presence in Africa allows Theroux to cast British efforts on the continent in a better light than the pathetic efforts of today's NGO workers. The endearingly intelligent and witty touch of Dickens helps legitimate Theroux's commemoration of the British presence in East Africa: memories of "God Save the Queen" being played before the screening of films at the local cinema (312); the availability of such quintessentially British condiments as a mustard pot and a jar of Branston Pickle (318); the very existence of Blantyre, Malawi, a town named for Scottish explorer David Livingston's birthplace (321). Whatever its failings, the British attempt to explore and civilize Africa, Theroux implies, should not be dismissed. It is not for nothing that Theroux imagines himself as a nineteenth-century traveler when sleeping next to ancient ruins in the Sudan (80–81), invokes Richard Francis Burton when visiting Harar, Ethiopia (102–4), and cites Livingston (69). This American writer sees Africa through a British lens.

What remains of British Africa seems valuable to Theroux not only for personal reasons — he taught in the former British colony of Nyasaland during the early 1960s — but also as a sign of the way Africa once managed to function. However dependent on "drudges and whipped serfs," Africa seems to have enjoyed a measure of security and stability under British colonial rule (176). Thus in his account of a return visit to Nairobi, Theroux quietly, but palpably, engages in his own version of imperial nostalgia. He mourns the loss of the Nairobi he knew in the early 1960s, describing the city as a "quiet market town of low shop houses and long verandas" (176). While he claims that the control of the masses typical of the British colonial administration has continued in the postindependence years, his narrative suggests, in fact, that things have gotten far worse.[20] If colonial Nairobi was "an English county town," but one that ran better due to the abundance of cheap labor (177), the Nairobi of the new millennium is "somewhat recognizable," still "a provincial place," but now "huge and dangerous and ugly." The replacement of the disciplinarian British colonial government by "corrupt African politicians" has brought violence and viciousness to the city.[21]

Theroux does not claim outright that the British colonial regime was superior to the current arrangement of African rule and NGO aid he finds central to Kenyan and indeed most African societies, but he intimates as much through gestures of sentiment and regret. When Theroux profiles two British colonial educators who ran a teacher's college in Nyasaland, for example, he affirms their mission and their capacities in such glowing terms that the reader seems encouraged to hope that some equally skilled colonials might replace them. Sir Martin Roseveare "was of the old breed, an educator, not an evangelist, someone who had come to Africa to serve, to call it home, and to die in the bush"(288); "Lady Margaret, was the same: sporty, intelligent, resourceful" (289). The antithesis of the pampered and officious NGO workers described by Theroux, the Roseveares suggest that white Westerns can play a useful productive role in Africa; or, more accurately, that they could do so in the past. For even as Theroux had long seen the two educators "as role models, vigorous retirees [he] might emulate" by "returning to Africa . . . and doing as they had done," the current state of Africa seems to militate against any such elder mission (289). In Theroux's view, independence has led, sadly, to a situation where this sort of white intervention, however charitable, leads to nothing more than disaster; Africa now no longer constitutes a place to which he might commit himself, heart and soul, but exists instead as a dangerous place with the tantalizing and deathly allure of the frontier.

Theroux recognizes that his image of an almost irredeemable Africa might suggest more than a nonfiction writer's commitment to the truth, however unpleasant, and thus reminds the reader from time to time that he loves Africa and Africans: that he is in no way a racist repeating the hackneyed comments of white supremacists. Ironically enough, he reveals his own anxiety over charges of racism most visibly by ascribing such attitudes to his former mentor and friend, the renowned Trinidadian writer, V. S. Naipaul.[22] According to Theroux, Naipaul "hated living in Africa" (207). Quoting his ex-comrade, Theroux writes, "he said: 'The weak and oppressed. They're terrible, man. They've got to be kicked. . . . That's the only thing Africans understand' " (209). The laziness and corruption Theroux seems to find endemic to contemporary Africa does not move him to make such brutal and insensitive comments; instead, the white American writer demonstrates a wisdom and restraint Naipaul cannot match. Or so Theroux would have us think. Yet as several moments in the book make clear, Theroux does come disturbingly close to matching his ex-friend's alleged dismissal of black Africans. Consider, for example, how Theroux slips into a weak approval of British racism that suggests biases similar to those ascribed to his famously anglophilic older ex-mentor. When meeting a friend in an old ex-colonial club in Zomba, Malawi, Theroux cites the comments of British racists on the importance of maintaining a segregated space:

> "Let Africans in here and they'll be tearing up the billiard table and getting drunk and bringing their snotty little piccanins in the bar. There'll be some African woman nursing her baby in the games room." This was considered rude and racist, yet in its offensive way it was fairly prescient, for the rowdy teenagers at the billiard table were stabbing their cues at the torn felt, the bar was full of drunks . . . and a woman was breast-feeding her baby under the dartboard. (306)

Theroux's impulse to admire the English colonial model extends to his almost deliberately outrageous affirmation of their racist predictions. With all their imperfections and biases, Theroux implies, the racist British colonials understood Africa far better than today's NGOs and their Western sponsors. The British colonial system, never criticized in the same manner as other institutions, stands as a flawed yet important template from which other white people might learn.[23]

Foremost among those whites are of course new-millennium Americans, the citizens of the nation that has inherited the British imperial mantle. Unlike the afore-cited imperialist cheerleaders such as Kaplan and Ferguson, Theroux never makes an explicit comparison between a US-dominated civilizing mission and previous British imperial enterprises. Instead he suggests parallels that the reader is free to draw on her or his own. When in Kenya, for example, Theroux runs across some clothing exporters who are taking full advantage of the new permissive trade rules legislated by the African Growth and Opportunity Act (AGOA) and sending products to the United States (188). Yet the people benefiting from this new trade law are not the Kenyans, but rather the Chinese and Indian manufacturers and the few locals who place Kenyan labels on the clothing. Instead of emerging as a new site of industrial capital, Kenya has become a way station — a place for packaging and shipment. A neoliberal trade policy designed to assist an African nation in the international market ends up benefiting Asian industrialists. The AGOA proves as ineffective for Africans as the aid that they receive from charitable organizations. Nothing could be further from the famed explorer David Livingstone's hope that his arduous journeys would help Africa develop a commercial relationship with Europe (343).

When Theroux compares US foreign and military policy in the region to that practiced by the British during the late nineteenth century, one senses again his quiet admiration for the older empire and his disdain for the new. At one point, Theroux finds himself in Khartoum, looking westward to Omdurman where the Mahdi and his dervishes killed General "Chinese" Gordon in 1885, and looking eastward to where the Clinton administration had destroyed a pharmaceutical factory in 1998 (58). While Theroux never openly endorses the vicious British attempts to defeat and control the Sudan, he represents the British engagements with the dervishes during the late nineteenth century in far more positive terms than he does the current US attempt to combat Osama bin Laden and al-Qaeda. The missile attack on the factory, an alleged site of bomb manufacture, prompts Theroux to remind the reader of Clinton's need to distract the nation from the Monica Lewinsky scandal. He also criticizes the US public for having little interest in where or whom we bomb (12). Yet Theroux's critique of US foreign policy does not extend to his representation to the British attempts to destroy the Mahdi, a fierce Islamic leader who in certain ways resembles a nineteenth-century Osama bin Laden. While Theroux paints the British as just as savage as the Africans—"Monkey" Gordon, the great general's nephew, disinters the Mahdi's body and takes his head on returning with General Herbert Kitchener's force thirteen years later—one senses in *Dark Star* a respect for the steadfast manner in which the old empire returned to a scene of defeat and completed the job (64–65). Here and throughout his text, Theroux's critique of British colonialism collapses before his greater admiration for British dedication: their willingness to stick things out, to fight until the end, stiff upper lip and all. If Theroux uses a British imperial past to indict a US imperial present, he does so, one suspects, not so much to reject the notion of an American imperium as to nudge the current administration into adopting a more practical, steadfast, ruthless—in a word, British—approach to the challenge of global governance: an approach that demands much of white imperialists, but far more of the people of color they have come to dominate and exploit.

If Paul Theroux stages his new African travel book as something of a return to familiar personal and literary territory, first-time author Alexandra Fuller frames her African memoir *Don't Let's Go to the Dogs Tonight* as a return of a very different sort, but one even more inflected by British colonialism. Raised in Zimbabwe, Malawi, and Zambia, but now living in Wyoming, Fuller is an expat British African, a colonial born after the end of the "Empire" (a word she always capitalizes), a white woman who loves the dark continent. She acknowledges her odd subject positioning at several places in the text. "My God," she writes in a mnemonic mode at one point, "I am the *wrong* color. . . . The way I stand out against the khaki bush like a large marshmallow to a gook with a gun. White. African. White-African" (10); and in the reader's guide that accompanies the recent paperback edition: "I am African by accident, not by birth. So while soul, heart, and the bent of my mind are African, my skin blaringly begs to differ and is resolutely white" (305). Yet a productive self-consciousness about racial, cultural, and geographic identity—sensitivity to the peculiarities of her version of whiteness — does not extend to Fuller's overall understanding of politics and history. Indeed, her family chronicle constitutes a narrative that displaces the political themes so often central to black African narrative. As she puts it at the end of the reader's guide, "It is not a political story or the story of Empire. It is the story of how one African came to terms with her family's troubled history; it is a love story for the continent" (308). The relationship between the last two sentences of this passage proves telling. To come to terms with "her family's troubled history" is for this author a way of expressing her "love" for Africa. For all their white skin and British origins, the eccentric, indeed somewhat mad, Fullers somehow parallel the wildness and insanity of the place in which they live. They endure poor food, disease, parasites, and most tragically, the loss of three children. As Fuller puts it at one point, "it starts to get hard for me to know where Mum's madness ends and the world's madness begins" (196–97). In order to accept her family, Fuller must also accept Africa, but an Africa from which the question of politics has somehow been removed, an Africa that belongs to her as completely as her family.

In her *New York Times* review of Fuller's most recent book *Scribbling the Cat* (2003), Laura Miller points out that *Don't Let's Go to the Dogs Tonight* includes all the elements of the classic English memoir: "The disorderly, impecunious household; the 'well-bred' and oppressively eccentric parents; lots of booze, lots of dogs and lots and lots of tea — all rendered with the dry tang of a gin and tonic. Tonic with extra quinine, that is, since 'Dogs' juiced up the old formula by transplanting it to a perilous setting, plagued with civil war, poisonous reptiles and tropical diseases."[24] Yet to set an English memoir replete with Scottish bagpipe records (12), C. S. Lewis novels (65), Land Rovers (121), and yes, gin and tonics (294) in the contested territory of the (former) British colonies has far greater resonance than Miller acknowledges. It is no accident that Fuller devotes more space to an appreciation of Paul Scott's *Staying On* than to any other text in the essay on suggested reading that accompanies the new paperback edition; the author Salman Rushdie singled out as one of the main contributors to the Raj revisionism of the 1980s provides Fuller with a literary antecedent for the imperial nostalgia so fundamental to her narrative.[25] The prominence of Scott and the notable absence of any black African author in this bibliographic essay suggest the extent to which Fuller uses

Africa as a frame for an intimate and insistently white story. While Fuller does at times prove sensitive to the delicate matter of racial and cultural difference, her decision to tell the necessarily controversial story of white Africans as a charming memoir—think Jessica Mitford, or, for that matter, Mary Karr, in Zimbabwe—helps license a suppression of black political critique and an affirmation of the white colonial presence.

Indeed, in Fuller's hands, the affective power of the memoir is used to invite the (white) liberal reader to rethink her or his usual horror at white colonialism and the people who perpetrate it. In one scene, for example, the family hosts a visiting liberal Englishman at their home and offers him a candid racist response to recent events; Mrs. Fuller bemoans the loss of the British colonies in Africa and describes all the newly independent African nations as "cock-ups." The narrator's representation of the Englishman's likely response is revealing: "The guest says nothing, but his smile is bemused. I can tell he's thinking, *Oh my God, they'll never believe this when I tell them back home.* He's saving this conversation for later" (20). We are encouraged to identify with the Fullers against this smug visitor who will most likely spend only two years in Zambia (20). And this strategy of urging the reader to bond with the Fullers regardless of their racism—or, indeed, perhaps because of it—extends throughout the entire text.

Such is the affective nature of her style that Fuller's anguished story cannot help but invite the reader, or at least the middle-class US reader, to commiserate with the lonely white people stranded in a terrifying world of color, poverty, and violence. Given the myriad losses that burden the Fullers—above all, the deaths of three young children—it is difficult for the reader not to think that they have suffered as much as any black African; that their lives, the lives with which we identify, would have been better had they succeeded in achieving the goal of, in Mrs. Fuller's words, keeping "*one* country in Africa white-run" so that there might have been "an oasis, a refuge" (19–20). By transforming Africa into the material of contemporary white memoir, Fuller invites us, consciously or not, to reconsider the meaning of the end of colonialism: to consider how its end might have been less a boon than a disaster for all concerned.

Like Theroux, Fuller refuses to validate attempts by white neoliberal policy makers (the Englishmen who come for dinner), white missionaries (the

Americans with whom they pray [80]), and white aid workers (the environmentalist German couple [242]) to help the Africans help themselves. The presence of these white charity providers appears far more burdensome to black Africa than the presence of white farmers such as the Fullers and their neighbors. Indeed, Fuller quietly suggests that some of what the new aid workers seek to do was already underway in the old colonial regime. Her mother ran an unofficial medical clinic from the back door of their Rhodesian home and helped support a local school; the coming of independence not only terminated such private efforts — as her mother tells a group of ailing black Africans, "don't you have your *comrades* at the hospital?" — it also ushered in the era of professional do-gooders from afar, who are less capable and more corrupt than their local white predecessors (153). British colonial Africa was unjust; Mrs. Fuller accepts a compliment for a meal their housekeeper Kelvin has cooked. But the author also suggests that the British expats provided local people with a level of guidance and common sense they seemed to lack and which aid workers seem unable or unwilling to provide; the same chapter includes a scene in which Mrs. Fuller rescues Kelvin after he has poisoned himself with insecticide (21).

Fuller, of course, hopes to downplay the controversy over white people in Africa, and she pursues this strategy through lyric invocations of what we might call mythic environmentalism. Fuller denounces the theft of African territory in what is now Zimbabwe by both the English and the Afrikaaners, yet her desire to somehow rise above the seeming pettiness of politics leads her to mythologize the land and discount the significance of its original inhabitants in a manner that recalls the ideologically charged aesthetics Mary Louise Pratt has identified in Enlightenment travel writing.[26] The very notion of any tribe, nation, or race naming and claiming this land strikes Fuller as absurd: "The land itself, of course, was careless of its name. It still is. You can call it what you like, fight all the wars you want in its name. Change its name altogether if you like. The land is still unblinking under the African sky. It will absorb white man's blood and the blood of African men. . . . It doesn't care" (26–27). Fuller treats the land as a mythic presence that transcends the attempts of any men to control and inscribe it. For her, white colonialism may be a crime against black Africans, but it is more importantly a crime against the land to which all inhabitants enjoy an intimate connection. In Fuller's view, everyone ("black, white, coloured, Indian, old-timers, newcomers") of Rhodesia has an undeniable and primal bond to the earth (149): "In Rhodesia, we are born and then the umbilical cord of each child is sewn straight from the mother onto the ground where it takes root and grows. Pulling away from the ground causes death by suffocation, starvation. That's what the people of this land believe. Deprive us of the land and you are depriving us of air, water, food, and sex" (149–50). However moving, Fuller's conflation of white colonists' claim on the land with all humanity's claim on the land abuses environmentalist conceptions of the commons for a specific political purpose: the covert representation of white Rhodesian lament for an oasis lost, the quiet appreciation of white African grief for lands now tilled by others.

Given Fuller's mythic celebration of the land beyond any question of ownership, it seems all too fitting that her memoir should end with a move to Wyoming. Her book, a tale of white settlers and angry natives, of fortified homes and violent raids, recalls the western narratives of her new home, a connection acknowledged when Fuller describes how she and her sister do a "Red Indian War Dance" as her father and his "boys" (black African servants) track a criminal through the Rhodesian bush (128).[27] In her hands, the everyday life of white British colonialists in Africa resembles nothing so much as the everyday life of white Americans on the frontier. Fuller argues that white Americans should feel just as much guilt over the dispossession and murder of Native Americans as she feels over her family's crimes in Kenya, Rhodesia, and beyond. As K., the soldier interlocutor of her new book *Scribbling the Cat* points out, white Americans treated the local people much as the white Africans did (22). Yet in *Don't Let's Go to the Dogs Tonight* Fuller's horrified reaction to white racist violence in Africa and the US West coexists with a countervailing impulse: the need to claim for her white African memoir the adventure and romance many Americans still associate with white settler history. Sensitive though she is to the history of white genocide in the new world, Fuller also seems to recognize that the aura of the savage frontier will render her narrative more appealing to a US readership. To link these spaces and these conquests does not constitute an act of radical critique so much as it testifies to Fuller's tacit endorsement of both American and British colonialisms.

That this tale of dedicated settlers and rebellious natives, of white life on the African frontier, has struck a chord with US readers during the age of

Islamic fundamentalism should not surprise us. In Fuller's hands, the contemporary threat of terrorism—"the neck-prickling-terrorist-under-the-bed creeps"—articulates the United States and Africa, white Americans and British expats, Native Americans and black Africans (6). Indeed, in her hands, the fear of impending attack by people of color has a transhistorical aura just as palpable as that of the land. Like the earth, always present regardless of who claims it, the racial Other is always there, waiting to strike, waiting to kill, waiting to annihilate all representatives of civilization. Whatever their presence in Africa means, Fuller suggests that her family resembles white Americans attempting to defend themselves against the inevitable eruption of alterity.[28] In the end, Fuller's chronicle of a childhood spent fearing and fighting terrorists of color seems much like an African version of what many white Americans witness today. For her, the affective properties of memoir do more than assuage family wounds; they help justify violence inflicted in defense of white power.

The return of Victorian Africa invoked by Robert Kaplan well describes Daniel Bergner's recent book *In the Land of Magic Soldiers*: a representation of the British attempt to rescue and redeem the nation of Sierra Leone at the turn of the millennium. Bergner offers readers a powerful portrait of Sierra Leone in crisis; his text includes deft and moving sketches of Lamin Jarka, a man who had his hands amputated by Revolutionary United Front (RUF) soldiers while attempting to protect his daughter; Michael Josiah, a medical student who also serves in the government army; Komba Gbanya, a teenage soldier who has committed atrocities; Neall Ellis, a white mercenary; and the Kortenhovens, a Michigan missionary family. Yet the heart of Bergner's project concerns the return of the British to their former colony; as he informs us, "I had come for this, the rescue. . . . Before I had learned much of anything, I began following the British" (19). The relationship of the British to Africa—their former involvement and current intervention—renders Bergner's text a vital metacommentary on empire: a metacommentary that opens the door to a reevaluation of imperial identity, British and American.

Predictably enough, Bergner finds the deployment of eight hundred British commandos evocative of a colonial past. On witnessing Sam Rosenfeld, a British army captain, bellow at a thousand Sierra Leone soldiers awaiting arms instruction, Bergner writes, "The scene, in the summer of 2000, appeared to rise out of the nineteenth century" (19). He opens his eighth chapter by citing Lord Frederick Lugard, "British imperial officer, subjugator, and ruler from Nigeria to Uganda" on the importance of the so-called civilizing mission: "The *Pax Brittanica* which shall stop this lawless raiding and constant inter-tribal war will be the greatest blessing that Africa has known since the flood" (96). Bergner rightly points out the way in which the turn-of-the-century rescue mission echoes Lugard's words and actions—the identification of malevolence in Africa, the display of awesome military firepower; "it was hard, a century later, not to sense reverberations of the past within the British" (96). The recognition that the British military presence in war-torn Sierra Leone provokes such "reverberations" forces Bergner to engage with problems of race and empire in a historicist frame. To "come for the rescue" is, in short, to come for history: a challenge that haunts Bergner's resolutely personal text.

To be sure, the British have returned not to reclaim their former possession or to exploit its resources, mainly diamonds, but rather to save Sierra Leone from itself. As Bergner describes it, the British plan is idealistic and ambitious: first, to create "an army that would drive the evil out of the jungle" (21); second, "to foster . . . an open and democratic society" (25). Reverting to some Victorian imperial past seems to have no place in Tony Blair's version of "the new military humanism."[29] Yet in Bergner's account, the Sierra Leoneans themselves respond to the intervention in a manner that cannot help but underscore the historical reverberations he feels everywhere around him. After discussing the British intervention with a variety of interlocutors, and finding almost no one who claims to resent the British for their former control of the community, Bergner realizes, surprisingly, that the people of Sierra Leone are delighted to have their former colonial rulers return: "Sierra Leone longed to be recolonized" (22).[30] Late in the volume Bergner will identify a shift in attitude toward British intervention among a few Sierra Leoneans—some of the locals are horrified by the temporary return of (neo)colonialism (195–96)—yet most people interviewed still view the British presence as a positive phenomenon. Understandably amazed by this popular affirmation of recolonization, Bergner looks unsuccessfully for any widespread resentment toward the British on the part of the Sierra Leoneans (22).

What Bergner discovers instead is a disturbing truth about himself: "A part of me recoiled, felt hollowed out from witnessing such an absence of pride, such an embrace of the imperial past. . . . But a smaller, covert part of me was exhilarated . . . a vague excitement born of racial dominance" (142). The Sierra Leoneans' willingness to turn back the clock — to say, "long live the British" (26) — helps Bergner to recognize that somewhere in his psyche, in his imaginary, he, too, would like to turn back the clock and revel openly in his whiteness: "I was drawn to Sierra Leone precisely because its terror and self-destruction offered me a kind of primal self-affirmation, a seductive proof, no matter how insidiously false, of the superiority of my own race" (141–42). Bergner may have been drawn to Sierra Leone for much the same reason that the white British military men find it appealing: as a means of confirming white civilization and black savagery or "sub-human intelligence" (153).

To be sure, of all the recent work on Africa by white US mass-market writers, Bergner's text is perhaps the most politically sensitive and racially self-conscious. He worries openly about his relationship to the Africans, to the white British troops and their rescue mission, and to empire as such. Unlike so many US commentators, he recognizes the racial implications of humanitarian intervention, whether American or British: "Always there was an unmitigated confidence, a sense of invincibility that, though I hadn't heard the men speak in explicitly racist terms, was surely at least tinged by race" (98). The Sierra Leoneans may believe in animistic magic, but Bergner knows all too well that that the British maintain a comparable faith in the almost supernatural capacities of Western whiteness. The "magic soldiers" of his title refers to both the African *and* the British troops. That such a candid examination of white identity proves refreshing given the recent glorification of imperial violence goes without saying. Yet Bergner's attempt to plumb the depths of white racial psychology in the neocolonial setting coexists with an incapacity to render a historical explanation for the deplorable state of Sierra Leone. For all his knowledge of modern atrocities in Europe (145), for all his study of colonial brutalities, modern historiography seems to offer no useful lessons about the origins of the current African crisis: "The stacks of books I read and tunnels of thinking I descended could never lead to understanding . . . those who offered theses were either desperate or deceitful . . . in this tiny sweltering wasteland saturated with rain and blood, all explanations were meaningless"

(147). If witnessing the violence of Sierra Leone firsthand inspires Bergner's racial self-consciousness, the brutal tableau of "rain and blood" also prompts his despairing claim that history cannot fathom such a tragedy.

Of course, if history fails Bergner in his attempt to come to terms with the violence of Sierra Leone, it is in large part because Africa fails history. As Bergner makes evident in his recent *New York Times Magazine* essay "The Most Unconventional Weapon," Africa defies the explanatory power of historical analysis: it "is a continent suspended, trapped somewhere closer to the ancient than to the modern, a continent where so many visas lead to places that feel utterly lost, not only for their wretched poverty and cataclysmic civil wars and devastating histories of exploitation and neglect but also for the primitive understanding their people have of all that happens in their world."[31]

Like countless Westerners before him, Bergner imagines Africa as "no historical part of the World"[32]—a tactic that not only denies Africans any substantive agency to change their lives but also relieves the Western intellectual of any responsibility to understand the current crisis in light of slavery, colonialism, and Cold War proxy militarism, among other factors. Rather than remind his readers of the many Western depredations endured by Africa, Bergner exiles historicism from his narrative: "The stacks of books . . . could never lead to understanding."[33] In his view, Africa manifests a relationship to history only by dint of its colonial ties to the West; even as he cites the British colonialist Lord Lugard, he never refers to any important Western African figures from the nineteenth century (e.g., Asantere Osei Banju or Edward Wilmot Blyden). The British intervention, in other words, promises not only to enforce a momentary peace in Sierra Leone but also to reconnect the violent nation to a world in which historical progress is possible. Without the West, Bergner suggests, the very possibility of an African future seems unlikely.

Bergner's inability to register and resist the powerful allure of such white mythologies informs his writing on US military intervention as well. His 2003 *New York Times Magazine* article, "Where the Enemy Is Everywhere and Nowhere," chronicles the challenges facing the US Army in Afghanistan in much the same way that *Magic Soldiers* details the difficulties confronting the British in Africa. Foremost among these problems is the sheer incomprehensibility of the people, the culture, and the land itself. Just as his book-length study of

Sierra Leone emphasizes the meaninglessness of historical explanations in a "tiny sweltering wasteland saturated with rain and blood," the magazine article admits to the futility of US attempts to understand Afghanistan. Bergner recognizes that US military personnel do not "comprehend the men they face . . . or the country that surrounds them," but he does not suggest that the soldiers and their superiors should take a different tack and attempt to study Afghanistan, let alone withdraw and allow the local inhabitants to build a nation on their own.[34] History seems no more relevant in Central Asia than it does in West Africa — a worldview that allows Bergner to register the incontrovertible odds facing the US even as he applauds the dedication and persistence of the soldiers on the ground. Like the British thousands of miles away, the US military men prove resolute in their dedication to bring progress to the "natives," regardless of the torpor they encounter at every turn.

Bergner's article on Afghanistan reveals, in effect, that his critical awareness of the Western fascination with an all-powerful white identity, so evident in certain moments of his Sierra Leone volume, fades before his profound faith in the West's connection to civilization. For all his self-consciousness about fictions of whiteness, Bergner still claims the forces of truth and history for the British and American troops and consigns the "natives" to violent and irrational stasis. The end of *Magic Soldiers* confirms this point, if in an inadvertent manner. After witnessing a display of supernatural talents by a Sierra Leone religious figure, Bergner informs us that Michael, a young Sierra Leonean medical student, wants to use "such power" to unite and heal "the world," to ensure that "the multitude" prospers (213). In this dream, Sierra Leone serves not as an object of rescue, but as a rescuer; the poor nation saves the world. Yet Bergner well knows that not destitute nations but Western empires act on the dream of healing and inspiring "the multitude" through aggressive intervention. His decision to end the volume with the quixotic aspirations of a poor African student affirms the usual stereotype of a dark continent trapped by superstition or, as Bergner puts in his article on Africa, "by the primitive understanding [the] people have of all that happens in their world." *Magic Soldiers* concludes with a description of black African magic, but this tableau constitutes less an endorsement of Michael's dream than a means of highlighting Bergner's real point: the need for the West to recognize its own extraordinary capacity to pull the dark continent into the narrative of history. If the supernatural power of whiteness appears little more than a fiction, the magic of Western civilization constitutes nothing less than a self-evident truth.

Surely it is indicative of today's Africanist writing that all three writers examined tend to dismiss the effectiveness of the United Nations, not to mention NGOs and their workers. Theroux engages in fond reminiscences of the British colonial presence as he castigates recent liberal and neoliberal attempts to reconstruct the continent. Fuller and Bergner, more diplomatic than Theroux, attempt to address their positions as whites writing about Africa, but ultimately endorse the value of some British interventions. Fuller offers a quiet defense of British expats, their private charities, and their deep connection to the land; Bergner sanctions the return of British troops as the only firewall between Sierra Leone and utter anarchy. For these writers, the only people capable of making a substantive difference in Africa, past and present, are white colonials. They would, I believe, agree with the account of the British Empire offered by one of their fellow white Africanists, the British writer Aidan Hartley. Writing about the disastrous confrontation between US forces and the Somalis in Mogadishu, Hartley argues,

> For all their arrogance, I believe the British had their feet on the ground in a way that the UN did not. My father learned about Africa and Arabia during the course of a lifetime. He became intimate with his countries, traveling among local people on foot or horseback, speaking their languages. UN officials staying in Somalia a few months at most and few saw the nation beyond the razor wire. . . . Soldiers pointed over the walls and said to me, "That's Skinnyland. Why the hell you want to live out there."[35]

As the colloquial American English cited by Hartley suggests, his critique has less to do with the multinational and multiracial UN force than it does with the US military. While the UN may be guilty of launching brief and uninformed missions, it is the United States that is most guilty of ignoring the lessons of their British predecessors. The tragedy of Mogadishu helps highlight Hartley's affirmation of the British mission in Africa and underscores his claim that Americans should engage more intimately with the burdens and boons of empire. Yet surely the right question to ask in the new millennium is not how the United States, the new "bully on the block," in Colin Powell's phrase, should emulate this forebear's example, but rather how the world's leading democracy can avoid pursuing the sort of British policies that have left so many former colonies crippled by "repressive laws and undemocratic institutions."[36] To revel in narratives that affirm the virtues of British governance is a historical error of grave proportions, one that allows Americans to delude themselves into thinking that European colonialism was exploitative *and* constructive, oppressive *and* educational.[37] That this error plays such a fundamental role in the way contemporary US liberals view the world reminds us of how imperial violence and humanitarian intervention are so often flip sides of the same coin. An "empire lite" necessarily depends on much the same set of colonial abuses that helped set the stage for the current crises in Africa.[38] However much Theroux, Fuller, and Bergner seek to disavow the uglier aspects of British imperialism and celebrate its value as a model for the new American century, they cannot escape the racist exploitation central to that legacy. Empire lite always suggests empire *white*; the burden is always the Africans' to bear. A critical relationship to history remains our best defense against the temptations of a nostalgia that leaves America at peace with imperialism itself.[39]

NOTES

Many thanks to the anonymous readers for Duke University Press, Ashley Dawson, Malini Johar Schueller, Neil Smith, and, above all, Kathy Lavezzo. A portion of this essay was presented at the American Studies Association conference in Hartford, CT, October 16, 2003.

1. See Felicia R. Lee's "Once upon a Time in Africa," *New York Times*, July 16, 2003. In her piece, an extended commentary on *Nelson Mandela's Favorite African Folktales*, Lee includes the following paraphrase of Gates's comments: "Things African—literature, music, art, food—are peaking in popularity and interest in the United States, reflecting social changes, Mr. Gates said. President Bush's trip to Africa this summer is evidence of that allure, he said, and of the sharpened acknowledgment of the intense connection between Africa and the Americas that began hundreds of years ago with slavery. 'I'm hoping that the Mandela book will popularize the folk tales, like the Brothers Grimm,' Mr. Gates said. 'Interest in Africa is at an all-time high.'"
2. It is worth comparing Kaplan's description of violence-prone contemporary Africa with that offered by Wole Soyinka. Writing about the Sudanese conflict, Soyinka argues, "In our own time, a culture is being raped, as if Africa had regressed to the battlefronts of the

thirteenth and fourteenth centuries." Whereas Kaplan uses the warfare of contemporary Africa to retroactively legitimate the civilizing mission of the Victorians, Soyinka recognizes that today's violence might be more fruitfully interpreted within an exclusively African history. See Wole Soyinka, *The Burden of Memory, the Muse of Forgiveness* (New York: Oxford, 1999), 63.

3. As Neil Smith has suggested, the recent US political, military, and cultural fascination with Africa may constitute an early sign that global capitalism is expanding into a heretofore neglected arena. In a future essay, I plan to address Smith's provocative thesis on global capital and the African question. See Neil Smith, "Response to 'Rethinking U.S. Imperialism'" (paper presented at the annual meeting of the American Studies Association, Hartford, CT, October 16, 2003).
4. Increasing interest in Africa on the part of both Clinton administrations and the current Bush administration has only reinforced the notion that for Americans, Africa is a space largely separate from our history that we nonetheless want to uplift. "Dubya" in particular has worked hard to prove himself an earnest Afrophile. The president has expanded and signed the African Growth and Opportunity Act (AGOA) first initiated by President Clinton, supported the New Partnership for African Development (NEPAD), started the Millennium Challenge Account, promised billions to combat the spread of HIV/AIDS, called for an end to the wars in the Sudan and Liberia, agreed to forgive billions in African debt under pressure from Tony Blair, hosted the greatest number of African leaders ever to visit the White House during a particular administration, and spent five days touring Senegal, South Africa, Botswana, Uganda, and Nigeria in 2003. For all their differences, both the Clinton and the Bush administrations shared an interest in putting Africa on the US map.
5. As I revise this article, the number one film in the United States is *Exorcist: The Beginning* (dir. Renny Harlin, 2004), a shoddy prequel which locates the devil in—where else?—Africa.
6. See Sebastian Junger, "Liberia's Savage Harvest," *Vanity Fair*, October 2003, 280.
7. It is hardly incidental that most of the recent popular accounts of Africa are by white Anglo-Americans. The past vogue for narratives in which black Americans rediscover their family origins or black Africans fight for freedom has been eclipsed by the new appeal of works in which white Americans and Brits describe the difficulty and strangeness of life in a space of violence, poverty, famine, and disease. Needless to say, recent films such as *Tears of the Sun* (dir. Antoine Fuqua, 2003), *Hotel Rwanda* (dir. Terry George, 2004), *Sahara* (dir. Breck Eisner, 2005), and *The Interpreter* (dir. Sydney Pollack, 2005) also testify to this dynamic.
8. Paul Theroux, *Dark Star Safari* (New York: Houghton Mifflin, 2003); Alexandra Fuller, *Don't Let's Go to the Dogs Tonight* (New York: Random House, 2002); Daniel Bergner, *In the Land of Magic Soldiers* (New York: Farrar, Straus and Giroux, 2003). Subsequent references to these books will be cited parenthetically in the text. Each of these writers examines a different part of Africa. Theroux focuses on eastern and southern Africa

from Cairo to Capetown; Fuller describes her experiences in Zimbabwe (Rhodesia), Zambia, and Malawi; Bergner restricts himself to an account of Sierra Leone. In my essay, I use the term *Africa* to refer to sub-Saharan Africa more generally—a rhetorical gesture that relinquishes historical and geographic specificity in order to offer an expansive analysis of contemporary US Africanist writing.

9. Johnson invokes the ancient Greeks, the Romans, the British, and the French in his desire to legitimate neocolonialism in sub-Saharan Africa and the Caribbean, among other parts of the world. See his "Colonialism's Back," *New York Times*, April 18, 1993. For an interesting analysis of the imperial tendency to invoke predecessors, see Vilashini Cooppan, "The Ruins of Empire: The National and Global Politics of America's Return to Rome," in *Postcolonial Studies and Beyond*, ed. Ania Loomba et al. (Durham, NC: Duke University Press, 2005), 80–100.
10. In the summer of 2005, both ABC and HBO premiered a miniseries about the Roman Empire—further evidence of an imperial self-consciousness in our public culture.
11. See Robert D. Kaplan, "Supremacy by Stealth," *Atlantic Monthly*, July/August 2003, 83.
12. See Max Boot, *The Savage Wars of Peace* (New York: Basic Books, 2002); Donnelly's various contributions to the Project for the New American Century; and Niall Ferguson's *Empire: The Rise and Demise of the British World Order* (New York: Basic Books, 2003). Other conservative intellectuals such as the columnist Charles Krauthhammer and the historian Donald Kagan also have made this argument.
13. Once again, our popular culture proves telling. From *Tarzan of the Apes* to the spate of colonialist films from the 1930s (e.g., *Sanders of the River*, *King Kong*) to the James Bond franchise, Americans cannot seem to get enough of the British Empire. And they much prefer celebrations of British pluck and determination to muckraking narratives of British brutality in India or Jamaica, let alone careful examinations of US violence against people of color in the West, the Philippines, and the Caribbean.
14. Twain delivered this bit of acerbic oratory when introducing a young Winston Churchill to an American audience at the Waldorf Astoria hotel.
15. See, for example, Ignatieff's recent essay "Who Are Americans to Think That Freedom is Theirs to Spread?" *New York Times*, June 26, 2005.
16. Joseph Nye, "Lessons in Imperialism," *Financial Times*, June 16, 2000.
17. Ibid.; Christopher Hitchens, "Pakistan: On the Frontier of Apocalypse," in *Love, Poverty, and War: Journeys and Essays* (New York: Nation Books, 2004), 446; Michael Ignatieff, "The Burden," *New York Times*, January 5, 2003.
18. See Renato Rosaldo, "Imperial Nostalgia," *Representations*, no. 26 (1989): 107–23.
19. See James Petras's important article, "Imperialism and NGOs in Latin America," *Monthly Review*, December 1997, 10–27.
20. Theroux offers another example of how Africa fared far better under white British colonialism in the postscript to the second edition of *Dark Star Safari*. Writing about the recent farm invasions in Zimbabwe, Theroux ends the new version of his text by pointing out that the African nation now has to import food grown by the very white farmers

it has forced across the border into nearby Malawi. Without these white farmers, Theroux suggests, this part of Africa would collapse; without the British colonialism that brought them there, East Africa might well be worse off than it is today.

21. In *The Ladies No. 1 Detective Agency* and the subsequent novels in the series, Alexander McCall Smith offers his twist on this argument by suggesting that contemporary citizens of Botswana have achieved a certain level of security and sustainability through their emulation of the British. The main example McCall presents is, of course, Precious Ramotswe, his detective protagonist who is nothing less than an African version of Agatha Christie's Miss Marple.
22. Theroux already had skewered the older writer in the tell-all book, *Sir Vidia's Shadow* (Boston: Houghton Mifflin, 1998).
23. Perhaps the oddest and yet most revealing example of this impulse emerges in Theroux's fragmented commentary on *Killing Rage* (1998), a memoir by the ex-IRA hit man Eamon Collins. On discovering the volume in a truck driven by a Yorkshireman, Theroux reads it and comments that the volume was "full of violence motivated by the sort of tribalism that would not have been out of place in Samburu land" (167). For this writer, the sectarian tensions of Northern Ireland somehow parallel the tribal hostilities of northern Kenya. He will compare the depressing folklore of this portion of Africa to the IRA narrative one page later (168). That one might draw such parallels is not surprising; comparativists of various disciplines frequently engage in such intellectual activity. Yet for Theroux to compare the IRA to an African tribe in the context of his appreciation of the British colonial enterprise means something else altogether. When he discusses the Collins memoir with an Irish traveler a bit later, Theroux discovers that the ex-IRA man was gunned down by his erstwhile comrades for writing the book. The insight Theroux gleans from this tragic bit of information: "And the gunmen, the Irish generally, would cluck about savagery in Africa" (268). For Theroux, the Irish are not only as hypocritical as their fellow Europeans; they are as violent and tribal as the Africans. The Irish stand here as a local dark star against which the greater light and purpose of the British slowly emerge.
24. See Laura Miller, "The Infantryman," *New York Times*, May 9, 2004.
25. See "Outside the Whale," *American Film*, no. 10 (1985): 16, 70, 72–73.
26. I refer to Pratt's claim that John Barrow evacuates the landscape of humans and human agency in his travel book on Africa. See Mary Louise Pratt, "Scratches on the Face of the Country; or, What Mr. Barrow Saw in the Land of the Bushmen," *Critical Inquiry* 12, no. 1 (1985): 119–43.
27. This steady invocation of white terror and vengeance on the high plains of Africa is riddled with references to narratives of segregation as well, but the western theme seems more integral to its appeal.
28. It is all too fitting, then, that Fuller's "The Soldier," a recent essay on the violent life of a middle-aged white Zimbabwean guerrilla, appeared in the *New Yorker* one issue before the magazine published Dan Baum's "The Casualty," a profile of a US Army specialist

recently wounded in Iraq. That the *New Yorker* might have switched the titles of these two essays suggests the writers' overlapping interests: not just a fascination with the military world but rather an urge to assess how past and present Western clashes with guerrillas of color demand a high price indeed of white military personnel. See Alexandra Fuller, "The Soldier," *New Yorker*, March 1, 2004, 54–68; and: Dan Baum, "The Casualty, *New Yorker*, March 8, 2004, 64–73.

29. I take the phrase "new military humanism" from Noam Chomsky's book of the same name. See his *The New Military Humanism* (Monroe, ME: Common Courage, 1999).
30. The claim that many average Africans hope to be recolonized has become something of a running motif in recent writing on empire. Thus in "Colonialism's Back," Paul Johnson claims that "recently in Liberia . . . a humble inhabitant of the capital . . . approached a marine guarding the United States Embassy and said, 'For God's sake come and govern us' " (22).
31. See Daniel Bergner, "The Most Unconventional Weapon," *New York Times*, October 26, 2003.
32. G. W. F. Hegel, *The Philosophy of History*, trans. J. Sibree (New York: Wiley, 1944), 99.
33. As V. I. Mudimbe has taught us, the very act of labeling Africa a place beyond history constitutes a historical statement, one which views the progress of civilization as identical to the expansion of Western power. See V. I. Mudimbe, *The Invention of Africa* (Bloomington: Indiana University Press, 1988), 20.
34. Daniel Bergner, "Where the Enemy Is Everywhere and Nowhere," *New York Times Magazine*, July 20, 2003, 40.
35. See Aidan Hartley, *The Zanzibar Chest* (New York: Atlantic Monthly Press, 2003), 289.
36. Caroline Elkins, "The Wrong Lesson," *Atlantic Monthly*, July–August 2005, 36.
37. Walter Rodney puts this idea to rest in his important book *How Europe Underdeveloped Africa* (Washington, DC: Howard University Press, 1974).
38. I refer to Michael Ignatieff's famous definition (and endorsement) of benevolent empire: "A global hegemony whose grace notes are free markets, human rights and democracy, enforced by the most awesome military power the world has ever known." See his "The Burden," *New York Times*, January 5, 2003.
39. For some recent examples of cultural texts that engage in critical historical practice with respect to Africa, see Barbara Kingsolver's novel *The Poisonwood Bible* (1998) and Raoul Peck's film *Lumumba* (2000). Both texts received considerable attention in the United States.

ASHLEY DAWSON

☆ ☆ ☆ New Modes of Anti-imperialism

Fanny Price, the main character in Jane Austen's *Mansfield Park*, experiences many indignities while living on the estate of her rich relation Sir Thomas Bertram. Despite the petty humiliations heaped on her by snotty relatives who consider themselves her social betters, she is shielded almost entirely from knowledge of the far more brutal social relations that characterize the colonial plantation system. Without Sir Bertram's plantation in Antigua, of course, the family would be unable to support the opulent lifestyle of the English landed gentry. Thanks to critics like C. L. R. James and Edward Said, we are now aware of the constitutive role of the colonial periphery in maintaining life in the metropole during the zenith of European imperial power.[1] If the colonies provided much of the economic foundation that sustained life for the wealthy classes depicted in Austen's novels, they also helped define European civilization itself by serving as an exotic and often phobic Other against which the imperial cultures could define themselves. Looking back on the parochial attitudes of Austen's characters, it seems difficult to believe that Europeans could sequester themselves so effectively from the imperial periphery that was bound to their world with ties of sugar, rum, gold, sweat, and blood.

And yet contemporary Americans appear to live under similarly insular illusions.[2] For instance, on September 11, 2001, blowback from US economic and political policies around the world reached the so-called American homeland.[3] Although the suicide attacks on New York and Washington punctured the bubble of US global supremacy, most Americans still have little understanding of what motivated al-Qaeda attackers and why people around the world feel animosity toward the US president George W. Bush, and his neocon policy makers have skillfully manipulated this naïveté, telling US citizens that they have come under attack because other people are jealous of the many freedoms Americans enjoy. The Bush administration has used 9/11 to articulate a vigilante rhetoric that divides the world into simplistic binary terms of good and evil, effectively making all attempts to explain and perhaps address the historical and material roots of anti-American animosity a form of treason.[4]

How is it possible for such illusions concerning US beneficence to be maintained, given the history of American involvement around the world over the past half century? The shock created by 9/11 derives in large measure from the fact that despite frequent exertions of military power, the defining characteristic of US imperialism is its informal nature. Unlike previous imperial powers such as Britain and France, that is, the United States has not relied predominantly on territorial conquest abroad. While the onset of a US imperium has often been dated to the Spanish-American War, the establishment of colonies in Puerto Rico and the Philippines and the annexation of Hawaii were in fact atypical of the economic, political, and ideological forms of domination that had already come to characterize US power. Instead of developing an extensive colonial apparatus, the United States asserted its imperial sway from the beginning of the twentieth century primarily through foreign direct investment and the modern corporate form, making its power distinct from previous European forms of hegemony.[5] The genius of US policy makers, beginning with Woodrow Wilson, has resided in their corresponding ability to represent America's informal empire in terms of a framework of universal rights. Thus a pamphlet inserted in *Fortune* magazine at the dawn of American global hegemony in 1942 could proclaim that "a new American 'imperialism,' if it is to be called that, will—or rather can—be quite different from the British type . . . American imperialism does not need extra-territoriality; it can get along better in Asia if the tuans and sahibs stay home."[6]

US hegemony following 1945 was expressed through what Peter Gowan calls a "protectorate system" in which the United States reconstructed the economic relations of the core capitalist nations and consolidated a hub-and-spokes network of links to the US security apparatus.[7] This new brand of informal empire, characterized by the penetration of nation-state borders rather than their dissolution, made the model of interimperial rivalry envisaged by Lenin seem outmoded for the past half century, at least within the capitalist nations.[8] This was particularly true during the period after 1970, when US neoliberal ideology rapidly dismantled nation-state borders in the name of free trade and so-called globalization. Despite this increasing interpenetration of capital and governance on a global scale, the informal character of US imperial power and its reliance on other states, both core and peripheral, to maintain global order has ensured that culture has remained largely national during the last half-century.[9] This observation applies both to US culture and to that of the nations who achieved their independence from European colonial domination under US tutelage after 1945. If, as Edward Said argues in *Culture and Imperialism*, empire remained a marginally visible presence in most European fiction of the nineteenth century, US global hegemony and the transnational economic, political, and ideological networks on which it relies have been virtually invisible in the realm of domestic cultural production.[10] Literature has thus helped reproduce the insularity that is the ironic corollary of informal US imperialism.

The essential task for a literature intent on challenging contemporary US hegemony is therefore to render visible the transnational networks of power that characterize American imperialism today. This is a particularly difficult role for the novel, which, unlike more recent media such as the Internet, was one of the primary technologies of print capitalism through which national consciousness was initially consolidated.[11] While the novel clearly played a vital role in articulating anticolonial nationalist consciousness, metropolitan novels that fail to provide cognitive maps for the transnational reach of US imperial hegemony participate in an ideological veiling of contemporary power relations.[12] In addition, because the contemporary global justice movement (GJM) is characterized by fresh organizational forms that remain based in particular nations but also develop significant transnational linkages, contemporary anti-imperial literature must extend its imaginative orientation to a similar transnational horizon. This new literature would constitute a revival of sorts of what Richard Wright called "the novelists' international," one that originates in the new forms of transnational organization associated with the GJM rather than the nationally based, hierarchical, and centralized forms of the

Second and Third International.[13] The greatest strength of the GJM is to have revived links between the dispossessed and marginalized of the global North and South. We need a radical popular culture that uses all genres, from the pamphlet to the blog to the novel, to articulate this new solidarity.[14] Furthermore, we should expect such a literature to extend the concerns of recent postcolonial literature, which has tended to focus both on the many failures of anticolonial nationalism and on the migration of people and culture across national boundaries.[15]

Although the outlines of such a literature are difficult to discern at this early stage, Robert Newman's recent novel *The Fountain at the Center of the World* offers a prototype for what such an anti-imperialist literature in the age of globalization might look like.[16] Using a Dickensian plot conceit of brothers separated at birth, Newman's epic novel traces the impact of what David Harvey calls "accumulation by dispossession," the privatization of the global commons that has been one of the primary facets of the neoliberal reconstruction of empire over the past quarter of a century.[17] In Newman's work, forms of accumulation by dispossession such as water privatization are represented in all their dislocating power, etching their disruptive impact on the alloy of individual and collective experience in multiple, interwoven geographical sites around the globe. While underlining the transnational networked power that sustains imperial power today, Newman's novel also traces the emergence of an anticapitalist "movement of movements" that links the dispossessed in the capitalist core and periphery. *The Fountain at the Center of the World* thus documents the emergence of new antisystemic social movements that over the past decade have come to constitute an important internationalist counterarticulation to global imperial power.[18]

ENCLOSING THE GLOBAL COMMONS

Newman's novel takes its title from a small fountain in the town of Tonalacapan, located in Mexico's northeastern state Tamaulipas, "the land of dead rivers." What justifies the notion that this fountain in a dusty provincial town in a far corner of Mexico could be at the center of the world? Tonalacapan's fountain may be a kind of seismograph, the novel's protagonist Chano Salgado speculates, "responding minutely to everything that's going on everywhere on earth."[19] Since the fountain is fed by underground springs, its gradually diminishing spurts serve as an index of the region's declining water table. This parched condition is hardly a result of natural causes. Instead, the fountain is in such a sad state because the area's groundwater is being siphoned off by the US-based Ethylclad corporation. Protests a year before the novel's action begins delayed construction of Ethylclad's "toxic-waste plant," but now a court has ruled that the people of Tamaulipas must pay compensation to the multinational for ten months of lost profit. In addition, the completed plant has begun pumping out sixty thousand gallons of groundwater a day, intensifying the already advanced process of desertification in Tamaulipas. Tonalacapan's fountain thus lies at the center of the world in as much as its fate serves as an index of the increasing disenfranchisement of the world's poor as they are stripped of communal water rights.[20] The seemingly innocuous fountain in Newman's novel thus stands as a symbol for the remorseless encroachment of the forces of privatization on the global commons and the dispossession of those who depend on the precious resources contained in the commons.

The cutting edge of imperialism over the past two decades has been what Naomi Klein calls "the privatization of every aspect of life, and the transformation of every activity and value into a commodity."[21] From water rights to peasants' land to the seeds they plant in that land and even the genetic makeup of indigenous peoples, virtually all aspects of life have been subjected to commodification during the neoliberal era. The neocon conquest of Iraq has merely intensified this pillaging of the public realm, as Klein herself noted in a powerful article on the unleashing of a radical free-market ideology during US-administered "reconstruction" efforts.[22] When activists such as Klein refer to the enclosure of the commons, they signal through this implicit reference to the rise of agrarian capitalism in eighteenth-century England that this process is not a new one.[23] Instead, the tide of privatization that has accelerated so dramatically during the neoliberal era in fact constitutes a structural aspect of capitalism. Conditions in the core capitalist countries have, however, led many analysts to overlook this fact. In his discussion of the new imperialism, David Harvey seeks to explain this blindness by differentiating between struggles over expanded reproduction and those over what he calls "accumulation by dispossession."[24] The organs of the organized working class in core capitalist nations tended to emphasize struggles over expanded reproduction, fighting through labor unions and political parties during the past two centuries for suffrage, shorter working hours, and access to health care, unemployment insurance, education, and other so-called benefits of advanced capitalism. As a result of this emphasis, the ongoing accumulation of capital through dispossession of commonly held assets such as land, water, and minerals tended to be ignored.[25] Had radicals in the industrialized world been more sensitive to the forms of dispossession unfolding in their nation's colonial possessions throughout the nineteenth and twentieth centuries, they might not have made such a dramatic conceptual and strategic error. Marx's description of this process as "primitive accumulation," developed from his analysis of the origins of agrarian capitalism in Britain, testifies to the Eurocentric character of much radical analysis. By suggesting that such acts took place in an isolated, long-distant temporal moment, Marx's analysis failed to attend to the geographical expansion of this structural component of capitalist accumulation around the world.

This ignorance concerning accumulation through dispossession helps explain the blindness of most commentators to the character of anti-imperialist struggle over the past two decades. Indeed, the very term *imperialism* dropped out of both radical and mainstream vocabulary in the core capitalist nations during the 1980s and 1990s. This is due in large part to the fact that the 1970s saw the last great wave of decolonization of the postwar period. However, if overt occupation of foreign territory such as occurred during the age of European colonialism in the nineteenth century or even during the Vietnam War seemed by and large a thing of the past by 1980, accumulation by dispossession or informal imperialism actually accelerated during this period. The increasing bias of the media in core countries toward exclusive coverage of parochial metropolitan issues also helped obscure the nature of the crisis and reconstruction of the capitalist order in the periphery.[26] Taken together, this increasing metropolitan narcissism and the theoretical shortcomings of many radical analysts impeded systemic analysis of the changes that took place during these years and put a brake on efforts to forge unity around common experiences of dispossession in wealthy and poor countries.

The new enclosures in poor nations took place under the sign of debt. Faced with a critical deterioration in trade terms for commodities and inflated energy prices as a result of the OPEC (Organization of Petroleum Exporting Countries) oil embargo in the 1970s, many developing countries borrowed heavily from metropolitan banks, which at the time were awash with petrodollars deposited by the wealthy regimes of the Middle East.[27] While a few countries such as South Korea and Taiwan developed quickly during the late 1970s and early 1980s, most poor countries found themselves facing escalating balance-of-payments crises that left them mired ever more deeply in debt. In response to this situation, international lending organizations such as the World Bank (WB) and the International Monetary Fund (IMF) began to intervene by making further loans subject to stringent internal fiscal reform policies. These policies, promoted in the name of stabilization or "structural adjustment," were widespread by the early 1980s. Their impact on poor countries was nothing short of devastating. Many of the central components of developmental states in both the second and third world — from price supports for commodity production to decent wages to health care and education — were eradicated in the name of structural adjustment. Although the changes that resulted from IMF-WB policies appeared to be purely economic, they were in fact also political and cultural since they involved a thorough reconfiguration of the relation between the state and civil society in poor countries.[28]

While channeling billions of dollars annually to banks in the core capitalist nations, structural adjustment dramatically deepened poverty in many nations in the second and third world during the 1980s and 1990s.[29] As a rule, these austerity measures could only be effectively imposed by relatively authoritarian regimes. Thus structural adjustment programs (SAPS) imposed by US-dominated institutions like the IMF and the WB succeeded both in worsening hunger and other forms of deprivation and in intensifying dictatorship in the majority of the countries where they were enforced. States that acquiesced to such policies were widely perceived to have broken the social contract they had established with their people. The predictable result of such perceptions was widespread discontent, which in many situations was translated into demonstrations that targeted both the international lending institutions that mandated SAPS and the local governments that implemented them. The insurrections that erupted in the majority of nations where SAPS were imposed were provoked, in other words, not simply by poverty but also by moral outrage at the perceived betrayal of the social contract by developmental states.[30] Taken together, these uprisings constitute an international strike wave that has lasted for nearly two decades.[31] The core capitalist nations have remained largely ignorant of these insurrections, in general congratulating themselves for the collapse of the Soviet Union and its satellites and for democratization in Latin America and Asia without understanding the deeper economic and social forces at work behind these watershed events.

Ironically, steps toward democratization in both second and third world nations subjected to SAPs have been accompanied by an intensification rather than by an alleviation of indebtedness and austerity. This has led many in these countries to question the character of democratization. For while it is true that liberal parliamentary democracy has swept the globe over the past decade, it also constitutes a form of rule that has proven itself incapable of restoring the social contract between state and people that led to anti-austerity protests in the first place. Nowhere is this failure more glaringly apparent than in the arrogant and largely unregulated conduct of multinational corporations in poor countries. Moving in droves to nations where wages are low and environmental legislation scarce since the 1970s, multinational corporations have benefited from the sanctity of private property within liberal democratic capitalism to evade popular pressures for regulation. Indeed, according to constitutional law in the United States, which has tended to set the ground rules for relations between state, business, and civil society around the world since the collapse of communism in 1990, corporations enjoy the legal status of persons. Governments are, as a result, obligated to grant corporations all of the rights to life, liberty, and the pursuit of profits enjoyed by private individuals, essentially gutting democratic governance.[32] This legal situation, along with the threat to pull up stakes and move to less politically obstructionist pastures, has given corporations unparalleled power. While transnational corporations have been able to employ human rights law to free themselves of unwanted government regulation, individuals have been impeded from challenging corporate conduct since human rights law is seen to regulate the behavior of states rather than individuals, even if these individuals happen to be corporations. The upshot has been that resistance to corporate power has increasingly been manifest not through government regulation but through forms of dissent within civil society, from the establishment of nongovernmental organizations (NGOs) to forms of civil disobedience such as nonviolent direct action (NVDA).

Faced with the privatization of water rights and with the failure of mass demonstrations to provoke government regulation of Ethylclad's plant, Chano

Salgado and his comrades in *The Fountain at the Center of the World* turn to the extralegal means of collective bargaining by sabotage. But not before Newman's novel has staged tactical debates between Chano and his friends about the political impact of the destruction of corporate property. With an implicit nod to Edward Abbey's classic novel *Monkey Wrench Gang*, Chano's friend Ayo argues that it is the despoiling corporations who are the terrorists and that sabotage of corporate property merely constitutes an act of self-defense (14). Chano resists this line, saying that violence loses the sympathy of the people. His hope that speaking truth to power will make a difference gradually evaporates, however, as Ayo reminds him of the many people whose livelihoods are being destroyed by Ethylclad's polluting practices.

Woven through Chano's fragmented thoughts as he tries to decide whether to help Ayo prepare a bomb to blow up the Ethylclad plant's pipes are memories of his life with his wife Marisa and their son Daniel. Marisa, we learn as the novel progresses, has been assassinated for her organizing activities in the factories — or maquiladoras — along the border between the United States and Mexico. Following her death, Chano is picked up by the military and disappeared, to live for two years in a distant prison and, consequently, to lose all trace of his son Daniel. These events help to explain his refusal to engage in political activities for ten years after he is released from jail. They also explain the emotional desolation that prevents him from believing in the power of the people to challenge Ethylclad's polluting practices. And they explain his decision to blow up the pipes that feed the region's groundwater into the Ethylclad plant.

Punctuating the narrative of Chano's sabotage of the Ethylclad plant and subsequent life underground, the story of Daniel's journey in search of his father offers a fragile counterpoint of hope to what might otherwise be a very pessimistic tale. Daniel is one of the many people uprooted by the disrupting power of the global financial system and rerouted across multiple borders. The paradox of a borderless economy that operates through increasingly barricaded borders figures repeatedly in Newman's novel, which is filled with border crossings.[33] Of course, the borders that impede the movement of human beings from state to state also make them illegal, subjecting them to intensified exploitation and hence functioning as an integral part of the global economy despite their apparently paradoxical character.

Seldom do metropolitan critics of immigration consider the role played by countries like the United States in disrupting economies in the third world, thereby creating strong push factors that contribute to migration. Most immigrants are, after all, simply refugees from the undeclared civil wars unleashed by neoliberalism around the globe. While SAPs have been a major force over the past two decades in undermining the livelihood of poor people around the world, they have not been the only factor. Another important source of migration, both internal and international, has been the green revolution. By introducing pesticides, fertilizers, intensive single-crop cultivation, and automated farming techniques, the green revolution increased productivity in many third world countries, but at the same time pushed poor farmers who could not afford to buy the new fossil fuel–based agricultural inputs out of business and off their land.[34] Beto, Daniel's adoptive father in Costa Rica, is experiencing precisely this fate since the exorbitant costs of pesticides, fertilizers, and gasoline are proving too high for a small landowning peasant like him. With no future to hold him in Costa Rica, Daniel joins the crew of a fishing boat named the *Jennifer Lopez* that is setting sail for Mexico. He is intent on finding his father.

When he arrives in Tonalacapan, Daniel encounters two groups of people, whom Newman uses to cast in high relief opposing values of human solidarity and exploitation. On the one hand, Daniel meets Chano's friends Oscar and Yolanda, who make a kind of surrogate son out of him. Their own son lived an agonizing life, having been born with fluid filling his skull as a result of Yolanda's work with toxic chemicals in the maquiladoras. Now, they struggle to protect Daniel without giving him information about his father that might endanger his life following the sabotage of the Ethylclad plant. Oscar and Yolanda embody the kind of generosity of spirit and political solidarity that Chano has lost sight of, and they do much to teach Daniel about these values. In particular, they include him in their efforts to organize their fellow workers and to bring about social change through political activism. When the army sends troops to arrest Daniel during a demonstration against neoliberalism that Yolanda and Oscar have invited him to attend, Oscar saves Daniel by warning him of the danger over his truck's loudspeaker (135). This heroic act costs Oscar his life: the soldiers shoot him down in cold blood.

With this scene, Newman's novel lays bare the nexus of corporate and state power. The attack on Ethylclad's property has set off an escalating confrontation between the people and their government, which is acting to protect corporate property rather than the environment on which the people depend. Oscar's murder signals that the stakes of opposing this nexus of power are high indeed and suggests that Chano's solitary act of sabotage has reverberations that go far beyond his own exile. More specifically, the killing of Oscar demonstrates that Chano's turn toward sabotage constituted a strategic error: it elided many other tactics that could have placed pressure on Ethylclad; it left no room for negotiation with the corporation; it had minimal impact; and, most of all, it helped legitimate state violence.[35] Ultimately, it is a peaceful demonstrator like Oscar who is made to pay for Chano's isolated act.

On the opposite pole from Yolanda and Oscar is Blas Mastrangelo, a canny but unscrupulous coyote, or smuggler of human cargo across the Rio Grande. Blas takes advantage of his compatriots who, desperate to make it to the United States, are willing to pay cash up front for safe passage. Once the *mojados*, or illegal immigrants, wade into the river, Blas releases the slipknot he's tied on their line and drowns them all (59). If Yolanda and Oscar offer living testimony to values of human solidarity, Blas symbolizes the greed and domination that increasingly define life in a world founded on neoliberalism.[36] When he meets Daniel, Blas quickly figures out who his father is and smells a way to gain leverage with the local police by turning him in. Throughout this section of the novel, Blas tries to outfox the new head of police, Ilan Cardenas, who embodies the new order ushered in by NAFTA. Immune to the corruption that once conferred immunity on coyotes such as Blas, Ilan believes strongly in free trade agreements such as NAFTA. In the new economic order envisioned by Ilan, the police play a key political role: securing the stability necessary to attract foreign investment. Of course, keeping the peace ultimately involves calling in the army, whose members murder Oscar. Prior to this denouement, however, Blas and Ilan, driven by their own selfish ambitions, each try to manipulate one another, using Daniel as a pawn in their power games. As a result of these egotistical machinations, both Daniel and Chano slip through Ilan's hands. Ilan responds by sending Blas to a prison where a death sentence at the hands of fellow prisoners awaits him.

Through the juxtaposition of Blas and Ilan with Oscar and Yolanda, Newman demonstrates that neoliberalism is not simply a set of economic policies but also a culture that emphasizes personal gain and hierarchical domination to the exclusion of broader values of social solidarity and mutuality. While Newman's contrast of these different groups of characters lends his novel the character of a strong morality play, the values embodied by such characters have a political valence that extends beyond the individual. For it is precisely the qualities of equality and solidarity that the austerity measures mandated by international lending institutions such as the IMF and the WB were perceived as violating by citizens in poor countries around the world over the past two decades. It was the abrogation of these social values that helped spark the uprisings against neoliberalism of the past two decades. And it is these same values of solidarity that are not simply animating the global justice movement today but also providing it with its unique organizational forms and political tactics.

GREENWASHING AND POPULAR POWER

If neoliberalism is not a set of economic policies alone but also a hegemonic ideology, then we should expect that one of its core modes of maintaining power would be the manufacture of consent. *The Fountain at the Center of the World* explores the role of such manipulation through the character of Evan Hatch, Chano's twin brother. Adopted by a middle-class British couple when the twins were four years old, Evan has grown up to be cynical about progressive social change and a master massager of public opinion.[37] The theme of brothers separated at birth that provides the narrative scaffolding for Newman's novel offers an inherent challenge to the contemporary reemergence of biological essentialism. As Newman himself notes, "the ancient trope of the prince and the pauper has as its moral that there is nothing intrinsic about the fortune the prince or pauper enjoys."[38] The dramatically different fortunes enjoyed by Chano and Evan are a product of chance and circumstance rather than of some inherent, genetic superiority of the latter, European-bred brother.[39] Newman's novel is thus predicated on an egalitarian structuring plot device, one that systematically unravels Evan's arrogant master-of-the-universe attitude. Admittedly, *The Fountain at the Center of the World* is certainly less radical in formal terms that other works associated with the global justice movement, including the anonymously authored, anticopyright novels of the Luther Blissett collective or the recent collaboration of the Zapatistas' Subcomandante Marcos and the Mexican novelist Paco Ignacio Taibo II. Nevertheless, despite its relatively traditional realist format, Newman's work affirms and embodies the egalitarianism that lies at the heart of the movement.[40]

At the novel's outset, Evan is working for a public relations firm whose mission statement asserts that it is easier to change the way people think than to change reality (4). In the society of the spectacle, that is, media-generated public impressions often matter far more than on-the-ground reality, particularly when it comes to events taking place in the distant countries in which transnational companies tend to set up shop.[41] While this has been true throughout the era of US global hegemony, the trend toward media concentration has intensified radically over the past decade, making the kind of manipulation engaged in by Evan particularly damaging to progressive causes. As critics such as Robert McChesney have documented, the 1990s proved a watershed era in which the corporate media moved from a nation-state platform to establish a global media system dominated by a handful of octopus-like megaconglomerates such as Time Warner, Disney, and Rupert Murdoch's News Corporation.[42] The convergence of telecommunications and computing with news media, in tandem with structural adjustment policies that pried open the domestic markets of poor nations, has helped create a new form of electronic imperialism of unprecedented power, undermining the public information function of the media around the world and disseminating neoliberal ideology into every crevice of the global economy.[43] Despite the utopian ballyhoo surrounding the Internet, opponents of corporate media in both the global North and South face tremendous odds as this new mode of communication is bent to overwhelmingly commercial ends in a manner that parallels the commodification of previous media such as radio and television.[44]

In the face of the overwhelming hegemony of the corporate media, members of the global justice movement have extended the tradition of strategic media-oriented activism that stretches back to avant-garde movements such as the Situationist International, whose radical culture jamming helped spark the uprisings of May 1968 in Paris.[45] Picking up on the situationists' critique of the media spectacle, contemporary media activists intervene both by deconstructing the central symbols of dominant discourse and by establishing alternative media and discourses. Inspired by anarchist traditions of autonomous, antihierarchical activism, members of the GJM in Robert Newman's home country of Britain created a vibrant counterculture of squatting, antiroad protests, raves, and alternative, do-it-yourself electronic media such as guerrilla radio and *Squall* magazine during the 1990s.[46] Although he strenuously eschews the mantle of leader, Newman has been an important protagonist in Britain's DIY movement through his immensely popular work as a political comedian, his writing for magazines such as *Squall*, his activism on behalf of groups like People's Global Action and the Dissent Network against the G8, and, now, his *Fountain at the Center of the World*.[47] A product and document of the media activism that characterizes DIY culture, Newman's novel identifies the means through which the corporate media manufactures consent in order to "dispute what is given to us as 'reality'" and thereby challenge the neoliberal mantra, "there is no alternative."[48]

In a powerful demonstration of the manipulation of public opinion, Evan Hatch and his PR flack colleagues feed stories to the media that help legitimate government support for right-wing regimes, cover up the environmentally destructive impact of corporate practices around the world, and generally foster the impression that there is no alternative to privatization. A good example of these strategies is Evan's clever use of greenwashing. Working for the Competitive Enterprise Institute in New York, Evan sets up front groups such as "the Clean Air Working Group (coal companies against the U.S. Clean Air Act), the Coalition for Sensible Regulation (developers), and the Sea Lion Defense Fund, a trawler consortium fighting limits on factory fishing" (31). When he finds himself in top form, Evan works not so much to repudiate the arguments of anticorporate activists as to sow doubt about the issues under debate to create apathy and passivity among the public.[49]

Evan prides himself on being a hard-nosed realist, someone who, like Blas and Ilan, knows the score and will not let anyone make a sucker out of him. His capacity to manipulate public opinion gives him a feeling of personal mastery that contrasts strongly with the self-doubt and vacillation that plagues his brother Chano in Mexico. Yet despite his arrogance, Evan's body harbors a fatal virus that shatters his feelings of invulnerability. Shortly after attending a meeting of the "social management working group," whose brief is to defuse opposition to water privatization, Evan is overcome by a paroxysm brought on by his illness (73). He abandons his BMW to stagger through flooded fields until he finds a place to vomit violently. When he returns, he finds that the flooding has submerged his sports car. This scene cleverly evokes the unstoppable power of the natural forces that Evan and the companies wish to commodify. In addition, Evan's fit, we learn later, is the result of Chagas disease, a tropical illness for which there is no remedy; since Chagas exclusively affects peasants in poor countries, drug companies have done no research to find a cure (317). As we learn later in the novel, Evan contracted his illness during his infancy in Mexico. Both elements of this scene — the flooding and Evan's disease — evoke a return of the natural and historical forces that neoliberal capitalism has repressed. Like the rioting provoked by neoliberal austerity regimes, they suggest that unrestrained capitalism generates powerful contradictions and counterforces. Moreover, the images of a virus and a flood attacking the capitalist body also presage the uprising that takes place during the World Trade Organization (WTO) meeting in Seattle in 1999.

Much of the second half of Newman's novel documents the so-called battle of Seattle. Evan, Chano, and Daniel all converge on Seattle before the WTO meeting in a series of encounters through which Newman explores the events that took place in the streets and hotel suites during this watershed moment. The collapse of the WTO negotiations in Seattle represented one of the most significant defeats for US trade policy since the establishment of the nation's global hegemony after 1945. Equally important, the demonstrations that disrupted the WTO brought the global justice movement to the attention of the public in the Northern hemisphere for the first time, in the process sealing long-developing bonds between social movements from the South and the North.[50] Evan Hatch ironically first evokes the GJM's transnational solidarity as a way of manipulating the CEOs he advises using fear. When he arrives in Seattle, however, he finds the events taking place to exceed his most inflated predictions. Evan, Chano, and Daniel find themselves in the midst of an uprising against neoliberalism that unites the disenfranchised and dispossessed of every continent into a movement of movements.

REPRESENTING THE FOURTH WORLD WAR

While austerity was imposed on poor countries during the 1980s and 1990s, similar forces were rolling back the social and economic entitlements won by social movements in the rich countries over the past two centuries.[51] The creation of a global assembly line during this period led to massive deindustrialization, structural unemployment, and the rise of the poorly paying service economy in the North. At the same time, new technology began to replace workers and allow the integration of financial transactions and communications on an unprecedented global scale. The common wealth — from physical assets such as clean air and pure water to public institutions like schools and parks to intangible assets like civil rights and liberties — came under assault by quickly accumulating corporate power. While governance was hollowed out on a local and national scale, insular, undemocratic institutions such as the WTO took over the role of regulating capital accumulation on a world scale.

Although this new post-Fordist regime led to unprecedented levels of accumulation for many large corporations and wealthy stockholders, it also deepened the contradictions of capitalism. Once unleashed, the forces of neoliberal globalization triggered a seemingly inexorable race toward the bottom that gutted democracy, spread poverty, degraded the environment, and fomented political instability around the planet. If the social movements that had opposed unfettered capitalism, including trade unions and social democratic governments, were completely outflanked by the forces of globalization, these same forces began to create common interests among those suffering from globalization. The intensifying inequality generated by capitalism in rut around the world over the past two decades therefore ironically helped social movements overcome national and interest-group boundaries. Thus it was the very power accumulated by corporate globalization during the past twenty years that set the stage for the appearance of the first genuinely global resistance to neoliberal capitalism.

One of the most important moments for this converging movement of movements was the Encuentro Intercontinental Contra El Neoliberalismo y Por La Humanidad (International Encounter against Neoliberalism and for Humanity) sponsored by the Zapatista Army for National Liberation (EZLN) in 1996. The Zapatistas emerged from the remote jungle of Chiapas in southwest Mexico on January 1, 1994, to protest the North American Free Trade Agreement's elimination of Article 27 of the Mexican constitution, a reform fought for during the revolution that created a nationwide system of collectively owned and cultivated land.[52] Using new technology such as the Internet that is central to corporate globalization, the Zapatistas spread their message of resistance to neoliberalism around the world and called on global civil society to support their uprising. In response, Zapatista solidarity groups sprang up around the world. The Encuentro of 1996 brought these and many other NGOs to the Lacandón rain forest to discuss strategies for working toward alternative, just forms of globalization. The following year, another meeting organized by the Zapatistas gave birth to People's Global Action, a network of grassroots social movements dedicated to resisting neoliberal globalization using direct action that helped to plan the demonstrations in Seattle.[53] At the same time, protests against the summit meetings through which the financial architecture of corporate globalization was being constructed became more frequent, beginning with demonstrations at the APEC (Asia-Pacific Economic Cooperation) summit in Manila in 1996. In addition, in core nations such as the United States, protest groups like ACT UP and Earth First! pioneered radical new strategies of dissent, putting their bodies on the line in spectacular image events that disrupted corporate business as usual. By 1999, the Zapatista slogan "Ya Basta!" (Enough!) had become a rallying cry picked up and amplified by these and other disenfranchised groups around the world.

The Zapatistas and the many other movements that developed alongside them or in their wake were organized along lines that represented a direct challenge not simply to the organs of corporate globalization but also to previous anticapitalist social movements. For in their struggle for social justice, the latter had unwittingly replicated some of the most pernicious structures of the former, including top-down, vanguardist leadership styles that are inherently antidemocratic. Instead of seeking to create a disciplined cadre bent on taking state power as had the guerrilla bands and radical movements of previous decades, the organizations of illegal immigrants, radical environmentalists, dispossessed peasants, and others who form the GJM embrace organizational forms that strive to embody egalitarianism and direct democracy.[54] The loosely organized affinity groups, clusters, and spokescouncils that characterize the GJM offer a stark contrast to the elitism of organizations such as the WTO.[55] Out of these new organizational forms come radically new tactics that initially left the forces of law and order, whose counterinsurgency techniques were based on tracking down movement leaders, in a quandary.[56] Media representations of the GJM during the battle of Seattle also hearkened back to the social movements of the 1960s, underscoring the mainstream media's ignorance of the transnational links characterizing today's movement of movements.[57] For the novel organization structures and tactics deployed on the streets of Seattle and elsewhere are grounded in new forms of anticapitalist political subjectivity that the GJM is generating in its struggle against neoliberal forces around the planet.

This radical new consciousness is exemplified in Newman's novel in the transformation that Chano and his son undergo while in Seattle. Chano arrives in the city masquerading as his brother in order to escape Mexico. When confronted with the massing affinity groups of the GJM, Chano secretly hopes that the demonstration will fail, thereby confirming his sense of hopelessness (244). In fact, as protesters lock down the streets around the Seattle Convention Center in order to prevent WTO delegates from attending their meetings, there are many moments when the movement seems on the verge of defeat. The leader of the AFL-CIO sells out the protesters who are attempting to shut down the WTO when presented with a paltry seat at the negotiating table (265). As a result, union marshals keep rank-and-file union members away from the area where protesters affiliated with the Direct Action Network (DAN) are occupying the streets in the face of police violence.[58] Chano is also infuriated by the naïveté of demonstrators from the United States and other affluent countries, who seem completely nonplussed when their creative expressions of nonviolent civil disobedience provoke the Seattle police department and the National Guard to acts of escalating, indiscriminate violence (285). Witnessing the incredible bravery and resilience of the DAN protesters in the face of police brutality, however, Chano recovers the optimism he felt when he first met his wife Marisa. After a hurricane had hit Tamaulipas, Chano had joined other members of the community in self-organized, autonomous groups that began to reconstruct the community from the ground up.[59] This grassroots activism offered an example of lived solidarity that Chano's experiences in Seattle help reactivate. The novel concludes with Chano remembering his wife Marisa's gentle reminder of the power of community solidarity (339).

Daniel undergoes a similar transformation in Seattle. Despite incessantly searching the teargas-filled streets for his father, he never has more than a fleeting encounter with Chano. Notwithstanding this failure to find the man who he hopes will provide him with a sense of roots, Daniel comes to understand the shape of his life by connecting it to the broader struggles against neoliberalism taking place in the streets of Seattle and around the world. At the close of the second day of demonstrations, during which National Guard soldiers fire rubber bullets and toxic CN gas at peaceful protesters, Daniel attends a meeting of a Latino group named Voces de la Frontera (Voices of the Border). Here, a speaker's words suddenly clarify the meaning of Daniel's life to him:

> If the Cold War was the Third World War, she was saying, then this is the Fourth. And it's a war being fought between private power and civil society, between corporations and people. The more that everything else was changing, the less uprooted Daniel felt . . . . And only a new reality—call it the Fourth World War—could, he felt, make sense of his own radically changing experience. It was the golden thread through the maze, the global maze he'd entered on first seeing Beto in a field no longer his own. (293)

The golden thread that Daniel picks up at this meeting and during the rest of the battle of Seattle is the grassroots struggle of the GJM for another world, a struggle that challenges the "there is no alternative" rhetoric of corporate globalization's advocates. Of course, by providing Daniel with this golden thread, the speaker at Voces de la Frontera also offers the novel's readers a cognitive map that clarifies the otherwise apparently random movements of the characters across national borders. By articulating the stakes in the battle of Seattle in the simple terms of private power versus civil society, the speaker offers a powerful slogan for the GJM that is precisely the sort of clear explanation necessary for the movement to reach a broader audience.[60] With this newfound understanding of the meaning of his experience in hand, Daniel embraces his father's struggle for a fuller sense of human possibility than that offered by neoliberalism. The last time we hear of Daniel, he has traveled to the town of Cochabamba in Bolivia to protest against the Bechtel Corporation's notorious privatization of water supplies.[61] By following Daniel and his father as they cross many national borders, Newman's *The Fountain at the Center of the World* links together the many diverse instances of commodification of the global commons. The novel thereby provides readers with a clear sense of the realities behind corporate globalization and of the alternative vision offered by the movement for global justice.

CONCLUSION

Although *The Fountain at the Center of the World* concludes on this optimistic note, the novel also devotes a great deal of attention to the repression experienced by GJM protesters in Seattle. By cataloguing in detail the various forms of gas, pepper spray, and beating to which members of DAN were subjected, Newman's novel offers a counternarrative to that offered by the corporate media. Both during the battle of Seattle and at subsequent GJM protests, the mainstream media tended to focus obsessively on the few instances of violence by demonstrators and to ignore the systematic forms of brutality deployed by the police and the National Guard.[62] The media's focus on the spectacle of demonstrators battling or being beaten up by police in the streets may have made for sensation viewing, but it completely silenced the reasons for the demonstrations, suggesting that the events in Seattle simply had to do with hooliganism versus law and order. The upshot of such media representation was to legitimate a popular authoritarian mentality in a significant segment of the US public that supports draconian infractions of constitutional rights to free speech and public dissent.[63]

The alarming character of this popular authoritarianism is perhaps most apparent in relation to pepper spray, to which many characters in Newman's novel are subjected. In 1997, a group of environmental protesters who had locked themselves together in the office of a California congressman were subjected to torture by the local sheriff's department. The policemen deliberately held the protesters' eyelids open and repeatedly applied the excruciatingly painful pepper spray onto their open tear ducts, despite the protesters' screams of agony. Notwithstanding their cries of pain, the protesters—all of whom were female—had no physical signs of abuse that might have offered "objective" evidence of police abuse. Pepper spray thus seems to be the ideal postmodern police device since it effectively ruptures the link between signifier (pepper spray) and signified (pain).[64] In fact, the screams of the protesters in reaction to the spray's application were characterized in the press as the overwrought reactions of "hysterical" women. Unlike the public reaction to Rodney King's beating earlier in the decade, the public and members of the jury who deadlocked on the case brought by the protesters against the police condoned police brutality because of the character of the torture inflicted. A

US district court judge subsequently ruled that the police had "acted reasonably," a ruling that still stands, legitimating the now ubiquitous application of pepper spray against demonstrators engaging in nonviolent civil disobedience in the United States.

The incidents of police violence assiduously recorded by Newman's novel suggest that neoliberalism, the cutting edge of US imperial culture over the past two decades, always contained within it the seeds of the neocon authoritarianism that the Bush administration has adopted both at home and around the world. As Antonio Gramsci stressed, consent and coercion are the two linchpins through which hegemony is maintained. However, the past two decades have demonstrated a consistent erosion of the mechanisms through which the state maintains consent in both the core capitalist countries and in poor nations. As a result, there has been an unrelenting shift toward forms of authoritarianism and repression in order to implement the neoliberal program of stripping the commons around the world. People in poor countries and in communities of color in wealthy nations such as the United States and the United Kingdom have recognized and sought to challenge this shift toward coercion for several decades. Since the battle of Seattle, however, the rise of popular authoritarianism has begun to affect not simply marginalized communities but the basic constitutional order of the United States and the universal civil liberties it purportedly upholds. Measures such as the USA PATRIOT Act and the now widespread practice of caging demonstrators in barbed-wire "free speech zones" many blocks away from the events they are protesting are in direct violation of the Bill of Rights.[65]

In her discussion of the origins of European fascism, Hannah Arendt stresses that the central doctrines and strategies of Nazism—including genocide—germinated in the colonies.[66] A very similar process is unfolding in the United States today. Just as neoliberal doctrines of structural adjustment led to uprisings, government repression, and resistance in many poor countries around the world over the past two decades, so the increasingly extreme implementation of free-market fundamentalism in the United States since the battle of Seattle has led to increasing resistance and authoritarianism. Particularly after 9/11, the GJM, which developed an unparalleled understanding of the workings of corporate globalization, has been faced with the new challenge of theorizing and implementing strategies to counteract a climate of intensifying state repression.[67] The challenges are immense. Almost all forms of dissent other than letter writing have now been criminalized in the United States.[68] The long-established tactic of nonviolent direct action, whose roots go back all the way to Henry David Thoreau and which has been the basis of vital movements for civil rights and peace in the United States, now provokes thinly veiled forms of torture by state authorities. As the media becomes ever more dominated by right-wing monopolies, it has proven increasingly difficult to articulate the grievances and goals of the GJM to a broader public. Notwithstanding these challenges, the GJM continues to develop radical alternative means of disseminating its message, from the development of the Internet-based Indymedia independent news service to the World Social Forums at which people from around the world have met to draft a platform for an alternative to the neoliberal order.[69] Robert Newman's *The Fountain at the Center of the World* constitutes an important part of this project to imagine a better world.

NOTES

1. Edward Said, *Culture and Imperialism* (New York: Knopf, 1993), 96; C. L. R. James, *The Black Jacobins: Toussaint L'Ouverture and the San Domingo Revolution* (New York: Knopf, 1989).
2. For an analysis of the domestic impact of previous US imperial policies, see Amy Kaplan, *Anarchy of Empire in the Making of U.S. Culture* (Cambridge, MA: Harvard University Press, 2002).
3. Chalmers Johnson, *Blowback: The Costs and Consequences of American Empire* (New York: Holt, 2000).
4. The campaign by groups such as the American Council of Trustees and Alumni (associated with Vice President Cheney's wife Lynne) against academics who seek to place 9/11 in historical perspective offers abundant evidence of this "you're either with us or against us" mentality.
5. Leo Panitch and Sam Gindin, "Global Capitalism and American Empire," in *The New Imperial Challenge: Socialist Register 2004*, ed. Panitch and Colin Leys (New York: Monthly Review Press, 2003), 10.
6. Quoted in ibid., 14.
7. Peter Gowan, *The Global Gamble: Washington's Faustian Bid for World Dominance* (New York: Verso, 1999)
8. Events since 9/11 have underlined the importance of an analysis of US state power and its problematic relation with other states, making the poststructuralist discussion in Michael Hardt and Antonio Negri's *Empire* (Cambridge, MA: Harvard University Press, 2000) seem particularly wrongheaded.

9. Michael Denning argues that an emphasis on a Gramscian national-popular also helped obscure transnational connections during what he calls the age of three worlds. See Michael Denning, *Culture in the Age of Three Worlds* (New York: Verso, 2004), 8.
10. Countries on the receiving end of US power have been all too aware of the penetration of American culture. For a classic reading of this cultural imperialism, see Ariel Dorfman and Armand Mattelart, *How to Read Donald Duck: Imperialist Ideology in the Disney Comic*, trans. David Kunzle (New York: International General, 1975).
11. Benedict Anderson, *Imagined Communities: Reflections on the Origin and Spread of Nationalism* (New York: New Left Books, 1991).
12. Cognitive mapping is discussed by Fredric Jameson in his chapter "Modernism and Imperialism" in Terry Eagleton, Fredric Jameson, and Edward Said, *Nationalism, Colonialism, and Literature* (Minneapolis: University of Minnesota Press, 1990), 43–68.
13. Denning, *Culture in the Age of Three Worlds*, 51.
14. Newman explicitly states that his novel is in conversation with other genres such as the pamphlet, the leaflet, and the political tract. The common thread that unites these genres is, according to Newman, that they "insist that truth is not what it is taken to be and that you will have to go off the beaten track to find it." Robert Newman, personal communication, July 1, 2005.
15. For criticism of the iconoclastic literature of nationalist disillusionment, see Tim Brennan, *Salman Rushdie and the Third World: Myths of the Nation* (New York: St. Martin's, 1991); and Neil Lazarus, *Nationalism and Cultural Practice in the Postcolonial World* (New York: Cambridge University Press, 1999). Such perspectives have been relatively marginal, however, with far more attention focused on alternatives to national identity through critical concepts such as diaspora.
16. The work of the Bolognese writers' collective that initially worked under the pseudonym Luther Blissett and currently operates as the Wu Ming Foundation offers another prototype of such fiction explicitly affiliated with the GJM. For examples, see Luther Blissett, *Q* (New York: Harcourt, 2004) and Wu Ming Foundation, *Fifty-four* (New York: Heinemann, 2005).
17. David Harvey, *The New Imperialism* (New York: Oxford University Press, 2003), 158.
18. For an illuminating discussion of the important distinctions between today's global justice movement and previous antisystemic movements, see Immanuel Wallerstein, "New Revolts against the System," in *A Movement of Movements: Is Another World Really Possible?*, ed. Tom Mertes (New York: Verso, 2004), 262–74.
19. Robert Newman, *The Fountain at the Center of the World* (New York: Soft Skull, 2004), 12. Further references to the novel will be cited parenthetically in the text.
20. Privatization of water resources is likely to become a source of intensifying inequality and conflict in the future. For recent discussions of this issue, see Marq de Villiers, *Water: The Fate of Our Most Precious Resource* (Boston: Houghton Mifflin, 2000); Vandana Shiva, *Water Wars: Privatization, Pollution, and Profit* (Cambridge, MA: South End, 2002); and Diana Raines Ward, *Water Wars: Drought, Flood, Folly and the Politics of Thirst* (New York: Riverhead, 2002).

21. Naomi Klein, "Reclaiming the Commons," in Mertes, *A Movement of Movements*, 220.
22. Naomi Klein, "Baghdad Year Zero: Pillaging Iraq in Pursuit of a Neocon Utopia," *Harper's*, September 2004, 43–53.
23. For a detailed discussion of agrarian capitalism in England, see Ellen Meiksins Wood, *The Origin of Capitalism: A Longer View* (New York: Verso, 2002).
24. Harvey, *New Imperialism*, 171.
25. Ibid.
26. Emma Miller, "Representing the South," in *Representing Resistance: Media, Civil Disobedience, and the Global Justice Movement*, ed. Andrew Opel and Donnalyn Pompper (Westport, CT: Praeger, 2003), 115–30.
27. It should be noted that poor countries only turned to borrowing because of the refusal of the wealthy nations to back progressive trade agreements such as those UNCTAD (United Nations Conference on Trade and Development) sought to implement. See Walden Bello, "UNCTAD: Time to Lead, Time to Challenge the WTO," in *Globalize This! The Battle against the WTO and Corporate Rule*, ed. Kevin Danaher and Roger Burbach (Monroe, ME: Common Courage, 2000), 163–70.
28. John Walton and David Seddon, *Free Markets and Food Riots: The Politics of Global Adjustment* (Cambridge, MA: Blackwell, 1994), 21.
29. John Walton and David Seddon stress that UN organizations were circulating studies showing the tendency for poverty to increase in nations subjected to structural adjustment programs from 1983 onward. This did not, however, lead to a dismantling of austerity programs. See ibid., 19.
30. Drawing on E. P. Thompson's reading of premodern food riots, Walton and Seddon emphasize the "moral economy" of modern anti-austerity protests. See ibid., 31.
31. Ibid., 23.
32. In a ruling in the 1886 case of *Santa Clara County v. Southern Pacific Railroad*, the US Supreme Court held that fourteenth amendment rights originally intended to protect emancipated slaves applied equally to corporations. Ten years later, the court rescinded those rights for black people but left them intact for corporations in *Plessy v. Ferguson*. For a discussion of the resulting corporate takeover of the ability to govern, see Georges Monbiot, "Corporations Behave as If They Are More Human Than We Are," *Guardian* October 5, 2000; and William Greider, *Who Will Tell The People: The Betrayal of American Democracy* (New York: Simon and Schuster, 1993). Newman refers to the *Plessy v. Ferguson* decision in *The Fountain at the Center of the World*, 151.
33. Commentators such as Arjun Appadurai have noted the multiple flows of capital, commodities, and information that are associated with globalization in *Modernity at Large: Cultural Dimensions of Globalization* (Minneapolis: University of Minnesota Press, 1996). Ironically, barriers to the movement of (poor) people have in most cases been strengthened despite the increasing freedom of movement in other sectors.
34. For a discussion of the impact of the green revolution, see Vandana Shiva, *The Violence of the Green Revolution: Third World Agriculture, Ecology, and Politics* (Atlantic Highlands, NJ: Zed, 1991); and Fred Magdoff, John Bellamy Foster, and Frederick H. Buttel, eds.,

Hungry for Profit: The Agribusiness Threat to Farmers, Food, and the Environment (New York: Monthly Review Press, 2000).

35. As Eddie Yuen puts it in a discussion of the Black Bloc's window smashing during the battle of Seattle, "clandestine activity invariably brings about a climate of spectatorship, repression, and paranoia that is anathema to movement building—and much more manageable by the state." See Eddie Yuen, introduction to in *The Battle of Seattle: The New Challenge to Capitalist Globalization*, ed. Yuen, Daniel Burton Rose, and George Katsiaficas (New York: Soft Skull, 2002), 12.
36. For a scathing discussion of the cultural shift from castigation to the celebration of materialism and greed, see Neal Wood, *Tyranny in America: Capitalism and National Decay* (New York: Verso, 2004).
37. Transnational adoption has received significant attention not simply as a way of imagining globalization but also as a problematic practice related to uneven development. See, for example, Toby Alice Volkman, "Embodying Chinese Culture: Transnational Adoption in North America," *Social Text* 21, no. 1 (2003): 29–56.
38. Robert Newman, personal communication, July 1, 2005.
39. Newman explained to me that he read *Biology as Ideology*, which contains a powerful critique of neo-Darwinian justifications for social inequality, while composing his novel. See Richard Lewontin, *Biology as Ideology* (New York: HarperPerennial, 1992).
40. As the *Ecologist* put it, Newman's work is "the first novel to explore the human story behind the placard waving and polemics of globalization." Jeremy Smith, "Review of *The Fountain at the Center of the World*," *Ecologist* 33, no.9 (2003): 60.
41. The classic work on this topic is, of course, Guy Debord's *Society of the Spectacle*, trans. Donald Nicholson-Smith (Boston: Zone, 1995).
42. Robert McChesney and John Nichols, *Our Media, Not Theirs: The Democratic Struggle against Corporate Media* (New York: Seven Stories, 2002).
43. Daya Kishan Thussu, "Infotainment International: A View from the South," in *Electronic Empires: Global Media and Local Resistance*, ed. Thussu (New York: Arnold, 1998): 63–77.
44. Peter Golding, "Worldwide Wedge: Division and Contradiction in the Global Information Infrastructure," in Thussu, *Electronic Empires*, 135–49.
45. For a discussion of the links between the GJM and the Situationist International, see Asa Wettergren, "Like Moths to a Flame: Culture Jamming and the Global Spectacle," in Opel and Pompper, *Representing Resistance*, 27–43.
46. Britain's DIY culture is described in George McKay, *DIY Culture: Party and Protest in 1990s Britain* (New York: Verso, 1998); and George McKay, *Senseless Acts of Beauty: Cultures of Resistance since the Sixties* (New York: Verso, 1996).
47. Many of these activities are documented on Newman's Web site at www.robertnewman.com. Note that Newman's novel was published in Britain by Verso, the imprint that has published the lion's share of GJM documents in English.
48. Robert Newman, personal communication, July 1, 2005.
49. Greenwashing has become a standard weapon in the corporate arsenal. See Eveline

Lubbers, *Battling Big Business: Countering Greenwashing, Front Groups, and Other Forms of Corporate Deception* (Monroe, ME: Common Courage, 2002); and Brian Tokar, *Earth for Sale: Reclaiming Ecology in the Age of Corporate Greenwash* (Boston: South End, 1997).

50. There are now many books documenting the battle of Seattle. In addition to Yuen, Burton Rose, and Katsiaficas's excellent book, readers should consult Alexander Cockburn and Jeffrey St. Clair, *Five Days that Shook the World: Seattle and Beyond* (New York: Verso, 2000); and Danaher and Burbach, *Globalize This!*

51. For a concise description of the most significant aspects of globalization, see Jeremy Brecher, Tim Costello, and Brendan Smith, *Globalization from Below: The Power of Solidarity* (Cambridge, MA: South End, 2000).

52. Notes from Nowhere, ed., *We Are Everywhere: The Irresistible Rise of Global Anticapitalism* (New York: Verso, 2003), 22.

53. Ibid., 24.

54. Yuen makes the important point that the GJM is a critique of both corporate globalization and of the New Left. See Yuen, "Introduction," 8.

55. For a discussion of the organization structures during the battle of Seattle, see Starhawk, "How We Really Shut Down the WTO," in Danaher and Burbach, *Globalize This!*, 37.

56. The RAND Corporation prepared a report for government counterinsurgency agencies that described the GJM as a "swarm." See Notes from Nowhere, *We Are Everywhere*, 66.

57. This ignorance also conveniently obscured the truly antisystemic character of the protests in Seattle. See George Katsiaficas, "Seattle Was Not the Beginning," in Yuen, Burton Rose, and Katsiaficas, *The Battle of Seattle*, 32.

58. Newman's book thus offers a challenge to the much ballyhooed notion of a coalition between unions and environmentalists. For a discussion of this aspect of the battle of Seattle, see John C. Berg, ed., *Teamsters and Turtles? U.S. Progressive Political Movements in the Twenty-first Century* (Lanham, MD: Rowman and Littlefield, 2003).

59. The GJM has strong roots in the historical anarchist movement and in more recent outgrowths such as the Italian *autonomia*. See David Graeber, "The New Anarchists," *New Left Review*, no. 13 (2002): 61–73.

60. Brecher, Costello, and Smith are particularly clear on the diverse strategies that the GJM needs to pursue in order to communicate its message to a broader audience. See their *Globalization from Below*, 91–106.

61. Bechtel's conduct in Cochabamba has become notorious among GJM activists. The company raised water rates as much as 200 percent after gaining the franchise to run the city's water system and forced barrio dwellers to pay for permits to gather rainfall off their own tin roofs. See Pratap Chatterjee, "The Earth Wrecker," *San Francisco Bay Guardian*, May 31, 2000, www.sfbg.com; and Kayla M. Starr, "The Blue Gold Rush," *Sentient Times*, December 2002/January 2003, www.sentienttimes.com.

62. For a discussion of how media representation effectively constituted the GJM as a subaltern public sphere, see Anne Marie Todd, "Whose Public Sphere? The Party and the Protests of America 2000," in Opel and Pompper, *Representing Resistance*, 99–108.

63. Stuart Hall and his colleagues at the Birmingham School of Cultural Studies developed the concept of popular authoritarianism in the context of British race riots during the 1970s. Their analysis unfortunately applies all too well to the contemporary United States. See Stuart Hall et al., *Policing the Crisis: Mugging, the State, and Law and Order* (London: Macmillan, 1978).

64. Andrew Opel, "Punishment before Prosecution: Pepper Spray as Postmodern Repression," in Opel and Pompper, *Representing Resistance*, 55.

65. For discussion of the USA PATRIOT Act's infringement on civil liberties, consult Cynthia Brown, ed., *Lost Liberties: Ashcroft and the Assault on Personal Freedom* (New York: New Press, 2003).

66. Hannah Arendt, *The Origins of Totalitarianism* (New York: Meridian, 1951), 206.

67. Walden Bello stresses that the GJM has tended to delink the economic logic of corporate globalization from the military industrial complex. See his "The Global South," in Mertes, *A Movement of Movements*, 57.

68. For a particularly passionate indictment of today's "jackboot state," see Cockburn and St. Clair, *Five Days That Shook the World*, 100–112.

69. On Indymedia, see Dorothy Kidd, "Become the Media: The Global IMC Network," in Opel and Pompper, *Representing Resistance*, 224–40.

ASHLEY DAWSON AND
MALINI JOHAR SCHUELLER

Coda: Information Mastery and the Culture of Annihilation

> We have entered a new American century, in which we will become still wealthier, culturally more lethal, and increasingly powerful. We will excite hatreds without precedent. . . . One of the defining bifurcations of the future will be the conflict between information masters and information victims. As more and more human beings are overwhelmed by information, or dispossessed by the effects of information-based technology, there will be more violence. Information victims will see no other resort . . . . There will be no peace. At any given moment for the rest of our lifetimes, there will be multiple conflicts in mutating forms around the globe. The *de facto* role of the U.S. armed forces will be to keep the world safe for our economy and open to our cultural assault. To those ends, we will do a fair amount of killing.—**P. Ralph Peters, Office of the Deputy Chief of Staff for Intelligence, "Constant Conflicts"**

How would Henry Luce—the publisher of *Time* magazine, the coiner of the term *American century*, and a proponent of an expansive role for the United States as the global good Samaritan — regard the *Pax Americana* were he alive today? One need look little further than the words of Major Ralph Peters, published in the US War College's journal *Parameters*, to gain a sense of the dystopian terminus of Luce's missionary position. Peters dispenses with lofty notions of the United States as an exporter of democracy or even as global cop, conjuring up instead an inegalitarian, atomistic, and violently Hobbesian world in which the country rules through naked violence. It seems that the futurists at the War College have been ingesting their Marx without much supervision, for the vision that emerges from Peters's prognostications is of a cultural superstructure—information—that not only controls but has also become isomorphic with the economic base. While the theoretical moorings of this vision may be somewhat shaky, Peters's emphasis on information mastery underlines the fact that the Right takes cultural supremacy as deadly serious. Peters's blood-soaked picture of the future offers what in retrospect appears to be a hard-boiled rejoinder to the rhetoric of the Project for the New American Century (PNAC), the right-wing–funded think tank spawned by the neocon leaders of current US imperial interventions.[1] Although both Peters and PNAC imagine an aggressively preemptive stance for the United States throughout this new century, the latter legitimates its endeavor in terms that, in echoing those of Luce, carefully excise the anti-imperialist movements of the 1960s and 1970s. To quote PNAC's list of fundamental propositions, "American leadership is good both for America and for the world . . . such leadership requires military strength, diplomatic energy and commitment to moral principle."[2] The boldness of this assertion of America's benevolent role on the world stage attests to the success of the Right's culture wars over the past two decades.

In August 2005, standing in the bed of a pickup truck beneath the sweltering central Texas sun, Cindy Sheehan, the mother of a soldier slain the previous year in Baghdad's vast Sadr City slum, challenged the vacationing president to explain to her and the rest of the nation what we are doing at war. "I want to taunt George Bush, I want to say that this is America standing in front of you, these are real people who disagree with you, those people exist and they're here."[3] Sheehan's vigil by the roadside outside Dubya's dude ranch attracted the attention of both the international and the US corporate press, serving as a lightning rod for domestic discontent with the worsening quagmire in Iraq. At that time, polls indicated that Americans already considered the war a mistake by a 54–44 percent margin, and 56 percent wanted some or all of the US troops withdrawn.[4] Since then, public opinion has further galvanized against the war. While it is obviously far too early to draw any conclusions concerning the mass appeal of the peace movement from these statistics or from Sheehan's success at galvanizing public attention during the dog days of August, the failures of the new US imperial foreign policy are increasingly manifest. The United States is currently conducting a disastrous campaign in Iraq that was originally sold to the domestic and international public as a battle against nuclear proliferation. Thousands of US troops and hundreds of thousands of Iraqi civilians have now died as a result of this war. Yet as a Downing Street memo, among other documents, has shown, the intelligence suggesting that Iraq was acquiring weapons of mass destruction (WMDS) was generated in order to legitimate an already established policy goal of the Bush administration to remove Saddam Hussein from power, rather than vice versa.[5] In addition, the specter of imminent annihilation weighs increasingly heavily on public imagination despite more than five years' worth of zealous prosecution of the so-called war on terror.

The Bush administration's fabrication of evidence legitimating bellicose US policies in the name of self-defense and just war is hardly novel. Even a cursory examination of the rhetoric that has accompanied US foreign policy since 1945 reveals a striking continuity. As Norman Solomon has recently documented, from Lyndon Johnson's manipulation of the media to justify the escalation of US involvement in Vietnam through Ronald Reagan's explanation for the attack on Grenada to the current president's argument for supposedly liberating Iraq, the propaganda that legitimates US aggression turns on a remarkably similar set of lies.[6] With few exceptions, post–World War II US administrations have successfully persuaded the public to engage in imperial interventions by casting our nation as the hapless victim of real or potential foreign aggression. Moreover, like previous administrations, the present Bush regime has relied on fundamentally decent but misplaced public sentiment concerning the noble intentions that animate the country's rulers. Despite the fact that the United States has bombed twenty-one different nations since 1948 and refuses to submit itself to international norms of conduct such as the International Criminal Court, a significant segment of the US populace has been willing to believe that Uncle Sam is always a force for good in the world. Such perceptions are all too easily yoked to racially coded perceptions of the Other. Drawing on the blatant Orientalism of pundits such as Samuel Huntington, for example, neocons in the Bush administration have prosecuted the war in Iraq under the name of a crusade against global terror, despite the fact that the country became a haven for supposed terrorists after, rather than before, the US invasion, and under the pretext of restoring democracy to the country, despite overseeing the implementation of policies that effectively hollowed out most significant institutions of civil society in postinvasion Iraq.[7]

At present, it is hard to miss the fact that the world's sole superpower has come to rely more and more on coercion rather than consent, placing an increasingly heavy burden on its citizens and on civilian populations in countries such as Afghanistan and Iraq. This is particularly apparent in relation to US military expenditure, which is roughly equivalent to that of the rest of world combined, while arms sales by thirty-eight North American companies (only one of which is based in Canada) account for more than 60 percent of world totals (up 25 percent since 2002).[8] In tandem with the Bush administration's tax cuts for the superrich, this militarist policy has provided effective cover for the shredding of what remained of the social safety net and has imposed a poverty draft on America's unfortunate working-class sons and daughters. The sole institutional solution to the rising tide of social discontent and dysfunction in the United States seems to be mass incarceration, particularly of its minorities.[9] Like the titan Saturn, US policy makers are consuming their own future, apparently oblivious to the fact that the reproduction of social relations depends ultimately on the consent of the governed.

Of course, the dismantling of the Keynesian welfare state is nothing new. It is becoming increasingly clear, however, that the war in Iraq has politicized and polarized the US populace to an extent not seen since the Vietnam War. Indeed, the 2004 presidential election saw a dramatic increase in voter turnout, indicating the abnormal seriousness with which the normally apathetic US populace took the contest.[10] While President Bush's reelection provoked tremendous despair among progressives and generated a map of electoral votes that suggests the onset of another civil war, it should be remembered that he won by a razor-thin margin, a significant anomaly for an incumbent in a time of war. Of course, one prominent reason for the Democrats' failure to topple Bush was their inability to depart from the imperialist script. Indeed, John Kerry's promise to run a more ruthlessly efficient campaign against Iraqi insurgents vividly underlined the bipartisan support for the US imperial mission. Having obtained this slight mandate, however, the neocons who took US forces into Iraq on trumped-up charges must now live with the increasingly sanguineous results of their arrogant drive to remake the Middle East in America's own image. Although the ability of presidential administrations to spin the media should never be underestimated, it has become demonstrably more difficult for Bush and company to dodge the human toll taken by their imperial overreach. When one bereaved mother can galvanize the press as Cindy Sheehan did by camping out on a fly-blown roadside near the president's ranch to demand a sensible explanation for the death of her son, it is clear that public credulity in US humanitarian imperialism is on the wane.

As the mask of consent begins to slip, the temptation to lash out at domestic dissent grows apace. Within the United States, we are currently witnessing a renewed spasm of the culture wars, this time in the form of a potent campaign to blacklist dissenting intellectuals and to turn university area studies programs into factories for the production of imperial factotums. Feeding off of the cultural production of insecurity and victimage since 9/11, several Right organizations have stepped up their efforts to legitimize the surveillance of knowledge production and to coerce academia to serve the ends of US imperialism. Key to this coercion is to characterize any questioning about the endless war on terror as unpatriotic and tantamount to treason, thus echoing within the nation George W. Bush's belligerent threat to the world: "Every nation in every region now has a decision to make: Either you are with us, or you are with the terrorists."[11] On the heels of 9/11, the American Council of Trustees and Alumni (ACTA), an organization founded by Lynne Cheney and Joseph Lieberman, issued a report entitled "Defending Civilization: How Our Universities Are Failing America and What Can Be Done about It." The report alleged that the failure of universities to glorify Western culture and American history had resulted in their inability to defend the values of civilization under attack on 9/11 and produced a climate of danger. The original version of the document blacklisted 117 faculty whose comments were deemed a danger to national security. Included were statements such as "ignorance breeds hate" and "there needs to be an understanding of why this kind of suicidal violence could be undertaken against our country."[12] A year later, Daniel Pipes would brazenly publish his list of "Profs Who Hate America" and include for illustration comments by MIT's Noam Chomsky that the impetus for the impending Iraqi invasion was the country's oil reserves, as well as the Columbia history professor Eric Foner's argument that preemptive war "takes us back to the notion of the jungle."[13]

Clearly, the Right's endeavor is to delegitimize any critical thinking about the war in Iraq. However, what distinguishes the current calls for academic surveillance from McCarthyism is that the target is not simply the political affiliations and activities of faculty but the very paradigms of knowledge production, so that faculty teaching and research become legitimate areas for state control, while knowledge that does not support the cause of US imperialism becomes suspect. Chief among the architects of academic monitoring has been David Horowitz who, as a master of Orwellian doublespeak, has pillaged the language of identity politics to promote his so-called Academic Bill of Rights. While seemingly innocuous in its promotion of diversity and veritably postmodern in its championing of the fluidity of knowledge, the bill urges administrative oversight of curricula and reading lists in the humanities and social sciences, as well as surveillance of invited speakers and conferences.[14] Ironically, to illustrate his support of diversity, Horowitz cites his visit to the political science department at the University of Colorado at Denver, where he objected to faculty posting cartoons ridiculing Republicans on their office doors. Horowitz sees the harboring of oppositional intellectuals in state-funded universities as a public outrage. As evidence he cites the UCLA senate's (April 2003) overwhelming condemnation of the invasion of Iraq after the United States had "liberated Iraq" and when 76 percent of the population supported the war.[15] Yet despite the absurdity of demanding that universities serve as mouthpieces of the state and become unthinking reflectors of public opinion at its most jingoist, the Academic Bill of Rights is pending legislation in over twenty states and has already been passed in Pennsylvania.

More important, right-wing organizations are seizing the current fear-induced moment as a propitious one to purge academia of the knowledge paradigms produced through the twin motors of decolonization and the new social movements of the sixties.[16] Students for Academic Freedom (SAF), the student arm of Horowitz's organization, for instance, explicitly instructs students to police course content and bias in all the race- and gender-based programs created in the wake of the third world movement and civil rights—"Women's Studies, African-American Studies, Chicano/Latino/Hispanic Studies, Lesbian/Gay/Bisexual/Transgender Studies, American-Indian Studies, and Asian-American Studies."[17] Also suspect are other programs involved in cultural production such as cultural studies and American studies and, to a lesser degree, departments of history and political science. Students for Academic Freedom, which urges students to press legislators to oversee curricula, has chapters in over 130 campuses across the country. Perhaps the strongest injunctions for knowledge production to serve as a conduit of empire have been reserved for area studies, particularly Middle East studies, in which both Orientalist and developmentalist models have been challenged with the introduction of postcolonial theory. Right-wing pundits such as Horowitz view the resultant interrogation of the imperative of knowledge about the Middle East to benefit US imperialism as tantamount to bias and treason. Thus, in September 2002, the right-wing columnist Daniel Pipes launched the Web site Campus Watch (www.campus-watch.org), in which he published dossiers of eight prominent professors of Middle East studies who supposedly promoted anti-Americanism. Each month, the Web site showcases a "Quote of the Month" that demonstrates the supposedly "terrorist" sympathies of a Middle East studies professor. More often than not, the targeted professors are Arabs or Arab sympathizers, thus reflecting Pipes's own racial paranoia.[18]

The most concerted attempt to monitor the very paradigms of knowledge came in the hearings for HR 3077, the International Studies in Higher Education Act, approved by the House Subcommittee on Select Education in September 2003. The act, which mandated that an advisory board from the Department of Homeland Security oversee course content of area studies centers, was based on the testimony of Stanley Kurtz, testimony that was largely devoted to denouncing the pernicious influence of postcolonial theorists such as Edward Said on Middle East studies. Kurtz urged departments to include readings by Orientalists such as Bernard Lewis. The sole authority Kurtz relied on in his report was Martin Kramer's *Ivory Towers on Sand*, which unambiguously affirms the role of Middle East studies as a promulgation of US imperialism. Scholars in the area, Kramer argues, should stress "that which is uniquely American in the American approach to the Middle East. The idea that the United States plays an essentially beneficent role in the world is at the very core of this approach."[19] While it is gratifying to note state interest in the minutiae of humanities scholarship, it is sobering to realize that the bill might well have passed Senate approval had it not been for massive faculty mobilization against it. Despite the temporary quashing of academic surveillance called for in HR 3077, there is need for a renewed vigilance on the part of educators to resist state attempts to recruit universities for the imperial mission. Section 103 of HR

609, a bill debated by Congress in 2005, included a clause to monitor all academic programs and based itself on Horowitz's Academic Bill of Rights. It also emphasized the obligation of foreign language and area studies programs to fulfill national security needs.[20]

Indeed, it is increasingly clear that the state regards all educational institutions as appendages of empire. As part of the No Child Left Behind Act of 2002, for instance, any K-12 institution receiving federal funds is obliged to reveal personal information about its students to military recruiters. The predatory stalking of students by recruiters, particularly in minority and low-income areas, speaks poignantly to the willed redirection of public welfare to military-imperial fare. Given the enormous role of culture and knowledge production in the apparatus of imperialism, it is imperative that academics, particularly those involved in the analysis and understanding of culture, be vigilant of right-wing attempts to take over or contain public discourse. Starved universities, depleted of funding, need not necessarily become allies of empire. Instead, they should strive to produce intellectuals whose role, as Said pointed out, is "to present alternative narratives and other perspectives on history than those provided by combatants on behalf of official memory and national identity and mission."[21] He continued, "The intellectual is perhaps a kind of counter-memory, with its own counter-discourse that will not allow conscience to look away or fall asleep."[22]

Such alternative narratives are already beginning to be heard. Military recruiters seeking fresh fodder for the Army are facing a formidable array of peace activists determined to deter recruiters from campuses. Across the nation, counter-recruitment workers are exposing the unjust nature of the so-called poverty draft imposed by the administration and attempting to deny the war machine the human resources it needs to continue its illegal occupation of Iraq. Teach-ins, coordinated university–high school counter-recruitment clubs, and peaceful demonstrations have successfully driven off recruiters or forced them to rely on police brutality to quell discontent. In March 2005, for instance, police arrested students at the City College of New York for demonstrating against recruiters at a career fair; at the University of California at Santa Cruz and the University of California at Berkeley, students organized campaigns to evict military recruiters from their schools. In high schools across the country, communities are challenging the state's unfettered right of access to personal student information through the No Child Left Behind Act by mobilizing parents to exercise their right to opt out of access to the military. Although it is difficult to fathom to what extent members of the working class seeking health care and access to higher education will join this fight, it is clear that these counter-recruitment efforts are gaining legitimacy. In Houston, Texas, for example, a Leave My Child Alone group successfully convinced five area school districts to mail opt-out forms to prospective parents.

It is crucial, however, that counter-recruitment efforts not be viewed as expedient ways of solving a local problem, but be seen as part of a larger, systemic challenge to the structures of imperialism and the militarization that undergirds them. Central to this rethinking is an interrogation of the university as a research appendage of the military and the neoliberal state, responsible therefore for producing knowledge in the service of the state. On the other hand, we also believe that the current Right-engineered calls for academic surveillance under the guise of diversity and tolerance are opportunities to be seized. They beckon us as educators to break the silence about the neoliberal imperial university and demand programs in worker's rights, Marxist economics, and imperialism along with those in capitalist marketing. They solicit us to constantly demystify, interrogate, and challenge the appropriation of the rhetoric of multiculturalism in the service of a ruthless militaristic imperialism. Just as urgently, they demand our participation in the creation of oppositional knowledges vitally linked to grassroots anti-imperial struggles around the world and that cannot be privatized as identity politics alone.

NOTES

1. PNAC is funded by the Sarah Scaife, the John M. Olin, and the Bradley Foundations, organizations that have played a key role in the reassertion of right-wing primacy in the US public sphere since the 1970s.
2. See the Project for the New American Century Web site, www.newamericancentury.org, August 18, 2005.
3. Cindy Sheehan, speech, August 13, 2005.
4. Robert Kuttner, "Battle Fatigue Is Setting In," *Boston Globe*, August 17, 2005.
5. Juan Cole, "The Lies That Led to War," www.salon.com, July 29, 2002.
6. Norman Solomon, *War Made Easy: How Presidents and Pundits Keep Spinning Us to Death* (New York: Wiley, 2005).
7. For a discussion of rampant neoliberalism in postinvasion Iraq, see Naomi Klein,

"Baghdad Year Zero: Pillaging Iraq in Pursuit of a Neocon Utopia," *Harper's*, September 2004, 43–53.

8. Noam Chomsky, "We Must Act Now to Prevent Another Hiroshima—Or Worse," *Independent*, August 6, 2005.
9. Christian Parenti, *Lockdown America: Police and Prisons in the Age of Crisis* (New York: Verso, 1999).
10. For statistics on increased voter turnout and other quantitative elements of the presidential campaign, see James E. Campbell, "Why Bush Won the Presidential Election of 2004: Incumbency, Ideology, Terrorism, and Turnout," *Political Science Quarterly* 120, no. 2 (2005): 219–42.
11. George W. Bush, "President's Address," September 20, 2001, www.angelsharleyevents.com/presidentialaddress.htm.
12. Quoted in Joel Beinin, "The New American McCarthyism: Polling Thought About the Middle East," *Race and Class* 46, no. 1 (2004): 103–4.
13. Daniel Pipes, "Profs Who Hate America," *New York Post*, November 12, 2002, www.danielpipes.org/article/923.
14. See "Academic Bill of Rights," www.studentsforacademicfreedom.org, July 18, 2006.
15. David Horowitz, "The Campus Blacklist," www.frontpagemag.com, April 18, 2003.
16. On the creation of an anti-imperial culture, particularly in the teaching of history, see Howard Zinn, "The Politics of History in the Era of the Cold War: Repression and Resistance" in *The Cold War and the University: Toward an Intellectual History of the Postwar Years* (New York: New Press, 1997), 35–71.
17. Sara Dogan, with Ryan Call and Lee Kaplan, *Students for Academic Freedom Handbook*, 31, www.studentsforacademicfreedom.org.
18. In an essay about immigration, Pipes wrote: "Fears of a Muslim influx have more substance than the worry about jihad. West European societies are unprepared for the massive immigration of brown-skinned peoples cooking strange foods and not exactly maintaining Germanic standards of hygiene." See Daniel Pipes, "The Muslims Are Coming! The Muslims Are Coming!" *National Review* 42, no. 22 (1990): 28–31. Yet the administration's support of Pipes was reflected in Bush's 2003 nomination of Pipes to the board of directors of the United States Institute of Peace despite massive opposition.
19. Martin Kramer, *Ivory Towers on Sand: The Failure of Middle Eastern Studies in America* (Washington, DC: Washington Institute for Near East Policy, 2001), 129.
20. The College Access and Opportunity Act, July 22, 2005, edworkforce.house.gov/issues/109th/education/hea/hr609bill.
21. Edward Said, *Humanism and Democratic Criticism* (New York: Columbia University Press, 2004), 141.
22. Ibid., 142.

Bibliography

Agamben, Giorgio. *Means without End: Notes on Politics*. Trans. Vincenzo Binetti and Cesare Cassarino. Minneapolis: University of Minnesota Press, 2000.

——. *State of Exception*. Trans. Kevin Attell. Chicago: University of Chicago Press, 2005.

Ali, Tariq. *Clash of Fundamentalisms: Crusades, Jihads, Modernity*. New York: Verso, 2002.

Ammerman, Nancy. "North American Protestant Fundamentalism." In *Media, Culture, and the Religious Right*, ed. Linda Kintz and Julie Lesage. Minneapolis: University of Minnesota Press, 1998. 55–114.

Amnesty International. "Afghanistan: No One Listens to Us and No One Treats Us as Human Beings: Justice Denied to Women." October 5, 2003.

Anderson, Benedict. *Imagined Communities: Reflections on the Origin and Spread of Nationalism*. New York: New Left Books, 1991.

Appadurai, Arjun. *Modernity at Large: Cultural Dimensions of Globalization*. Minneapolis: University of Minnesota Press, 1996.

Appiah, Anthony. *The Ethics of Identity*. Princeton, NJ: Princeton University Press, 2005.

Archibugi, Daniele, David Held, and Martin Köhler, eds. *Re-imagining Political Community: Studies in Cosmopolitan Democracy*. Stanford, CA: Stanford University Press, 1998.

Arendt, Hannah. *The Origins of Totalitarianism*. New York: Harcourt Brace Jovanovich, 1973.

Ariel, Yaakov. "How Are Jews and Israel Portrayed in the *Left Behind* Series?: A Historical Discussion of Jewish-Christian Relations." In *Rapture, Revelation, and the End Times: Exploring the Left Behind Series*, ed. Bruce David Forbes and Jeanne Halgren Kilde. New York: Palgrave Macmillan, 2004. 131–66.

Asad, Talal. *Genealogies of Religion: Disciplines and Reasons of Power in Christianity and Islam*. Baltimore, MD: Johns Hopkins University Press, 1993.

Bacevich, Andrew. *American Empire: The Realities and Consequences of U.S. Diplomacy*. Cambridge, MA: Harvard University Press, 2002.

Badran, Margot. *Feminists, Islam, and Nation: Gender and the Making of Modern Egypt*. Princeton, NJ: Princeton University Press, 1995.

Balmer, Randall. *Mine Eyes Have Seen the Glory: A Journey through the Evangelical Subculture in America*. New York: Oxford University Press, 1993.

Balmer, Randall, and Lauren F. Winner. *Protestantism in America*. New York: Columbia University Press, 2002.

Baritz, Loren. *City on a Hill: A History of Ideas and Myths in America*. New York: Wiley, 1964.

Basher, Brenda. *Give Me That Online Religion*. San Francisco: Jossey-Bass, 2001.

Baudrillard, Jean. *La guerre du Golfe n'a pas eu lieu*. Paris: Galilée, 1991.

———. *The Gulf War Did Not Take Place*. Trans. Paul Patton. Bloomington: Indiana University Press, 1995.

———. "War Porn." Trans. Paul A. Taylor. *International Journal of Baudrillard Studies* 2, no. 1 (2005): n.p.

Bausch, Richard. *Hello to the Cannibals: A Novel*. New York: HarperCollins, 2002.

Beiner, Ronald. *What's the Matter with Liberalism?* Berkeley: University of California Press, 1992.

Beinin, Joel. "The New American McCarthyism: Policing Thought About the Middle East." *Race and Class* 46, no.1 (2004): 101–15.

Beitz, Charles R. *Political Theory and International Relations*. Princeton, NJ: Princeton University Press, 1979.

Bell, David, and Barbara M. Kennedy, eds. *The Cybercultures Reader*. New York: Routledge, 2000.

Benvenisti, Meron, et al. *Abu Ghraib: The Politics of Torture*. Berkeley, CA: North Atlantic Books, 2004.

Berg, John C., ed. *Teamsters and Turtles? U.S. Progressive Political Movements in the Twenty-first Century*. Lanham, MD: Rowman and Littlefield, 2003.

Bergner, Daniel. *In the Land of Magic Soldiers*. New York: Farrar, Straus and Giroux, 2003.

———. "Where the Enemy is Everywhere and Nowhere." *New York Time Magazine*, July 20, 2003, 38–47.

Binnendijk, Hans. Introduction to *Transforming America's Military*. Washington, DC: NDU Press/US Government Printing Office, 2002.

Blissett, Luther. *Q*. New York: Harcourt, 2004.

Boot, Max. *The Savage Wars of Peace*. New York: Basic Books, 2002.

Boyer, Paul. *When Time Shall Be No More: Prophecy Belief in Modern American Culture*. Cambridge, MA: Harvard University Press, 1992.

Brecher, Jeremy, Tim Costello, and Brendan Smith. *Globalization from Below: The Power of Solidarity*. Cambridge, MA: South End Press, 2000.

Brennan, Tim. *Salman Rushdie and the Third World: Myths of the Nation*. New York: St. Martin's, 1991.

Brilmayer, Lea. *American Hegemony: Political Morality in a One-Superpower World*. New Haven, CT: Yale University Press, 1994.

Brodsky, Anne E. *With All Our Strength: The Revolutionary Association of the Women of Afghanistan*. New York: Routledge, 2003.

Brown, Chris. "Universal Human Rights: A Critique." In *Human Rights in Global Politics*, ed. Tim Dunne and Nicholas J. Wheeler. Cambridge: Cambridge University Press, 1999. 103–27.

Brown, Cynthia, ed. *Lost Liberties: Ashcroft and the Assault on Personal Freedom*. New York: New Press, 2003.

Buchanan, Allen. *Justice, Legitimacy, and Self-Determination: Moral Foundations for International Law*. Oxford: Oxford University Press, 2004.

Calleo, David. *The Bankrupting of America: How the Federal Budget Is Impoverishing the Nation*. New York: Morrow, 1992.

Campbell, James E. "Why Bush Won the Presidential Election of 2004: Incumbency, Ideology, Terrorism, and Turnout." *Political Science Quarterly* 120, no. 2 (2005): 219–42.

Castells, Manuel. *The Power of Identity*. Malden, MA: Blackwell, 1997.

Chandler, David. "The Road to Military Humanism: How the Human Rights NGOs Shaped a New Humanitarian Agenda." *Human Rights Quarterly* 21, no.3 (2001): 678–800.

Chatterjee, Piya. *A Time for Tea: Women, Labor, and Post/Colonial Politics on an Indian Plantation*. Durham, NC: Duke University Press, 2001.

Chaudhuri, Nupur, and Margaret Strobel, eds. *Western Women and Imperialism: Complicity and Resistance*. Bloomington: Indiana University Press, 1992.

Chomsky, Noam. *Hegemony or Survival: America's Quest for Global Dominance*. New York: Metropolitan, 2003.

———. *The New Military Humanism*. Monroe, ME: Common Courage, 1999.

Chomsky, Noam, et al. *The Cold War and the University: Toward an Intellectual History of the Postwar Years*. New York: New Press, 1997.

Chopra, Jarat, and Thomas Weiss. "Sovereignty Is No Longer Sacrosanct: Codifying Humanitarian Intervention." *Ethics and International Affairs* 6 (1992): 95–118.

Cockburn, Alexander, and Jeffrey St. Clair. *Five Days That Shook the World: Seattle and Beyond*. New York: Verso, 2000.

Cole, David. *Enemy Aliens: Double Standards and Constitutional Freedoms in the War on Terrorism*. New York: New Press, 2003.

Cooppan, Vilashini. "The Ruins of Empire: The National and Global Politics of America's Return to Rome." In *Postcolonial Studies and Beyond*, ed. Ania Loomba et al. Durham, NC: Duke University Press, 2005. 80–100.

Corcoran, Bill, dir. *Left Behind II: Tribulation Force*. Cloud Ten Pictures, 2002.

Crotty, William. *The Politics of Terror: The US Response to 9/11*. Boston: Northeastern University Press, 2004.

Dahbour, Omar, and Micheline R. Ishay, eds. *The Nationalism Reader*. Atlantic Highlands, NJ: Humanities Press, 1995.

Damrosch, Lori Fisler, and David J. Scheffer, eds. *Law and Force in the New International Order*. Boulder, CO: Westview, 1991.

Danaher, Kevin, and Roger Burbach, eds. *Globalize This! The Battle against the WTO and Corporate Rule*. Monroe, ME: Common Courage, 2000.

Danner, Mark. *Torture and Truth: America, Abu Ghraib, and the War on Terror*. New York: New York Review Books, 2004.

Davis, Angela Y. *Are Prisons Obsolete?* New York: Seven Stories, 2003.

Davis, Mike. *Prisoners of the American Dream: Politics and Economy in the History of the US Working Class*. New York: Verso, 1986.

Debord, Guy. *Society of the Spectacle*. Trans. Donald Nicholson-Smith. Boston: Zone, 1995.

DeMar, Gary. *End Time Fiction: A Biblical Consideration of the Left Behind Theology*. Nashville, TN: Thomas Nelson, 2001.

Denning, Michael. *Culture in the Age of Three Worlds*. New York: Verso, 2004.

De Villiers, Marq. *Water: The Fate of Our Most Precious Resource*. Boston: Houghton Mifflin, 2000.

Dixon, Wheeler. *Film and Television after 9/11*. Carbondale: University of Southern Illinois Press, 2004.

Dogan, Sara, with Ryan Call and Lee Kaplan. *Students for Academic Freedom Handbook*, www.studentsforacademicfreedom.org.

Donnelly, Jack. *Universal Human Rights in Theory and Practice*. Ithaca, NY: Cornell University Press, 1989.

Donnelly, Thomas. "Rebuilding America's Defenses: Strategy, Forces, and Resources for a New Century." Project for the New American Century, September 2000.

Dorfman, Ariel, and Armand Mattelart. *How to Read Donald Duck: Imperialist Ideology in the Disney Comic*. Trans. David Kunzle. New York: International General, 1975.

Douhet, Giulio. *The Command of the Air*. Washington, DC: Office of Air Force History, 1983.

Doyle, Michael W. *Empires*. Ithaca, NY: Cornell University Press, 1986.

Dudziak, Mary L., ed. *September 11 in History: A Watershed Moment*. Durham, NC: Duke University Press, 2003.

Dugard, Martin. *Into Africa: The Epic Adventures of Stanley and Livingstone*. New York: Doubleday, 2002.

Eagleton, Terry, Fredric Jameson, and Edward Said. *Nationalism, Colonialism, and Literature*. Minneapolis: University of Minnesota Press, 1990.

Easton, Dossie, and Catherine A. Liszt. *The Topping Book; or, Getting Good at Being Bad*. San Francisco: Greenery, 1995.

Emerson, Michael, and Christian Smith. *Divided by Faith: Evangelical Religion and the Problem of Race in America*. New York: Oxford University Press, 2002.

Etienne, Mona, and Eleanor Leacock, eds. *Women and Colonization*. New York: Praeger, 1980.

Ferguson, Niall. *Colossus: The Price of America's Empire*. New York: Penguin, 2004.

———. *Empire: The Rise and Demise of the British World Order*. New York: Basic Books, 2003.

Foden, Giles. *Mimi and Toutou's Big Adventure: The Bizarre Battle of Lake Tanganyika*. New York: Knopf, 2005.

Forbes, Bruce David. "How Popular are the *Left Behind* Books and Why?" In *Rapture, Revelation, and the End Times: Exploring the Left Behind Series*, ed. Bruce David Forbes and Jeanne Halgren Kilde. New York: Palgrave Macmillan, 2004. 5–32.

Forbes, Bruce David, and Jeanne Halgren Kilde, eds. *Rapture, Revelation, and the End Times: Exploring the Left Behind Series*. New York: Palgrave Macmillan, 2004.

Foucault, Michel. *Discipline and Punish: The Birth of the Prison*. Trans. Alan Sheridan. New York: Vintage, 1979.

Frank, Thomas. *One Market under God: Extreme Capitalism, Market Populism, and the End of Economic Democracy*. New York: Doubleday, 2000.

———. *What's the Matter with Kansas? How Conservatives Won the Heart of America*. New York: Henry Holt, 2004.

Freeman, Samuel, ed. *The Cambridge Companion to Rawls*. Cambridge: Cambridge University Press, 2003.

Friedberg, Anne. *Window Shopping: Cinema and the Postmodern*. Berkeley: University of California Press, 1993.

Friedman, Norman. "War Game Raises Questions." *United States Naval Institute: Proceedings* 128, no. 10 (2002): 4–11.

Friedman, Thomas. *The Lexus and the Olive Tree*. New York: Farrar, Straus and Giroux, 1999.

Frykholm, Amy Johnson. *Rapture Culture: Left Behind in Evangelical America*. New York: Oxford University Press, 2004.

Fukuyama, Francis. *The End of History and the Last Man*. New York: Free Press, 1992.

Fulbright, J. W. Foreword to *The Fourth Dimension of Foreign Policy: Educational and Cultural Affairs*, by Philip H. Coombs. New York: Harper/Council on Foreign Relations, 1964.

Fuller, Alexandra. *Don't Let's Go to the Dogs Tonight: An African Childhood*. New York: Random House, 2002.

———. *Scribbling the Cat: Travels with an African Soldier*. New York: Penguin, 2004.

Gallagher, John, and Robinson, Ronald. "The Imperialism of Free Trade." *Economic History Review*, new series, 6, no.2 (1953): 1–25.

Garland, David. *Punishment and Modern Society: A Study in Social Theory*. Chicago: University of Chicago Press, 1990.

Gauntlett, David, ed. *Web Studies: Rewiring Media Studies for the Digital Age*. New York: Oxford University Press, 2000.

Gewirth, Alan. *The Community of Rights*. Chicago: University of Chicago Press, 1996.

Goldberg, Jonathan. *Sodometries: Renaissace Text, Modern Sexualities*. Stanford: Stanford Univeristy Press, 1992.

Gorenberg, Gershom. *The End of Days: Fundamentalism and the Struggle for the Temple Mount*. New York: Free Press, 2000.

Gowan, Peter. *The Global Gamble: Washington's Faustian Bid for World Dominance*. New York: Verso, 1999.

Graeber, David. "The New Anarchists." *New Left Review*, no. 13 (2002): 61–73.

Greider, William. *Who Will Tell The People? The Betrayal of American Democracy*. New York: Simon and Schuster, 1993.

Guha, Ranajit. "Domination without Hegemony and Its Historiography." In *Subaltern Studies 6: Writings on South Asian History and Society*, ed. Guha. Delhi: Oxford University Press, 1989. 229–32.

Hall, Stuart. *The Hard Road to Renewal: Thatcherism and the Crisis of the Left*. New York: Verso, 1988.

Hall, Stuart, et al. *Policing the Crisis: Mugging, the State, and Law and Order*. London: Macmillan, 1978.

Haraway, Donna J. *Simians, Cyborgs, and Women: The Reinvention of Nature*. New York: Routledge, 1991.

Harding, Susan. *The Book of Jerry Falwell: Fundamentalist Language and Politics*. Princeton, NJ: Princeton University Press, 2000.

Hardt, Michael, and Antonio Negri. *Empire*. Cambridge, MA: Harvard University Press, 2000.

Harney, Stefano. *State Work: Public Administration and Mass Intellectuality*. Durham, NC: Duke University Press, 2002.

Hartley, Aidan. *The Zanzibar Chest: A Story of Life, Love, and Death in Foreign Lands*. New York: Atlantic Monthly Press, 2003.

Harvey, David. *The New Imperialism*. New York: Oxford University Press, 2003.

Hauerwas, Stanley, and Frank Lentricchia, eds. *Dissent from the Homeland: Essays after September 11*. Durham, NC: Duke University Press, 2003.

Hawkins, William R. "Imposing Peace: Total versus Limited Wars, and the Need to Put Boots on the Ground." *Parameters* 30, no. 2 (2000): 72–83.

Hegel, G. W. F. *The Philosophy of History*. Trans. J. Sibree. New York: Willey, 1944.

Hendershot, Heather. *Shaking the World for Jesus: Media and Conservative Evangelical Culture*. Chicago: University of Chicago Press, 2004.

Henkin, Louis. *The Age of Rights*. New York: Columbia University Press, 1990.

——. *How Nations Behave: Law and Foreign Policy*. New York: Columbia University Press, 1979.

Henkin, Louis, et al. *Right v. Might: International Law and the Use of Force*. New York: Council on Foreign Relations Press, 1989.

Hennessey, Rosemary. *Materialist Feminism and the Politics of Discourse*. New York: Routledge, 1993.

Henwood, Doug, *After the New Economy*. New York: New Press, 2003.

Hietala, Thomas R. *Manifest Design: Anxious Aggrandizement in Late Jacksonian America*. Ithaca, NY: Cornell University Press, 1985.

Hill, Felicity, Mikele Abotiz, and Sara Poehlman-Doumbouya. "Non-governmental Organizations' Role in the Buildup and Implementation of Security Council Resolution 1325." *Signs* 28, no. 4 (2003): 1255–70.

Hinsley, M. H. *Sovereignty*. 2nd ed. Cambridge: Cambridge University Press, 1986.

Hitchens, Christopher. "Pakistan: On the Frontier of Apocalypse." In *Love, Poverty, and War: Journeys and Essays*. New York: Nation Books, 2004. 437–50.

Hobsbawm, Eric. *The Age of Empire, 1875–1914*. New York: Vintage, 1987.

Hoffman, F. G. "Joint Vision 2010: A Marine Perspective." *Joint Force Quarterly* 17 (1997): 32–38.

———. "Transforming for the Chaordic Age." *Marine Corps Gazette* 86, no. 11 (2002): 44–56.

———. "Why the Critique? An Author's Response." *National Security Studies Quarterly* 4, no.1 (1999): 90–98.

Hoganson, Kristin L. *Fighting for American Manhood: How Gender Politics Provoked the Spanish-American and Philippine-American Wars*. New Haven, CT: Yale University Press, 1998.

Horkheimer, Max, and Theodor Adorno. *Dialectic of Enlightenment*. Trans. John Cumming. New York: Continuum, 1988.

Human Rights Watch Report. *Climate of Fear: Sexual Violence and Abduction of Women and Girls in Baghdad.* New York: Human Rights Watch, 2003.

———. *We Want to Live as Humans: Repression of Women and Girls in Western Afghanistan*. New York: Human Rights Watch, 2002.

Hunt, Michael H. *Ideology and U.S. Foreign Policy*. New Haven, CT: Yale University Press, 1987.

Hunter, James. "The Evangelical Worldview since 1890." In *Piety and Politics: Evangelicals and Fundamentalists Confront the World*, ed. Richard John Neuhaus and Michael Cromartie. Washington, DC: Ethics and Public Policy Center, 1987. 19–53.

Huntington, Samuel P. "The Clash of Civilizations," *Foreign Affairs* 72, no. 3 (1993): 22–49.

Husak, Douglas N. "Why There Are No Human Rights." *Social Theory and Practice* 10, no. 2 (1984): 125–41.

Hyam, Ronald. *Empire and Sexuality: The British Experience*. Manchester: Manchester University Press, 1990.

Ignatieff, Michael. *Human Rights as Politics and Idolatry*. Princeton, NJ: Princeton University Press, 2001.

International Commission on Intervention and State Sovereignty. *The Responsibility to Protect*. Ottawa: International Development Research Centre, 2001.

James, C. L. R. *The Black Jacobins: Toussaint L'Ouverture and the San Domingo Revolution*. New York: Knopf, 1989.

JanMohamed, Abdul. "Sexuality on/of the Racial Border: Foucault, Wright, and the Articulation of Racialized Sexuality." In *Discourses of Sexuality: From Aristotle to AIDS*, ed. Domna C. Stanton. Ann Arbor: University of Michigan Press, 1992. 94–116.

Jayawardena, Kumari. *The White Women's Other Burden: Western Women and South Asia during British Rule*. New York: Routledge, 1995.

Jeffords, Susan. *The Remasculinization of America: Gender and the Vietnam War*. Bloomington: Indiana University Press, 1989.

Jeffords, Susan, and Lauren Rabinovitz, eds. *Seeing through the Media: The Persian Gulf War*. New Brunswick, NJ: Rutgers University Press, 1994.

Jenkins, Philip. *The Next Christendom: The Coming of Global Christianity*. New York: Oxford University Press, 2002.

Jensen, Robert. *Citizens of Empire: The Struggle to Reclaim Our Humanity*. San Francisco: City Lights, 2004.

Johnson, Chalmers. *Blowback: The Costs and Consequences of American Empire*. New York: Holt, 2000.

———. *The Sorrows of Empire: Militarism, Secrecy, and the End of the Republic*. New York: Metropolitcan, 2004.

Johnstone, Diana. *The Politics of Euromissiles: Europe's Role in America's World*. London: Verso, 1984.

———. "Seeing Yugoslavia Through a Dark Glass: Politics, Media, and the Ideology of Globalization." *Covert Action Quarterly* 65 (1998).

Jones, Frank L. "Marine Corps Civil Affairs and the Three Block War." *Marine Corps Gazette* 86, no. 3 (2002): 33–37.

Kagan, Robert. *Of Paradise and Power: America and Europe in the New World Order*. New York: Random House, 2003.

Kaplan, Amy. *Anarchy of Empire in the Making of U.S. Culture*. Cambridge, MA: Harvard University Press, 2002.

———. "Homeland Insecurities: Reflections on Language and Space." *Radical History Review*, no. 85 (2003): 82–93.

Kaplan, Amy, and Donald E. Pease, eds. *Cultures of United States Imperialism*. Durham, NC: Duke University Press, 1993.

Kelly, John D. "U.S. Power, after 9/11 and before It: If Not an Empire, Then What?" *Public Culture* 15, no. 2 (2003): 347–69.

Kennedy, Paul. *The Rise and Fall of the Great Powers: Economic Change and Military Conflict*. New York: Random House, 1987.

Khattak, Saba Gul. "In/Security: Afghan Refugees and Politics in Pakistan." *Critical Asian Studies* 35, no. 2 (2003): 195–208.

Kiernan, V. G. *America, the New Imperialism: From White Settlement to World Hegemony.* London: Zed, 1978.

King, Dan H. *Skeletons on the Zahara: A True Story of Survival.* New York: Little, Brown, and Company, 2004.

Kintz, Linda, and Julie Lesage, eds. *Media, Culture, and the Religious Right.* Minneapolis: University of Minnesota Press, 1998.

Klare, Michael T. *Resource Wars: The New Landscape of Global Conflict.* New York: Metropolitan, 2001.

Klein, Christina. *Cold War Orientalism: Asia in the Middlebrow Imagination, 1945–1961.* Berkeley: University of California Press, 2003.

Klein, Naomi. *No Logo: Taking Aim at the Brand Bullies.* New York: Picador, 2000.

Kolko, Gabriel. *Another Century of War?* New York: New Press, 2002.

Kramer, Martin. *Ivory Towers on Sand: The Failure of Middle Eastern Studies in America.* Washington, DC: Washington Institute for Near East Policy, 2001.

Kristeva, Julia. *Powers of Horror: An Essay on Abjection.* Trans. Leon S. Roudiez. New York: Columbia University Press, 1982.

Kugler, Richard. "Dissuasion as a Strategic Concept." *Strategic Forum*, no. 196 (2002): 1–8.

Kwon, Insook . "'The New Women's Movement' in 1920s Korea: Rethinking the Relationship between Imperialism and Women." *Gender and History* 10, no. 3 (1998): 358–80.

LaHaye, Tim, and Jerry Jenkins. *Assassins.* Wheaton, IL: Tyndale House, 1999.

———. *Apollyon.* Wheaton, IL: Tyndale House, 1999.

———. *Armaggedon.* Wheaton, IL: Tyndale House, 2003.

———. *Desecration.* Wheaton, IL: Tyndale House, 2001.

———. *Glorious Appearing.* Wheaton, IL: Tyndale House, 2004.

———. *The Indwelling.* Wheaton, IL: Tyndale House, 2000.

———. *Left Behind: A Novel of the Earth's Last Days.* Wheaton, IL: Tyndale House, 1995.

———. *The Mark.* Wheaton, IL: Tyndale House, 2000.

———. *Nicolae.* Wheaton, IL: Tyndale House, 1997.

———. *The Remnant.* Wheaton, IL: Tyndale House, 2002.

———. *The Rising: Before They Were Left Behind.* Wheaton, IL: Tyndale House, 2005.

———. *Soul Harvest.* Wheaton, IL: Tyndale House, 1998.

———. *Tribulation Force.* Wheaton, IL: Tyndale House, 1996.

Lazarus, Neil. *Nationalism and Cultural Practice in the Postcolonial World.* New York: Cambridge University Press, 1999.

Lenin, V. I. *Imperialism, the Highest Stage of Capitalism: A Popular Outline.* New rev. trans. New York: International Publishers, 1939.

Levine, Andrew. *Rethinking Liberal Equality: From a "Utopian" Point of View.* Ithaca, NY: Cornell University Press, 1998.

Levine, Phillipa. *Prostitution, Race, and Politics: Policing Venereal Disease in the British Empire.* New York: Routledge, 2003.

Lewontin, Richard. *Biology as Ideology*. New York: HarperPerennial, 1992.

Liebowitz, David, and Charles Pearson. *The Last Expedition: Stanley's Mad Journey Through the Congo*. New York: Norton, 2005.

Lindsey, Hal, with C. C. Carlson. *The Late Great Planet Earth*. Grand Rapids, MI: Zondervan, 1970.

Liotta, P. H. "Chaos as Strategy." *Parameters* 32, no.2 (2002): 47–56.

Lorelei, Mistress. *The Mistress Manual: The Good Girl's Guide to Female Dominance*. San Francisco: Greenery, 2000.

Lowe, Lisa. "Imagining Los Angeles in the Production of Multiculturalism." In *Mapping Multiculturalism*, ed. Avery F. Gordon and Christopher Newfield. Minneapolis: University of Minnesota Press, 1996. 413–23.

Lubbers, Eveline. *Battling Big Business: Countering Greenwashing, Front Groups, and Other Forms of Corporate Deception*. Monroe, ME: Common Courage, 2002.

Lukács, Georg. *History and Class Consciousness: Studies in Marxist Dialectics*. Trans. Rodney Livingstone. Cambridge, MA: MIT Press, 1971.

Lulofs, Madelon H. *Coolie*. New York: Oxford University Press, 1987.

———. *Rubber*. New York: Oxford University Press, 1987.

Luper-Foy, Steven, ed. *Problems of International Justice*. Boulder, CO: Westview, 1988.

Magdoff, Fred, John Bellamy Foster, and Frederick H. Buttel, eds. *Hungry for Profit: The Agribusiness Threat to Farmers, Food, and the Environment*. New York: Monthly Review Press, 2000.

Mann, Michael. *Incoherent Empire*. New York: Verso, 2003.

Martin, William. *With God on Our Side: The Rise of the Religious Right in America*. New York: Broadway Books, 1996.

Marx, Karl. *Capital: A Critique of Political Economy*. Trans. Ben Fowkes. 2 vols. London: Penguin, 1977.

Marx, Karl, and Friedrich Engels. *The German Ideology*. Ed. C. J. Arthur. New York: International Publishers, 1970.

Maynes, Charles William. "The Perils of (and for) an Imperial America." *Foreign Policy* 111 (1998): 36–49.

McAlister, Melani. *Epic Encounters: Culture, Media, and U.S. Interests in the Middle East since 1945*. Rev. ed. Berkeley: University of California Press, 2005.

McCarthy, Anna. *Ambient Television: Visual Culture and Public Space*. Durham, NC: Duke University Press, 2001.

McChesney, Robert, and John Nichols. *Our Media, Not Theirs: The Democratic Struggle against Corporate Media*. New York: Seven Stories, 2002.

McKay, George. *DIY Culture: Party and Protest in 1990s Britain*. New York: Verso, 1998.

———. *Senseless Acts of Beauty: Cultures of Resistance since the Sixties*. New York: Verso, 1996.

McNeill, Willliam H. "The Care and Repair of Public Myth" *Foreign Affairs* 61, no. 1 (1982): 1–14.

Mehta, Uday Singh. *Liberalism and Empire: A Study in Nineteenth-Century British Liberal Thought*. Chicago: University of Chicago Press, 1999.

Meron, Theodor. "The Humanization of Humanitarian Law." *American Journal of International Law* 94, no. 2 (2000): 239–78.

Mertes, Tom, ed. *A Movement of Movements: Is Another World Really Possible?* New York: Verso, 2004.

Mertus, Julie. *Bait and Switch: Human Rights and U.S. Foreign Policy*. New York: Routledge, 2004.

Metz, Steven, and James Kievit. "Strategy and the Revolution in Military Affairs: From Theory to Policy." Paper presented at the Strategic Studies Institute of the US Army War College, Carlisle Barracks, June 27, 1995.

Midgley, Clare. *Women against Slavery: The British Campaigns, 1780–1870*. New York: Routledge, 1992.

——, ed. *Gender and Imperialism*. Manchester: Manchester University Press, 1998.

Mill, John Stuart. *Considerations on Representative Government*. 1861. Reprint, Amherst, NY: Prometheus, 1991.

Mitchell, W. J. T. "Cloning Terror." Talk given at MALS Symposium, Dartmouth College, July 21, 2004.

Mommsen, Wolfgang J. *Theories of Imperialism*. Trans. P. S. Falla. Chicago: University of Chicago Press, 1982.

Mosse, George L. *Nationalism and Sexuality: Middle-Class Morality and Sexual Norms in Modern Europe*. Madison: University of Wisconsin Press, 1985.

Mudimbe, V. I. *The Invention of Africa*. Bloomington: Indiana University Press, 1988.

Neuhaus, Richard, and Michael Cromartie, eds. *Piety and Politics: Evangelicals and Fundamentalists Confront the World*. Washington DC: Ethics and Public Policy Center, 1987.

Newman, Robert. *The Fountain at the Center of the World*. New York: Soft Skull, 2004.

Nickel, James W. *Making Sense of Human Rights: Philosophical Reflections on the "Universal Declaration of Human Rights."* Berkeley: University of California Press, 1987.

Niebuhr, H. Richard. *The Kingdom of God in America*. 1937. Middletown, CT: Wesleyan University Press, 1988.

Ninkovich, Frank. *The United States and Imperialism*. Malden, MA: Blackwell, 2001.

Noll, Mark A. *The Scandal of the Evangelical Mind*. Grand Rapids, MI: W. B. Eerdmans, 1994.

Norton, Anne. *Leo Strauss and the Politics of American Empire*. New Haven, CT: Yale University Press, 2004.

Notes from Nowhere, ed. *We Are Everywhere: The Irresistible Rise of Global Anticapitalism*. New York: Verso, 2003.

Opel, Andrew, and Donnalyn Pompper, eds. *Representing Resistance: Media, Civil Disobedience, and the Global Justice Movement*. Westport, CT: Praeger, 2003.

Panitch, Leo, and Colin Leys, eds. *The New Imperial Challenge: Socialist Register 2004*. New York: Monthly Review Press, 2003.

Paolini, Albert, Anthony Jarvis, and Christian Reus-Smit, eds. *Between Sovereignty and Good Governance: The United Nations, the State, and Civil Society*. New York: St. Martin's, 1998.

Parenti, Christian. *Lockdown America: Police and Prisons in the Age of Crisis*. New York: Verso, 1999.

Parry, Benita. "The Postcolonial: Conceptual Category or Chimera?" *Yearbook of English Studies*, no. 27 (1997): 3–21.

Patai, Raphael. *The Arab Mind*. Hatherleigh Press, 2002.

Peters, P. Ralph. "Constant Conflict." *Parameters* 27, no. 2 (1997): 4–14.

Petras, James, and Henry Veltmeyer, *Globalization Unmasked: Imperialism in the Twenty-first Century*. London: Zed, 2001.

Pipes, Daniel. "The Muslims Are Coming! The Muslims Are Coming!" *National Review* 42, no.22 (1990): 28–31.

Piven, Frances Fox. *The War at Home: Domestic Consequences of Bush's Militarism*. New York: New Press, 2004.

Pogge, Thomas W. "The Moral Demands of Global Justice." *Dissent* 47, no. 4 (2000): 37–43.

——. *Realizing Rawls*. Ithaca, NY: Cornell University Press, 1989.

Poster, Mark. *What's the Matter with the Internet?* Minneapolis: University of Minnesota Press, 2001.

Pratt, Mary Louise. "Scratches on the Face of the Country; or, What Mr. Barrow Saw in the Land of the Bushmen." *Critical Inquiry* 12, no. 1 (1985): 119–43.

Quinby, Lee. *Millennial Seduction: A Skeptic Confronts Apocalyptic Culture*. Ithaca, NY: Cornell University Press, 1999.

——. "Women and the Techno-Millennium." *Review of Education/Pedagogy/Cultural Studies*, 21, no.4 (1999): 281–301.

Ramsay, Maureen. *What's Wrong with Liberalism? A Radical Critique of Liberal Political Philosophy*. London: Leicester University Press, 1997.

Rancière, Jacques. *Disagreement: Politics and Philosophy*. Trans Julie Rosen. Minneapolis: University of Minnesota Press, 1999.

Rawls, John. *The Law of Peoples*. Cambridge, MA: Harvard University Press, 1999.

——. *Political Liberalism*. New York: Columbia University Press, 1993.

Record, Jeffrey. "The Creeping Irrelevance of US Force Planning." Carlisle Barracks, PA: Strategic Studies Institute of the US Army War College, May 19, 1998.

Rehnand, Elisabeth, and Ellen Johnson Sirleaf. *World Progress of Women 2002*. Vol. 1, *Women, War, and Peace*. Bloomfield, CT: Kumarian, 2003.

Rejali, Darius M. *Torture and Modernity: Self, Society, and State in Modern Iran*. Boulder, CO: Westview, 1994.

Rieff, David. *A Bed for the Night: Humanitarianism in Crisis*. New York: Simon and Schuster, 2002.

Robbins, Kevin. "Cyberspace and the World We Live In." In *The Cybercultures Reader*, ed. David Bell and Barbara M. Kennedy. London: Routledge, 2000. 77–95.

Rodney, Walter. *How Europe Underdeveloped Africa*. Washington, DC: Howard University Press, 1974.

Rosaldo, Renato. "Imperial Nostalgia." *Representations*, no. 26 (1989): 107–23.

Rosenberg, Emily. *Financial Missionaries to the World: The Politics and Culture of Dollar Diplomacy, 1900–1930*. Cambridge, MA: Harvard University Press, 1999.

Rosenthal, John. "Kosovo and 'the Jewish Question.'" *Monthly Review* 51, no. 9 (2000): 24–42.

Rossing, Barbara. *The Rapture Exposed: The Message of Hope in the Book of Revelation*. Boulder, CO: Westview, 2004.

Rowe, John Carlos. *Literary Culture and U.S. Imperialism: From the Revolution to World War II*. New York: Oxford University Press, 2000.

——. *The New American Studies*. Minneapolis: University of Minnesota Press, 2002.

Roy, Arundhati. *Power Politics*. 2nd ed. Cambridge, MA: South End, 2001.

Rupp, Lila. *Worlds of Women: The Making of an International Women's Movement*. Princeton, NJ: Princeton University Press, 1997.

Rushdie, Salman. "Outside the Whale." *Granta* 11 (1984): 123–38.

Said, Edward. *Culture and Imperialism*. New York: Knopf, 1993.

——. "Globalizing Literary Study." *PMLA* 116, no. 1 (2001): 64–68.

——. *Humanism and Democratic Criticism*. New York: Columbia University Press, 2004.

——. *Orientalism*. New York: Vintage, 1978.

Salecl, Renata. *Spoils of Freedom: Psychoanalysis and Feminism after the Fall of Socialism*. New York: Routledge, 1994.

Samary, Catherine. *Yugoslavia Dismembered*. New York: Monthly Review Press, 1995.

Sandel, Michael. *Liberalism and the Limits of Justice*. Cambridge: Cambridge University Press, 1982.

Sarin, Vic, dir. *Left Behind*. Cloud Ten Pictures, 2000.

Scales, Robert H., Jr. "America's Army: Preparing for Tomorrow's Security Challenges." Carlisle Barracks, PA: Strategic Studies Institute of the US Army War College, December 1998.

Schake, Kori N. "Do European Union Defense Initiatives Threaten NATO?" *Strategic Forum*, no. 184 (2001): 1–6.

Schama, Simon. *The Embarrassment of Riches*. New York: Vintage, 1987.

Scheffer, David J. "Toward a Modern Doctrine of Humanitarian Intervention." *University of Toledo Law Review* 23, no. 2 (1992): 253–94.

Schueller, Malini Johar. *U.S. Orientalisms: Race, Nation, and Gender in Literature, 1790–1890*. Ann Arbor: University of Michigan Press, 1998.

Scraton, Phil, "The Politics of Morality." In *Beyond September 11: An Anthology of Dissent*, ed. Scraton. London: Pluto, 2002. 40–46.

Seager, Joni. *The Penguin Atlas of Women in the World*. New York: Penguin, 2003.

Sen, Amartya. *Development as Freedom*. New York: Knopf, 1999.

Sheer, Owen. *The Dust Diaries: Seeking the African Legacy of Arthur Cripps*. New York: Houghton Mifflin, 2004.

Shiva, Vandana. *The Violence of the Green Revolution: Third World Agriculture, Ecology, and Politics*. Atlantic Highlands, NJ: Zed, 1991.

———. *Water Wars: Privatization, Pollution, and Profit*. Cambridge, MA: South End, 2002.

Shue, Henry. *Basic Rights: Subsistence, Affluence, and U.S. Foreign Policy*. Princeton, NJ: Princeton University Press, 1980.

Singer, Peter. *One World: The Ethics of Globalization*. New Haven, CT: Yale University Press, 2002.

Sinha, Mrinalini, Donna J. Guy, and Angela Woolacott, eds. "Feminisms and Internationalism." Special issue, *Gender and History* 10, no. 3 (1998).

Slotkin, Richard. "Myth and the Production of History." In *Ideology and Classic American Literature*, ed. Sacvan Bercovitch and Myra Jehlen. New York: Cambridge University Press, 1986. 70–90.

———. *Regeneration through Violence: The Mythology of the American Frontier, 1600–1860*. Middletown, CT: Wesleyan University Press, 1973

Smith, Alexander McCall. *The No. 1 Ladies' Detective Agency*. New York: Pantheon, 2005.

Smith, Henry Nash. *Virgin Land: The American West in Symbols and Myth*. Cambridge, MA: Harvard University Press, 1950.

Smith, Jeremy. "Review of *The Fountain at the Center of the World*." *Ecologists* 33, no.9 (2003): 60.

Smith, Neil. *American Empire: Roosevelt's Geographer and the Prelude to Globalization*. Berkeley: University of California Press, 2003.

———. *The Endgame of Globalization*. New York: Routledge, 2005.

Snowball, David. *Continuity and Change in the Rhetoric of the Moral Majority*. New York: Praeger, 1991.

Sokolsky, Richard D. "Beyond Containment: Defending U.S. Interests in the Persian Gulf." *Strategic Forum* special report, (2002), 1–8.

Solomon, Norman. *War Made Easy: How Presidents and Pundits Keep Spinning Us to Death*. New York: Wiley, 2005.

Soyinka, Wole. *The Burden of Memory, the Muse of Forgiveness*. New York: Oxford, 1999.

Spees, Pam. "Women's Advocacy in the Creation of the International Criminal Court." *Signs* 28, no. 4 (2003): 1233–54.

Spigel, Lynn. "Entertainment Wars: Television Culture after 9/11." *American Quarterly* 56, no. 2 (2004): 235–70.

Spivak, Gayatri Chakravorty. "Terror: A Speech after 9/11." *boundary 2* 31, no. 2 (2004): 81–111.

Steger, Manfred B. *Globalism: The New Market Ideology*. Lanham, MD: Rowan and Littlefield, 2002.

Steinmetz, George. "The State of Emergency and the Revival of Imperialism: Toward an Authoritarian Post-Fordism." *Public Culture* 15, no. 2 (2003): 323–45.

Stiglitz, Joseph E. *Globalization and Its Discontents*. New York: Norton, 2002.

Stoler, Ann Laura. *Carnal Knowledge and Imperial Power: Race and the Intimate in Colonial Rule*. Berkeley: University of California Press, 2002.

——. *Race and the Education of Desire: Foucault's History of Sexuality and the Colonial Order of Things*. Durham, NC: Duke University Press, 1995.

Strober, Jerry, and Ruth Tomczak. *Jerry Falwell: Aflame for God*. Nashville, TN: Thomas Nelson, 1979.

Swofford, Anthony. *Jarhead: A Marine's Chronicle of the Gulf War*. New York: Scribner, 2003.

Tabb, William. *Economic Governance in the Age of Globalization*. New York: Columbia University Press, 2004.

Taylor, Charles. *The Ethics of Ambiguity*. Cambridge, MA: Harvard University Press, 1991.

Taylor, Jeffrey. *Facing the Congo: A Modern Journey into the Heart of Darkness*. St. Paul, MN: Ruminator, 2000.

Theroux, Paul. *Dark Star Safari*. New York: Houghton Mifflin, 2003.

——. *Sir Vidia's Shadow*. Boston: Houghton Mifflin, 1998.

Theweleit, Klaus. *Male Fantasies*. Trans. Stephen Conway. Minneapolis: University of Minnesota Press, 1987.

Thussu, Daya Kishan, ed. *Electronic Empires: Global Media and Local Resistance*. New York: Arnold, 1998.

Todd, Emmanuel. *After the Empire: The Breakdown of the American Order*. New York: Columbia University Press, 2003.

Tokar, Brian. *Earth for Sale: Reclaiming Ecology in the Age of Corporate Greenwash*. Boston: South End, 1997.

Ullman, Harlan K., and James P. Wade Jr. *Shock and Awe: Achieving Rapid Dominance*. National Defense University Press, 1996.

Volkman, Toby Alice. "Embodying Chinese Culture: Transnational Adoption in North America." *Social Text* 21, no. 1 (2003): 29–56.

Volpp, Leti. "The Citizen and the Terrorist." In *September 11 in History: A Watershed Moment*, ed. Mary L. Dudziak. Durham, NC: Duke University Press, 2003. 147–62.

Wallerstein, Immanuel. *The Capitalist World-Economy: Essays*. New York: Cambridge University Press, 1979.

——. *The Decline of American Power: The US in a Chaotic World*. New York: New Press, 2003.

Walt, Stephen M. "American Primacy: Its Prospects and Pitfalls." *Naval War College Review* 55, no.2 (2002): 9–29.

Walton, John, and David Seddon. *Free Markets and Food Riots: The Politics of Global Adjustment*. Cambridge, MA: Blackwell, 1994.

Walzer, Michael. "Governing the Globe: What Is the Best We Can Do?" *Dissent* 47, no. 4 (2000): 44–52.

Ward, Diana Raines. *Water Wars: Drought, Flood, Folly, and the Politics of Thirst*. New York: Riverhead, 2002.

Ware, Vron. *Beyond the Pale: White Women, Racism, and History*. London: Verso, 1991.

Watson, Tim. "Is the 'Post' in the Postcolonial the US in American Studies? The US Beginnings of Commonwealth Studies." *Ariel* 31, no. 1 (2000): 51–72.

Wexler, Laura. *Tender Violence: Domestic Visions in an Age of U.S. Imperialism*. Chapel Hill, NC: University of North Carolina Press, 2000.

Whittington, Sherrill. "Gender and Peacekeeping: The United Nations Transitional Administration in East Timor." *Signs* 28, no. 4 (2003): 1283–88.

Wiegman, Robyn. "Missiles and Melodrama (Masculinity and the Televisual War)." In *Seeing through the Media: The Persian Gulf War*, ed. Susan Jeffords and Lauren Rabinovitz. New Brunswick, NJ: Rutgers University Press, 1994. 171–87.

Wildenthal, Lora. *German Women for Empire, 1884–1945*. Durham, NC: Duke University Press, 2001.

Williams, William Appleman. *Empire as a Way of Life*. New York: Oxford University Press, 1980.

——. *The Tragedy of American Diplomacy*. New York: Dell, 1959.

Wolfee, Alan. *The Transformation of American Religion: How We Actually Live Our Faith*. New York: Free Press, 2003.

Wood, Ellen Meiksins. *Empire of Capital*. New York: Verso, 2003.

——. *The Origin of Capitalism: A Longer View*. New York: Verso, 2002.

Wood, Neal. *Tyranny in America: Capitalism and National Decay*. New York: Verso, 2004.

Woodward, Susan. *Balkan Tragedy: Chaos and Dissolution after the Cold War*. Washington, DC: Brookings Institution, 1995.

Wu Ming Foundation. *Fifty-four*. New York: Heinemann, 2005.

Wuthnow, Robert. *After Heaven: Spirituality in America since the 1950s*. Berkeley: University of California Press, 1998.

Young, Louise. *Japan's Total Empire: Manchuria and the Culture of Wartime Imperialism*. Berkeley: University of California Press, 1998.

Yuen, Eddie, Daniel Burton Rose, and George Katsiaficas, eds. *The Battle of Seattle: The New Challenge to Capitalist Globalization*. New York: Soft Skull, 2002.

Zinni, Anthony C. "A Military for the Twenty-first Century: Lessons from the Recent Past." *Strategic Forum*, no. 181 (2001): 1–4.

Žižek, Slavoj. *The Ticklish Subject: The Absent Centre of Political Ontology*. New York: Verso, 1999.

Contributors

Omar Dahbour is the author of *Illusion of the Peoples: A Critique of National Self-Determination* (2003), the editor of *Philosophical Perspectives on National Identity* (1997), and a coeditor of *The Nationalism Reader* (1995), and has published articles on self-determination, national identity, international law, just war, the ethics of terrorism, and other topics. He teaches philosophy at Hunter College and the Graduate Center of the City University of New York and is affiliated with CUNY's Center for Place, Culture, and Politics.

Ashley Dawson is an associate professor of English at the City University of New York's Graduate Center and the College of Staten Island. He is author of *Mongrel Nation: Diasporic Culture and the Making of Postcolonial Britain* (2006), as well as of numerous articles on postcolonial culture.

Cynthia Enloe is a professor of government at Clark University. She is the author of nine books, including *The Morning After: Sexual Politics at the End of the Cold War* (1993), *Bananas, Beaches, and Bases: Making Feminist Sense of International Politics* (2000), *Maneuvers: The International Politics of Militarizing Women's Lives* (2000), and *The Curious Feminist: Searching for Women in a New Age of Empire* (2004). She has written for *Ms.* magazine and *Village Voice* and has appeared on National Public Radio and the BBC.

Melani McAlister is an associate professor of American studies and international affairs at George Washington University. She is the author of *Epic Encounters: Culture, Media, and U.S. Interests in the Middle East since 1945* (2001). She is currently working on a study of Christian evangelicals, popular culture, and foreign relations, tentatively titled "Our God in the World: The Global Vision of American Evangelicals." She has written for the *New York Times*, the *Washington Post*, and the *Nation* and has been interviewed with CNN, BBC, Voice of America, and NPR.

Christian Parenti writes for the *Nation* and is the author of several books including *Lockdown America: Police and Prisons in the Age of Crisis* (2000), *The Soft Cage: Surveillance in America from Slavery to the War on Terror* (2003), and *The Freedom: Shadows and Hallucinations in Occupied Iraq* (2004). He received a PhD in sociology from the London School of Economics.

Donald E. Pease is Avalon Foundation Chair of the Humanities and the chair of the Liberal Studies Program at Dartmouth College. He is the author of *Visionary Compacts: American Renaissance Writing in Cultural Context* and the editor of eight volumes, including *The American Renaissance Reconsidered* (with Walter Benn Michaels), *Cultures of US Imperialism* (with Amy Kaplan), *New Americanists: Revisionist Interventions into the American Canon*, *United States National Identities and Post-Americanist Narratives*, and *The Futures of American Studies* (with Robyn Wiegman).

John Carlos Rowe is USC Associate's Chair in Humanities and a professor of English and American studies and ethnicity at the University of Southern California. His recent books include *The New American Studies* (2002) and *Literary Culture and U.S. Imperialism: From the Revolution to World War II* (2000).

Malini Johar Schueller is a professor of English at the University of Florida. She is the author of *The Politics of Voice: Liberalism and Social Criticism from Franklin to Kingston* (1992) and *U.S. Orientalisms: Race, Nation, and Gender in Literature, 1790–1890*. She has edited a scholarly edition of a slave's travel narrative, *A Colored Man Round the World*, by David F. Dorr (1999), and coedited (with Edward Watts) *Messy Beginnings: Postcoloniality and Early American Studies* (2003).

Harilaos Stecopoulos teaches in the English department at the University of Iowa. He has coedited (with Michael Uebel) *Race and the Subject of Masculinities* (1997) and published articles on Stuart Hall, Richard Wright, and William Faulkner.

Index

Library of Congress Cataloging-in-Publication Data
Exceptional state : contemporary U.S. culture and the new imperialism /
edited by Ashley Dawson and Malini Johar Schueller.
p. cm. — (New Americanists)
Includes bibliographical references and index.
ISBN 978-0-8223-3805-5 (cloth : alk. paper)
ISBN 978-0-8223-3820-8 (pbk. : alk. paper)
1. United States — Foreign relations — 2001–. 2. Political culture — United States.
3. United States — Civilization — 1970–. 4. Popular culture — United States.
5. Imperialism. 6. Militarism — United States. 7. United States — Military policy.
8. Globalization — Political aspects — United States. 9. Millennialism — Political aspects —
United States. 10. Imperialism in literature. I. Dawson, Ashley. II. Schueller,
Malini Johar.
E902.E96 2007
973.931 — dc22 2006101128